SECOND EDIT

SELECTIONS FROM

— The OLD —
Testament
MADE EASIER

PART TWO:
EXODUS 25 THROUGH 2 SAMUEL

SECOND EDITION

SELECTIONS FROM

—THE OLD—
TESTAMENT
MADE EASIER

PART TWO:
EXODUS 25 THROUGH 2 SAMUEL

DAVID J. RIDGES

CFI
An Imprint of Cedar Fort, Inc.
Springville, Utah

© 2014 by David J. Ridges

ISBN: 978-1-4621-1493-1

Published by CFI, an imprint of Cedar Fort, Inc., 2373 W. 700 S., Springville, UT 84663
Distributed by Cedar Fort, Inc., www.cedarfort.com

The Library of Congress has cataloged the first volume of this set as follows:

Ridges, David J., author.
Your study of the Old Testament made easier / David J. Ridges. -- Second edition.
   pages cm
Includes bibliographical references.
Summary: Study guide for the King James Version of the Old Testament.
ISBN 978-1-4621-1492-4
1. Bible. Old Testament--Commentaries. I. Title.

BS1151.52.R53 2014
221.071--dc23

                      2014007358

Cover design by Shawnda T. Craig
Cover design © 2014 Lyle Mortimer
Edited and typeset by Emily S. Chambers

Printed in the United States of America

10 9 8 7 6 5 4 3 2 1

Printed on acid-free paper

BOOKS BY DAVID J. RIDGES

The Gospel Study Series:

- Your Study of The Book of Isaiah Made Easier, Second Edition

- The New Testament Made Easier, Part 1 (Second Edition)

- The New Testament Made Easier, Part 2 (Second Edition)

- Your Study of The Book of Mormon Made Easier, Part 1

- Your Study of The Book of Mormon Made Easier, Part 2

- Your Study of The Book of Mormon Made Easier, Part 3

- Book of Mormon Made Easier, Family Deluxe Edition, Vols. 1 and 2

- Your Study of The Doctrine and Covenants Made Easier, Part 1

- Your Study of The Doctrine and Covenants Made Easier, Part 2

- Your Study of The Doctrine and Covenants Made Easier, Part 3

- The Old Testament Made Easier, Part 1

- The Old Testament Made Easier, Part 2—Selections from the Old Testament

- The Old Testament Made Easier, Part 3—Selections from the Old Testament

- Your Study of the Pearl of Great Price Made Easier

- Your Study of Jeremiah Made Easier

- Your Study of The Book of Revelation Made Easier, Second Edition

Our Savior, Jesus Christ: His Life and Mission to Cleanse and Heal

Mormon Beliefs and Doctrines Made Easier

The Proclamation on the Family: The Word of the Lord on More Than 30 Current Issues

Using the Signs of the Times to Strengthen Your Testimony

Doctrinal Details of the Plan of Salvation: From Premortality to Exaltation

CONTENTS

FOREWORD

IN THE SECOND edition of volumes 1–3 of this Old Testament study guide, I have added many additional verses, along with notes and explanations not found in the original edition. For example, every verse of Exodus is included in the second edition of volume one and volume two, which was not the case in the first edition.

By the way, the bolded words and phrases are for teaching emphasis and allow the reader to glean the main ideas and concepts at a glance.

In over 40 years of teaching in the Church and for the Church Educational System, I have found that members of the Church encounter some common problems when it comes to understanding the scriptures. One problem is understanding the language of the scriptures themselves. Another is understanding symbolism. Another common concern is how best to mark their own scriptures and perhaps make brief notes in them. Yet another concern is how to understand what the scriptures are actually teaching. In other words, what are the major messages being taught by the Lord through His prophets?

This book is designed to address each of the concerns mentioned above. One of my objectives in these "Teacher in Your Hand" Gospel Studies Series books is to teach the language of the scriptures. Many Latter-day Saints struggle with the beautiful language of the scriptures. There is a special Spirit that attends it. The Brethren use it often to bring us the word

of God, matched to our exact needs by the Holy Ghost. Therefore, I add brackets on occasion within the verses, for the purpose of defining difficult scriptural terms. I hope that as you read and study this work, you will get to the point that you do not need these definitions in brackets anymore. When that happens, please be patient because others may still need them.

The format is intentionally simple, with some license taken with respect to capitalization and punctuation in order to minimize interruption of the flow. It is intended to help readers to

- Quickly gain a basic understanding of these scriptures as they read, through the use of brief explanatory notes in brackets within the verses as well as occasional notes between verses. This paves the way for even deeper testimony and understanding later.

- Better understand the beautiful language of the scriptures. This is accomplished in this book with in-the-verse notes that define difficult terms.

- Mark their scriptures and put brief notes in the margins that will help them understand now and remember later what particular passages of scripture teach.

- Better understand symbolism.

Over the years, one of the most common expressions of gratitude from my students has been "Thanks for the notes you had

1

us put in our scriptures." This book is dedicated to that purpose. Sources for the notes given in this work are as follows:

- The standard works of The Church of Jesus Christ of Latter-day Saints.

- Footnotes in the Latter-day Saint version of the King James Bible.

- The Joseph Smith Translation of the Bible.

- The Bible Dictionary in the back of our Bible.

- Various dictionaries.

- Various student manuals provided for our institutes of religion.

- Other sources as noted in the text and in the "Sources" section.

I hope that this study guide will serve effectively for members of the Church, as well as others, as they seek to increase their understanding of the writings and teachings contained in these portions of the Old Testament. Above all, if this work serves to bring increased understanding and testimony of the Atonement of Christ, all the efforts to put it together will have been far more than worth it. A special thanks goes to my wife, Janette, and to my daughters and sons, who have encouraged me every step of the way.

DAVID J. RIDGES

THE JST

(THE JOSEPH SMITH TRANSLATION OF THE BIBLE)

REFERENCES USED IN
STUDY GUIDES BY DAVID J. RIDGES

BE AWARE THAT some of the JST references I use in my study guides are not found in the footnotes nor in the JST section at the back of our LDS version of the King James Bible (the one we use in the English-speaking part of the Church). The reason for this, as explained to me some years ago while writing curriculum materials for the Church, is simply that there is not enough room, for practical purposes, to include all of the JST additions and changes. As you can imagine, as was likewise explained to me, there were difficult decisions that had to be made by the Scriptures Committee and Church leaders as to which JST contributions were included and which were not.

The Joseph Smith Translation of the Bible in its entirety can generally be found in LDS bookstores or ordered through them. It was originally published under the auspices of the Reorganized Church of Jesus Christ of Latter Day Saints in Independence, Missouri. The version of the JST that I prefer to use is a parallel column version, entitled, *Joseph Smith's "New Translation" of the Bible*, published by Herald Publishing House,

Independence, Missouri, in 1970. This parallel column version compares the King James Bible with the JST side by side and includes only the verses that have changes, additions, or deletions made by the Prophet Joseph Smith.

By the way, some members of the Church have wondered whether we can trust the JST since it was published by a breakaway faction from our church who retained the original manuscripts after the martyrdom of the Prophet Joseph Smith. They worry that some changes to the Prophet's original manuscript might have been made to support doctrinal differences between the RLDS Church (the Reorganized Church of Jesus Christ of Latter Day Saints) and us. This is not the case. Many years ago, Robert J. Matthews of the Brigham Young University Religion Department was teaching a summer school class I attended. He told us that he was given permission by leaders of the RLDS Church to come to their Independence, Missouri, headquarters to see their publication of the JST. Brother Matthews was thus able to verify that they had been meticulously true to the Prophet's original work.

EXODUS 25

DURING THE "FORTY days and forty nights," spoken of at the end of chapter 24, Moses was instructed to build a portable tabernacle. Chapters 25–30 contain these instructions. The actual construction of the Tabernacle and all that pertains to it will be described in Exodus, chapters 36–39. Because the people were still traveling toward the promised land, it had to be completely portable. The instructions given to Moses in chapters 25–30 could be considered to be "blueprints" or the "'planning phase" of the Tabernacle.

This tabernacle was designed as a central focus for worship during the years the children of Israel would spend wandering in the wilderness. It was, in effect, a portable temple.

You will see much plan of salvation and Atonement symbolism, in the plans for building and using the tabernacle. In fact, it can be surprising how many parallels there are between worship associated with the tabernacle and temple worship in our day.

Before we do our verse-by-verse study of the next six chapters, we will provide a quick overview of the Tabernacle and its contents. This will help you better visualize and understand what Moses is told by the Lord to build, in chapters 25–30.

THE LAYOUT OF THE TABERNACLE

You can read a summary about the tabernacle in the Bible Dictionary at the back of your LDS version of the Bible, under "Tabernacle." The structure of the Tabernacle itself was thirty cubits long, ten cubits wide and ten cubits high. A cubit was about eighteen inches; therefore, the tabernacle was about forty-five feet long by fifteen feet wide by fifteen feet high. It was divided into two compartments by a veil. The first compartment, the "Holy Place," was thirty feet long. The second room, the "Most Holy Place" or "Holy of Holies," was fifteen feet long and thus was a perfect cube. The whole structure was covered by a tent that was forty cubits (sixty feet) long.

A fenced, outer courtyard surrounded the tabernacle. This courtyard was one hundred cubits by fifty cubits and the fence was five cubits high. In other words, the courtyard was about 150 feet by 75 feet with a 7½-foot-high portable fence around it. The entrance to the courtyard was thirty feet wide (twenty cubits) and was placed in the fence on the east side.

Thus, there were three main areas in the tabernacle complex:

1. The outer courtyard

2. The first room in the tabernacle itself, known as the Holy Place.

3. The second room in the tabernacle, known as the Holy of Holies.

The craftsmanship and decoration became progressively more beautiful and ornate from the outer courtyard to the Holy of Holies, symbolizing that life becomes more and more meaningful and beautiful as we journey from the world toward the presence of God.

Similarly, the three main areas of the tabernacle complex symbolized the telestial kingdom (outer courtyard), the terrestrial kingdom (the Holy Place), and the celestial kingdom (the Holy of Holies). These three areas were "types," in other words, symbolic of the telestial room, the terrestrial room, and the celestial room of modern temples.

THINGS WITHIN THE TABERNACLE AND GROUNDS

The first thing the people saw as they entered through the east gate into the tabernacle grounds was the altar of burnt offerings (the altar of sacrifice), upon which animal sacrifices were offered. It was about 7½ feet square and 4½ feet high and was symbolic of the obedience and sacrifice required to progress toward entrance into the presence of God (the Holy of Holies).

Between the altar of sacrifice and the tabernacle itself was a basin made of brass placed on a base of brass and filled with water. When Solomon built a permanent temple, he built such a basin and placed it on the backs of statues of twelve oxen. Before entering the Holy Place in the tabernacle, the priests were required to wash their hands and feet. This basin can be symbolic of washing, including baptism, before entering the presence of God.

There were three things in the Holy Place (the first room in the tabernacle itself):

1. **The Altar of Incense**, placed near the veil that separated the Holy Place from the Holy of Holies. This altar was placed at the middle of the veil. Incense was burned morning and evening upon it. Incense symbolized the prayers of the people (Revelation 5:8).

2. **The Golden Candlestick** stood to the left of the Altar of Incense It was called "menorah" in Hebrew. It was made of pure gold. When you read about

it in Exodus 25:31-40, you will see that it is actually seven candlesticks, a center column with three columns curving out on each side. But, you will also notice that even though it is called a "candlestick," it was formed with seven cups at the top of the columns, in which pure olive oil was burned, providing light for the tabernacle. The oil used for this "candlestick" had to be beaten from the olives (Exodus 27:20-21). This can symbolize that Christ, who is the source of light for us, was beaten (John 19:1) before he was crucified. Pure olive oil can also represent healing. Furthermore, olive oil symbolized the light and guidance of the Holy Ghost in the parable of the ten virgins (Doctrine and Covenants 45:56-57).

3. The Table of Shewbread (Hebrew: "bread of the face" or "presence bread," meaning bread, in the presence of God) stood to the right of the Altar of Incense. It was about three feet long, eighteen inches wide, and twenty-seven inches high. Upon this table were twelve round, unleavened loaves of bread, made of fine flour, weighing about ten pounds each, arranged in two stacks. They were symbolic of each of the twelve tribes of Israel. The loaves presented each tribe perpetually "before the face of God" (see Bible Dictionary, under "Shewbread"). Frankincense was put by each pile of loaves and was later burned on the Altar of Incense. These loaves were replaced each Sabbath, and the old ones were eaten by the priests in a place set aside for that holy purpose. Jewish tradition says that wine was also placed on the table with the bread (*Old Testament Student Manual*, page 149.) Thus, the elements of the sacrament bread and wine were symbolically represented on this table.

THE ARK OF THE COVENANT

Only one special item was in the Holy of Holies. It was the ark of the covenant (the box or chest containing the stone tablets on which the Ten Commandments and other things were written by the finger of the Lord). The ark thus contained the commandments of God, which the people accepted by covenant—Exodus 24:7-8. The ark was also referred to as "the ark of the testimony."

It was a chest or box about three feet nine inches long, two feet three inches wide, and two feet three inches high. It was overlaid with pure gold, inside and out. In addition to the second set of stone tablets (see JST Exodus 34:1-2) given by the Lord to Moses on Sinai, the ark eventually held a container of manna and Aaron's rod.

The mercy seat was a solid slab of gold formed to fit as the lid of the ark (Exodus 25:17, footnote a, in your Bible). See also *Old Testament Student Manual*, p 148. Statues of two cherubim were placed on it, one at each end. They were of gold, and their wings spread toward each other, covering the mercy seat. While we know that angels don't actually have wings, we know from Doctrine and Covenants 77:4 that wings symbolize power to move and act in the work of the Lord.

Another name for the mercy seat was "seat of atonement" (*Old Testament Student Manual*, page 148). Blood from sacrifices representing Christ's blood was sprinkled on the mercy seat (Leviticus 16:15–16). The symbolism is that of the blood of the Savior providing mercy for us.

We will now proceed with our verse-by-verse study of these "blueprint" chapters for the construction of the Tabernacle and its contents.

FIRST, IN CHAPTER 25, verses 1-9, the Lord instructs Moses to have the people give donations of materials for the project. One of the things you will notice as you read these chapters is that the children of Israel were commanded by the Lord to put the very best, costliest, and finest materials into the construction of the tabernacle. You will see much of gold, silver, brass, fine linen, blue, purple, scarlet, beautiful wood, and so forth. This can be symbolic of putting our best work and best efforts into living the gospel and our worship of God. It also reminds us of putting the finest materials into our temples today.

Note the emphasis in verse 2 on "willingly." We know from the Book of Mormon that in order for an offering to be acceptable to the Lord, it must be given willingly (Moroni 7:6–8).

1 AND the LORD spake unto Moses, saying,

2 Speak unto the children of Israel, that they bring me an offering [*donations for the building of the Tabernacle*]: of every man that giveth it **willingly** with his heart ye shall take my offering.

3 And this is the offering which ye shall take of them; gold, and silver, and brass,

4 And blue, and purple, and scarlet, and fine linen, and goats' hair,

5 And rams' skins dyed red, and badgers' skins, and shittim wood,

"Shittim" wood, or acacia wood (see Exodus 25, footnote 5b in your Bible), is a hard, close-grained wood, orange-brown in color. It can be highly polished. It lends itself to beautiful cabinet work. Acacia trees found in Bible lands were often 3 to 4 feet in diameter. See *Smith's Bible Dictionary*, p 624.

6 Oil for the light, spices for anointing oil, and for sweet incense,

7 Onyx stones, and stones to be set in the ephod [*vest or apron worn*

by the high priest, worn over a blue robe], and in the breastplate [see note following Exodus 39:7 in this study guide].

8 And let them make me a sanctuary; that I may dwell among them.

9 According to all that I shew thee, after the pattern ["blueprint"] of the tabernacle, and the pattern of all the instruments thereof, even so shall ye make it.

10 ¶ And they shall make an ark [a chest (the ark of the covenant) to hold the ten commandment stone tables and, later, other sacred items,] of shittim wood: two cubits and a half [3 feet, 9 inches] shall be the length thereof, and a cubit and a half the breadth [2 feet, 3 inches wide] thereof, and a cubit and a half the height thereof.

11 And thou shalt overlay it with pure gold, within and without [inside and out] shalt thou overlay it, and shalt make upon it a crown of gold round about [a gold molding around the top].

Next, Moses is instructed to create a system for carrying the ark. It will consist of rings of gold, two on each side of the chest, and poles to insert through them to serve as handles for carrying it.

12 And thou shalt cast four rings of gold for it, and put them in the four corners thereof; and two rings shall be in the one side of it, and two rings in the other side of it.

13 And thou shalt make staves [poles] of shittim wood, and overlay them with gold.

14 And thou shalt put the staves into the rings by the sides of the ark, that the ark may be borne [carried] with them.

15 The staves shall be in the rings of the ark: they shall not be taken from it.

16 And thou shalt put into the ark the testimony [the stone tablets containing the Ten Commandments, etc.] which I shall give thee.

Next, Moses is told to make a lid of pure gold for the chest. It will be referred to as the "mercy seat."

17 And thou shalt make a mercy seat of pure gold: two cubits and a half [3 feet, 9 inches] shall be the length thereof, and a cubit and a half [2 feet, 3 inches] the breadth thereof.

The revealed "blueprint" next specifies that two cherubim be hammered as one piece with the gold lid and that they face each other from opposite ends of the lid. As you can well imagine, this will be an incredible artistic feat by inspired craftsmen!

18 And thou shalt make two cherubims [figures representing heavenly

creatures—see Bible Dictionary under "Cherubim] of gold, of beaten [hammered] work shalt thou make them, in the two ends of the mercy seat.

19 And make one cherub on the one end, and the other cherub on the other end: even of [one piece with] the mercy seat shall ye make the cherubims on the two ends thereof.

20 And the cherubims shall stretch forth their wings on high, covering the mercy seat with their wings, and their faces shall look one to another; toward the mercy seat shall the faces of the cherubims be.

21 And thou shalt put the mercy seat above upon the ark; and in the ark thou shalt put the testimony [the stone tablets containing the Ten Commandments, etc.] that I shall give thee.

Next, the Savior tells Moses that when the ark with its mercy seat lid is completed and in place in the Tabernacle, it will serve as a place where the Lord will meet Moses and commune with him.

22 And there I will meet with thee, and I will commune with thee from above the mercy seat, from between the two cherubims which are upon the ark of the testimony, of all things which I will give thee in commandment unto the children of Israel.

Next, the "blueprint" is provided for the table of shewbread (pronounced "showbread").

23 ¶ Thou shalt also make a table of shittim [acacia] wood: two cubits [about 3 feet] shall be the length thereof, and a cubit [about 18 inches] the breadth thereof, and a cubit and a half [about 27 inches] the height thereof.

24 And thou shalt overlay it with pure gold, and make thereto a crown [a top border or rim] of gold round about.

25 And thou shalt make unto it a border of an hand breadth round about, and thou shalt make a golden crown to the border thereof round about.

Next, as was the case for carrying the ark of the covenant, Moses is given the plans for carrying the table of shewbread. It likewise will have four gold rings with gold covered poles with which to carry it.

26 And thou shalt make for it four rings of gold, and put the rings in the four corners that are on the four feet thereof.

27 Over against the border shall the rings be for places of the staves [poles] to bear the table.

28 And thou shalt make the staves of shittim wood, and overlay them with gold, that the table may be borne with them.

Next, we see that various items of gold are to be made for use on the table of shewbread.

29 And thou shalt make the dishes thereof, and spoons thereof, and covers thereof, and bowls thereof, to cover withal: of pure gold shalt thou make them.

30 And thou shalt set upon the table shewbread before me alway.

Finally, the "blueprints" for the golden candlestick or "menorah" are given. It will have a center branch with three curved branches extending out from the center on each side. At the top of each branch a cup or container will be formed which will hold olive oil. With a wick in place in each cup, seven flames will provide light in the Holy Place. "Seven," in Old Testament symbolism, symbolizes perfection or wholeness. Thus, among other things, the menorah represents the perfect light from God, which, if followed, will lead us to become perfect like Him (Matthew 5:48.)

31 ¶ And thou shalt make a candlestick of pure gold: of beaten [*hammered*] work shall the candlestick be made: his shaft, and his branches, his bowls, his knops [*spherical decorations*], and his flowers, shall be of the same [*shall likewise be made of pure gold*].

32 And six branches shall come out of the sides of it; three branches of the candlestick out of the one side, and three branches of the candlestick out of the other side:

33 Three bowls made like unto almonds [*almond blossoms*], with a knop [*crown-shaped circlets—see footnote 33a in your Bible*] and a flower in one branch; and three bowls made like almonds in the other branch, with a knop and a flower: so in the six branches that come out of the candlestick.

34 And in the candlestick shall be four bowls made like unto almonds, with their knops and their flowers.

35 And there shall be a knop under two branches of the same, and a knop under two branches of the same, and a knop under two branches of the same, according to the six branches that proceed out of the candlestick.

36 Their knops and their branches shall be of the same: all it shall be one beaten work of pure gold.

37 And thou shalt make the seven lamps thereof: and they shall light the lamps thereof, that they may give light over against it.

Next, Moses is instructed to make pure gold utensils for use with the menorah.

38 And the tongs thereof, and the snuffdishes [*trays for the wick trimmings*] thereof, shall be of pure gold.

39 Of a talent [*NIV: about 75*

pounds] of pure gold shall he make it, with all these vessels.

> Finally, in the last verse of this chapter, Moses is strictly instructed to follow the pattern or "blueprint" shown him while he was on Mount Sinai communicating with the Lord.

40 And look that thou make them after their pattern, which was shewed thee in the mount.

EXODUS 26

THIS CHAPTER IS a continuation of instructions from the Lord in chapters 25–30, given to Moses concerning the building of the Tabernacle (see background notes for chapter 25). Verses 1–14 are the patterns given by the Lord for the layers of fabric used to make the curtains that would cover the wall panels and open ceiling of the Tabernacle. We will include the following quote from the *Old Testament Student Manual* to help with these verses.

"Exodus 26:1–14; 36:8–38. The Coverings for the Tabernacle

"Because the Israelites were wandering in the wilderness at this time, the tabernacle had to be portable. The walls were formed of panels that could be joined together (see Exodus 25:15–16). Then the walls and open ceiling were covered with four different layers of fabric. The inner fabric was made of fine-twined linen. The Hebrew word translated "linen" signifies not only the fabric but also "whiteness" (Wilson, *Old Testament Word Studies*, s.v. "linen," p. 255; see also Fallows, Bible Encyclopedia, s.v. "linen," 2:1068). Scholars believe it was either a fine cotton fabric or one made from flax. Because of the length of the tabernacle, ten curtains, or pieces of fabric, were needed to cover it. This inner layer was to have cherubim (angels) embroidered upon it and was to incorporate, besides the whiteness, the colors blue, purple, and scarlet.

"The selvage [*the woven edge of the fabric*] of these curtains was a special border at the edge of each woven piece that prevented raveling. This border was usually of different size threads and was sometimes of a different weave than the rest of the curtain. By means of golden clasps or pins called taches, the selvages of adjacent curtain segments were joined together, creating the appearance of a single drape over the tabernacle. The other three fabrics consisted of goats' hair, rams' skins dyed red, and badgers' skins (see Exodus 26:7, 14). The nature of the last kind of fabric is not clear; scholars seem to agree only that it was not the skin of badgers. The Hebrew word implies the color of, more than the kind of, fabric (see Wilson, *Old Testament Word Studies*, s.v. "badger," p. 27). Some scholars believe it may have been the skins of porpoises or seals from the Red Sea which would have given the tabernacle a waterproof outer covering (see Keil and Delitzsch, Commentary, 1:2:163)." (*Old Testament Student Manual, Genesis–2 Samuel,* p. 150–51)

With the above quote in mind, you

can better appreciate the great skill of the weavers in creating the fabrics and intricate designs to be used in this part of the Tabernacle. Also, be aware that there are many differences among scholars and artists' renditions as to exactly how the curtains were put together to form the Tabernacle.

1 MOREOVER thou shalt make the tabernacle with ten curtains of fine twined linen, and blue, and purple, and scarlet: with cherubims [*depictions of angelic beings*] of cunning [*skilled*] work shalt thou make them.

2 The length of one curtain shall be eight and twenty cubits, and the breadth of one curtain four cubits: and every one of the curtains shall have one measure [*have the same measurements*].

3 The five curtains shall be coupled together one to another; and other five curtains shall be coupled one to another.

Next, the Lord tells Moses how the curtains or lengths of fabric are to be joined together to provide the covering for the wall frames and ceiling of the Tabernacle.

4 And thou shalt make loops of blue upon the edge of the one curtain from the selvedge in the coupling; and likewise shalt thou make in the uttermost edge of another curtain, in the coupling of the second.

5 Fifty loops shalt thou make in the one curtain, and fifty loops shalt thou make in the edge of the curtain that is in the coupling of the second; that the loops may take hold one of another.

6 And thou shalt make fifty taches [*clasps*] of gold, and couple the curtains together with the taches: and it shall be one tabernacle [*so that the whole Tabernacle is one unit*].

7 ¶ And thou shalt make curtains of goats' hair to be a covering upon the tabernacle: eleven curtains shalt thou make.

8 The length of one curtain shall be thirty cubits, and the breadth of one curtain four cubits: and the eleven curtains shall be all of one measure [*the same dimensions*].

9 And thou shalt couple five curtains by themselves, and six curtains by themselves, and shalt double the sixth curtain in the forefront of the tabernacle.

10 And thou shalt make fifty loops on the edge of the one curtain that is outmost in the coupling, and fifty loops in the edge of the curtain which coupleth the second.

11 And thou shalt make fifty taches [*clasps or fasteners*] of brass, and put the taches into the loops, and couple the tent together, that it may be one.

12 And the remnant that remaineth of the curtains of the tent, the half curtain that remaineth, shall hang over the backside of the tabernacle.

13 And a cubit on the one side, and a cubit on the other side of that which remaineth in the length of the curtains of the tent, it shall hang over the sides of the tabernacle on this side and on that side, to cover it.

14 And thou shalt make a covering for the tent of rams' skins dyed red, and a covering above of badgers' skins.

15 ¶ And thou shalt make boards for the tabernacle of shittim wood standing up [*make upright frames*].

16 Ten cubits shall be the length of a board [*panel frame*], and a cubit and a half shall be the breadth of one board [*frame for a panel*].

Next, the Lord instructs Moses in how to support the frames upright in bases. A quote from the *Old Testament Student Manual* helps here:

"The tenon was one of two large rectangular dowels at the bottom end of each board. The tenon fitted into a double base support called a socket that could slip up and down each tenon independently. Since all of the boards were fastened firmly side to side, making a rigid wall, every socket could rest on the ground even when it was irregular. One is immediately impressed with the detail that the Lord gave Moses concerning His dwelling place." (*Old Testament Student Manual, Genesis-2 Samuel*, p. 151.)

17 Two tenons shall there be in one board, set in order one against another: thus shalt thou make for all the boards of the tabernacle.

18 And thou shalt make the boards [*frames*] for the tabernacle, twenty boards on the south side southward.

19 And thou shalt make forty sockets [*bases*] of silver under the twenty boards; two sockets under one board for his two tenons, and two sockets under another board for his two tenons.

20 And for the second side of the tabernacle on the north side there shall be twenty boards [*frames*]:

21 And their forty sockets [*bases*] of silver; two sockets under one board, and two sockets under another board.

22 And for the sides of the tabernacle westward thou shalt make six boards.

23 And two boards shalt thou make for the corners of the tabernacle in the two sides.

24 And they shall be coupled together beneath, and they shall be coupled together above the head of it unto one ring: thus shall it be for them both; they shall be for the two corners.

25 And they shall be eight boards, and their sockets of silver, sixteen sockets; two sockets under one board, and two sockets under another board.

26 ¶ And thou shalt make bars of shittim wood [*crossbars of acacia wood*]; five for the boards [*frames*] of the one side of the tabernacle,

27 And five bars for the boards of the other side of the tabernacle, and five bars for the boards of the side of the tabernacle, for the two sides westward.

28 And the middle bar [*center crossbar*] in the midst of the boards shall reach from end to end.

29 And thou shalt overlay the boards with gold, and make their rings of gold for places for the bars: and thou shalt overlay the bars with gold.

Imagine how breathtaking it would be to see the Tabernacle with gold leaf on all of the frames and crossbars!

30 And thou shalt rear up [*set up*] the tabernacle according to the fashion thereof which was shewed thee in the mount.

Next, Moses is given the plans or pattern for making the veil or curtain that will separate the Holy Place from the Holy of Holies, in which the ark of the covenant will be placed.

31 ¶ And thou shalt make a vail of blue, and purple, and scarlet, and fine twined linen of cunning [*high quality, skilled*] work: with cherubims shall it be made:

32 And thou shalt hang it upon four pillars of shittim [*acacia*] wood overlaid with gold: their hooks shall be of gold, upon the four sockets [*bases*] of silver.

33 ¶ And thou shalt hang up the vail under the taches [*from the clasps*], that thou mayest bring in thither [*into the Holy of Holies*] within the vail the ark of the testimony [*the ark of the covenant containing the stone tables*]: and the vail shall divide unto you between the holy place and the most holy.

34 And thou shalt put the mercy seat [*the gold lid for the ark with cherubim on it*] upon the ark of the testimony in the most holy place.

35 And thou shalt set the table [*of shewbread*] without the veil [*outside of the Holy of Holies, on the Holy Place side of the veil*], and the candlestick [*menorah*] over against the table on the side of the tabernacle toward the south: and thou shalt put the table on the north side.

Next, Moses is given instructions for making and hanging the curtain for the entrance to the Tabernacle.

36 And thou shalt make an hanging

for the door of the tent, of blue, and purple, and scarlet, and fine twined linen, wrought with needlework.

37 And thou shalt make for the hanging five pillars of shittim wood, and overlay them with gold, and their hooks shall be of gold: and thou shalt cast five sockets [bases] of brass for them.

EXODUS 27

THIS CHAPTER IS a continuation of instructions from the Lord, recorded in chapters 25-30, given to Moses on Mt. Sinai, concerning the building of the Tabernacle (see background notes for chapter 25).

Here in chapter 27, Moses receives instructions for the building of the altar of sacrifice (verses 1-8), for the construction of the outer courtyard of the Tabernacle (verses 9-19), and for the production and donation of pure olive oil (verses 20-21).

As mentioned above, the first 8 verses of this chapter are the "blueprints" for the altar of burnt offerings or altar of sacrifice. It was to be the first thing the people saw as they entered through the east gate onto the tabernacle grounds. It would be upon this altar that animal sacrifices would be offered. It was to be about 7½ feet square and 4½ feet high and was symbolic of the obedience and sacrifice required to progress toward entrance into the presence of God (symbolized by the Holy of Holies).

1 AND thou shalt make an altar of shittim [acacia] wood, five cubits long [7½ feet], and five cubits broad [in other words, square]; the altar shall be foursquare [square]: and the height thereof shall be three cubits [4½ feet].

2 And thou shalt make the horns [symbolic of power] of it upon the four corners thereof: his horns shall be of the same [NIV: the horns and the altar are to be of one piece]: and thou shalt overlay it with brass [bronze— see footnote 2c in your Bible].

Next, the plans for the tools and implements to be used with this altar are given.

3 And thou shalt make his pans to receive his ashes, and his shovels, and his basons, and his fleshhooks, and his firepans: all the vessels thereof thou shalt make of brass.

4 And thou shalt make for it a grate of network of brass [a bronze grate]; and upon the net shalt thou make four brasen rings in the four corners thereof [for transporting it—see also verse 7].

5 And thou shalt put it under the compass [ledge—see footnote 5a in your Bible] of the altar beneath, that the net may be even to the midst of the altar [half way up the altar].

6 And thou shalt make staves for

the altar [*poles for purposes of carrying it*], staves of shittim wood, and overlay them with brass.

7 And the staves shall be put into the rings, and the staves shall be upon the two sides of the altar, to bear it.

8 Hollow with boards shalt thou make it: as it was shewed thee in the mount [*on Mt. Sinai*], so shall they make it.

Next, in verses 9–19, we see the plans for the outer courtyard which was to be 150 feet long and 75 feet wide, surrounded by a seven-and-a-half foot high fence made of pillars and panels of fine white linen.

Be aware that the Tabernacle and outer courtyard were rectangular shaped, oriented east and west, such that the entrance to the courtyard was on the east end and the entrance to the Tabernacle itself was likewise on the east end. "East" often symbolized "heaven" or "being influenced by heaven," in biblical symbolism. The Savior will come from the east at the time of the second coming—see Joseph Smith—Matthew 1:26.

9 ¶ And thou shalt make the court of the tabernacle: for the south side southward there shall be hangings [*curtains or panels*] for the court of fine twined linen [*fine white linen*] of an hundred cubits [*150 feet*] long for one side:

10 And the twenty pillars thereof and their twenty sockets [*bases*] shall be of brass; the hooks of the pillars and their fillets [*rectangular bands around the pillars for protection of the wood and for beauty*] shall be of silver.

11 And likewise for the north side [*the north wall of the courtyard*] in length there shall be hangings of an hundred cubits long, and his twenty pillars and their twenty sockets of brass; the hooks of the pillars and their fillets of silver.

12 ¶ And for the breadth of the court on the west side shall be hangings of fifty cubits [*75 feet*]: their pillars ten, and their sockets ten.

13 And the breadth of the court on the east side eastward shall be fifty cubits.

14 The hangings [*panels*] of one side of the gate [*entrance*] shall be fifteen cubits: their pillars [*posts*] three, and their sockets [*bases*] three.

15 And on the other side shall be hangings fifteen cubits: their pillars three, and their sockets three.

Imagine the beauty of the thirty-foot-wide curtain in the east wall, spoken of in verse 16, next, with its beautiful colors and intricate needlework, that will form the entrance to the outer courtyard!

16 ¶ And for the gate [*the entrance to the courtyard, in the east wall*]

of the court shall be an hanging [*curtain*] of twenty cubits [*30 feet*], of blue, and purple, and scarlet, and fine twined linen, wrought with needlework: and their pillars shall be four, and their sockets four.

17 All the pillars round about the court shall be filleted with silver; their hooks shall be of silver, and their sockets of brass [*bronze*].

18 ¶ The length of the court shall be an hundred cubits, and the breadth fifty every where, and the height five cubits of fine twined linen, and their sockets of brass.

19 All the vessels [*NIV: "All the other articles"*] of the tabernacle in all the service thereof, and all the pins [*tent pegs*] thereof, and all the pins of the court [*pegs the wall pillars are tied to*], shall be of brass.

In verses 20–21, we see that the people themselves are to provide the pure olive oil that will be used in the seven lamps of the golden candlestick, or menorah, which will be located in the Holy Place. This could be similar in privilege to that of our members who provide beautiful altar cloths for our temples today.

20 ¶ And thou shalt command the children of Israel, that they bring thee pure oil olive beaten for the light, to cause the lamp [*menorah*] to burn always.

21 In the tabernacle of the congregation without the vail, which is before the testimony [*outside of the veil which will screen the Holy of Holies and the ark of the testimony— ark of the covenant—from view from the Holy Place*], Aaron and his sons shall order it from evening to morning before the LORD: it shall be a statute for ever unto their generations on the behalf of the children of Israel.

EXODUS 28

THIS CHAPTER IS a continuation of instructions from the Lord, recorded in chapters 25–30, given to Moses while he was Mt. Sinai. It is a continuation of the plans or "blueprints" for building the Tabernacle and preparing all things pertaining to worship in it. Specifically, chapter 28 deals with consecrating and anointing Aaron (Moses's older brother by three years—see Exodus 7:7) and his sons to minister in the priest's office. It also gives details about special sacred clothing for such ministering.

1 AND take thou unto thee Aaron thy brother, and his sons with him, from among the children of Israel, that he may minister unto me in the priest's office, even Aaron, Nadab and Abihu, Eleazar and Ithamar, Aaron's sons.

Next, we see that special "holy" clothing is to be made for Aaron, who will serve as the high priest (of the Aaronic Priesthood) and for his sons, who will serve as priests.

The priests wore four articles of sacred clothing, a plain white robe, a sash, a turban or cap, and special underpants or "linen breeches to cover their nakedness" (verse 42). In addition, the high priest wore a blue robe over the basic white robe, an ephod or "apron," as it is sometimes translated" (*Old Testament Student Manual*, p 152), a breastplate made of fabric (the lower half folded up to form a pocket into which the Urim and Thummim could be placed) , and a gold plate on the front of his mitre or cap, on which was inscribed "HOLINESS TO THE LORD."

2 And thou shalt make holy garments for Aaron thy brother for glory and for beauty.

In verse 3, next, Moses is instructed to assign the making of this special clothing to those who are sensitive to inspiration.

3 And thou shalt speak unto all that are wise hearted, whom I have filled with the spirit of wisdom, that they may make Aaron's garments to consecrate him, that he may minister unto me in the priest's office.

4 And **these** *are* **the garments** which they shall make; a **breastplate** [*functioned also as a holder for the Urim and Thummim that Aaron had—see verse 30*], and an **ephod** [*apron—see* Old Testament Student Manual, *page 152*], and a **robe**, and

a **broidered coat**, a **mitre** [*a cap*], and a **girdle** [*NIV: a sash*]: and they shall make holy garments for Aaron thy brother, and his sons, that he may minister unto me in the priest's office.

5 And they shall take gold, and blue, and purple, and scarlet, and fine linen.

6 ¶ And they shall make the ephod [*vest or apron worn by the high priest, worn over a blue robe*] of gold, of blue, and of purple, of scarlet, and fine twined linen, with cunning [*skillful, artistic*] work.

7 It shall have the two shoulderpieces [*straps*] thereof joined at the two edges thereof; and so it shall be joined together.

8 And the curious [*beautifully woven*] girdle [*waistband or sash*]of the ephod, which is upon it, shall be of the same [*same fabric as the ephod*], according to the work thereof; even of gold, of blue, and purple, and scarlet, and fine twined linen.

Next, we see that two onyx stones set in gold are to be crafted, one for each shoulder strap of the ephod, engraved with the names of the sons of Jacob (Israel), six on one stone and the other six on the other stone.

9 And thou shalt take two onyx stones, and grave on them the names of the children of Israel:

10 Six of their names on one stone, and the other six names of the rest on the other stone, according to their birth.

11 With the work of an engraver in stone, like the engravings of a signet [*like the engravings on a signet ring or seal*], shalt thou engrave the two stones with the names of the children of Israel: thou shalt make them to be set in ouches of gold [*gold settings*].

12 And thou shalt put the two stones upon the shoulders of the ephod for stones of memorial unto the children of Israel [*to serve as symbols or reminders of Israel and God's covenants with them*]: and Aaron shall bear their names before the LORD upon his two shoulders for a memorial.

13 ¶ And thou shalt make ouches [*settings*] of gold;

Next, we see that the fabric breastplate will be attached to the ephod with gold chains fastened to the settings in which the two engraved onyx stones were placed.

14 And two chains of pure gold at the ends; of wreathen [*braided*] work shalt thou make them, and fasten the wreathen chains to the ouches.

Next, Moses is shown the pattern or plans for the cloth breastplate. It will have twelve precious stones, representing the twelve tribes of Israel and will be attached to the high priest's ephod with gold chains and fasteners. It is to be made of beautiful fabric, the same material as was used in making the ephod. Its length will be twice its width, and the bottom half will be folded up to make a pocket for the Urim and Thummim used by the high priest. It is interesting that the breastplate given to Joseph Smith (Doctrine and Covenants 17:1) was likewise used to hold the Urim and Thummim given to him (Joseph Smith—History 1:35). However, the breastplate made for Aaron was of fabric, whereas the breastplate given to Joseph Smith was made of metal (*Old Testament Student Manual*, p 152).

15 ¶ And thou shalt make the breastplate of judgment [*NIV: for making decisions*] with cunning [*skilled, careful*] work; after the work [*using the same fabric*] of the ephod thou shalt make it; of gold, of blue, and of purple, and of scarlet, and of fine twined linen, shalt thou make it.

16 Foursquare [*square*] it shall be being doubled [*when it is folded*]; a span [*NIV: about 9 inches*] shall be the length thereof, and a span shall be the breadth thereof.

The precious stones to be attached to the breastplate are described in verses 17–20.

17 And thou shalt set in it settings

of stones, even four rows of stones: the first row shall be a sardius, a topaz, and a carbuncle [*a red precious stone*]: this shall be the first row.

18 And the second row shall be an emerald, a sapphire, and a diamond.

19 And the third row a ligure [*NIV: jacinth*], an agate, and an amethyst.

20 And the fourth row a beryl, and an onyx, and a jasper: they shall be set in gold in their inclosings.

> We see in verse 21, next, that each stone is to have the name of one of the tribes of Israel engraved on it.

21 And the stones shall be with the names of the children of Israel, twelve, according to their names, like the engravings of a signet; every one with his name shall they be according to the twelve tribes.

> Next, Moses is given the plans for attaching the breastplate to the high priest's vest or apron.

22 ¶ And thou shalt make upon the breastplate chains at the ends of wreathen [*braided*] work of pure gold.

23 And thou shalt make upon the breastplate two rings of gold, and shalt put the two rings on the two ends of the breastplate.

24 And thou shalt put the two wreathen chains of gold in the two rings which are on the ends of the breastplate.

25 And the other two ends of the two wreathen chains thou shalt fasten in the two ouches [*sockets or fasteners*], and put them on the shoulderpieces [*shoulder straps*] of the ephod [*the high priests' vest or apron*] before it [*in the front*].

26 ¶ And thou shalt make two rings of gold, and thou shalt put them upon the two ends of the breastplate in the border thereof, which is in the side of the ephod inward.

27 And two other rings of gold thou shalt make, and shalt put them on the two sides of the ephod underneath, toward the forepart thereof, over against the other coupling thereof, above the curious girdle of the ephod.

28 And they shall bind the breastplate by the rings thereof unto the rings of the ephod with a lace of blue, that it may be above the curious girdle of the ephod, and that the breastplate be not loosed from the ephod [*so that the breastplate will not flop around when the high priest is moving about*].

> Next, we see that when Aaron, the high priest of the Aaronic Priesthood, is wearing the breastplate with its 12 stones, it will symbolize that the twelve tribes of Israel are close to his

heart. Likewise, it will symbolize that the people of covenant Israel are close to the heart of the Savior, the "High Priest of our profession, Christ Jesus." (Hebrews 3:1.)

29 And Aaron shall bear the names of the children of Israel in the breastplate of judgment upon his heart, when he goeth in unto the holy place, for a memorial before the LORD continually.

Verse 30, next, explains that one of the functions of the breastplate will be that of a Urim and Thummim holder, as explained in the note following verse 14.

30 ¶ And thou shalt put in the breastplate of judgment the Urim and the Thummim; and they shall be upon Aaron's heart, when he goeth in before the LORD [*when he goes into the Holy of Holies in the Tabernacle*]: and Aaron shall bear the judgment of the children of Israel upon his heart before the LORD continually.

We will add a note from the Bible Dictionary here regarding the Urim and Thummim (bold added for emphasis):

Bible Dictionary: Urim and Thummim
"Hebrew term that means Lights and Perfections. An instrument prepared of God to assist man in obtaining revelation from the Lord and in translating languages. See Ex. 28:30; Lev. 8:8; Num. 27:21; Deut. 33:8; 1 Sam. 28:6; Ezra 2:63; Neh. 7:65; JS–H 1:35.

"Using a Urim and Thummim is the special prerogative of a seer, and it would seem reasonable that such instruments were used from the time of Adam. However, the earliest mention is in connection with the brother of Jared (Ether 3:21–28). Abraham used a Urim and Thummim (Abr. 3:1–4), as did Aaron and the priests of Israel, and also the prophets among the Nephites (Omni 1:20–21; Mosiah 8:13–19; 21:26–28; 28:11–20; Ether 4:1–7). There is more than one Urim and Thummim, but we are informed that Joseph Smith had the one used by the brother of Jared (Ether 3:22–28; Doctrine and Covenants 10:1; 17:1). (See Seer.) A partial description is given in JS–H 1:35. Joseph Smith used it in translating the Book of Mormon and in obtaining other revelations.

"This earth in its celestial condition will be a Urim and Thummim, and many within that kingdom will have an additional Urim and Thummim (Doctrine and Covenants 130:6–11)."

Next, Jehovah gives Moses the pattern for the special blue robe Aaron will wear as he officiates in the office of the high priest. It is to be one piece, woven without seams, with a hole for his head to go through.

The Savior, the "Great High Priest," was dressed in a similar seamless cloak before His crucifixion according to John 19:23.

31 ¶ And thou shalt make the robe of the ephod all of blue.

32 And there shall be an hole in the top of it, in the midst thereof: it shall have a binding of woven work round about the hole of it, as it were the hole of an habergeon [*a sleeveless coat of mail*], that it be not rent [*so it wouldn't tear*].

Verses 33-34 tell us about the alternating gold bells and fringes woven to look like pomegranates that were to be attached to the hem of the robe.

33 ¶ And beneath upon the hem of it thou shalt make pomegranates of blue, and of purple, and of scarlet, round about the hem thereof; and bells of gold between them round about:

34 A golden bell and a pomegranate, a golden bell and a pomegranate [*alternating*], upon the hem of the robe round about.

Imagine the reverent hush that would come upon the people who were close enough to hear the bells when Aaron went into the Holy Place!

35 And it shall be upon Aaron to minister: and his sound shall be heard when he goeth in unto the holy place before the LORD, and when he cometh out, that he die not.

Verses 36-38 describe the special pure gold plate to be made for the front of the high priest's turban or cap, on which "HOLINESS TO THE LORD" will be inscribed. This symbolizes being consecrated to the Lord (Exodus 28:36, footnote b, in your Bible). It is also symbolic of Christ, the Great High Priest, who is perfectly holy before the Father. We see this inscription on the outside of our temples today.

36 ¶ And thou shalt make a plate of pure gold, and grave upon it, like the engravings of a signet, HOLINESS TO THE LORD.

Next, a blue cord is to be made by which the gold plate is to be attached to the cap.

37 And thou shalt put it on a blue lace, that it may be upon the mitre [*cap or turban*]; upon the forefront of the mitre it shall be.

38 And it shall be upon Aaron's forehead, that Aaron may bear the iniquity of the holy things, which the children of Israel shall hallow in all their holy gifts; and it shall be always upon his forehead, that they may be accepted before the LORD.

39 ¶ And thou shalt embroider the coat of fine linen, and thou shalt make the mitre of fine linen, and thou shalt make the girdle of needlework.

According to verses 40-43, Aaron's sons are also to have

special, sacred clothing made for them when they offici- ate as priests. They will have a white robe or coat, a girdle or sash, a cap or turban, and "linen breeches" (underpants or undergarments), as mentioned in verse 42.

40 ¶ And for Aaron's sons thou shalt make coats, and thou shalt make for them girdles, and bonnets shalt thou make for them, for glory and for beauty.

In verse 41, next, Moses is told that he is to anoint, consecrate, and sanctify Aaron and his sons, when the time comes, so that they may be enabled to minister in their priestly offices. You will see more about this in chapter 29.

41 And thou shalt put them upon Aaron thy brother, and his sons with him; and shalt anoint them, and consecrate them, and sanctify them [*make them pure and holy, fit to be in the presence of God*], that they may minister unto me in the priest's office.

42 And thou shalt make them linen breeches to cover their nakedness; from the loins even unto the thighs they shall reach:

43 And they shall be upon Aaron, and upon his sons, when they come in unto the tabernacle of the con- gregation, or when they come near unto the altar to minister in the holy place; that they bear not iniquity

[*"do not incur guilt"—see footnote 43c, in your Bible*], and die: it shall be a statute for ever unto him and his seed after him.

EXODUS 29

THIS CHAPTER IS a continuation of instructions from the Lord, recorded in Exodus, chapters 25–30, given to Moses while he was Mt. Sinai communicating with Jehovah. It is a continuation of the plans or "blueprints" for building the Tabernacle and preparing all things pertaining to worship in it.

According to verses 1–9, Aaron and his sons are to be washed, anointed, and consecrated, preparatory for their sacred work in conjunction with the Tabernacle. Verses 10–42 are instruc- tions for various sacrifices and offer- ings to be made when the Tabernacle is finished and put in service. Verses 43–46 assure the people that the Lord's presence will dwell with them through their obedience to His instructions.

1 And this *is* the thing that thou shalt do unto them **to hallow** [*sanc- tify, make pure and holy, fit to be in the presence of God*] **them,** to minister unto me in the priest's office: Take one young bullock, and two rams **without blemish** [*symbolic of Jesus and His perfect life*],

2 And unleavened bread, and cakes unleavened tempered with oil, and wafers unleavened anointed with oil: of wheaten flour shalt thou make them.

3 And thou shalt put them into one basket, and bring them in the basket, with the bullock and the two rams.

4 And Aaron and his sons thou shalt bring unto the door of the tabernacle of the congregation, and shalt wash them with water.

In verses 5-6, next, instructions are given for clothing Aaron in the sacred clothing described in chapter 28, in preparation for his ministering in the office of high priest of the Aaronic Priesthood. These instructions will be carried out in chapter 40, after the Tabernacle is completed.

5 And thou shalt take the garments, and put upon Aaron the coat, and the robe of the ephod, and the ephod, and the breastplate, and gird him [*clothe him*] with the curious [*beautifully woven*] girdle of the ephod:

6 And thou shalt put the mitre [*cap*] upon his head, and put the holy crown [*the gold plate engraved with "Holiness to the Lord," as described in chapter 28, verses 36–38*] upon the mitre.

7 Then shalt thou take the anointing oil, and pour it upon his head, and anoint him.

8 And thou shalt bring his sons, and put coats upon them.

9 And thou shalt gird them with girdles, Aaron and his sons, and put the bonnets [*caps*] on them: and the priest's office shall be theirs for a perpetual statute: and thou shalt consecrate Aaron and his sons.

In the following verses, there is much Atonement symbolism. You will see the priests place their hands upon the head of the animals to be sacrificed, symbolizing that our sins would be placed upon the Savior as He submitted to being sacrificed to pay the price for our salvation.

You will see the blood of sacrificial animals sprinkled upon the altar of sacrifice, symbolic of Christ's blood, shed for us.

You will see parts of the sacrificial animals burned upon the altar. Bruce R. McConkie explained the symbolism in this:

"Fire is a cleansing agent. Filth and disease die in its flames. The baptism of fire, which John promised Christ would bring, means that when men receive the actual companionship of the Holy Spirit, then evil and iniquity are burned out of their souls as though by fire. The sanctifying power of that member of the Godhead makes them clean. In similar imagery, all the fires on all the altars of the past, as they burned the flesh of animals, were signifying that spiritual purification would come by the Holy Ghost, whom the Father would send because of the Son." (*The Promised Messiah*, pp. 431–432.)

25

10 And thou shalt cause a bullock to be brought before the tabernacle of the congregation: and Aaron and his sons shall put their hands upon the head of the bullock.

11 And thou shalt kill the bullock before the LORD, by the door of the tabernacle of the congregation.

12 And thou shalt take of the blood of the bullock, and put it upon the horns of the altar with thy finger, and pour all the blood beside the bottom of the altar.

13 And thou shalt take all the fat that covereth the inwards, and the caul [*membrane*] that is above the liver, and the two kidneys, and the fat that is upon them, and burn them upon the altar.

14 But the flesh of the bullock, and his skin, and his dung, shalt thou burn with fire without the camp [*outside of the camp of the Israelites*]: it is a sin offering.

15 ¶ Thou shalt also take one ram; and Aaron and his sons shall put their hands upon the head of the ram.

16 And thou shalt slay the ram, and thou shalt take his blood, and sprinkle it round about upon the altar [*symbolic of the shedding of Christ's blood in Gethsemane and on the cross*].

17 And thou shalt cut the ram in pieces, and wash the inwards of him, and his legs, and put them unto his pieces, and unto his head.

18 And thou shalt burn the whole ram upon the altar [*symbolic of being cleansed by fire and the Holy Ghost*]: it is a burnt offering unto the LORD: it is a sweet savour, an offering made by fire unto the LORD.

19 ¶ And thou shalt take the other ram; and Aaron and his sons shall put their hands upon the head of the ram.

20 Then shalt thou kill the ram, and take of his blood, and put it upon the tip of the right ear of Aaron, and upon the tip of the right ear of his sons, and upon the thumb of their right hand, and upon the great toe of their right foot, and sprinkle the blood upon the altar round about.

The symbolism in verse 20, above, is explained in a commentary on the Bible quoted in the *Old Testament Student Manual, Genesis-2 Samuel*, p 153, as follows:

"The priest put some of [the] blood [from the offering] upon the tip of the right ear, the right thumb, and the great toe of the right foot of the person to be consecrated, in order that the organ of hearing, with which he hearkened to the word of the Lord, and those used in acting and walking according to His commandments, might thereby be sanctified through the power of the atoning blood of the sacrifice" (Keil and Delitzsch, Commentary, 1:2:387-88).

In verse 7, earlier in this chapter, you saw an instruction for the use of "anointing oil," to be carried out when the Tabernacle is completed and put into service. We see "anointing oil" again in verse 21, next. We will quote from the *Old Testament Student Manual*, pp 153-54, this time in reference to the use of pure olive oil in anointing.

"Pure olive oil was a sacred symbol of the Spirit of the Lord (see Doctrine and Covenants 45:56-57), and its use signified the sanctification of the person or object anointed (see Exodus 30:29). The use of the oil can also be an indication of the existing purity of the person, since the Spirit of the Lord will not dwell in an unclean tabernacle. President Joseph Fielding Smith said: 'The olive tree from the earliest times has been the emblem of peace and purity. It has, perhaps, been considered more nearly sacred than any other tree or form of vegetation by the inspired writers of all ages through whom we have received the word of the Lord. In parables in the scriptures the House of Israel, or the people who have made covenant with the Lord, have been compared to the olive tree.' (*Doctrines of Salvation*, 3:180.) Thus, to anoint even these inanimate objects with oil suggests that the tabernacle and all connected with it were sanctified by the Spirit in preparing them for service to God."

21 And thou shalt take of the blood that is upon the altar, and of the anointing oil, and sprinkle it upon Aaron, and upon his garments, and upon his sons, and upon the garments of his sons with him: and he shall be hallowed [*cleansed, made pure and holy*], and his garments, and his sons, and his sons' garments with him.

As mentioned in the Background to this chapter, verses 10-42 are instructions for various sacrifices and offerings to be made when the Tabernacle is finished and put in service. You may wish to study more about some of these rites in the Bible Dictionary in your English edition of the LDS Bible, under "Feasts."

22 Also thou shalt take of the ram the fat and the rump, and the fat that covereth the inwards, and the caul above the liver, and the two kidneys, and the fat that is upon them, and the right shoulder; for it is a ram of consecration:

23 And one loaf of bread, and one cake of oiled bread, and one wafer out of the basket of the unleavened bread that is before the LORD:

24 And thou shalt put all in the hands of Aaron, and in the hands of his sons; and shalt wave them for a wave offering [*lift them up to heaven as an offering—see footnote 24a, in your Bible*] before the LORD.

25 And thou shalt receive them of their hands, and burn them upon the altar for a burnt offering, for a sweet savour before the LORD: it is an offering made by fire unto the LORD.

26 And thou shalt take the breast of the ram of Aaron's consecration, and wave it for a wave offering before the LORD: and it shall be thy part.

27 And thou shalt sanctify the breast of the wave offering, and the shoulder of the heave offering, which is waved, and which is heaved up [*waved and lifted up before the Lord*], of the ram of the consecration, even of that which is for Aaron, and of that which is for his sons:

28 And it shall be Aaron's and his sons' by a statute for ever from the children of Israel: for it is an heave offering: and it shall be an heave offering from the children of Israel of the sacrifice of their peace offerings, even their heave offering unto the LORD.

In verse 29, next, Jehovah tells Moses that Aaron's sacred clothing is to be passed on to his male descendents so that they, too, can be anointed and ordained in them.

29 ¶ And the holy garments of Aaron shall be his sons' after him, to be anointed therein, and to be consecrated in them.

30 And that son that is priest in his stead shall put them on seven days, when he cometh into the tabernacle of the congregation to minister in the holy place.

31 ¶ And thou shalt take the ram of the consecration, and seethe [*cook*] his flesh in the holy place.

32 And Aaron and his sons shall eat the flesh of the ram, and the bread that is in the basket, by the door of the tabernacle of the congregation.

33 And they shall eat those things wherewith the atonement was made, to consecrate and to sanctify them: but a stranger shall not eat thereof, because they are holy.

34 And if ought of the flesh of the consecrations, or of the bread, remain unto the morning, then thou shalt burn the remainder with fire: it shall not be eaten, because it is holy.

In verse 35, next, Moses is told that the rites of consecration for Aaron and his sons are to take seven days. The number seven, in biblical symbolism, means several things, including perfection and completeness, the work of the Lord. Thus, these priests have the role of helping to perfect the people and bring them home to God.

35 And thus shalt thou do unto Aaron, and to his sons, according to all things which I have commanded thee: seven days shalt thou consecrate them.

36 And thou shalt offer every day [*each of the seven days*] a bullock for a sin offering for atonement: and thou shalt cleanse the altar, when thou hast made an atonement for it, and thou shalt anoint it, to sanctify it.

37 Seven days thou shalt make an atonement for the altar, and sanctify it; and it shall be an altar most holy: whatsoever toucheth the altar shall be holy.

Once the Tabernacle is up and running, the authorized priests are to offer a daily sacrifice, as explained in verses 38–41. According to verse 42, this daily sacrifice is to continue throughout the generations.

38 ¶ Now this is that which thou shalt offer upon the altar; two lambs of the first year day by day continually.

39 The one lamb thou shalt offer in the morning; and the other lamb thou shalt offer at even:

40 And with the one lamb a tenth deal of flour mingled with the fourth part of an hin [*NIV: probably about one quart*] of beaten oil; and the fourth part of an hin of wine for a drink offering.

41 And the other lamb thou shalt offer at even, and shalt do thereto according to the meat offering of the morning, and according to the drink offering thereof, for a sweet savour, an offering made by fire unto the LORD.

42 This shall be a continual burnt offering throughout your generations at the door of the tabernacle of the congregation before the LORD: where I will meet you, to speak there unto thee.

Verses 43–46 assure the people that the Lord's presence will dwell with them through their obedience to His instructions.

43 And there I will meet with the children of Israel, and the tabernacle shall be sanctified [*cleansed and made holy*] by my glory.

44 And I will sanctify the tabernacle of the congregation, and the altar: I will sanctify also both Aaron and his sons, to minister to me in the priest's office.

45 ¶ And I will dwell among the children of Israel, and will be their God.

46 And they shall know that I am the LORD their God, that brought them forth out of the land of Egypt, that I may dwell among them: I am the LORD their God.

EXODUS 30

THIS CHAPTER IS the last of a series of chapters (Exodus 25-30) recording instructions from the Lord, given to Moses on Mt. Sinai, revealing the plans or "blueprints" for building the Tabernacle and preparing all things pertaining to worship in it.

Verses 1-10 are the plans for the altar of incense that will be placed just outside of the veil separating the Holy of Holies from the Holy Place. When this altar is built and placed in the completed Tabernacle, hot coals will be placed on it each morning and evening on which the high priest will burn incense. Included in the symbolism here is the idea that a person can approach God through prayer, thus, in effect, piercing the veil and communicating with God. Revelation 5:8 teaches that incense symbolizes the prayers of the saints rising up to God.

1 AND thou shalt make an altar to burn incense upon: of shittim [acacia] wood shalt thou make it.

> This altar will be 18 by 18 inches square and 3 feet high. It will have horns (a symbol of power) one at each top corner. It will be covered with pure gold.

2 A cubit [about 18 inches] shall be the length thereof, and a cubit the breadth thereof; foursquare [square] shall it be: and two cubits shall be the height thereof: the horns thereof shall be of the same.

3 And thou shalt overlay it with pure gold, the top thereof, and the sides thereof round about, and the horns thereof; and thou shalt make unto it a crown [border] of gold round about.

> It will have two gold rings on each side, just under the top border, through which gold covered poles will be inserted for purposes of transporting it.

4 And two golden rings shalt thou make to it under the crown of it, by the two corners thereof, upon the two sides of it shalt thou make it; and they shall be for places for the staves to bear it withal [with which to carry it].

5 And thou shalt make the staves [poles] of shittim wood, and overlay them with gold.

6 And thou shalt put it before the vail that is by the ark of the testimony [outside of the veil that is next to the ark of the covenant], before the mercy seat [the lid of the ark of the covenant] that is over the testimony [the stone tablets housed in the ark of the covenant, on which the Ten Commandments were written by the finger of the Lord], where I will meet with thee.

7 And Aaron shall burn thereon sweet incense every morning: when he dresseth the lamps, he shall burn incense upon it.

8 And when Aaron lighteth the lamps at even [*in the evening*], he shall burn incense upon it, a perpetual incense before the LORD throughout your generations.

This is to be a limited use altar, as indicated in verse 9.

9 Ye shall offer no strange incense thereon, nor burnt sacrifice, nor meat offering; neither shall ye pour drink offering thereon.

In verse 10, next, instructions are given to Moses by Jehovah, the premortal Christ, for a yearly symbolic representation of His own Atonement. It is to be performed by Aaron, the Aaronic Priesthood high priest. It will point the minds of the Israelites to the future Atonement of Christ, the Great High Priest, for the sins of all.

10 And Aaron shall make an atonement upon the horns of it once in a year with the blood of the sin offering of atonements: once in the year shall he make atonement upon it throughout your generations: it is most holy unto the LORD.

Much more detail about this yearly sacrifice is given in Leviticus 16 and elsewhere in the Old Testament. In the New Testament, the Apostle Paul refers to it in Hebrews.

Hebrews 9:7

7 But into the second [*the Holy of Holies*] went the high priest alone once every year, not without blood, which he offered for himself, and for the errors of the people:

We read more about this in the New Testament student manual used by Institutes of Religion of the Church:

"Each division of the tabernacle was regarded as a sacred sanctuary. While priests might enter the outer chamber [*the Holy Place*] every day as required by priestly duty, only the high priest (i.e., the presiding priest, who was to be of the tribe of Levi and a firstborn son of a direct descendent of Aaron) might enter the Holy of Holies, and that but once a year on Yom Kippur, or the Day of Atonement. This is the most sacred of all days in the Jewish year and had for its purpose the offering up of a special sacrifice within the Holy of Holies for the sins of the people. The ritual involved a series of events, the first two of which were to prepare the high priest for his solemn duties. First he would make sacrifices for himself and his brother priests so as to make them symbolically worthy to perform their sacred functions. Then he would lay aside his priestly robes, don a simple white tunic in preparation for the sacrifice itself, and return to the outer court. Taking two pure and unblemished male goats, he would dedicate one to Jehovah and one to the evil one, Azazel, or the devil. The goat dedicated to Jehovah was then sacrificed in the outer court. Its blood was taken into the Holy of Holies and sprinkled on the mercy-seat and before the ark of the covenant. This symbolized that Israel's sins were atoned for by sacrifice." (*The Life And Teachings of Jesus & His Apostles*, 1979, p 390.)

In verses 11-16, next, a sum of money (called "atonement money" in verse 16) is levied which will provide funds for the operation of the Tabernacle.

11 ¶ And the LORD spake unto Moses, saying,

12 When thou takest the sum [*a count or census*] of the children of Israel after their number, then shall they give every man a ransom for his soul [*symbolic of the Savior's Atonement, which "ransoms" our souls*] unto the LORD, when thou numberest them; that there be no plague among them, when thou numberest them.

13 This they shall give, every one that passeth among them that are numbered, half a shekel [*NIV: about* 1/5 *ounce, probably of silver, see Exodus 38:25–26*] after the shekel of the sanctuary: (a shekel is twenty gerahs:) an half shekel shall be the offering of the LORD.

This levy applies to those 20 years and older.

14 Every one that passeth among them that are numbered, from twenty years old and above, shall give an offering unto the LORD.

It is interesting to note, in verse 15, next, that no distinction is made based on ability to pay.

This may be a reminder that all people are of equal value before the Lord.

15 The rich shall not give more, and the poor shall not give less than half a shekel, when they give an offering unto the LORD, to make an atonement for your souls.

16 And thou shalt take the atonement money of the children of Israel, and shalt appoint it [*use it*] for the service of the tabernacle of the congregation; that it may be a memorial unto the children of Israel before the LORD, to make an atonement for your souls.

Next, in verses 17-21, Moses is instructed to have a bronze basin made and placed in the outer courtyard near the Tabernacle. Aaron and his sons will use it for washing their hands and feet, in order to be ceremonially clean before officiating.

17 ¶ And the LORD spake unto Moses, saying,

18 Thou shalt also make a laver [*basin*] of brass, and his foot [*its base*] also of brass, to wash withal [*for use in washings—see footnote 18a in your Bible*]: and thou shalt put it between the tabernacle of the congregation and the altar, and thou shalt put water therein.

19 For Aaron and his sons shall wash their hands and their feet thereat:

20 When they go into the tabernacle of the congregation, they shall wash with water, that they die not; or when they come near to the altar to minister, to burn offering made by fire unto the LORD:

21 So they shall wash their hands and their feet, that they die not: and it shall be a statute for ever to them, even to him and to his seed throughout their generations.

In verses 22-33, Moses is told how to make special anointing oil to be used in ritual cleansing and making holy. Perhaps you are aware that one of the uses of anointing is that of preparation for coming blessings (such as in the case of anointing before sealing the anointing, when a sick person is administered to by Melchizedek Priesthood holders.)

22 ¶ Moreover the LORD spake unto Moses, saying,

23 Take thou also unto thee principal spices, of pure myrrh five hundred shekels [NIV: about 12½ pounds], and of sweet cinnamon half so much, even two hundred and fifty shekels, and of sweet calamus two hundred and fifty shekels,

24 And of cassia five hundred shekels, after the shekel of the sanctuary, and of oil olive an hin [NIV: about four quarts]:

25 And thou shalt make it an oil of holy ointment, an ointment compound after the art of the apothecary: it shall be an holy anointing oil.

Next, Moses is instructed how to use the holy oil, after it is made, to prepare the Tabernacle and all associated with it for service.

26 And thou shalt anoint the tabernacle of the congregation therewith, and the ark of the testimony [ark of the covenant],

27 And the table and all his vessels, and the candlestick and his vessels, and the altar of incense,

28 And the altar of burnt offering with all his vessels, and the laver and his foot.

29 And thou shalt sanctify them, that they may be most holy: whatsoever toucheth them shall be holy.

30 And thou shalt anoint Aaron and his sons, and consecrate them, that they may minister unto me in the priest's office.

31 And thou shalt speak unto the children of Israel, saying, This shall be an holy anointing oil unto me throughout your generations.

Next, in verses 32-33, we see a strict warning against misusing this holy oil.

32 Upon man's flesh shall it not be poured, neither shall ye make any other like it, after the composition of it: it is holy, and it shall be holy unto you.

33 Whosoever compoundeth any like it, or whosoever putteth any of it upon a stranger, shall even be cut off [*excommunicated*] from his people.

> Verses 34–38 instruct Moses how to formulate the incense that will be used on the altar of incense in the Holy Place.

34 ¶ And the LORD said unto Moses, Take unto thee sweet spices, stacte, and onycha, and galbanum; these sweet spices with pure frankincense: of each shall there be a like weight [*equal amounts of each*]:

35 And thou shalt make it a perfume, a confection after the art of the apothecary, tempered together, pure and holy:

36 And thou shalt beat some of it very small, and put of it before the testimony in the tabernacle of the congregation, where I will meet with thee: it shall be unto you most holy.

37 And as for the perfume which thou shalt make, ye shall not make to yourselves according to the composition thereof: it shall be unto thee holy for the LORD.

38 Whosoever shall make like unto that, to smell thereto, shall even be cut off [*excommunicated*] from his people.

EXODUS 31

THE PLANS OR "blueprints" for the Tabernacle have now been given to Moses by the Lord as they communed on Mt. Sinai (chapters 25-30). Now, the focus is on preparations for actually constructing the Tabernacle. In verses 1-11, the Lord explains that He will inspire certain craftsmen as they work on the tabernacle and its furnishings. We see much of this type of inspiration in the design and construction of our modern temples.

1 AND the LORD spake unto Moses, saying,

2 See, I have called by name Bezaleel the son of Uri, the son of Hur, of the tribe of Judah:

3 And **I have filled him with the spirit of God, in wisdom, and in understanding, and in knowledge, and in all manner of workmanship**,

4 To devise cunning works [*skilled construction techniques*], to work in gold, and in silver, and in brass,

5 And in cutting of stones, to set them, and in carving of timber, to work in all manner of workmanship.

6 And I, behold, I have given with him Aholiab, the son of Ahisamach, of the tribe of Dan: and in the hearts of all that are wise hearted [*all the other workers who are subject to inspiration*] I have put wisdom, that they may make all that I have commanded thee;

Next, the Lord describes some of the projects these inspired craftsmen will work on.

7 The tabernacle of the congregation, and the ark of the testimony, and the mercy seat that is thereupon, and all the furniture of the tabernacle,

8 And the table and his furniture, and the pure candlestick with all his furniture, and the altar of incense,

9 And the altar of burnt offering with all his furniture, and the laver and his foot,

10 And the cloths of service, and the holy garments for Aaron the priest, and the garments of his sons, to minister in the priest's office,

11 And the anointing oil, and sweet incense for the holy place: according to all that I have commanded thee shall they do.

Next, we are clearly taught that the Sabbath is a special sign of a covenant between the Lord and His people. This certainly applies to us.

12 ¶ And the LORD spake unto Moses, saying,

13 Speak thou also unto the children of Israel, saying, Verily **my sabbaths ye shall keep**: for it *is* **a sign between me and you** throughout your generations; **that *ye* may know that I *am* the LORD that doth sanctify you** [*the Savior is the means by which we can be sanctified—in other words, made pure, clean, and holy, worthy to return to the Father's presence to live forever in celestial glory*].

14 **Ye shall keep the sabbath therefore** [*because it is the sign of the covenant between us and the Lord*]; **for it *is* holy unto you**: every one that defileth it shall surely be put to death [*breaking the Sabbath was a capital offence, punishable by death; this is a reminder of how important keeping the Sabbath is*]: for whosoever doeth *any* work therein, that soul shall be cut off from among his people.

15 **Six days may work be done; but in the seventh *is* the sabbath of rest, holy to the LORD**: whosoever doeth *any* work in the sabbath day, he shall surely be put to death.

16 **Wherefore** [*this is the reason why*] **the children of Israel shall keep the sabbath**, to observe the sabbath throughout their generations, *for* **a perpetual covenant.**

17 **It *is* a sign between me and the children of Israel for ever**: for *in* six days the LORD made heaven and earth, and on the seventh day he rested, and was refreshed.

As the forty days and forty

35

nights (Exodus 24:18) of instruction came to a close, Jesus gave Moses a set of stone tablets containing commandments and laws, written by His own finger.

18 And he gave unto Moses, when he had made an end of communing with him upon mount Sinai, **two tables of testimony, tables of stone, written with the finger of God.**

EXODUS 32

THIS CHAPTER DEALS with making and worshipping the golden calf. While Moses was on the mountain being instructed by Jehovah, the premortal Christ, his people down below were becoming restless. It seems that they were afflicted with what might be called the "re-deciding syndrome." They had trouble with long-term loyalty to the Lord, and kept "re-deciding" whether or not to keep the covenants they had made with Him such as the covenant they made as recorded in Exodus 24:3–8.

Sometimes, members of the Church find themselves similarly afflicted. They keep "re-deciding" whether or not to attend church, pay tithing, keep the word of wisdom, and so forth. Such lack of complete commitment takes a heavy toll on spirituality and peace of mind.

One of the symptoms of the "re-deciding syndrome" is lack of patience with the Lord and His servants. Some people want instant results and tend to grow critical when their perceived needs are not met according to their timetable. Faith is often developed and strengthened in an environment of delayed blessings. Impatience tends to damage faith.

In the case of the children of Israel, we see that they have become impatient with the long absence of Moses as he communes with the Lord on Sinai, and they turn to idol worship, likely learned in Egypt, instead of waiting faithfully for the Lord and His prophet.

There is another serious, difficult-to-understand problem with the apostate behavior of the Israelites here. Even though they have become impatient and are complaining that Moses has not returned, they can plainly see the glory of the Lord on Mount Sinai during the forty days he is gone (Exodus 24:17–18). Thus, they are in open rebellion, building and worshiping the golden calf while they have an obvious witness that the presence of the Lord is close by. He has not forgotten them. Perhaps you've noticed that wickedness does not promote rational thought!

We will now study the verses relating to the golden calf.

1 And when the people saw that Moses delayed to come down out of the mount, the people gathered themselves together **unto Aaron** [*Moses's brother*], **and said unto him, Up** [*a demand*], **make us gods** [*completely forbidden by the Ten Commandments, so recently received* and agreed to by covenant—see Exodus 20:4, 24:3–8], **which shall go before us** [to lead us]; **for** as for **this Moses, the man** [a put-down; they are distancing themselves from Moses; they should refer to him as the Lord's prophet] **that brought us up out of the land of Egypt, we wot not** [we don't know] **what is become of him.**

2 And Aaron said unto them, **Break off** [NIV: "take off"] **the golden earrings,** which are in the ears of your wives, of your sons, and of your daughters, and **bring** them **unto me.**

3 And all the people brake off [took out] **the golden earrings** which were in their ears, **and brought** them **unto Aaron.**

4 And he received them **at their hand,** and fashioned it with a graving tool, after **he had made** it **a molten calf: and they said, These** be **thy gods, O Israel, which brought thee up out of the land of Egypt.**

What we have here is stark contrast. On the one hand, Moses is on the mountain in the presence of the true God, being instructed in the building of the tabernacle in which true worship of Jehovah can take place. Among other things, he is being told to have the people donate their treasures and wealth for the building of the tabernacle.

In contrast, Aaron is giving in to the wicked demands of the people to build an idol, in direct violation of the very recently given second commandment, "Thou shalt not make unto thee any graven image" (Exodus 20:4). The people are invited to bring their wealth as offerings to be used in creating this abomination (verse 2).

This is an example of Satan's efforts to create a counterfeit culture of worship, in open rebellion against the ways of God.

Notice, next, that Aaron includes elements of true worship of Jehovah in this apostate worship, such as an altar and burnt offerings.

5 And when Aaron saw it, he built an altar before it; and Aaron made proclamation, and said, To morrow is a feast to the LORD.

6 And they rose up early on the morrow, and offered burnt offerings, and brought peace offerings [counterfeits of the offerings used in worshiping the true God]; and the people sat down to eat and to drink, and rose up to play [to participate in crudeness and sexual immorality—see verse 25].

We find ourselves feeling sorry for Moses as the Lord tells him what is going on down below.

7 ¶ And the LORD said unto Moses, Go, get thee down; for thy people, which thou broughtest out of the land of Egypt, have corrupted themselves:

8 They have turned aside quickly out of the way which I commanded them [*they have apostatized quickly*]: **they have made them a molten calf** [*they have melted gold and made a golden calf out of it*]**, and have worshipped it**, and **have sacrificed thereunto**, and **said, These** *be* **thy gods, O Israel, which have brought thee up out of the land of Egypt** [*they are claiming that an idol has rescued Israel from Egypt*].

> Next, in verses 9–10, the Lord proposes to Moses that He will destroy the children of Israel because of pride and wickedness so that He can start over with a new group of covenant people to lead.

9 And the LORD said unto Moses, I have seen this people, and, behold, it *is* **a stiffnecked** [*prideful*] **people:**

10 Now therefore let me alone [*step aside*]**, that my wrath** [*anger*] **may wax** [*grow*] **hot against them, and that I may consume them: and I will make of thee a great nation** [*I will start over with you and make a great covenant nation*].

> Watch in verses 11–13 as Moses reacts and pleads that his people be given another chance. Here, Moses is a "type" of Christ. In other words, he becomes symbolic of the Savior and His "pleading" our cause (Doctrine and Covenants 45:3), to give us additional opportunities to wake up spiritually, repent, and be successful.

The JST changes the whole meaning of the last part of verse 12, and solves a problem in which it looks like Moses tells the Lord to repent.

11 And Moses besought [*pled with*] **the LORD his God**, and said, LORD, why doth thy wrath wax hot against thy people, which thou hast brought forth out of the land of Egypt with great power, and with a mighty hand?

12 Wherefore [*why*] should the Egyptians speak [*gossip about us*], and say, For mischief [*with evil intent*] did he [*the god of the Israelites*] bring them out, to slay them in the mountains, and to consume them from the face of the earth? **Turn from thy fierce wrath, and repent of this evil against thy people.**

<u>JST Exodus 32:12</u>
12 Wherefore should the Egyptians speak, and say, For mischief did he bring them out, to slay them in the mountains, and to consume them from the face of the earth? **Turn from thy fierce wrath. Thy people will repent of this evil; therefore come thou not out against them.**

As you can see from the JST change, Moses assures the Lord that the people will repent and pleads that they be given another chance.

Moses continues, reasoning with the Lord about the role his people can play in the fulfilling of the promises Jehovah made to Abraham, Isaac, and Jacob.

13 Remember Abraham, Isaac, and Israel [*Jacob*], **thy servants, to whom thou swarest** [*made covenants*] **by thine own self, and saidst** unto them, **I will multiply your seed as the stars of heaven, and all this land** that I have spoken of **will I give unto your seed** [*posterity*], **and they shall inherit** *it* **for ever.**

In his role here, Moses can remind us of the servant in the allegory of the olive trees, found in Jacob, chapter five, of the Book of Mormon. There, the servant (symbolic of God's prophets) initially simply carries out the Lord's instructions (for example, Jacob 5:10). But as the allegory continues, he begins to take a more active role (for instance, Jacob 5:21). Yet farther along in the parable, when the Lord instructs that the wicked branches be cast into the fire, the servant pleads with the Lord to give the people another chance (Jacob 5:26–27).

Moses is being taught principles of compassionate leadership by the Master Teacher, which will ultimately lead to his becoming a god.

The JST makes very significant changes to verse 14, next. The whole verse is different than it stands in the Bible.

14 And the LORD repented of the evil which he thought to do unto his people.

JST Exodus 32:14

14 And the Lord said unto Moses, **If they will repent** of the evil which they have done, **I will spare them,** and turn away my fierce wrath; **but,** behold, **thou shalt execute judgment upon all that will not repent** [*Moses must play an unpleasant role in punishing the unrepentant wicked among his people—he will, in verses 25–29*] of this evil this day. **Therefore, see thou do this thing that I have commanded thee** [*you do it*], **or I will execute all that which I had thought to do unto my people.**

Moses hurries down the mountain, joined by Joshua who has been waiting part way up the mountain during the forty days and nights (Exodus 24:18).

Next, we get a description of the stone tablets, engraved by the finger of God.

15 ¶ And Moses turned, and went down from the mount, and the two tables of the testimony *were* in his hand: **the tables** *were* **written on both their sides;** on the one side and on the other *were* they written.

16 And **the tables** *were* **the work of God, and the writing** *was* **the writing of God,** graven [*engraved*] upon the tables.

Moses has already been told by the Lord what is going on below, in verses 7-8, but Joshua does not yet know.

17 And **when Joshua heard the noise of the people as they shouted, he said** unto Moses, *There is a* **noise of war in the camp** [*someone has attacked our people*].

18 And **he** [*Moses*] **said, *It is* not the voice of *them that* shout for mastery** [*it is not enemy voices crying for victory*], **neither *is it* the voice of *them that* cry for being overcome** [*nor the voice of victims being overpowered*]: **but the noise of *them that* sing do I hear** [*rather, it is riotous singing*].

Next, Moses breaks the tablets, which symbolizes, among other things, that the people have broken their covenant with God.

19 ¶ And it came to pass, as soon as he came nigh [*near*] unto the camp, that **he saw the calf, and the dancing** [*the riotous partying—see verse 25*]: and Moses' anger waxed hot, **and he cast the tables out of his hands, and brake them** beneath the mount.

Watch the punishment which Moses now metes out. The gold calf is melted down, ground into powder, and the people are forced to drink it.

20 And **he took the calf which they had made, and burnt** *it* **in the fire, and ground** *it* **to powder, and** strawed [*scattered*] it upon the water, and **made the children of Israel drink** *of it*.

Next, Aaron is called to accountability as Moses asks him what happened.

21 And Moses said unto Aaron, **What did this people unto thee, that thou hast brought so great a sin upon them?**

22 And **Aaron said, Let not the anger of my lord** [*a respectful term used by Aaron to address his younger brother, Moses*] **wax hot** [*don't get mad at me*]: **thou knowest the people, that they *are set* on mischief** [*you know how prone these people are to do evil*].

23 For **they said unto me, Make us gods, which shall go before us:** for *as for this Moses*, the man that brought us up out of the land of Egypt, **we wot not** [*know not*] **what is become of him.**

It seems that Aaron's explanation for how the gold calf came to be in verse 24, next, is about as good as some of our excuses for not keeping the commandments.

Remember that Aaron, too, is learning, and that he will repent and go on to play a great role among the children of Israel.

24 And I said unto them, Whosoever hath any **gold**, let them break *it* off [*take it off*]. So **they gave** *it* me: then **I cast it into the fire, and there came out this calf.**

25 ¶ And when Moses saw that **the people *were* naked** [*the Hebrew word*

for this can mean "bare, uncovered," or "unrestrained, let loose, wild"]; (for **Aaron had made them naked unto *their* shame** among their enemies:)

We will provide two quotes for extra help here:

"Moses sought out those who were 'on the Lord's side' from those whom Aaron had made 'naked.' (The Hebrew word used here may mean either 'bare, uncovered' or 'unruly, broken loose.') 'Naked' can be understood in the same sense as when Adam was ashamed and hid himself from God because he was naked. The expression can also mean 'exposed in guilt before God's wrath.' Compare the feeling of Alma as he described such exposure, in Alma 36:14-22. On the other hand, that Israel had 'broken loose' and become 'unruly' under Aaron's lead was obviously true. Both conditions would be to the shame of a people who were supposed to be religious" (Rasmussen, *Introduction to the Old Testament*, 1:93).

"Some have wondered why Aaron, who played a key role in the golden calf episode, came out with no condemnation. Though he did not record it in Exodus, Moses later indicated that Aaron also was nearly destroyed and was saved only through Moses's intercession in his behalf (see Deuteronomy 9:20)" (*Old Testament Student Manual: Genesis–2 Samuel*, page 142).

Remember that in the JST version of verse 14, above, Moses was told that if he wanted the Lord to spare the people, he would have to carry out his part of punishing the unrepentant. In verses 26-27, next, Moses is obedient. He instructs all who are willing to repent and follow the Lord to come to him.

26 Then Moses stood in the gate of the camp, and said, Who *is* on the LORD's side? *let him come unto me.* And all the sons of Levi gathered themselves together unto him.

Apparently, those who desired to repent, including the sons of Levi, came to Moses while the rest remained in camp. Then the sons of Levi (verse 26, above) were sent out into the camp to destroy those who were still rebellious.

27 And he said unto them [*the sons of Levi in verse 26*], **Thus saith the LORD God of Israel, Put every man his sword by his side, *and* go in and out from gate to gate throughout the camp, and slay every man his brother,** and every man his **companion,** and every man his **neighbour** [*anyone who refuses to repent*].

28 And the children of Levi did according to the word of Moses: and **there fell of the people that day about three thousand men** [*about three thousand were executed for refusing to repent*].

29 For Moses had said, Consecrate yourselves to day to the LORD,

even every man upon his son, and upon his brother; **that he may bestow upon you a blessing this day.**

> In verses 30–33, Moses asks the Lord to forgive the people for their sins committed in worshiping the golden calf. He is a mediator, seeking to help his people make peace with God. He is a "type" of Christ—symbolic of the Savior as he seeks to atone for the sins of his people, the Israelites.

30 ¶ And it came to pass on the morrow, that **Moses said** unto the people, **Ye have sinned a great sin:** and now **I will go up unto the LORD; peradventure I shall** [*perhaps I will be able to*] **make an atonement for your sin.**

31 And **Moses returned unto the LORD, and said, Oh, this people have sinned a great sin**, and have made them gods of gold.

> Next, in verse 32, we see the total dedication of Moses to his people. He is willing to give his all for his people. This too is a "type" of the total dedication of the Savior, who gave His all for us.

32 Yet now, **if thou wilt forgive their sin—;** and **if not, blot me, I pray thee, out of thy book** which thou hast written.

> The "book which thou hast written" is the book of life (Exodus 32:32, footnote d, in your Bible). It is mentioned also in

Revelation 3:5 and symbolizes the records kept in heaven of the names of the faithful, those who earn exaltation in celestial glory. See Bible Dictionary, under "Book of Life."

Thus, Moses is saying, in effect, that if his people can be forgiven, fine, but if not, then please destroy him with them. This is total commitment on his part to his people, just as the Savior had total commitment to all people, including the most vile of sinners.

Next, the Savior teaches Moses a simple doctrine, namely, that salvation is ultimately a matter of individual choice and use of agency.

33 And the LORD said unto Moses, **Whosoever hath sinned against me** [*and not repented*]**, him will I blot out of my book.**

> This doctrine is the same as that which the Lord taught Nephi when he prayed for the souls of Laman and Lemuel, his brothers. The Lord's answer to him was, in effect, the same answer He gave Moses.
>
> **1 Nephi 2:18–21**
> 18 But, behold, **Laman and Lemuel would not hearken unto my words; and being grieved because of the hardness of their hearts I cried unto the Lord for them.** 19 And it came to pass that **the Lord spake unto me,** saying: **Blessed art thou, Nephi, because of thy faith,** for thou hast sought me diligently, with lowliness of heart.

20 And **inasmuch as ye shall keep my commandments, ye shall prosper**, and shall be led to a land of promise; yea, even a land which I have prepared for you; yea, a land which is choice above all other lands.

21 And **inasmuch as thy brethren shall rebel against thee, they shall be cut off from the presence of the Lord.**

Next, the Lord tells Moses to go ahead and lead the people, but that there will have to be some punishment for the blatant sin they committed.

34 Therefore now **go, lead the people** unto *the place* of which I have **spoken unto thee:** behold, mine Angel shall go before thee: **nevertheless in the day when I visit** [*in a day of punishment*] **I will visit their sin upon them** [*they will have to pay a consequence for their sin*].

As you are likely aware, there is forgiveness for grievous sin, such as that committed by the children of Israel in violating covenants and participating in the riotous worshipping of the golden calf. However, even though complete forgiveness is ultimately available, there is often a severe price to pay by way of consequences before this complete forgiveness comes. Such is apparently the case here for the rebellious Israelites.

35 And the LORD plagued the people, because **they made the calf,** which Aaron made.

JST Exodus 32:35
35 And the Lord plagued the people because **they worshiped the calf**, which Aaron made.

EXODUS 33

THE ISRAELITES WERE slow to learn their lessons. Because of their rebellions and disobedience, it was necessary for the Lord to curtail some of the blessings and privileges they had enjoyed up to now. In verse 1, Moses is told to have the people leave this area and start toward the promised land. In verses 2 and 3, the people are scolded and told that an angel will replace the direct presence of the Lord and lead them for fear that they might be destroyed by the close presence of the Lord.

1 And the LORD said unto Moses, **Depart, *and* go up** hence, thou and the people which thou hast brought up out of the land of Egypt, **unto the land which I sware** [*promised*] **unto Abraham, to Isaac, and to Jacob, saying, Unto thy seed** [*posterity*] **will I give it:**

JST Exodus 33:1
1 And the Lord said unto Moses, Depart, and go up hence, thou and the people which thou hast brought up out of the land of Egypt, unto **a land flowing with milk and honey** [*in other words, a rich land where you can prosper*], the land which I sware unto

Abraham, to Isaac, and to Jacob, saying, Unto thy seed will I give it;

2 And **I will send an angel before thee**; and I will drive out the Canaanite, the Amorite, and the Hittite, and the Perizzite, the Hivite, and the Jebusite [*the current inhabitants of the promised land*]:

3 Unto a land flowing with milk and honey: **for I will not go up in the midst of thee; for thou** *art* **a stiffnecked people**: lest I consume thee in the way.

4 ¶ And **when the people heard these evil tidings** [*this bad news*], **they mourned**: and no man did put on him his ornaments [*rings, jewelry, and so forth that indicate prosperity and well-being*].

5 For [*because*] **the LORD had said** unto Moses, Say unto the children of Israel, **Ye** *are* **a stiffnecked people**: I will come up into the midst of thee in a moment, and consume thee [*if the Lord were to come among them, see footnote 5b in your Bible, they would all die instantly—they are not worthy to be in His presence*]: therefore now put off thy ornaments from thee, that I may know what to do unto thee.

6 And the children of Israel stripped themselves of their ornaments by the mount Horeb.

Next, Moses sets up a tent outside of camp, which was to serve temporarily as a holy place for the presence of the Lord to be manifest. We see this in verses 7-10, next.

7 And **Moses took the tabernacle** [*a temporary tent, not* the *Tabernacle, which has not yet been constructed and won't be finished until chapter 40*], **and pitched it** without [*outside of*] the camp, **afar off from the camp**, and **called it the Tabernacle of the congregation**. And it came to pass, *that* every one which sought the LORD went out unto the tabernacle of the congregation, which *was* without the camp.

The *Old Testament Student Manual*, page 142, quotes a Bible commentary to further explain verse 7, above (**bold** added for emphasis):

"Moses then took a tent, and pitched it outside the camp, at some distance off, and called it 'tent of meeting.' The 'tent' is neither the sanctuary of the tabernacle described in [Exodus 25-30], which was not made till after the perfect restoration of the covenant [Exodus 35-40], nor another sanctuary that had come down from their forefathers and was used before the tabernacle was built, . . . but a tent belonging to Moses, which was made into a temporary sanctuary by the fact that the pillar of cloud came down upon it, and Jehovah talked with Moses there, and which was called by the same name as the tabernacle . . . because

Jehovah revealed Himself there, and every one who sought Him had to go to this tent outside the camp. (Keil and Delitzsch, *Commentary*, 1:2:233-34.)"

8 And it came to pass, when Moses went out unto the tabernacle, *that* all the people rose up, and stood every man *at* his tent door, and looked after Moses, until he was gone into the tabernacle.

9 And it came to pass, as Moses entered into the tabernacle, the cloudy pillar descended, and stood *at* the door of the tabernacle, and *the Lord* talked with Moses.

10 And **all the people saw the cloudy pillar stand *at* the tabernacle door: and all the people rose up and worshipped, every man *in* his tent door.**

Any time people challenge you about Joseph Smith and the First Vision, in which Joseph saw the Father and the Son, telling you that the Bible says that no one can see God (John 1:18), you may wish to gently tell them that Moses saw Him face-to-face, as recounted in verse 11, next.

11 And **the LORD spake unto Moses face to face, as a man speaketh unto his friend.** And he turned again into the camp: but his servant Joshua, the son of Nun, a young man, departed not out of the tabernacle.

As you read the next verses, you will see that Moses desires further reassurance that he is still in good favor with the Lord, and that his people still have a chance to continue being the Lord's covenant people.

12 ¶ And Moses said unto the LORD, See, thou sayest unto me, Bring up this people: and thou hast not let me know whom thou wilt send with me. Yet thou hast said, I know thee by name [*You know me personally and know my fears, hopes, and desires*], and thou hast also found grace in my sight [*You told me that I am in good standing with Thee*].

Next, Moses pleads with the Lord that these people can still be considered the Lord's covenant people.

13 Now therefore, I pray thee, if I have found grace in thy sight, shew me now thy way, that I may know thee, that I may find grace in thy sight: and consider that this nation is thy people.

14 And he said, My presence shall go with thee, and I will give thee rest.

Moses has obviously been badly shaken by the open rebellion of many of his people. He is seeking to cover every possibility. Next, he pleads that if, by any chance, the Lord cannot continue with him, that they might remain in this area.

15 And he said unto him, If thy presence go not with me, carry us not up hence.

16 For wherein shall it be known here that I and thy people have found grace in thy sight? is it not in that thou goest with us? so shall we be separated, I and thy people, from all the people that are upon the face of the earth.

17 And the LORD said unto Moses, I will do this thing also that thou hast spoken: for thou hast found grace in my sight, and I know thee by name.

> Next, Moses desires yet additional reassurance.

18 And he said, I beseech thee, shew me thy glory.

19 And he said, I will make all my goodness [*mercy, graciousness, patience, etc.,—see Exodus 34:6*] pass before thee, and I will proclaim the name of the LORD before thee; and will be gracious to whom I will be gracious, and will shew mercy on whom I will shew mercy.

> When you get to verse 20, there is a problem. It contradicts verse 11, where Moses saw God face to face. We will use the JST to solve this concern.

20 And he said, Thou canst not see my face: for **there shall no man see me, and live.**

JST Exodus 33:20
20 And he said unto Moses, Thou canst not see my face **at this time,** lest mine anger be kindled against thee also, and I destroy thee, and thy people; for there shall no man among them see me **at this time,** and live, for they are exceeding sinful. And **no sinful man hath at any time, neither shall there be any sinful man at any time, that shall see my face and live.**

> You may wish to put a cross reference to JST Exodus 33:20 next to John 1:18 in your Bible. The JST also helps with the next three verses.

21 And the LORD said, Behold, *there is* a place by me, and thou shalt stand upon a rock:

JST Exodus 33:21
21 And the Lord said, Behold, thou shalt stand upon a rock, and I will prepare a place by me for thee.

22 And it shall come to pass, while my glory passeth by, that I will put thee in a **clift** of the rock, and will cover thee with my hand while I pass by:

JST Exodus 33:22
22 And it shall come to pass, while my glory passeth by, that I will put thee in a **cleft** of a rock, and cover thee with my hand while I pass by.

23 And I will take away mine hand, and thou shalt see my back parts: but my face shall not be seen.

JST Exodus 33:23
23 And I will take away mine

hand, and thou shalt see my back parts, but my face shall not be seen, **as at other times; for I am angry with my people Israel.**

As you can see, Moses is still learning and growing in his calling as a prophet. Certainly, we all continue learning and growing throughout our lives, as we strive to serve faithfully.

EXODUS 34

MOSES BROKE THE first set of stone tablets, given him by the Lord, when he saw the children of Israel worshiping the golden calf (Exodus 32:19). Jehovah made the first set (Exodus 24:12), but Moses was instructed to make the second set, and then the Lord would write on them. When we read the first two verses of Exodus 34 in the Bible, it sounds like the two sets of stone tablets contained the same writings. This is not the case. The JST makes a vital change in the first two verses of Exodus 34.

1 And the LORD said unto Moses, Hew thee [*chisel out*] two tables of stone like unto the first: and **I will write upon *these* tables the words that were in the first tables, which thou brakest.**

2 And be ready in the morning, and **come up in the morning unto mount Sinai, and present thyself there to me** in the top of the mount.

JST Exodus 34:1–2

1 And the Lord said unto Moses, Hew thee two other tables of stone, like unto the first, and **I will write upon them also, the words of the law, according as they were written at the first on the tables which thou brakest; but it shall not be according to the first, for I will take away the priesthood out of their midst; therefore my holy order, and the ordinances thereof, shall not go before them; for my presence shall not go up in their midst, lest I destroy them.**

2 But I will give unto them the law as at the first, but it shall be after the law of a carnal commandment; for I have sworn in my wrath, that they shall not enter into my presence, into my rest, in the days of their pilgrimage. Therefore do as I have commanded thee, and be ready in the morning, and come up in the morning unto mount Sinai, and present thyself there to me, in the top of the mount.

As you can see, there is a big difference between the Bible translation and the JST, which says:

1. The Melchizedek Priesthood ("my holy order") was to be taken away from the people in general.

2. The ordinances of the Melchizedek Priesthood were no longer available to them.

3. The higher laws and ordinances were to be replaced by a lesser law, known as the "law of carnal commandments."

We see this same difference between the two sets pointed out in Deuteronomy, some forty years later as Moses reviewed the event of getting the second set of stone tablets. First, we will quote the Bible, then the JST:

Deuteronomy 10:2

2 And I will write on the tables the words that were in the first tables which thou brakest, and thou shalt put them in the ark.

JST Deuteronomy 10:2

2 And I will write on the tables the words that were on the first tables, which thou breakest, **save** [*except for*] **the words of the everlasting covenant of the holy priesthood**, and thou shalt put them in the ark.

Thus, it appears that temple marriage and other ordinances pertaining to the "everlasting covenant of the holy priesthood" (Melchizedek Priesthood), which were included on the first set of tablets, were taken away and not included on the second set. This was a big loss, but, sadly, the people had thoroughly demonstrated that they were neither worthy nor ready to take upon themselves the covenants and ordinances pertaining to the Melchizedek Priesthood.

Next, in verses 3–28, you will see that Moses chiseled out another set of stone tables (which would require much work and sweat on his part—similar to what the Brother of Jared did in preparing the 16 small stones to take up onto the mountain for the Lord to touch—Ether 3:1-2), and then climbed the mountain again, this time carrying the heavy tablets.

You will see Moses plead for forgiveness for his people. Jehovah will give him strict instructions to give to the people that they are not to join in wicked practices of society that will be common among the inhabitants of the promised land when they get to it. Furthermore, in these next verses, some of the Ten Commandments as well as several laws of Moses will be stated again.

Next, Moses is given strict instructions to come back up the mount alone.

3 And no man shall come up with thee, neither let any man be seen throughout all the mount; neither let the flocks nor herds feed before that mount.

4 ¶ And **he hewed two tables of stone like unto the first**; and Moses rose up early in the morning, and went up unto mount Sinai, as the LORD had commanded him, and took in his hand the two tables of stone.

5 And the LORD descended in the cloud, and stood with him there, and proclaimed the name of the LORD.

6 And the LORD passed by before him, and proclaimed, The LORD, The LORD God, merciful and gracious, longsuffering, and abundant in goodness and truth,

7 Keeping mercy for thousands, forgiving iniquity and transgression and sin, and that will by no means clear the **guilty**; visiting the iniquity of the fathers upon the children, and upon the children's children, unto the third and to the fourth generation.

JST Exodus 34:7
7 Keeping mercy for thousands, forgiving iniquity and transgression and sin, and that will by no means clear the **rebellious**; visiting the iniquity of the fathers upon the children, and upon the children's children, unto the third and to the fourth generation.

8 And Moses made haste, and bowed his head toward the earth, and worshipped.

9 And he said, If now I have found grace in thy sight, O Lord, let my Lord, I pray thee, go among us; for it is a stiffnecked people; and pardon our iniquity and our sin, and take us for thine inheritance.

10 ¶ And he said, Behold, I make a covenant: before all thy people I will do marvels, such as have not been done in all the earth, nor in any nation: and all the people among which thou art shall see the work of the LORD: for it is a terrible thing that I will do with thee.

11 Observe thou that which I command thee this day: behold, I drive out before thee the Amorite, and the Canaanite, and the Hittite, and the Perizzite, and the Hivite, and the Jebusite.

12 Take heed to thyself, lest thou make a covenant with the inhabitants of the land whither thou goest, lest it be for a snare in the midst of thee:

Next, the children of Israel are commanded to destroy all things associated with idol worship when they arrive in the promised land.

13 But ye shall destroy their altars, break their images, and cut down their groves [*havens for idol worship*]:

The JST makes an important change in verse 14.

14 For thou shalt worship no other god: for the LORD, whose name is **Jealous**, is a jealous God [*does not allow His people to worship other gods, idols, etc.—see verses 15–16*]:

JST Exodus 34:14
14 For thou shalt worship no other god; for the Lord, whose name is **Jehovah**, is a jealous God.

In verses 15–16, next, you can see

that idol worship is, in effect, called spiritual adultery. It involves "stepping out on God."

15 Lest thou make a covenant with the inhabitants of the land, and **they go a whoring after their gods** , and do sacrifice unto their gods, and one call thee, and thou eat of his sacrifice [*participate in idol worship*];

16 And thou take of their daughters unto thy sons, and their daughters **go a whoring after their gods,** and make thy sons **go a whoring after their gods.**

17 Thou shalt make thee no molten gods [*idols*].

18 ¶ The feast of unleavened bread shalt thou keep. Seven days thou shalt eat unleavened bread, as I commanded thee, in the time of the month Abib: for in the month Abib thou camest out from Egypt.

> For help with verses 19–20, next, see notes associated with Exodus 13:12–13, in this study guide.

19 All that openeth the matrix [*womb*] is mine; and every firstling among thy cattle, whether ox or sheep, that is male.

20 But the firstling of an ass thou shalt redeem with a lamb: and if thou redeem him not, then shalt thou break his neck. All the firstborn of thy sons thou shalt redeem. And none shall appear before me empty.

21 ¶ Six days thou shalt work, but on the seventh day thou shalt rest: in earing time and in harvest thou shalt rest.

22 ¶ And thou shalt observe the feast of weeks, of the firstfruits of wheat harvest, and the feast of ingathering at the year's end.

23 ¶ Thrice in the year shall all your men children appear before the Lord GOD, the God of Israel.

24 For I will cast out the nations before thee, and enlarge thy borders: neither shall any man desire thy land, when thou shalt go up to appear before the LORD thy God thrice in the year.

> Next, the Lord commands them not to offer anything that contains yeast (leaven) in combination with their sacrifices involving blood. In some settings, leaven was symbolic of evil and corruption.

25 **Thou shalt not offer the blood of my sacrifice with leaven;** neither shall the sacrifice of the feast of the passover be left unto the morning.

26 The first of the firstfruits of thy land thou shalt bring unto the house of the LORD thy God. Thou shalt not seethe a kid in his mother's milk [*don't cook a young goat in its mother's milk, a ritual food used in idol worship by fertility cults—see footnote 26b in your Bible*].

27 And the LORD said unto Moses, Write thou these words: for after the tenor of these words [*with these words as the foundation*] I have made a covenant with thee and with Israel.

28 And he was there with the LORD forty days and forty nights; he did neither eat bread, nor drink water. And he wrote upon the tables the words of the covenant, the ten commandments.

> After this period of forty days and forty nights, Moses will come down off the mountain again, unaware that the glory of the Lord is still shining from his face. The light radiating from his face is so intense that his people are afraid to approach him (verse 30). As a result, he will veil his face as he speaks to them (verse 33).

29 ¶ And it came to pass, when Moses came down from mount Sinai with the two tables of testimony in Moses' hand, when he came down from the mount, that Moses wist that the skin of his face shone while he talked with him not [*knew not that his face was shining*]

30 And when Aaron and all the children of Israel saw Moses, behold, the skin of his face shone; and they were afraid to come nigh him.

31 And Moses called unto them; and Aaron and all the rulers of the congregation returned unto him: and Moses talked with them.

32 And afterward all the children of Israel came nigh: and he gave them in commandment all that the LORD had spoken with him in mount Sinai.

33 And *till* Moses had done speaking with them, he put a vail on his face.

> According to verses 34–35, next, it appears that Moses wore the veil for some time afterward, but that he took it off whenever he went into the temporary sanctuary (Exodus 33:7) to commune with the Lord.

34 But when Moses went in before the LORD to speak with him, he took the vail off, until he came out. And he came out, and spake unto the children of Israel *that* which he was commanded.

35 And the children of Israel saw the face of Moses, that the skin of Moses' face shone: and Moses put the vail upon his face again, until he went in to speak with him [*the Lord, in the temporary sanctuary*].

JST Exodus 34:35
35 And the children of Israel saw the face of Moses, that the skin of Moses's face shone; and Moses put the veil upon his face again, until he went in to speak with the Lord.

EXODUS 35

IN EXODUS, CHAPTERS 25-30, Moses received detailed instructions from Jehovah for building the tabernacle. Those chapters can be referred to as the "blueprints" for the Tabernacle. Now, preparations for the actual construction are getting under way. In chapter 35, Moses requests donations and invites skilled craftsmen to use their skills in building the Tabernacle and furnishing it.

First, though, in verses 1-3, the people are again reminded of the vital importance of keeping the Sabbath day holy.

1 AND Moses gathered all the congregation of the children of Israel together, and said unto them, These are the words which the LORD hath commanded, that ye should do them.

2 Six days shall work be done, but on the seventh day there shall be to you an holy day, a sabbath of rest to the LORD: whosoever doeth work therein shall be put to death.

3 Ye shall kindle no fire throughout your habitations upon the sabbath day.

Next, in verses 4-9, the people are told what kind of things they need to donate for the construction and furnishing of the Tabernacle.

4 ¶ And Moses spake unto all the congregation of the children of Israel, saying, This is the thing which the LORD commanded, saying,

5 Take ye from among you an offering unto the LORD: whosoever is of a willing heart [see also verse 21], let him bring it, an offering of the LORD; gold, and silver, and brass,

Did you notice, in verse 5, above, that any donations to the building of the Tabernacle must be given with a "willing heart"? Reluctant giving is not acceptable to the Lord. This principle is explained in the Book of Mormon.

Moroni 7:6–8
6 For behold, God hath said a man being evil cannot do that which is good; for if he offereth a gift, or prayeth unto God, except he shall do it with real intent it profiteth him nothing.
7 For behold, it is not counted unto him for righteousness.
8 For behold, if a man being evil giveth a gift, **he doeth it grudgingly; wherefore it is counted unto him the same as if he had retained the gift**; wherefore he is counted evil before God.

6 And blue, and purple, and scarlet, and fine linen, and goats' hair,

7 And rams' skins dyed red, and badgers' skins, and shittim wood [acacia wood, a hard, beautiful wood that has a high luster when polished],

8 And oil for the light, and spices

for anointing oil, and for the sweet incense,

9 And onyx stones, and stones to be set for the ephod [*a piece of sacred clothing worn by high priests officiating in the Levitical Priesthood*], and for the breastplate.

We will quote from the Old Testament Student Manual for an explanation of the breastplate mentioned in verse 9, above.

"Attached to the ephod with golden chains and ouches (sockets or fasteners) was the breastplate. The breastplate worn by Aaron and subsequent high priests should not be confused with the one used by the Prophet Joseph Smith in translating the Book of Mormon. Aaron's breastplate was made of fabric rather than of metal and was woven of the same material that was used in making the ephod. It was twice as long as it was wide and when folded became a square pocket into which the Urim and Thummim was placed. Upon the exposed half of the breastplate were precious stones inscribed with the names of each of the tribes of Israel." (Old Testament Student Manual, Genesis-2 Samuel, p 152.)

Next, in verses 10-19, Moses issues a call for men and women skilled in the crafts and trades needed.

10 And **every wise hearted among you** shall **come, and make all that the LORD hath commanded;**

11 The tabernacle, his tent, and his covering, his taches [*hooks*], and his boards, his bars, his pillars, and his sockets,

12 The ark [*the ark of the covenant*], and the staves thereof, with the mercy seat, and the vail of the covering,

13 The table, and his staves, and all his vessels, and the shewbread [*twelve loaves of bread made with finely ground flour, weighing about ten pounds each—see Old Testament Student Manual, Genesis to 2 Samuel, p 149*],

14 The candlestick also for the light, and his furniture, and his lamps, with the oil for the light,

15 And the incense altar, and his staves, and the anointing oil, and the sweet incense, and the hanging for the door at the entering in of the tabernacle,

16 The altar of burnt offering, with his brasen grate, his staves, and all his vessels, the laver [*basin*] and his foot [*stand or base*],

17 The hangings of the court, his pillars, and their sockets, and the hanging for the door of the court,

18 The pins of the tabernacle, and the pins of the court, and their cords,

19 The cloths of service, to do

service in the holy place, **the holy garments for Aaron the priest, and the garments of his sons,** to minister in the priest's office.

20 ¶ And all the congregation of the children of Israel departed from the presence of Moses.

> Note the emphasis again on serving with a willing heart in verses 21–29.

21 And they came, **every one whose heart stirred him up, and every one whom his spirit made willing,** and they brought the LORD's offering to the work of the tabernacle of the congregation, and for all his service, and for the holy garments.

22 And **they came, both men and women, as many as were willing hearted,** and brought bracelets, and earrings, and rings, and tablets, all jewels of gold: and every man that offered offered an offering of gold unto the LORD.

23 And every man, with whom was found blue, and purple, and scarlet, and fine linen, and goats' hair, and red skins of rams, and badgers' skins, brought them.

24 Every one that did offer an offering of silver and brass brought the LORD's offering: and every man, with whom was found shittim wood for any work of the service, brought it.

25 And all the women **that were wise hearted** did spin with their hands, and brought that which they had spun, both of blue, and of purple, and of scarlet, and of fine linen.

26 And all the women **whose heart stirred them up in wisdom** spun goats' hair.

27 And the rulers brought onyx stones, and stones to be set, for the ephod, and for the breastplate;

28 And spice, and oil for the light, and for the anointing oil, and for the sweet incense.

29 The children of Israel **brought a willing offering** unto the LORD, every man and woman, **whose heart made them willing** to bring for all manner of work, which the LORD had commanded to be made by the hand of Moses.

> Next, Moses announces to the whole congregation of Israel the names of two especially skilled men who would help supervise the work and teach others.

30 ¶ And Moses said unto the children of Israel, See, the LORD hath called by name **Bezaleel** the son of Uri, the son of Hur, of the tribe of Judah;

31 And he hath filled him with the spirit of God, in wisdom, in understanding, and in knowledge, and in all manner of workmanship;

32 And to devise curious [*artistic, beautiful*] works, to work in gold, and in silver, and in brass,

33 And in the cutting of stones, to set them, and in carving of wood, to make any manner of cunning [*skilled*] work.

34 And he hath put in his heart that he may teach, both he, and **Aholiab**, the son of Ahisamach, of the tribe of Dan.

35 **Them hath he filled with wisdom of heart, to work all manner of work**, of the engraver, and of the cunning [*skilled*] workman, and of the embroiderer, in blue, and in purple, in scarlet, and in fine linen, and of the weaver, even of them that do any work, and of those that devise cunning work.

EXODUS 36

IN THIS CHAPTER, the actual work on the Tabernacle gets underway. Verse 1 informs us that there was much inspiration from the Lord upon many skilled people working under the direction of Bezaleel and Aholiab, who were called to help supervise the work (Exodus 35:30–35).

1 THEN wrought Bezaleel and Aholiab, and every wise hearted man, **in whom the LORD put wisdom and understanding** to know how to work all manner of work

for the service of the sanctuary, according to all that the LORD had commanded.

2 And Moses called Bezaleel and Aholiab, and every wise hearted man, **in whose heart the LORD had put wisdom, even every one whose heart stirred him up to come unto the work to do it:**

Next, in verse 3, we see that the people generously and enthusiastically donated from their means to the building of the Tabernacle.

3 And they received of Moses all the offering, which the children of Israel had brought for the work of the service of the sanctuary, to make it withal. And they brought yet unto him free [*freely given*] offerings every morning.

A rather wonderful problem now arises. The people are bringing so much for the building of the Tabernacle that the craftsmen and artisans have to leave their work and seek out Moses to ask him to call a halt to the donations.

4 And all the wise men, that wrought all the work of the sanctuary [*tabernacle*], came every man from his work which they made;

5 ¶ And they spake unto Moses, saying, **The people bring much more than enough** for the service of the work, which the LORD commanded to make.

6 And **Moses gave commandment,** and they caused it to be proclaimed throughout the camp, saying, **Let neither man nor woman make any more work for the offering of the sanctuary.** So **the people were restrained from bringing.**

7 For the stuff they [*the workers*] had was sufficient for all the work to make it, and too much.

> The next verses detail the work now being accomplished on the portable tabernacle. You can see that it required much intricate craftsmanship.

8 ¶ And every wise hearted man among them that wrought the work of the tabernacle made ten curtains of fine twined linen, and blue, and purple, and scarlet: with cherubims of cunning work made he them.

9 The length of one curtain was twenty and eight cubits [*one cubit is about 18 inches*], and the breadth of one curtain four cubits: the curtains were all of one size.

10 And he coupled the five curtains one unto another: and the other five curtains he coupled one unto another.

11 And he made loops of blue on the edge of one curtain from the selvedge in the coupling: likewise he made in the uttermost side of another curtain, in the coupling of the second.

12 Fifty loops made he in one curtain, and fifty loops made he in the edge of the curtain which was in the coupling of the second: the loops held one curtain to another.

13 And he made fifty taches [*clasps*] of gold, and coupled the curtains one unto another with the taches: so it became one tabernacle [*to hold the Tabernacle together as one unit*].

14 ¶ And he made curtains of goats' hair for the tent over the tabernacle: eleven curtains he made them.

15 The length of one curtain was thirty cubits, and four cubits was the breadth of one curtain: the eleven curtains were of one size.

16 And he coupled five curtains by themselves, and six curtains by themselves.

17 And he made fifty loops upon the uttermost edge of the curtain in the coupling, and fifty loops made he upon the edge of the curtain which coupleth the second.

18 And he made fifty taches of brass to couple the tent together, that it might be one.

19 And he made a covering for the tent of rams' skins dyed red, and a covering of badgers' skins above that.

20 ¶ And he made boards for the tabernacle of shittim wood, standing up.

21 The length of a board was ten cubits, and the breadth of a board one cubit and a half.

22 One board had two tenons [*rectangular dowels for inserting into a base*], equally distant one from another: thus did he make for all the boards of the tabernacle.

23 And he made boards [*frames*] for the tabernacle; twenty boards for the south side southward:

24 And forty sockets [*bases*] of silver he made under the twenty boards; two sockets under one board for his two tenons, and two sockets under another board for his two tenons.

25 And for the other side of the tabernacle, which is toward the north corner, he made twenty boards,

26 And their forty sockets of silver; two sockets under one board, and two sockets under another board.

27 And for the sides of the tabernacle westward he made six boards.

28 And two boards made he for the corners of the tabernacle in the two sides.

29 And they were coupled beneath, and coupled together at the head thereof, to one ring: thus he did to both of them in both the corners.

30 And there were eight boards; and their sockets were sixteen sockets of silver, under every board two sockets.

31 ¶ And he made bars [*crossbars*] of shittim [*acacia*] wood; five for the boards of the one side of the tabernacle,

32 And five bars for the boards of the other side of the tabernacle, and five bars for the boards of the tabernacle for the sides westward.

33 And he made the middle bar to shoot [*extend*] through the boards from the one end to the other.

34 And he overlaid the boards with gold, and made their rings of gold to be places for the bars, and overlaid the bars with gold.

35 ¶ And he made a vail of blue, and purple, and scarlet, and fine twined linen: with cherubims made he it of cunning [*highly skilled*] work.

36 And he made thereunto four pillars of shittim wood, and overlaid them with gold: their hooks were of gold; and he cast for them four sockets [*bases*] of silver.

> Imagine the beauty of the entrance curtain for the Tabernacle, as described next in verse 37! It can easily remind us of the beautiful work that goes into building our temples today.

37 ¶ And he made an hanging [*curtain*] for the tabernacle door of blue, and purple, and scarlet, and fine twined linen, of needlework;

38 And the five pillars of it with their hooks: and he overlaid their chapiters [*ornate tops of the pillars*] and their fillets with gold: but their five sockets were of brass.

EXODUS 37

IN VERSES 1-2, Bezaleel (Exodus 31:1-5) makes the ark of the covenant. It is an oblong chest made of acacia wood, overlaid with pure gold inside and out. It will be about three feet eight or nine inches long by two feet three inches wide and high. It will contain the stone tablets (1 Kings 8:9) on which the Ten Commandments and other things were written by the finger of the Lord. Later, it will also contain a pot of manna as well as Aaron's rod (Hebrews 9:4). When the Tabernacle is completed, the ark will be placed in the Holy of Holies (the west room of the Tabernacle, which formed a perfect cube of 15 feet by 15 feet by 15 feet).

1 AND Bezaleel made the ark of shittim wood: two cubits and a half was the length of it, and a cubit and a half the breadth of it, and a cubit and a half the height of it:

2 And he overlaid it with pure gold within and without, and made a crown of gold to it round about.

> Next, he makes rings, through which poles can be inserted by which to carry the ark or chest, without actually touching it.

3 And he cast for it four rings of gold, to be set by the four corners of it; even two rings upon the one side of it, and two rings upon the other side of it.

4 And he made staves [*poles*] of shittim wood, and overlaid them with gold.

5 And he put the staves into the rings by the sides of the ark, to bear the ark.

> Next, he makes a very beautiful lid for the ark out of solid gold. Two cherubim (symbolic of angelic beings, guardians or protectors of sacred things) of gold are made and placed on top. This lid will be known as the "mercy seat." The Lord promised Moses that He would meet him above the mercy seat and commune with him (Exodus 25:21–22).

6 ¶ And he made the mercy seat of pure gold: two cubits and a half was the length thereof, and one cubit and a half the breadth thereof.

7 And he made two cherubims of gold, beaten [*hammered*] out of one piece made he them, on the two ends of the mercy seat;

8 One cherub on the end on this side, and another cherub on the other end on that side: out of the mercy seat made he the cherubims on the two ends thereof. [*Typical biblical repetition*]

9 And the cherubims spread out their wings on high, and covered with their wings over the mercy seat, with their faces one to another; even to the mercy seatward were the faces of the cherubims.

As you know, we do not believe that angels have wings. However, we know from modern revelation that depicting angels with wings is symbolic of power to move and act. Joseph Smith, answering questions about beings mentioned in Revelation, chapter four, gave us the following.

Doctrine and Covenants 77:4

4   Q. What are we to understand by the eyes and wings, which the beasts had [*in Revelation 4:8*]?

A. Their eyes are a representation of light and knowledge, that is, they are full of knowledge; and **their wings are a representation of power, to move, to act, etc.**

Next, the constructing of the table of shewbread (Exodus 25:23-30) is described.

10 ¶ And he made the table of shittim wood: two cubits [*about 36 inches*] was the length thereof, and a cubit the breadth thereof, and a cubit and a half the height thereof:

11 And he overlaid it with pure gold, and made thereunto a crown of gold round about.

12 Also he made thereunto a border of an handbreadth round about; and made a crown of gold for the border thereof round about.

Rings with poles through them will be used to carry this ornate table.

13 And he cast for it four rings of gold, and put the rings upon the four corners that were in the four feet thereof.

14 Over against the border were the rings, the places for the staves [*poles*] to bear the table.

15 And he made the staves of shittim wood, and overlaid them with gold, to bear the table.

16 And he made the vessels which were upon the table, his dishes, and his spoons, and his bowls, and his covers to cover withal, of pure gold.

The table of shewbread, pronounced "showbread," will eventually hold the things mentioned in verse 16, above, plus twelve ten pound loaves of unleavened bread representing the twelve tribes of Israel, in two stacks of six each.

Next, the candlestick with seven branches is made. In Hebrew, it is called "menorah" and means "the place of lights." It will have no candles, rather seven arms with a cup-shaped container at the top of each arm, which will be filled with pure olive oil. A wick in each will be lit and the menorah will be the source of light for the Tabernacle.

The number "seven" symbolizes wholeness or perfection (example: 2 Kings 5:10–14). Thus, the light from the menorah can symbolize the perfect light from God.

As you have probably noticed, much of the construction of these furnishings for the Tabernacle uses pure gold. In biblical symbolism, "gold" symbolizes the best (example: Revelation 4:4). Thus, it can symbolize the highest the Lord has for us, in other words, exaltation.

17 ¶ And he made the candlestick **of pure gold**: of beaten work [*hammered gold*] made he the candlestick; his shaft, and his branch, his bowls, his knops, and his flowers [*NIV: "its flowerlike cups, buds and blossoms"*], were of the same [*were all made from the same piece of gold*]:

Next, we see that there was a center shaft with three branches going out on each side.

18 And six branches going out of the sides thereof; three branches of the candlestick out of the one side thereof, and three branches of the candlestick out of the other side thereof:

19 Three bowls made after the fashion of almonds in one branch, a knop and a flower [*NIV: 'Three cups shaped like almond flowers with buds and blossoms were on one branch'*]; and three bowls made like almonds in another branch, a knop and a flower: so throughout the six branches going out of the candlestick.

20 And in the candlestick were four bowls made like almonds, his knops, and his flowers:

21 And a knop under two branches of the same, and a knop under two branches of the same, and a knop under two branches of the same, according to the six branches going out of it.

22 Their knops and their branches were of the same: **all of it was one beaten work of pure gold**.

23 And he made his seven lamps, and his snuffers [*NIV: "wick trimmers"*], and his snuffdishes [*trays for the wick trimmings*], of pure gold.

24 Of a talent [*NIV: "about 75 pounds"*] of pure gold made he it, and all the vessels thereof.

Next, the altar of incense was made. It was the third piece of furniture placed in the Holy Place (not the Holy of Holies). The other two furnishings were the menorah and the table of shewbread. In biblical times, the smoke of burning incense symbolized prayers rising up to God (example Revelation 5:8). The altar of incense was placed directly in front of the veil that separated the Holy Place from the Holy of Holies. It was overlaid with gold and had rings and poles by which it was carried.

25 ¶ And he made the incense altar of shittim wood: the length of it was a cubit, and the breadth of it a cubit; it was foursquare; and two cubits was the height of it; the horns thereof were of the same.

26 And he overlaid it with pure gold, both the top of it, and the sides thereof round about, and the horns of it: also he made unto it a crown of gold round about.

27 And he made two rings of gold for it under the crown thereof, by the two corners of it, upon the two sides thereof, to be places for the staves to bear it withal.

28 And he made the staves of shittim wood, and overlaid them with gold.

> Next, sacred anointing oil and pure incense are made, for use in the rites.

29 ¶ And he made the **holy anointing oil**, and the **pure incense** of sweet spices, according to the work of the apothecary.

EXODUS 38

CHAPTER 37 GAVE an account of making the furnishings for the Holy of Holies and the Holy Place, which composed the inside of the Tabernacle itself. Remember that the Tabernacle was 45 feet long, 15 feet wide, and 15 feet high (see Bible Dictionary, under "Tabernacle"). The Holy of Holies or most holy place was a perfect cube of 15 feet by 15 feet by 15 feet. The Holy Place was 30 feet long by 15 feet wide by 15 feet high. A tent was spread over the Tabernacle.

In this chapter, we have the account of constructing the items for the outer courtyard, which was 150 feet long and 75 feet wide, surrounded by a seven and a half foot high fence made of pillars and fine white linen panels.

Perhaps you have noticed that there are strong similarities between the Tabernacle and our temples. The outer courtyard of the Tabernacle could remind us of our temple grounds. It could also symbolize the world or the telestial room of our temples. The Holy Place could symbolize the terrestrial room and the Holy of Holies the celestial room. These symbols can remind us of the progression we are invited by our loving Father in Heaven to make from the world back into His presence.

The first thing one encountered upon entering the outer courtyard was the altar of sacrifice. Starting with verse one, we have the account of its construction. It represented sacrifice and strict obedience to God's laws and commandments, the first major step in our progression back into the presence of God.

1 AND he made the altar of burnt offering of shittim wood: five cubits [*seven and a half feet*] was the length thereof, and five cubits the breadth thereof; it was foursquare [*it was square*]; and three cubits [*four and a half feet*] the height thereof.

2 And he made the horns thereof on the four corners of it; the horns thereof were of the same: and he overlaid it with brass [*bronze—see footnote 2b in your Bible*].

3 And he made all the vessels of the altar, the pots, and the shovels, and the basons, and the fleshhooks, and the firepans: all the vessels thereof made he of brass.

4 And he made for the altar a brasen grate of network under the compass thereof beneath unto the midst of it. [*NIV: "They made a grating for the altar, a bronze network, to be under its ledge, halfway up the altar."*]

> Next, in verses 5–7, bronze rings and acacia wood poles, overlaid with bronze, are made for carrying the altar of sacrifice.

5 And he cast four rings for the four ends of the grate of brass, to be places for the staves [*poles*].

6 And he made the staves of shittim wood, and overlaid them with brass.

7 And he put the staves into the rings on the sides of the altar, to bear it withal [*carry it*]; he made the altar hollow with boards.

> Next, a bronze basin is made. It will hold water for washing and cleansing of hands and feet (see *Old Testament Student Manual*, p 151) before entering the holy place. When Solomon made his temple, he placed a laver or basin on the backs of twelve oxen (1 Kings 7:25). There is clear symbolism of baptism here.

8 ¶ And he made the laver of brass, and the foot of it of brass, of the lookingglasses [*mirrors*] of the women assembling, which assembled at the door of the tabernacle of the congregation.

> Next, the fence for the outer courtyard and the curtains for the entrance are made.

9 ¶ And he made the court: on the south side southward the hangings of the court were of fine twined linen [*fine white linen*], an hundred cubits [*150 feet long*]:

10 Their pillars were twenty, and their brasen sockets [*bases*] twenty; the hooks of the pillars and their fillets [*rectangular bands around the pillars to protect the wood and for beauty*] were of silver.

11 And for the north side the hangings were an hundred cubits, their pillars were twenty, and their sockets of brass twenty; the hooks of the pillars and their fillets of silver.

12 And for the west side were hangings of fifty cubits [*75 feet*], their pillars ten, and their sockets ten; the hooks of the pillars and

their fillets of silver.

13 And for the east side eastward fifty cubits.

14 The hangings [curtains] of the one side of the gate were fifteen cubits; their pillars three, and their sockets three.

15 And for the other side of the court gate, on this hand and that hand, were hangings of fifteen cubits; their pillars three, and their sockets three.

16 All the hangings of the court round about were of fine twined linen.

17 And the sockets for the pillars were of brass; the hooks of the pillars and their fillets of silver; and the overlaying of their chapiters [decorative tops] of silver; and all the pillars of the court were filleted with silver.

18 And the hanging [curtain] for the gate of the court was needlework, of blue, and purple, and scarlet, and fine twined linen: and twenty cubits was the length, and the height in the breadth was five cubits, answerable to the hangings of the court.

19 And their pillars were four, and their sockets of brass four; their hooks of silver, and the overlaying of their chapiters [decorated tops of the pillars] and their fillets of silver.

20 And all the pins of the tabernacle,

and of the court round about, were of brass.

21 ¶ This is the sum of [total of things used in] the tabernacle, even of the tabernacle of testimony, as it was counted, according to the commandment of Moses, for the service of the Levites, by the hand of Ithamar [NIV: "by the Levites under the direction of Ithamar"], son to Aaron the priest.

Verses 22–23, next, emphasize that the Lord's commandments had been obeyed. It is a good example for us.

22 And Bezaleel the son of Uri, the son of Hur, of the tribe of Judah, **made all that the LORD commanded Moses.**

23 **And with him was Aholiab,** son of Ahisamach, of the tribe of Dan, an engraver, and a cunning workman, and an embroiderer in blue, and in purple, and in scarlet, and fine linen.

In the next verses, we are told how much gold and silver was used in building and furnishing the Tabernacle. A "talent" was about 75 pounds (see Bible Dictionary, under "Weights and Measures").

24 All the gold that was occupied for the work in all the work of the holy place, even the gold of the offering, was twenty and nine talents [over 2,175 pounds], and seven hundred and thirty shekels, after

the shekel of the sanctuary.

25 And the silver of them that were numbered of the congregation was an hundred talents [*over 7,500 pounds*], and a thousand seven hundred and threescore and fifteen shekels, after the shekel of the sanctuary:

26 A bekah for every man, that is, half a shekel [*NIV: "about one fifth ounce"*], after the shekel of the sanctuary, for every one that went to be numbered [*counted in the census*], from twenty years old and upward, for six hundred thousand and three thousand and five hundred and fifty men.

The next two verses tell what the silver was used for.

27 And of the hundred talents of silver were cast the sockets of the sanctuary, and the sockets of the vail; an hundred sockets of the hundred talents, a talent for a socket.

28 And of the thousand seven hundred seventy and five shekels he made hooks for the pillars, and overlaid their chapiters, and filleted them.

The last three verses tell what the bronze was used for.

29 And the brass of the offering was seventy talents [*over 5,000 pounds*], and two thousand and four hundred shekels.

30 And therewith he made the sockets to [*bases for*] the door of the tabernacle of the congregation, and the brasen altar, and the brasen grate for it, and all the vessels of the altar,

31 And the sockets [*bases*] of the court round about, and the sockets of the court gate, and all the pins [*NIV: "tent pegs"*] of the tabernacle, and all the pins of the court round about.

From the large amounts of precious metal and the number of articles made for the Tabernacle, mentioned in the above verses, it is not hard to imagine what a huge undertaking it was to build the Tabernacle. No doubt, large numbers of Israelites were kept wonderfully involved working under the supervision of Bezaleel and Aholiab—see verses 22–23, above, plus the heading to chapter 38 in your Bible.

EXODUS 39

THIS CHAPTER RE-CORDS the making of "holy garments" (verse 1), sacred articles of clothing for Aaron, the high priest, and the priests, to be worn as they served. This can remind us of the temple garments worn by endowed members of the Church today and of special articles of sacred clothing worn during temple worship.

The priests wore four articles of sacred clothing, a plain white robe, a sash, a turban or cap, and special underpants or "linen breeches to cover their nakedness" (Exodus 28:42). In addition, the high priest wore a blue robe over the basic white robe, an ephod or "apron," as it is sometimes translated" (*Old Testament Student Manual*, p 152), a breastplate (the lower half folded up to form a pocket into which the Urim and Thummim could be placed), and a gold plate on the front of his mitre or cap, on which was inscribed "holiness to the Lord."

Crafting the breastplate worn by Aaron and succeeding high priests (in the Aaronic Priesthood) is also recorded here. At the end of this chapter, all things pertaining to the Tabernacle have been completed and are brought to Moses.

1 AND of the blue, and purple, and scarlet, they made cloths of service, to do service in the holy place, and made the **holy garments** for Aaron; as the LORD commanded Moses.

2 And he made the **ephod** [*vest or apron worn by the high priest, worn over a blue robe*] of gold, blue, and purple, and scarlet, and fine twined linen.

> We can't help but have high respect and admiration for the skilled artisans who beat gold into thin sheets, cut it into thin threads, and then wove it into the fabric, as described in verse 3, next.

3 And they did beat the gold into thin plates, and cut it into wires,

to work it in the blue, and in the purple, and in the scarlet, and in the fine linen, with cunning [*skillful*] work.

4 They made shoulderpieces [*straps*] for it, to couple it together [*to fasten the ephod at each shoulder*]: by the two edges was it coupled together.

5 And the curious [*beautifully woven*] **girdle** [*band or sash*] of his ephod [*apron*], that was upon it, was of the same [*was one piece*], according to the work thereof; of gold, blue, and purple, and scarlet, and fine twined linen; as the LORD commanded Moses.

> Next, we see them craft two onyx stones set in gold, one for each shoulder strap of the ephod, with the names of the sons of Jacob (Israel), six on one stone and the other six on the other stone.

6 ¶ And they wrought [*made*] onyx stones inclosed in ouches [*settings*] of gold, graven, as signets are graven, with the names of the children of Israel [*with the names of the twelve sons of Jacob, six on each stone*].

7 And he put them on the shoulders of the ephod, that they should be stones for a memorial to the children of Israel; as the LORD commanded Moses.

> Next, the breastplate is crafted. It will be attached to the high priest's ephod (vest or apron)

with gold chains and fasteners. It is made of beautiful fabric, the same material as was used in making the ephod. Its length was twice its width, and the bottom half could be folded up to make a pocket for the Urim and Thummim. It is interesting that the breastplate given to Joseph Smith (Doctrine and Covenants 17:1) was likewise used to hold the Urim and Thummim given to him (Joseph Smith—History 1:35). However, the breastplate made for Aaron was of fabric, whereas the breastplate given to Joseph Smith was made of metal (*Old Testament Student Manual*, p 152).

8 ¶ And he made the **breastplate** of cunning work, like the work of the ephod; of gold, blue, and purple, and scarlet, and fine twined linen.

9 It was foursquare; they made the breastplate double: a span was the length thereof, and a span the breadth thereof, being doubled. [*It was twice as long as it was wide and when folded, formed a square.*]

Next, four rows of three precious stones each were attached to the breastplate, representing the twelve tribes of Israel. Each stone has the name of one of the tribes of Israel engraved on it. We see symbolism here. Just as the high priest of the Aaronic Priesthood here among the children of Israel wears the names of the tribes of Israel on his chest, close to his heart, so also the Great High Priest of the Melchizedek Priesthood, Jesus Christ (see BD, under "High Priest"), holds His people close to His heart.

The precious stones are described in verses 10–13.

10 And they set in it four rows of stones: the first row was a sardius [*ruby*], a topaz, and a carbuncle [*possibly a hard, deep red gemstone*]: this was the first row.

11 And the second row, an emerald, a sapphire, and a diamond.

12 And the third row, a ligure [*opal*], an agate, and an amethyst.

13 And the fourth row, a beryl, an onyx, and a jasper: they were inclosed in ouches [*settings*] of gold in their inclosings.

14 And the stones were according to the names of the children of Israel, twelve, according to their names, like the engravings of a signet, every one with his name, according to the twelve tribes.

Next, in verses 15–21, the system for attaching the breastplate to the high priest's ephod is described.

15 And they made upon the breastplate chains at the ends, of wreathen [*braided*] work of pure gold.

16 And they made two ouches [*settings*] of gold, and two gold rings; and put the two rings in the two ends of the breastplate.

17 And they put the two wreathen

chains of gold in the two rings on the ends of the breastplate.

18 And the two ends of the two wreathen chains they fastened in the two ouches, and put them on the shoulderpieces [*shoulder straps*] of the ephod, before it.

19 And they made two rings of gold, and put them on the two ends of the breastplate, upon the border of it, which was on the side of the ephod inward.

20 And they made two other golden rings, and put them on the two sides of the ephod underneath, toward the forepart of it, over against the other coupling thereof, above the curious girdle of the ephod.

21 And they did bind the breastplate by his rings unto the rings of the ephod with a lace of blue, that it might be above the curious girdle of the ephod, and that the breastplate might not be loosed [*wouldn't swing out*] from the ephod; as the LORD commanded Moses.

The weaving of the blue robe for the high priest is described next. It was woven as one piece with no seams, with a hole for the head to go through. The Savior, the Great High Priest, was dressed in a similar seamless cloak before His crucifixion according to John 19:23.

22 ¶ And he made the robe of the ephod of woven work, all of blue.

23 And there was an hole in the midst of the robe, as the hole of an habergeon [*a sleveless coat of mail*], with a band round about the hole, that it should not rend [*so it wouldn't tear*].

Verses 24–26 tell us about the bells of gold and fringes woven to look like pomegranates that were attached to the hem of the robe.

24 And they made upon the hems of the robe pomegranates of blue, and purple, and scarlet, and twined linen.

25 And they made bells of pure gold, and put the bells between the pomegranates upon the hem of the robe, round about between the pomegranates;

26 A bell and a pomegranate, a bell and a pomegranate, round about the hem of the robe to minister in; as the LORD commanded Moses.

Next, we see tunics, turbans, caps, undergarments, and sashes made for Aaron and his sons.

27 ¶ And they made coats [*tunics*] of fine linen of woven work for Aaron, and for his sons,

28 And a mitre [*turban*] of fine linen, and goodly bonnets [*caps*] of fine linen, and linen breeches [*NIV: "undergarments"*] of fine twined linen,

29 And a girdle [*NIV: "sash"*] of fine twined linen, and blue, and purple, and scarlet, of needlework; as the LORD commanded Moses.

Verses 30–31 describe the special pure gold plate, for the front of the high priest's turban or cap, on which "holiness to the Lord" was inscribed.

30 ¶ And they made the plate of the holy crown of pure gold, and wrote upon it a writing, like to the engravings of a signet [*a seal used to mark official documents*], HOLINESS TO THE LORD.

31 And they tied unto it a lace of blue, to fasten it on high upon the mitre; as the LORD commanded Moses.

Verses 32–42 describe how all the materials completed for the Tabernacle are now presented to Moses for his inspection and approval.

32 ¶ Thus was all the work of the tabernacle of the tent of the congregation finished: and the children of Israel did according to all that the LORD commanded Moses, so did they.

33 ¶ And they brought the tabernacle unto Moses, the tent, and all his furniture, his taches [*clasps*], his boards, his bars, and his pillars, and his sockets,

34 And the covering of rams' skins dyed red, and the covering of badgers' skins, and the vail of the covering,

35 The ark of the testimony [*the ark of the covenant*], and the staves [*poles for carrying it*] thereof, and the mercy seat [*the lid for the ark of the covenant*],

36 The table [*table of shewbread*], and all the vessels thereof, and the shewbread,

37 The pure candlestick [*manorah*], with the lamps thereof, even with the lamps to be set in order, and all the vessels thereof, and the oil for light,

38 And the golden altar, and the anointing oil, and the sweet incense, and the hanging [*curtain*] for the tabernacle door,

39 The brasen altar [*the altar of sacrifice*], and his grate of brass, his staves, and all his vessels, the laver and his foot,

40 The hangings of the court [*the white linen panels for the outer courtyard fence*], his pillars, and his sockets, and the hanging for the court gate, his cords, and his pins, and all the vessels of the service of the tabernacle, for the tent of the congregation,

41 The cloths of service to do service in the holy place, and the holy garments for Aaron the priest, and his sons' garments, to minister in the priest's office.

42 According to all that the LORD commanded Moses, so the children of Israel made all the work.

> We can feel the joy in the hearts of the people as well as Moses as he accepts the work and blesses the people. Only those who willingly give strict obedience to the commandments of the Lord can experience such satisfaction.

43 And Moses did look upon all the work, and, behold, **they had done it as the LORD had commanded, even so had they done it: and Moses blessed them.**

EXODUS 40

NOW THAT ALL the components for the Tabernacle have been completed and accepted, the Lord gives Moses exact instructions as to when it is to be erected, in verse 2. It is to be "on the first day of the first month of the second year (i.e., one year less 14 days from the exodus)"—see Bible Dictionary under "Tabernacle."

After it is set up and all the furnishings are put in their proper places, the glory of the Lord will fill the Tabernacle (verse 34). A cloud, signifying the presence of the Lord, will cover it by day and fire will rest on it during the night.

The Tabernacle will serve the Israelites for more than 200 years, until Solomon builds the temple in Jerusalem.

1 AND the LORD spake unto Moses, saying,

2 On the first day of the first month shalt thou set up the tabernacle of the tent of the congregation.

> Next, Jehovah instructs Moses to set up all the furnishings.

3 And thou shalt put therein the ark of the testimony [*place the ark of the covenant in the Holy of Holies*], and cover the ark with the vail [*hang the veil between the Holy Place and the Holy of Holies so that it shields the ark from view from the Holy Place*].

4 And thou shalt bring in the table [*table of shewbread*], and set in order the things that are to be set in order upon it [*and arrange everything properly that is to be upon it*]; and thou shalt bring in the candlestick [*the menorah*], and light the lamps thereof.

5 And thou shalt set the altar of gold for the incense [*altar of incense*] before the ark of the testimony [*near the ark of the covenant but in the Holy Place, outside the veil that shields the ark in the Holy of Holies from view*], and put the hanging [*curtain*] of the door to the tabernacle.

6 And thou shalt set the altar of the burnt offering [*the altar of sacrifice in* *the outer courtyard*] before the door of the tabernacle of the tent of the congregation [*another name for the Tabernacle*].

7 And thou shalt set the laver [*the bronze basin*] between the tent of the congregation and the altar [*altar of sacrifice*], and shalt put water therein.

8 And thou shalt set up the court round about [*set up the outer courtyard*], and hang up the hanging at the court gate [*hang the curtain at the entrance to the courtyard*].

In verses 9–16, the Lord instructs Moses to anoint the Tabernacle and all its furnishings in preparation for putting them into service. There is much symbolism here. Pure olive oil symbolized spirituality and worthiness to be in the presence of the Lord, as seen, for example, in the parable of the ten virgins (Matthew 25:1–13).

Anointing with pure olive oil was also used to prepare for coming blessings. We see this today in the anointing of the sick by Melchizedek Priesthood holders. It is done in preparation for the blessing to come in conjunction with sealing the anointing. Thus, among other things, we see the anointing of the Tabernacle and its furnishings as purifying them for the presence of the Lord and preparation for the many great blessings that would thus be available to His people.

9 And thou shalt take the anointing oil, and anoint the tabernacle, and all that is therein, and shalt hallow it, and all the vessels thereof: and it shall be holy.

10 And thou shalt anoint the altar of the burnt offering, and all his vessels, and sanctify the altar: and it shall be an altar most holy.

11 And thou shalt anoint the laver and his foot [*base*], and sanctify it.

Next, we see Aaron and his sons "washed and anointed" (see heading to chapter 40 in your Bible) and clothed in special, sacred clothing.

12 And thou shalt bring Aaron and his sons unto the door of the tabernacle of the congregation, and **wash them with water.**

13 And thou shalt **put upon Aaron the holy garments, and anoint him,** and sanctify him; that he may minister unto me in the priest's office.

14 And thou shalt bring his sons, and **clothe them with coats:**

15 And thou shalt **anoint them,** as thou didst anoint their father, that they may minister unto me in the priest's office: for their anointing shall surely be an everlasting priesthood throughout their generations.

16 Thus did Moses: according to all that the LORD commanded him, so did he.

Having been instructed as to

what to do on this momentous day, Moses now proceeds to do it. You are seeing much repetition here between the first several verses in this chapter and those that follow. It is typical of scripture in ancient times.

Imagine how many people were involved under his supervision to accomplish all this! Imagine also the feelings in their hearts as all the intense labor and dedication of the past year takes shape before their eyes!

Notice the emphasis on strict and pure obedience, in several verses now that say, one way or another, "as the Lord commanded."

17 ¶ And it came to pass in the first month in the second year, on the first day of the month, that **the tabernacle was reared up.**

18 And Moses reared up the tabernacle, and fastened his sockets, and set up the boards thereof, and put in the bars thereof, and reared up his pillars.

19 And he spread abroad the tent over the tabernacle, and put the covering of the tent above upon it; **as the LORD commanded Moses.**

Next, in verses 20-21, we see the stone tablets, with the Ten Commandments and other writings on them, placed in the ark of the covenant. Then the mercy seat (the lid) is put in place on top of the chest, the Ark is positioned in the Holy of Holies (it is the only piece of furniture in that room) and the

veil is put up between the Holy of Holies and the Holy Place.

20 ¶ And he took and put the testimony into the ark, and set the staves [*poles for carrying it*] on the ark, and put the mercy seat above upon the ark:

21 And he brought the ark into the tabernacle, and set up the vail of the covering, and covered the ark of the testimony; **as the LORD commanded Moses.**

22 ¶ And he put the table [*of shewbread*] in the tent of the congregation, upon the side of the tabernacle northward, without [*outside of*] the vail.

23 And he set the bread [*shewbread*] in order [*in two stacks of six loaves each*] upon it before the LORD; **as the LORD had commanded Moses.**

24 ¶ And he put the candlestick in the tent of the congregation, over against the table [*opposite the table of shewbread*], on the side of the tabernacle southward.

25 And he lighted the lamps [*the seven lamps at the top of the seven branches of the menorah*] before the LORD; **as the LORD commanded Moses.**

26 ¶ And he put the golden altar [*the altar of incense*] in the tent of the congregation before the vail:

27　And he burnt sweet incense thereon; **as the LORD commanded Moses.**

28　¶ And he set up the hanging [*curtain*] at the door of the tabernacle.

29　And he put the altar of burnt offering by the door of the tabernacle of the tent of the congregation, and offered upon it the burnt offering and the meat offering; **as the LORD commanded Moses.**

30　¶ And he set the laver between the tent of the congregation and the altar, and put water there, to wash withal.

31　And Moses and Aaron and his sons washed their hands and their feet thereat:

32　When they went into the tent of the congregation [*the Tabernacle*], and when they came near unto the altar, they washed; **as the LORD commanded Moses.**

33　And he reared up the court [*the white linen panels forming the fence around the outer court*] round about the tabernacle and the altar, and set up the hanging [*the entrance curtain to the outer courtyard*] of the court gate. So **Moses finished the work.**

Can you imagine the scene, next, as the Lord shows His acceptance of their efforts and work! Similar manifestations attended the dedication of the Kirtland Temple.

34　¶ **Then a cloud covered the tent of the congregation, and the glory of the LORD filled the tabernacle.**

35　And Moses was not able to enter into the tent of the congregation, because the cloud abode thereon, and the glory of the LORD filled the tabernacle.

Next, Moses (the author of Genesis through Deuteronomy) summarizes how the Israelites knew when to travel on and when to stay put, as they journeyed to the promised land.

36　And **when the cloud was taken up from over the tabernacle,** the children of Israel went onward in all their journeys:

37　But **if the cloud were not taken up,** then they journeyed not till the day that it was taken up.

Last, we see the cloud by day and fire by night, representing the presence of the Lord, referred to often in the scriptures and in works of art.

38　For the **cloud** of the LORD was upon the tabernacle by day, and **fire** was on it by night, in the sight of all the house of Israel, throughout all their journeys.

LEVITICUS

L EVITICUS GETS ITS
name from the tribe of Levi, the
tribe of Israel chosen to perform
Aaronic Priesthood rites and ceremonies among the children of Israel. It
is the third of the five books written
by Moses, known as Genesis, Exodus,
Leviticus, Numbers, and Deuteronomy.
These five books are often referred to
as the Pentateuch, which is a Greek
word meaning "the fivefold book" (see
Bible Dictionary, under "Pentateuch").

Leviticus could easily be called "the
handbook of instructions" for the
Levites in administering the Law of
Moses. Elder Mark E. Petersen described
the Law of Moses as "a preparatory
course of lesser commandments as
a foundation upon which they could
build an acceptance of the higher laws"
(*Moses, Man of Miracles*, page 100).

The Bible Dictionary in your LDS Bible
gives a description of the book of
Leviticus as follows (**bold** added for
emphasis):

> **Bible Dictionary: Leviticus**
> "Contains the following: (1)
> The sacrificial ordinances
> (chs. 1–7): (a) the burnt
> offering (1:1–17); (b) the
> meat offering (2:1–16); (c) the
> peace offering (3:1–17); (d)
> the sin offering (4:1–5:13); (e)
> the guilt-offering (5:14–6:7);
> and (f) various sacrifices
> for the priests (6:8–7:38).
> (2) The ritual observed in
> the consecration of priests,

together with an account
of the deaths of Nadab and
Abihu because they offered
strange fire (chs. 8–10). (3)
Laws relating to ceremonial
uncleanness (chs. 13–15).
(4) The ritual of the Day of
Atonement (ch. 16). (5) The
law of holiness (chs. 17–26),
containing a systematic code of
laws dealing with religious and
social observances. Chapter 27
is supplementary, dealing with
vows and the redemption of
'devoted' things.
"The book of Leviticus
represents the priestly religious
life of Israel. **Its dominant
thought** is the presence of a
holy God in the midst of a holy
people dwelling in a holy land.
Its object is to teach religious
truth to the minds of men
through the medium of a stately
ritual, sacrifices representing
the need of atonement and
communion, the consecration
of the priesthood teaching the
need of the consecration of the
life of every worshipper who
would draw nigh to God, and
the law of clean and unclean
teaching that **God requires
the sanctification of the
whole man, body as well as
spirit.**"

In the notes and commentary provided
for Exodus in this study guide, we gave
many details about the rites, rituals,
and animal sacrifices that accompanied
the Law of Moses. They served as a
"schoolmaster" law (see Galatians 3:24),
pointing the minds of the Israelites

toward the atoning sacrifice, yet future, of the Son of God. The Law of Moses contained far more by way of reference to the Savior and His Atonement than most Bible students realize.

As mentioned above, much of Leviticus gives instructions for the implementation of the Law of Moses among the Israelites. It is indeed a detailed handbook of instructions for the priests of the tribe of Levi. Our goal for these first ten chapters of Leviticus is to emphasize how the daily performance of the Law of Moses was designed to point the people's minds to the Savior and His atoning sacrifice. We will point this out by quickly going through these chapters, using **bold** to draw your attention to the frequent use of Atonement symbolism in Law of Moses ritual and sacrifice. While there will likely be many details of the rites and rituals that you will not understand, it is hoped that you will see that Jesus Christ and His Atonement are very much present in this part of the Old Testament. Once you see what we are doing, you will no doubt find more symbolism than we highlight.

Before we begin pointing out Atonement symbolism with **bold** in Leviticus, chapters 1–10, let's look at some examples that you will see:

ATONEMENT SYMBOLISM

1. **Without blemish** (symbolic of the Savior's perfect life).

2. **Voluntary** (symbolic of the fact that He voluntarily gave His life and that we must voluntarily submit our lives to Him).

3. **Make atonement for the sinner** (the whole goal of the Atonement is to make it possible for us to become clean and able to return to the presence of the Father).

4. **Blood** (symbolic of the cleansing blood of Christ, given for us).

5. **Body** of animals placed upon the altar (symbolic of the Savior's body being given for us as a sacrifice for sin).

6. **Bread** (spiritual nutrition; Jesus is the "bread of life"—see John 6:35).

7. **The priest** (symbolic of Christ; also priesthood leaders with keys to judge and help us).

8. **Altar** (symbolic of Christ's atoning sacrifice for us).

9. **Wood** (symbolic of the cross upon which Christ was sacrificed).

10. **Fire** (symbolic of the Holy Ghost—we are "cleansed by fire"; also, the Holy Ghost leads us as we strive to follow the Savior. Even though at this time the Israelites lost the ordinances of the Melchizedek Priesthood, which would include the gift of the Holy Ghost, the fire used in sacrificing could point their minds to cleansing and purifying through the Savior's Atonement).

11. **Washed in water** (can be symbolic of baptism and of the "living water," the Savior—see John 4:10–14).

12. **Oil** (pure olive oil, symbolic of the Savior, His healing power, the light that comes to us from Him, and so forth).

13. **Frankincense** (symbolic of the

prayers of the righteous; it was also a gift to the young Jesus from the Wise Men).

14. Unleavened bread (symbolizes that we must hurry to worship the true God; unleavened bread was used in the Passover, symbolizing that the people did not have time to wait for the bread to rise before being obedient to the Lord's commands; also, leaven sometimes symbolizes the corruption and evil in the world).

15. Anointing (symbolizing that Christ was the "Anointed One"—in other words, the Messiah—and that we are anointed with oil as part of being administered to when sick, symbolizing being anointed with the healing power of the Savior).

16. Salt (symbolizing that we are to be the salt of the earth).

17. Seven times ("seven" symbolizes completeness and perfection in biblical numerical symbolism; in other words, when we choose to allow the Savior's Atonement to work for us, we become "complete," or perfect, worthy to enter celestial exaltation as gods).

18. Laying hands upon the head of the sacrificial animal (transferring the sins to the sacrificial animal, symbolic of the fact that the Savior was "ordained" to take upon Him our sins that we might be forgiven).

19. A sin offering (symbolic of the Savior's Atonement).

20. Restitution (part of the repentance process for us).

21. Law of sacrifice (symbolizing the Savior's sacrifice for us and the need for us to sacrifice whatever is necessary to follow Christ).

22. Third day (can be symbolic of the Savior's body lying three days in the tomb).

23. Being sanctified (symbolic of being made clean, pure, and holy through the Savior).

24. Consecration (symbolic of dedicating our lives to the Lord).

25. Not drinking wine or strong drink (on the part of the priests when they were officiating in the tabernacle—symbolic of special dedication to the Lord).

You may wish to mark several of these words and phrases in your own Bible, perhaps using an asterisk out to the side of the verses to quickly indicate that they pertain to symbolism about the Savior and His Atonement.

Remember also, as previously stated, that much of the actual ritual and sacrifice may seem foreign and even repugnant to modern readers. Keep in mind that ancient biblical culture was a different culture from ours and that it was set in a different time. They routinely slaughtered their own animals for eating. It was daily life for them, whereas most of us buy our meat neatly shrink-wrapped in the grocery store.

Again, the point of doing a quick run through these ten chapters is to call your attention to the constant Atonement symbolism infused into the daily lives of these often-reluctant covenant people as an invitation and opportunity from our merciful Savior to progress to the level of following Him and accepting His Atonement for them. Each word or phrase reminds us of the Savior and what He did for us. As stated in the above list of symbolism, the priest represents Christ as he performs the sacrifice for individuals and for the people as a whole.

As a teaching technique, we will provide the first ten chapters without notes. Read only the words and phrases in **bold** in order to get the big picture of Atonement symbolism and the Savior's role in redeeming us from sin. You will see that there was constant repetition of this vital symbolism among the children of Israel, just as there is constant repetition of the Savior's mission in our scriptures, lessons in church, general conferences, and so forth.

LEVITICUS 1

1 And the LORD called unto Moses, and spake unto him out of the tabernacle of the congregation, saying,

2 Speak unto the children of Israel, and say unto them, If any man of you bring an **offering** unto the LORD, ye shall bring your **offering** of the cattle, *even* of the herd, and of the flock.

3 If his offering *be* a burnt sacrifice of the herd, let him offer **a male without blemish**: he shall offer it **of**

his own voluntary will at the door of the tabernacle of the congregation before the LORD.

4 And he shall put his hand upon the head of the burnt offering; and it shall be accepted for him **to make atonement for him.**

5 And he shall kill the bullock before the LORD: and the priests, Aaron's sons, shall bring the **blood**, and sprinkle the blood round about upon the **altar** that *is by* the door of the tabernacle of the congregation.

6 And he shall flay the burnt offering, and cut it into his pieces.

7 And the sons of Aaron the priest shall put **fire** upon the **altar**, and lay the **wood** in order upon the **fire**:

8 And the priests, Aaron's sons, shall lay the parts, the head, and the fat, in order upon the **wood** that *is* on the **fire** which *is* upon the **altar**:

9 But his inwards and his legs shall he **wash in water**: and the priest shall burn all on the **altar**, *to be* a burnt **sacrifice**, an offering **made by fire**, of a sweet savour unto the LORD.

10 ¶ And if his offering *be* of the flocks, *namely*, of the sheep, or of the goats, for a burnt sacrifice; he shall bring it **a male without blemish**.

11 And he shall kill it on the side of the **altar** northward before the

LORD: and the priests, Aaron's sons, shall sprinkle his **blood** round about upon the **altar.**

12 And he shall cut it into his pieces, with his head and his fat: and the priest shall lay them in order on the **wood** that *is* on the **fire** which *is* upon the **altar:**

13 But he shall **wash** the inwards and the legs **with water:** and the priest shall bring *it* all, and burn *it* upon the **altar:** it *is* a burnt sacrifice, **an offering made by fire,** of a sweet savour unto the LORD.

14 ¶ And if the burnt sacrifice for his offering to the LORD *be* of fowls, then he shall bring his offering of turtledoves, or of young pigeons.

15 And the priest shall bring it unto the **altar,** and wring off his head, and burn *it* on the **altar;** and the **blood** thereof shall be wrung out at the side of the **altar:**

16 And he shall pluck away his crop with his feathers, and cast it beside the altar on the east part, by the place of the ashes:

17 And he shall cleave it with the wings thereof, *but* shall not divide *it* asunder: and the priest shall burn it upon the **altar,** upon the **wood** that *is* upon the **fire:** it *is* a burnt sacrifice, an offering made by **fire,** of a sweet savour unto the LORD.

LEVITICUS 2

1 And when any will offer a meat offering unto the LORD, his offering shall be *of* fine flour; and he shall pour **oil** upon it, and put frankincense thereon:

2 And he shall bring it to Aaron's sons the priests: and he shall take thereout his handful of the flour thereof, and of the **oil** thereof, with all the **frankincense** thereof; and the priest shall burn the memorial of it upon the **altar,** *to be* an offering made by **fire,** of a sweet savour unto the LORD:

3 And the remnant of the meat offering *shall be* Aaron's and his sons': *it is* a thing most holy of the offerings of the LORD made by **fire.**

4 ¶ And if thou bring an oblation of a meat offering baken in the oven, *it shall be* **unleavened cakes** of fine flour mingled with **oil,** or **unleavened** wafers **anointed with oil.**

5 ¶ And if thy oblation *be* a meat offering *baken* in a pan, it shall be *of* fine flour **unleavened,** mingled with **oil.**

6 Thou shalt part it in pieces, and pour **oil** thereon: it *is* a meat offering.

7 ¶ And if thy oblation *be* a meat offering *baken* in the fryingpan, it

shall be made *of* fine flour with **oil**.

8 And thou shalt bring the meat offering that is made of these things unto the LORD: and when it is presented unto the priest, he shall bring it unto the **altar**.

9 And the priest shall take from the meat offering a memorial thereof, and shall burn *it* upon the **altar**: *it is* an offering made by **fire**, of a sweet savour unto the LORD.

10 And that which is left of the meat offering *shall be* Aaron's and his sons': *it is* a thing most holy of **the offerings of the LORD made by fire.**

11 No meat offering, which ye shall bring unto the LORD, shall be made with **leaven**: for ye shall burn no leaven, nor any honey, in any offering of the LORD made by **fire**.

12 ¶ As for the oblation of the firstfruits, ye shall offer them unto the LORD: but they shall not be burnt on the **altar** for a sweet savour.

13 And every oblation of thy meat offering shalt thou season with **salt**; neither shalt thou suffer the **salt** of the covenant of thy God to be lacking from thy meat offering: with all thine offerings thou shalt offer **salt**.

14 And if thou offer a meat offering of thy firstfruits unto the LORD, thou shalt offer for the meat offering of thy firstfruits green ears of corn dried by the **fire**, *even* corn beaten out of full ears.

15 And thou shalt put **oil** upon it, and lay **frankincense** thereon: it *is* a meat offering.

16 And the priest shall burn the memorial of it, *part* of the beaten corn thereof, and *part* of the **oil** thereof, with all the **frankincense** thereof: *it is* an offering made by **fire** unto the LORD.

LEVITICUS 3

1 And if his oblation *be* a sacrifice of peace offering, if he offer *it* of the herd; whether *it be* a male or female, he shall offer it **without blemish** before the LORD.

2 And he shall **lay his hand upon the head of his offering**, and kill it *at* the door of the tabernacle of the congregation: and Aaron's sons the priests shall sprinkle the **blood** upon the **altar** round about.

3 And he shall offer of the sacrifice of the peace offering an offering made by **fire** unto the LORD; the fat that covereth the inwards, and all the fat that *is* upon the inwards,

4 And the two kidneys, and the fat that *is* on them, which *is* by the flanks, and the caul above the liver, with the kidneys, it shall he take away.

5 And Aaron's sons shall burn it on the **altar** upon the burnt sacrifice, which *is* upon the **wood** that *is* on the **fire**: *it is* an offering made by **fire**, of a sweet savour unto the LORD.

6 ¶ And if his offering for a sacrifice of peace offering unto the LORD *be* of the flock; male or female, he shall offer it **without blemish**.

7 If he offer a lamb for his offering, then shall he offer it before the LORD.

8 And he shall **lay his hand upon the head of his offering**, and kill it before the tabernacle of the congregation: and Aaron's sons shall sprinkle the **blood** thereof round about upon the **altar**.

9 And he shall offer of the sacrifice of the peace offering an offering made by **fire** unto the LORD; the fat thereof, *and* the whole rump, it shall he take off hard by the backbone; and the fat that covereth the inwards, and all the fat that *is* upon the inwards,

10 And the two kidneys, and the fat that *is* upon them, which *is* by the flanks, and the caul above the liver, with the kidneys, it shall he take away.

11 And the priest shall burn it upon the **altar**: *it is* the food of the offering made by **fire** unto the LORD.

12 ¶ And if his offering *be* a goat, then he shall offer it before the LORD.

13 And he shall **lay his hand upon the head of it**, and kill it before the tabernacle of the congregation: and the sons of Aaron shall sprinkle the **blood** thereof upon the **altar** round about.

14 And he shall offer thereof his offering, *even* an offering made by **fire** unto the LORD; the fat that covereth the inwards, and all the fat that *is* upon the inwards,

15 And the two kidneys, and the fat that *is* upon them, which *is* by the flanks, and the caul above the liver, with the kidneys, it shall he take away.

16 And the priest shall burn them upon the **altar**: *it is* the food of the offering made by **fire** for a sweet savour: all the fat *is* the LORD's.

17 *It shall be* a perpetual statute for your generations throughout all your dwellings, that ye eat neither fat nor blood.

LEVITICUS 4

1 And the LORD spake unto Moses, saying,

2 Speak unto the children of Israel, saying, If a soul shall sin through

ignorance against any of the commandments of the LORD *concerning things* which ought not to be done, and shall do against any of them:

3 If the priest that is anointed do sin according to the sin of the people; then let him **bring for his sin, which he hath sinned**, a young bullock **without blemish** unto the LORD for **a sin offering**.

4 And he shall bring the bullock unto the door of the tabernacle of the congregation before the LORD; and shall **lay his hand upon the bullock's head**, and kill the bullock before the LORD.

5 And **the priest that is anointed** shall take of the bullock's **blood**, and bring it to the tabernacle of the congregation:

6 And the priest shall dip his finger in the **blood**, and sprinkle of the **blood seven times** before the LORD, before the vail of the sanctuary.

7 And the priest shall put *some* of the **blood** upon the horns of the altar of sweet incense before the LORD, which *is* in the tabernacle of the congregation; and shall pour all the **blood** of the bullock at the bottom of the altar of the burnt offering, which *is at* the door of the tabernacle of the congregation.

8 And he shall take off from it all the fat of the bullock for the sin offering; the fat that covereth the inwards, and all the fat that *is* upon the inwards,

9 And the two kidneys, and the fat that *is* upon them, which *is* by the flanks, and the caul above the liver, with the kidneys, it shall he take away,

10 As it was taken off from the bullock of the sacrifice of peace offerings: and the priest shall burn them upon the **altar** of the burnt offering.

11 And the skin of the bullock, and all his flesh, with his head, and with his legs, and his inwards, and his dung,

12 Even the whole bullock shall he carry forth without the camp unto a clean place, where the ashes are poured out, and burn him on the **wood** with **fire**: where the ashes are poured out shall he be burnt.

13 ¶ And if the whole congregation of Israel sin through ignorance, and the thing be hid from the eyes of the assembly, and they have done *somewhat against* any of the commandments of the LORD *concerning things* which should not be done, and are guilty;

14 When the sin, which they have sinned against it, is known, then the congregation shall **offer a young**

bullock for the sin, and bring him before the tabernacle of the congregation.

15 And the elders of the congregation shall **lay their hands upon the head of the bullock** before the LORD: and the bullock shall be killed before the LORD.

16 And **the priest that is anointed** shall bring of the bullock's **blood** to the tabernacle of the congregation:

17 And the priest shall dip his finger *in some* of the **blood**, and sprinkle *it* **seven times** before the LORD, *even* before the vail.

18 And he shall put *some* of the **blood** upon the horns of the altar which *is* before the LORD, that *is* in the tabernacle of the congregation, and shall pour out all the **blood** at the bottom of the **altar** of the burnt offering, which *is at* the door of the tabernacle of the congregation.

19 And he shall take all his fat from him, and burn *it* upon the **altar**.

20 And he shall do with the bullock as he did with the bullock for **a sin offering**, so shall he do with this: and **the priest shall make an atonement for them, and it shall be forgiven them.**

21 And he shall carry forth the bullock without the camp, and burn him as he burned the first bullock: it *is* a sin offering for the congregation.

22 ¶ When a ruler hath sinned, and done *somewhat* through ignorance *against* any of the commandments of the LORD his God *concerning things* which should not be done, and is guilty;

23 Or if his sin, wherein he hath sinned, come to his knowledge; he shall bring his offering, a kid of the goats, **a male without blemish:**

24 And he shall **lay his hand upon the head of the goat,** and kill it in the place where they kill the burnt offering before the LORD: it *is* **a sin offering.**

25 And the priest shall take of the **blood** of the sin offering with his finger, and put *it* upon the horns of the **altar** of burnt offering, and shall pour out his **blood** at the bottom of the altar of burnt offering.

26 And he shall burn all his fat upon the altar, as the fat of the sacrifice of peace offerings: and **the priest shall make an atonement for him** as concerning his sin, and **it shall be forgiven him.**

27 ¶ And if any one of the common people sin through ignorance, while he doeth *somewhat against* any of the commandments of the LORD *concerning things* which ought not to be done, and be guilty;

28 Or if his sin, which he hath sinned, come to his knowledge: then he shall bring his offering, a kid of the goats, a female **without blemish**, for his sin which he hath sinned.

29 And he shall **lay his hand upon the head of the sin offering**, and slay the sin offering in the place of the burnt offering.

30 And the priest shall take of the **blood** thereof with his finger, and put *it* upon the horns of the **altar** of burnt offering, and shall pour out all the **blood** thereof at the bottom of the **altar**.

31 And he shall take away all the fat thereof, as the fat is taken away from off the sacrifice of peace offerings; and the priest shall burn *it* upon the **altar** for a sweet savour unto the LORD; and **the priest shall make an atonement for him**, and **it shall be forgiven him**.

32 And if he bring a lamb for a sin offering, he shall bring it a female **without blemish**.

33 And **he shall lay his hand upon the head of the sin offering**, and **slay it for a sin offering** in the place where they kill the burnt offering.

34 And the priest shall take of **the blood of the sin offering** with his finger, and put *it* upon the horns of the **altar** of burnt offering, and shall pour out all the **blood** thereof at the bottom of the **altar**:

35 And he shall take away all the fat thereof, as the fat of the lamb is taken away from the sacrifice of the peace offerings; and the priest shall burn them upon the **altar**, according to the offerings made by **fire** unto the LORD: and **the priest shall make an atonement for his sin** that he hath committed, and **it shall be forgiven him**.

LEVITICUS 5

1 And **if a soul sin**, and hear the voice of swearing, and *is* a witness, whether he hath seen or known *of it*; if he do not utter *it*, then he shall bear his iniquity.

2 Or if a soul touch any unclean thing, whether *it be* a carcase of an unclean beast, or a carcase of unclean cattle, or the carcase of unclean creeping things, and *if* it be hidden from him; he also shall be unclean, and guilty.

3 Or if he touch the uncleanness of man, whatsoever uncleanness *it be* that a man shall be defiled withal, and it be hid from him; when he knoweth *of it*, then he shall be guilty.

4 Or if a soul swear, pronouncing with *his* lips to do evil, or to do good, whatsoever *it be* that a man shall pronounce with an oath, and it be hid from him; when he knoweth *of it*, then he shall be guilty in one of these.

5 And it shall be, when he shall be guilty in one of these *things*, that **he shall confess that he hath sinned** in that *thing*:

6 And he shall bring his **trespass offering** unto the LORD **for his** sin which he hath sinned, a female from the flock, a lamb or a kid of the goats, for a sin offering; and **the priest shall make an atonement for him concerning his sin.**

7 And if he be not able to bring a lamb, then he shall bring for his trespass, which he hath committed, two turtledoves, or two young pigeons, unto the LORD; one for **a sin offering**, and the other for a burnt offering.

8 And he shall bring them unto the priest, who shall offer *that* which *is* for the sin offering first, and wring off his head from his neck, but shall not divide *it* asunder:

9 And he shall sprinkle of the **blood** of the sin offering upon the side of the **altar**; and the rest of the **blood** shall be wrung out at the bottom of the **altar**: it *is* a sin offering.

10 And he shall offer the second *for* a burnt offering, according to the manner: and **the priest shall make**

an atonement for him for his sin which he hath sinned, and **it shall be forgiven him.**

11 ¶ But if he be not able to bring two turtledoves, or two young pigeons, then he that sinned shall bring for his offering the tenth part of an ephah of fine flour for a sin offering; he shall put no oil upon it, neither shall he put *any* frankincense thereon: for it *is* a sin offering.

12 Then shall he bring it to the priest, and the priest shall take his handful of it, *even* a memorial thereof, and burn *it* on the **altar**, according to the offerings made by **fire** unto the LORD: it *is* a sin offering.

13 And **the priest shall make an atonement for him** as touching his sin that he hath sinned in one of these, **and it shall be forgiven him:** and *the remnant* shall be the priest's, as a meat offering [*the priest and his family get what is left over from the offering to feed themselves*].

14 ¶ And the LORD spake unto Moses, saying,

15 **If a soul commit a trespass,** and sin through ignorance, in the holy things of the LORD; then he shall bring for his trespass unto the LORD **a ram without blemish** out of the flocks, with thy estimation by shekels of silver, after the shekel of the sanctuary, **for a trespass offering:**

16 And **he shall make amends** for the harm that he hath done in the holy thing, and shall add the fifth part thereto, and give it unto the priest: and **the priest shall make an atonement for him** with the ram of the trespass offering, **and it shall be forgiven him.**

17 ¶ And **if a soul sin**, and commit any of these things which are forbidden to be done by the commandments of the LORD; though he wist *it* not, yet is he guilty, and shall bear his iniquity.

18 And he shall bring **a ram without blemish** out of the flock, with thy estimation, **for a trespass offering**, unto the priest: and **the priest shall make an atonement for him** concerning his ignorance wherein he erred and wist *it* not, **and it shall be forgiven him.**

19 It *is* a trespass offering: he hath certainly trespassed against the LORD.

LEVITICUS 6

1 And the LORD spake unto Moses, saying,

2 If a soul sin, and commit a trespass against the LORD, and lie unto his neighbour in that which was delivered him to keep, or in fellowship, or in a thing taken away by violence, or hath deceived his neighbour;

3 Or have found that which was lost, and lieth concerning it, and sweareth falsely; in any of all these that a man doeth, sinning therein:

4 Then it shall be, because he hath sinned, and is guilty, that **he shall restore that which he took** violently away, or the thing which he hath deceitfully gotten, or that which was delivered him to keep, **or the lost thing which he found,**

5 Or all that about which he hath sworn falsely; he shall even restore it in the principal, and shall add the fifth part more thereto, *and* give it unto him to whom it appertaineth, in the day of his trespass offering.

6 And he shall bring his trespass offering unto the LORD, **a ram without blemish** out of the flock, with thy estimation, **for a trespass offering**, unto the priest:

7 And **the priest shall make an atonement for him** before the LORD: **and it shall be forgiven him** for any thing of all that he hath done in trespassing therein.

8 ¶ And the LORD spake unto Moses, saying,

9 Command Aaron and his sons, saying, This *is* the law of the burnt offering: It *is* the burnt offering, because of the burning upon the **altar** all night unto the morning, and the **fire** of the **altar** shall be burning in it.

10 And the priest shall put on his linen garment, and his linen breeches shall he put upon his flesh, and take up the ashes which the **fire** hath consumed with the burnt offering on the **altar**, and he shall put them beside the **altar**.

11 And he shall put off his garments, and put on other garments, and carry forth the ashes without the camp unto a clean place.

12 And the **fire** upon the **altar** shall be burning in it; it shall not be put out: and the priest shall burn **wood** on it every morning, and lay the burnt offering in order upon it; and he shall burn thereon the fat of the peace offerings.

13 The **fire** shall ever be burning upon the **altar**; it shall never go out.

14 ¶ And this *is* the law of the meat offering: the sons of Aaron shall offer it before the LORD, before the altar.

15 And he shall take of it his handful, of the flour of the meat offering, and of the **oil** thereof, and all the **frankincense** which *is* upon the meat offering, and shall burn *it* upon the **altar** *for* a sweet savour, *even* the memorial of it, unto the LORD.

16 And the remainder thereof shall Aaron and his sons eat: with **unleavened bread** shall it be eaten in the holy place; in the court of the tabernacle of the congregation they shall eat it.

17 It shall not be baken with leaven. I have given it *unto them for* their portion of my offerings made by fire; it *is* most holy, as *is* the **sin offering**, and as the **trespass offering**.

18 All the males among the children of Aaron shall eat of it. *It shall be* a statute for ever in your generations concerning **the offerings of the LORD made by fire**: every one that toucheth them shall be holy.

19 ¶ And the LORD spake unto Moses, saying,

20 This *is* the offering of Aaron and of his sons, which they shall offer unto the LORD in the day when he is **anointed**; the tenth part of an ephah of fine flour for a meat offering perpetual, half of it in the morning, and half thereof at night.

21 In a pan it shall be made with **oil**; *and when it is* baken, thou shalt bring it in: *and* the baken pieces of the meat offering shalt thou offer *for* a sweet savour unto the LORD.

22 And the priest of his sons that is **anointed** in his stead shall offer it: *it is* a statute for ever unto the LORD, it shall be wholly burnt.

23 For every meat offering for the priest shall be wholly burnt: it shall not be eaten.

24 ¶ And the LORD spake unto Moses, saying,

25 Speak unto Aaron and to his sons, saying, This *is* the law of **the sin offering**: In the place where the burnt offering is killed shall **the sin offering** be killed before the LORD: **it** *is* **most holy.**

26 The priest that offereth it for sin shall eat it: in the holy place shall it be eaten, in the court of the tabernacle of the congregation.

27 Whatsoever shall touch the flesh thereof shall be holy: and when there is sprinkled of the **blood** thereof upon any garment, thou shalt **wash** that whereon it was sprinkled in the holy place.

28 But the earthen vessel wherein it is sodden shall be broken: and if it be sodden in a brasen pot, it shall be both scoured, and rinsed in water.

29 All the males among the priests shall eat thereof: it *is* most holy.

30 And no **sin offering**, whereof *any* of the **blood** is brought into the tabernacle of the congregation to reconcile *withal* in the holy *place,* shall be eaten: it shall be burnt in the **fire.**

LEVITICUS 7

1 Likewise this *is* **the law of the trespass offering: it** *is* **most holy.**

2 In the place where they kill the burnt offering shall they kill the trespass offering: and the **blood** thereof shall he sprinkle round about upon the **altar.**

3 And he shall offer of it all the fat thereof; the rump, and the fat that covereth the inwards,

4 And the two kidneys, and the fat that *is* on them, which *is* by the flanks, and the caul *that is* above the liver, with the kidneys, it shall he take away:

5 And the priest shall burn them upon the **altar** *for* an offering made by **fire** unto the LORD: it *is* **a trespass offering.**

6 Every male among the priests shall eat thereof: it shall be eaten in the holy place: it *is* most holy.

7 As the **sin offering** *is*, so *is* the **trespass offering**: *there is* one law for them: the priest that maketh **atonement** therewith shall have *it.*

8 And the priest that offereth any man's burnt offering, *even* the priest shall have to himself the skin of the burnt offering which he hath offered.

9 And all the meat offering that

is baken in the oven, and all that is dressed in the fryingpan, and in the pan, shall be the priest's that offereth it.

10 And every meat offering, mingled with **oil**, and dry, shall all the sons of Aaron have, one *as much* as another.

11 And this *is* **the law of the sacrifice** of peace offerings, which he shall offer unto the LORD.

12 If he offer it for a thanksgiving, then he shall offer with the sacrifice of thanksgiving **unleavened cakes** mingled with **oil**, and unleavened wafers **anointed with oil**, and cakes mingled with **oil**, of fine flour, fried.

13 Besides the cakes, he shall offer *for* his offering leavened **bread** with the sacrifice of thanksgiving of his peace offerings.

14 And of it he shall offer one out of the whole oblation *for* an heave offering unto the LORD, *and* it shall be the priest's that sprinkleth the **blood** of the peace offerings.

15 And the flesh of the sacrifice of his peace offerings for thanksgiving shall be eaten the same day that it is offered; he shall not leave any of it until the morning.

16 But if the sacrifice of his offering *be* **a vow**, or **a voluntary offering**, it shall be eaten the same day that he offereth his sacrifice: and on the morrow also the remainder of it shall be eaten:

17 But the remainder of the flesh of the sacrifice on the third day shall be burnt with **fire**.

18 And if *any* of the flesh of the sacrifice of his peace offerings be eaten at all on **the third day**, it shall not be accepted, neither shall it be imputed unto him that offereth it: it shall be an abomination, and the soul that eateth of it shall bear his iniquity.

19 And the flesh that toucheth any unclean *thing* shall not be eaten; it shall be burnt with **fire**: and as for the flesh, all that be clean shall eat thereof.

20 But the soul that eateth *of* the flesh of the sacrifice of peace offerings, that *pertain* unto the LORD, having his uncleanness upon him, even that soul shall be cut off from his people.

21 Moreover the soul that shall touch any unclean *thing, as* the uncleanness of man, or *any* unclean beast, or any abominable unclean *thing*, and eat of the flesh of the sacrifice of peace offerings, which *pertain* unto the LORD, even that soul shall be cut off from his people.

22 ¶ And the LORD spake unto Moses, saying,

23 Speak unto the children of Israel, saying, Ye shall eat no manner of fat, of ox, or of sheep, or of goat.

24 And the fat of the beast that dieth of itself, and the fat of that which is torn with beasts, may be used in any other use: but ye shall in no wise eat of it.

25 For whosoever eateth the fat of the beast, of which men offer an offering made by fire unto the LORD, even the soul that eateth *it* shall be cut off from his people.

26 Moreover ye shall eat no manner of blood, *whether it be* of fowl or of beast, in any of your dwellings.

27 Whatsoever soul *it be* that eateth any manner of blood, even that soul shall be cut off from his people [*excommunicated*].

28 ¶ And the LORD spake unto Moses, saying,

29 Speak unto the children of Israel, saying, He that offereth the sacrifice of his peace offerings unto the LORD shall bring his oblation unto the LORD of the sacrifice of his peace offerings.

30 His own hands shall bring the offerings of the LORD made by **fire**, the fat with the breast, it shall he bring, that the breast may be waved *for* a wave offering before the LORD.

31 And the priest shall burn the fat upon the **altar**: but the breast shall be Aaron's and his sons.'

32 And the right shoulder shall ye give unto the priest *for* an heave offering of the sacrifices of your peace offerings.

33 He among the sons of Aaron, that offereth the **blood** of the peace offerings, and the fat, shall have the right shoulder for *his* part.

34 For the wave breast and the heave shoulder have I taken of the children of Israel from off the sacrifices of their peace offerings, and have given them unto Aaron the priest and unto his sons by a statute for ever from among the children of Israel.

35 ¶ This *is the portion* of the anointing of Aaron, and of the anointing of his sons, out of the offerings of the LORD made by **fire**, in the day *when* he presented them to minister unto the LORD in the priest's office;

36 Which the LORD commanded to be given them of the children of Israel, in the day that he **anointed** them, *by* a statute for ever throughout their generations.

37 This *is* the law of the burnt offering, of the meat offering, and of the **sin offering**, and of the **trespass offering**, and of the **consecrations**,

and of the **sacrifice** of the peace offerings;

38 Which the LORD commanded Moses in mount Sinai, in the day that he commanded the children of Israel to offer their oblations unto the LORD, in the wilderness of Sinai.

LEVITICUS 8

1 And the LORD spake unto Moses, saying,

2 Take Aaron and his sons with him, and the garments, and the **anointing oil**, and a bullock for the **sin offering**, and two rams, and a basket of **unleavened bread**;

3 And gather thou all the congregation together unto the door of the tabernacle of the congregation.

4 And Moses did as the LORD commanded him; and the assembly was gathered together unto the door of the tabernacle of the congregation.

5 And Moses said unto the congregation, This *is* the thing which the LORD commanded to be done.

6 And Moses brought Aaron and his sons, and **washed them with water**.

7 And he put upon him the coat, and girded him with the girdle, and clothed him with the robe, and put the ephod upon him, and he girded him with the curious girdle of the ephod, and bound *it* unto him therewith.

8 And he put the breastplate upon him: also he put in the breastplate the Urim and the Thummim.

9 And he put the mitre upon his head; also upon the mitre, *even* upon his forefront, did he put the golden plate, the holy crown; as the LORD commanded Moses.

10 And Moses took the **anointing oil**, and anointed the tabernacle and all that *was* therein, and **sanctified** them.

11 And he sprinkled thereof upon the altar **seven times**, and anointed the **altar** and all his vessels, both the laver and his foot, **to sanctify them**.

12 And **he poured of the anointing oil upon Aaron's head**, and **anointed him, to sanctify him**.

13 And Moses brought Aaron's sons, and put coats upon them, and girded them with girdles, and put bonnets upon them; as the LORD commanded Moses.

14 And he brought the bullock for the **sin offering**: and Aaron and his sons laid their hands upon the head of the bullock for the **sin offering**.

15 And he slew *it*; and Moses took the **blood**, and put *it* upon the horns of the **altar** round about with his finger, and purified the **altar**, and poured the **blood** at the bottom of the **altar**, and **sanctified** it, **to make reconciliation upon it.**

16 And he took all the fat that *was* upon the inwards, and the caul *above* the liver, and the two kidneys, and their fat, and Moses burned *it* upon the **altar.**

17 But the bullock, and his hide, his flesh, and his dung, he burnt with **fire** without the camp; as the LORD commanded Moses.

18 ¶ And he brought the ram for the burnt offering: and Aaron and his sons **laid their hands upon the head of the ram.**

19 And he killed *it*; and Moses sprinkled the **blood** upon the altar round about.

20 And he cut the ram into pieces; and Moses burnt the head, and the pieces, and the fat.

21 And he **washed** the inwards and the legs **in water**; and Moses burnt the whole ram upon the **altar**: it *was* a burnt sacrifice for a sweet savour, *and* an offering made by **fire** unto the LORD; as the LORD commanded Moses.

22 ¶ And he brought the other ram, the ram of **consecration**: and Aaron and his sons **laid their hands upon the head of the ram.**

23 And he **slew** *it*; and Moses took of the **blood** of it, and put *it* **upon the tip of Aaron's right ear, and upon the thumb of his right hand, and upon the great toe of his right foot.**

24 And he brought Aaron's sons, and Moses put of the **blood upon the tip of their right ear, and upon the thumbs of their right hands, and upon the great toes of their right feet**: and Moses sprinkled the **blood** upon the **altar** round about.

25 And he took the fat, and the rump, and all the fat that *was* upon the inwards, and the caul *above* the liver, and the two kidneys, and their fat, and the right shoulder:

26 And out of the basket of **unleavened bread**, that *was* before the LORD, he took one **unleavened cake**, and a cake of **oiled bread**, and one wafer, and put *them* on the fat, and upon the right shoulder:

27 And he put all upon Aaron's hands, and upon his sons' hands, and waved them *for* a wave offering before the LORD.

28 And Moses took them from off their hands, and burnt *them* on the altar upon the burnt offering: they *were* **consecrations** for a sweet savour: it *is* an offering made by **fire** unto the LORD.

29 And Moses took the breast, and waved it *for* a wave offering before the LORD: *for* of the ram of **consecration** it was Moses' part; as the LORD commanded Moses.

30 And Moses took of the **anointing oil**, and of the **blood** which *was* upon the **altar**, and sprinkled *it* upon Aaron, *and* upon his garments, and upon his sons, and upon his sons' garments with him; and **sanctified** Aaron, *and* his garments, and his sons, and his sons' garments with him.

31 ¶ And Moses said unto Aaron and to his sons, Boil the flesh *at* the door of the tabernacle of the congregation: and there eat it with the **bread** that *is* in the basket of **consecrations**, as I commanded, saying, Aaron and his sons shall eat it.

32 And that which remaineth of the flesh and of the **bread** shall ye burn with fire.

33 And ye shall not go out of the door of the tabernacle of the congregation *in* **seven days**, until the days of your **consecration** be at an end: for **seven days** shall he **consecrate** you.

34 As he hath done this day, *so* the LORD hath commanded to do, **to make an atonement for you.**

35 Therefore shall ye abide *at* the door of the tabernacle of the congregation day and night **seven days**, and keep the charge of the LORD, that ye die not: for so I am commanded.

36 So Aaron and his sons did all things which the LORD commanded by the hand of Moses.

LEVITICUS 9

1 And it came to pass on the eighth day, *that* Moses called Aaron and his sons, and the elders of Israel;

2 And he said unto Aaron, Take thee a young calf for a **sin offering**, and a ram for a burnt offering, **without blemish**, and offer *them* before the LORD.

3 And unto the children of Israel thou shalt speak, saying, Take ye a kid of the goats for a **sin offering**; and a calf and a lamb, *both* of the first year, **without blemish**, for a burnt offering;

4 Also a bullock and a ram for peace offerings, **to sacrifice before the LORD**; and a meat offering mingled with **oil**: for to day the LORD will appear unto you.

5 ¶ And they brought *that* which Moses commanded before the tabernacle of the congregation: and all the congregation drew near and

stood before the LORD.

6 And Moses said, This *is* the thing which the LORD commanded that ye should do: and the glory of the LORD shall appear unto you.

7 And Moses said unto Aaron, Go unto the **altar**, and offer thy **sin offering**, and thy burnt offering, and make an **atonement** for thyself, and for the people: and offer the **offering** of the people, and make an **atonement** for them; as the LORD commanded.

8 ¶ Aaron therefore went unto the **altar**, and slew the calf of the **sin offering**, which *was* for himself.

9 And the sons of Aaron brought the **blood** unto him: and he dipped his finger in the **blood**, and put *it* upon the horns of the **altar**, and poured out the **blood** at the bottom of the **altar**:

10 But the fat, and the kidneys, and the caul above the liver of the sin offering, he burnt upon the **altar**; as the LORD commanded Moses.

11 And the flesh and the hide he burnt with **fire** without the camp.

12 And he slew the burnt offering; and Aaron's sons presented unto him the **blood**, which he sprinkled round about upon the **altar**.

13 And they presented the burnt offering unto him, with the pieces thereof, and the head: and he burnt *them* upon the **altar**.

14 And he did **wash** the inwards and the legs, and burnt *them* upon the burnt offering on the **altar**.

15 ¶ And he brought the people's offering, and took the goat, which *was* the **sin offering for the people**, and slew it, and **offered it for sin**, as the first.

16 And he brought the burnt offering, and offered it according to the manner.

17 And he brought the meat offering, and took an handful thereof, and burnt *it* upon the **altar**, beside the burnt sacrifice of the morning.

18 He slew also the bullock and the ram *for* a sacrifice of peace offerings, which *was* for the people: and Aaron's sons presented unto him the **blood**, which he sprinkled upon the **altar** round about,

19 And the fat of the bullock and of the ram, the rump, and that which covereth *the inwards*, and the kidneys, and the caul *above* the liver:

20 And they put the fat upon the breasts, and he burnt the fat upon the **altar**:

21 And the breasts and the right shoulder Aaron waved *for* a wave offering before the LORD; as Moses commanded.

22 And Aaron lifted up his hand toward the people, and blessed them, and came down from offering of the **sin offering**, and the burnt offering, and peace offerings.

23 And Moses and Aaron went into the tabernacle of the congregation, and came out, and blessed the people: and the glory of the LORD appeared unto all the people.

24 And there came a **fire** out from before the LORD, and consumed upon the **altar** the burnt offering and the fat: *which* when all the people saw, they shouted, and fell on their faces.

LEVITICUS 10

1 And Nadab and Abihu, the sons of Aaron, took either of them his censer, and put fire therein, and put incense thereon, and offered strange fire [*unauthorized, apostate form of sacrifice*] before the LORD, which he commanded them not.

2 And there went out fire from the LORD, and devoured them, and they died before the LORD.

3 Then Moses said unto Aaron, This *is it* that the LORD spake, saying, I will be sanctified in them that come nigh me, and before all the people I will be glorified. And Aaron held his peace.

4 And Moses called Mishael and Elzaphan, the sons of Uzziel the uncle of Aaron, and said unto them, Come near, carry your brethren from before the sanctuary out of the camp.

5 So they went near, and carried them in their coats out of the camp; as Moses had said.

6 And Moses said unto Aaron, and unto Eleazar and unto Ithamar, his sons, Uncover not your heads, neither rend your clothes; lest ye die, and lest wrath come upon all the people: but let your brethren, the whole house of Israel, bewail the burning which the LORD hath kindled.

7 And ye shall not go out from the door of the tabernacle of the congregation, lest ye die: for the **anointing oil** of the LORD *is* upon you. And they did according to the word of Moses.

8 ¶ And the LORD spake unto Aaron, saying,

9 **Do not drink wine nor strong drink, thou, nor thy sons with thee, when ye go into the tabernacle of the congregation** [*to perform their Aaronic Priesthood functions*], **lest ye die: *it shall be* a statute for ever throughout your generations:**

10 And **that ye may put difference between holy and unholy, and**

between unclean and clean;

11 And that ye may teach the children of Israel all the statutes which the LORD hath spoken unto them by the hand of Moses.

12 ¶ And Moses spake unto Aaron, and unto Eleazar and unto Ithamar, his sons that were left, Take the meat offering that remaineth of the offerings of the LORD made by **fire**, and eat it **without leaven** beside the **altar**: for it *is* most holy:

13 And ye shall eat it in the holy place, because it *is* thy due, and thy sons' due, of the sacrifices of the LORD made by **fire**: for so I am commanded.

14 And the wave breast and heave shoulder shall ye eat in a clean place; thou, and thy sons, and thy daughters with thee: for *they be* thy due, and thy sons' due, *which* are given out of the sacrifices of peace offerings of the children of Israel.

15 The heave shoulder and the wave breast shall they bring with the offerings made by fire of the fat, to wave *it for* a wave offering before the LORD; and it shall be thine, and thy sons' with thee, by a statute for ever; as the LORD hath commanded.

16 ¶ And Moses diligently sought [*demanded*] the goat of the **sin offering**, and, behold, it was burnt:

and he was angry with Eleazar and Ithamar, the sons of Aaron *which were* left *alive,* saying,

17 Wherefore [*why*] have ye not eaten the **sin offering** in the holy place, seeing it *is* most holy, and *God* hath given it you **to bear the iniquity of the congregation, to make atonement** for them before the LORD?

18 Behold, the **blood** of it was not brought in within the holy *place:* ye should indeed have eaten it in the holy *place,* as I commanded.

19 And Aaron said unto Moses, Behold, this day have they offered their **sin offering** and their burnt offering before the LORD; and such things have befallen me: and *if* I had eaten the **sin offering** to day, should it have been accepted in the sight of the LORD?

20 And when Moses heard *that,* he was content.

LEVITICUS 11

THIS CHAPTER IS basically a "Word of Wisdom" for the Children of Israel. Just as the Lord has given the Word of Wisdom to His saints in our day, so also He gave ancient Israel a law of health, the keeping of which would help them in being a holy people (Leviticus 11:44-45). It was a spiritual law as well as a physical law.

If friends or acquaintances ever challenge you on our Word of Wisdom, you might gently remind them that the Israelites had one which was even more detailed than ours.

In this chapter, Jehovah is very specific about what the Israelites should and should not eat. They were protected from several types of illness by adhering to this law of health. You will note that some of the things they were not to eat, we are permitted to eat today because of better sanitation and cooking techniques. They were basically divided into "clean" and "unclean" foods

1 And the LORD spake unto Moses and to Aaron, saying unto them,

Permitted ("clean" foods)

2 Speak unto the children of Israel, saying, **These** *are* **the beasts which ye shall eat** among all the beasts that *are* on the earth.

3 Whatsoever parteth the hoof, and **is clovenfooted,** *and* **cheweth the cud**, among the beasts, that shall ye eat.

Things not to eat ("unclean")

4 Nevertheless **these shall ye not eat** of them that chew the cud, or of them that divide the hoof: *as* the **camel**, because he cheweth the cud, but divideth not the hoof; he *is* unclean unto you.

5 And the **coney** [*a marmot-like or badger-like creature*], because he cheweth the cud, but divideth not the hoof; he *is* unclean unto you.

6 And the **hare**, because he cheweth the cud, but divideth not the hoof; he *is* unclean unto you.

7 And the **swine**, though he divide the hoof, and be clovenfooted, yet he cheweth not the cud; he *is* unclean to you.

8 Of their flesh shall ye not eat, and their carcase shall ye not touch; they *are* **unclean to you.**

Clean

9 ¶ **These shall ye eat** of all that *are* in the waters: **whatsoever hath fins and scales in the waters**, in the seas, and in the rivers, them shall ye eat.

Unclean

10 And **all that have not fins and scales** in the seas, and in the rivers, of all that move in the waters, and of any living thing which *is* in the waters, they *shall be* an abomination unto you:

11 They shall be even an abomination unto you; **ye shall not eat** of their flesh, but ye shall have their carcases in abomination.

12 Whatsoever hath no fins nor scales in the waters, that *shall be* an abomination unto you.

13 ¶ And these *are they which* ye shall have in abomination **among**

the fowls; they **shall not be eaten,** they *are* an abomination: the **eagle,** and the **ossifrage** [*bearded vulture*], and the **ospray,**

14 And the **vulture,** and the **kite** [*hawk*] after his kind;

15 Every **raven** after his kind;

16 And the **owl,** and the **night hawk,** and the **cuckow,** and the **hawk** after his kind,

17 And the **little owl,** and the **cormorant,** and the **great owl,**

18 And the **swan,** and the **pelican,** and the **gier eagle,**

19 And the **stork,** the **heron** after her kind, and the **lapwing,** and the **bat.**

20 **All fowls that creep, going upon** *all* **four** [*NIV: "flying insects"*]**,** *shall* be an abomination unto you.

Clean

21 Yet **these may ye eat** of every **flying creeping thing that goeth upon** *all* **four, which have legs above their feet, to leap withal upon the earth;**

22 *Even* these of them ye may eat; the **locust** after his kind, and the **bald locust** after his kind, and the **beetle** after his kind, and the **grasshopper** after his kind.

Unclean

23 But **all** *other* **flying creeping things, which have four feet,** *shall* be an abomination unto you.

Avoid touching carcasses

24 And **for these ye shall be unclean: whosoever toucheth the carcase of them shall be unclean** until the even [*until evening*].

25 And **whosoever beareth** [*carries*] *ought* [*any part of*] **of the carcase of** them **shall wash his clothes, and be unclean until the even.**

26 *The carcases* **of every beast which divideth the hoof, and** *is* **not clovenfooted, nor cheweth the cud,** *are* **unclean unto you:** every one that toucheth them shall be unclean.

27 And **whatsoever goeth upon his paws, among all manner of beasts that go on** *all* **four, those** *are* **unclean unto you:** whoso toucheth their carcase shall be unclean until the even.

28 And **he that beareth the carcase of them shall wash his clothes, and be unclean until the even:** they *are* unclean unto you.

Unclean

29 ¶ **These also** *shall be* **unclean** unto you among the creeping things that creep upon the earth; the **weasel,** and the **mouse,** and the **tortoise** after his kind,

30 And the **ferret**, and the **chameleon**, and the **lizard**, and the **snail**, and the **mole**.

31 These *are* unclean to you among all that creep: **whosoever doth touch them, when they be dead,** shall be unclean until the even.

Things a carcass touches become unclean

32 And **upon whatsoever** *any* **of them, when they are dead, doth fall, it shall be unclean;** whether *it be* any vessel of wood, or raiment, or skin, or sack, whatsoever vessel *it be,* wherein *any* work is done, **it must be put into water, and it shall be unclean until the even; so it shall be cleansed.**

33 And **every earthen vessel** [*clay pot*], **whereinto** *any* **of them falleth,** whatsoever *is* in it **shall be unclean; and ye shall break it.**

34 Of all meat which may be eaten, *that* **on which** *such* **water cometh shall be unclean** [*if water from a contaminated vessel touches food, it becomes unclean—in other words, unsafe to eat*]: and **all drink that may be drunk in every** *such* **vessel shall be unclean.**

35 And **every** *thing* **whereupon** *any* **part of their carcase falleth shall be unclean;** *whether it be* oven, or ranges for pots, they shall be broken down: *for* they *are* unclean, and shall

be unclean unto you.

36 Nevertheless **a fountain** [*spring*] **or pit** [*well—see footnote 36a in your Bible*], **wherein there is plenty of water, shall be clean:** but that which toucheth their carcase shall be unclean.

Clean

37 And **if** *any part* **of their carcase fall upon any sowing seed** [*seed for planting*] which is to be sown, **it** *shall* **be clean.**

Unclean

38 But **if** *any* **water be put upon the seed, and** *any part* **of their carcase fall thereon, it** *shall be* **unclean** unto you.

39 And if any beast, of which ye may eat [*any clean animals*], die; **he that toucheth the carcase thereof shall be unclean until the even.**

40 And **he that eateth of the carcase of it shall wash his clothes, and be unclean until the even:** he also that beareth the carcase of it shall wash his clothes, and **be unclean until the even.**

41 And every creeping thing that creepeth upon the earth *shall be* an abomination; it shall not be eaten.

42 **Whatsoever goeth upon the belly,** and whatsoever goeth upon *all* four, or **whatsoever hath more feet** [*such as a millipede—see footnote*

42a in your Bible] among all creeping things that creep upon the earth, them **ye shall not eat**; for they *are* an abomination.

43 Ye shall not make yourselves abominable with any creeping thing that creepeth, neither shall ye make yourselves unclean with them, that ye should be defiled thereby.

You are to be a holy people.

Here again, as we see in verses 44–45, next, the physical laws given to preserve the Israelites had a spiritual aspect. By strictly obeying the Lord, the people would become holy.

44 For I *am* the LORD your God: ye shall therefore **sanctify yourselves, and ye shall be holy; for I *am* holy: neither shall ye defile yourselves** with any manner of creeping thing that creepeth upon the earth.

45 For I *am* the LORD that bringeth you up out of the land of Egypt, to be your God: **ye shall therefore be holy, for I *am* holy.**

In verses 46–47, next, the Lord summarizes what He has told them in the previous verses.

46 This *is* the law of the beasts, and of the fowl, and of every living creature that moveth in the waters, and of every creature that creepeth upon the earth:

47 To make a difference between the unclean and the clean, and between the beast that may be eaten and the beast that may not be eaten.

LEVITICUS 12

THIS CHAPTER DEALS with circumcising male newborns eight days after their birth, and with ritual cleansing after childbirth.

Circumcision was a sign of the Abrahamic covenant (see Genesis 17:9–14). Even the laws of ritual cleansing for a woman after childbirth were highly symbolic of Christ and the new birth that comes upon being "born again" through His Atonement.

Be careful not to come to the conclusion that having children is a sin. The blood associated with childbirth is part of the mortal condition. The symbolism is that of being cleansed from the sins that attend mortality.

If you do the math in verses 1–5, you will see that the days of uncleanness and purification for a woman after giving birth to a male total 40 and after bring forth a female baby, the total is 80 days. While we don't have a good explanation for this, it is important not to draw incorrect doctrinal conclusions on the relative worth of males and females in the eyes of God. We will include a quote from the *Old Testament Student Manual*:

"Why Was the Period of Uncleanness

Longer When a Female Child Was Born? Many things in the Mosaic law are puzzling at first but become clear and understandable upon further investigation. This question, however, is one that seems to have no key at present for its correct interpretation. An obvious implication, quickly taken up by some modern critics, is that this rule is a reflection of the inferior status of women anciently, a status which they regard as supported by the law. This conclusion is fallacious for two reasons. First, elsewhere in the law and the Old Testament, there is evidence that women had high status and their rights were protected. In fact, 'women appear to have enjoyed considerably more freedom among the Jews than is now allowed them in western Asia' (Fallows, *Bible Encyclopedia*, s.v. "woman," 3:1733; this reference includes numerous scriptural references in support of this statement; see also Hastings, ed., *Dictionary of the Bible*, s.v. "woman," pp. 976–77). Second, these laws were not the product of men's attitudes but were direct revelation from the Lord. God does not view women as inferior in any way, although the roles of men and women are different. Speculation on why the Lord revealed different requirements for ceremonial purifying after the birth of male and female children is pointless until further revelation is received on the matter." (*Old Testament Student Manual Genesis–2 Samuel*, pp 174–75.)

1 AND the LORD spake unto Moses, saying,

2 Speak unto the children of Israel, saying, If a woman have conceived seed, and **born a man child**: then she shall be unclean **seven days;** according to the days of the separation for her infirmity shall she be unclean.

3 And in the eighth day the flesh of his foreskin shall be circumcised.

4 And she shall then **continue** in the blood of her purifying **three and thirty** days; she shall touch no hallowed thing, nor come into the sanctuary, until the days of her purifying be fulfilled.

5 But if she **bear a maid child,** then she shall be unclean **two weeks,** as in her separation: and she **shall continue** in the blood of her purifying **threescore and six days** [66 *more days*].

Notice that in verses 6–8, next, the offerings to be brought for either a son or a daughter are the same. The Atonement symbolism is very clear in these verses.

6 And when the days of her purifying are fulfilled, for a son, or for a daughter, she shall bring a lamb [*symbolic of Christ*] of the first year for a burnt offering, and a young pigeon, or a turtledove, for a sin offering, unto the door of the tabernacle of the congregation, unto the priest:

7 Who shall offer it before the LORD, and make an atonement for

her; and she shall be cleansed from the issue of her blood. This *is* the law for her that hath born a male or a female.

8 And if she be not able to bring a lamb, then she shall bring two turtles, or two young pigeons; the one for the burnt offering, and the other for a sin offering: and **the priest** [*symbolic of Christ*] **shall make an atonement for her, and she shall be clean.**

SELECTIONS FROM LEVITICUS

We will select a few significant excerpts to finish our study of Leviticus.

LEVITICUS 14

Selection: verses 1–20

IF YOU WERE to study nothing else but these few verses in Leviticus, you would be far ahead of most people regarding appreciation of the powerful Atonement symbolism contained in the laws and rituals given the children of Israel through Moses. When you view their rites and ceremonies through the eyes of symbolism, you see them in an entirely different light than you otherwise could.

As you can see, in the Bible, Leviticus, chapter 13, gives rules and laws for detecting leprosy and for preventing it from spreading. Chapter 14 shows how a person who once had leprosy but has healed can be cleansed and allowed back among the Lord's people.

Atonement symbolism in the ritual cleansing of the leper.

Under the Law of Moses, as seen in Leviticus 14, the ritual cleansing of a person once afflicted with leprosy who is now well and can be pronounced "clean" is used to symbolically represent each of us in terms of our need to be cleansed and healed from sin. Under the Law of Moses, lepers were prohibited from direct physical contact with others (because of fear of spreading the disease) and were required to live outside the camp of the children of Israel during their years in the wilderness. Later, after Israel had entered the promised land, lepers were forbidden to enter walled cities.

Leprosy itself was a contagious, much-dreaded disease of the skin, considered to be "a living death" (see Bible Dictionary, under "Leper"). It led to nerve paralysis and deformation of the extremities of the body. The cleansing of the ten lepers who were standing "afar off" from Christ is not only an example of the Savior's power over physical disease but also represents His miraculous power to heal us spiritually through our faith in Him (Luke 17:12–19). We see His power to cleanse and heal us symbolized in these verses. Keep in mind that there are many different ways to view and interpret symbols. What we present here exemplifies the power of symbolism in the Old Testament.

1 And the LORD spake unto Moses, saying,

2 This shall be **the law of the leper** [*the rules for being made clean; symbolic of serious sin and great need for help and cleansing*] **in the day of his cleansing** [*symbolic of the desire to be made spiritually clean and pure*]: **He shall be brought unto the priest** [*authorized servant of God who holds the keys of authority to act for God*]:

3 And **the priest shall go forth out of the camp** [*the person with leprosy did not have fellowship with the Lord's people and was required to live outside the main camp of the children of Israel; the bishop, symbolically, goes out of the way to help sinners who want to repent*]; and **the priest shall look, and, behold, if the plague of leprosy be healed in the leper** [*a bishop today serves as a judge to see if the repentant sinner is ready to return to full membership privileges*];

4 Then shall the priest command to take for him that is to be cleansed [*the person who has repented*] **two birds** [*one represents the Savior during His mortal mission; the other represents the person who has repented*] alive *and* clean, and **cedar wood** [*symbolic of the cross*], and **scarlet** [*associated with mocking Christ before his crucifixion, Mark 15:17*], and **hyssop** [*associated with Christ on the cross—John 19:29*]:

5 And the priest shall command that **one of the birds** [*symbolic of the Savior*] be **killed in an earthen vessel** [*Christ was sent to earth to die for us*] **over running water** [*Christ offers living water, the gospel of Jesus Christ—John 7:37–38—which cleanses us when we come unto Him*]:

6 As for the living bird [*representing the person who has repented*], **he** [*the priest, symbolic of the bishop, stake president, one who holds the keys of judging*] shall take it [*the living bird*], **and the cedar wood**, and the **scarlet**, and the **hyssop** [*all associated with the Atonement*], **and shall dip them and the living bird in the blood of the bird** *that was* **killed over the running water** [*representing the cleansing power of the Savior's blood, which was shed for us*]:

7 And he shall **sprinkle upon him that is to be cleansed from the leprosy** [*symbolically, being cleansed from sin*] **seven times** [*seven is the number that, in biblical numeric symbolism, represents completeness, perfection*], **and shall pronounce him clean** [*he has been forgiven*], **and shall let the living bird** [*the person who has repented*] **loose into the open field** [*representing the wide open opportunities again available in the kingdom of God for the person who truly repents*].

8 And **he that is to be cleansed**

shall wash his clothes [*symbolic of cleaning up one's life from sinful ways and pursuits—compare with Isaiah 1:16*], and shave off all his hair [*symbolic of becoming like a newborn baby; having a fresh start*], and wash himself in water [*symbolic of baptism*], that he may be clean [*cleansed from sin*]: and after that he shall come into the camp [*rejoin the Lord's covenant people*], and shall tarry abroad out of his tent seven days.

9 But it shall be on the seventh day, that he shall shave all his hair off his head and his beard and his eyebrows, even all his hair he shall shave off [*symbolic of being born again*]: and he shall wash his clothes [*clean up his life*], also he shall wash his flesh in water [*symbolic of baptism*], and he shall be clean [*a simple fact—namely that we can truly be cleansed and healed by the Savior's Atonement*].

10 And on the eighth day he shall take two he lambs without blemish [*symbolic of the Savior's perfect life*], and one ewe lamb of the first year without blemish, and three tenth deals of fine flour *for* a meat offering, mingled with oil [*pure olive oil, symbolic of healing, of light from Christ, of the Holy Ghost—Doctrine and Covenants 45:55–57—of the Savior's suffering in Gethsemane (the "oil press") under the pressure and weight of our sins*], and one log of oil.

11 And the priest that maketh *him* clean [*symbolic of Christ*] shall present the man that is to be made clean, and those things, before the LORD, *at* the door of the tabernacle of the congregation:

12 And the priest shall take one he lamb [*symbolic of Christ*], and offer him for a trespass offering [*an atonement*], and the log of oil, and wave them *for* a wave offering [*see Bible Dictionary, under "Feasts," for an explanation of several types of "offerings" associated with ritual feasts*] before the LORD:

13 And he shall slay the lamb in the place where he shall kill the sin offering and the burnt offering, in the holy place: for as the sin offering *is* the priest's, *so is* the trespass offering: it *is* most holy:

14 And the priest shall take *some* of the blood of the trespass offering [*the blood of the Lamb*], and the priest shall put *it* upon the tip of the right ear [*symbolic of hearing and obeying the Lord*] of him that is to be cleansed, and upon the thumb [*symbolic of actions, behaviors*], of his right hand [*the covenant hand; symbolic of making covenants with God*], and upon the great toe of his right foot [*symbolic of walking in the ways of God*]:

15 And **the priest shall take** *some* **of the log of oil, and pour** *it* **into the palm of his own left hand:**

16 And the priest shall dip his right finger in the oil that *is* in his left hand, and shall sprinkle of the oil with his finger **seven** [*symbolic of becoming perfect through Christ*] times before the LORD:

17 And of the rest of the **oil** that *is* in his hand shall the priest put **upon the tip of the right** ear of him that is to be cleansed, and **upon the thumb of his right hand,** and **upon the great toe of his right foot,** upon the blood of the trespass offering [*among many possible symbols, one can be that, as we take upon us the cleansing blood of Christ through baptism, the Holy Ghost follows up by guiding us to hear, act, and walk in His ways*]:

18 And the remnant of **the oil that** *is* **in the priest's hand he shall pour upon the head of him that is to be cleansed** [*symbolic of being anointed in preparation for great blessings from the Lord*]: and **the priest shall make an atonement for him** before the LORD.

19 And **the priest** [*symbolizing the Savior*] **shall offer the sin offering, and make an atonement for him that is to be cleansed** from his uncleanness; and afterward he shall kill the burnt offering:

20 And the priest shall offer the burnt offering and the meat offering upon the **altar:** and the priest shall make **an atonement for him, and he shall be clean.**

The last four words of verse 20, above, are a simple statement of a marvelous eternal truth. We can indeed become completely clean and worthy through the Savior's Atonement!

Two More Selections

As you study the rest of Leviticus in your Bible, you will continue to see much of this Atonement symbolism, a reminder that, by design, the Law of Moses kept Christ and His atoning sacrifice before the eyes of the people constantly.

We will do two more chapters of Leviticus before we move on to Numbers. One, chapter 18, will provide a rather stark and sobering definition of what it means for a nation to become "ripe in iniquity." The other, chapter 19, will provide a chance for us to see once more that the laws of Moses were rather high laws and embodied many of the behaviors required of a Zion people.

LEVITICUS 18

Selection: all verses

WE OFTEN SEE the phrase "ripe in iniquity" in the scriptures (Ether 2:9; 9:20; Helaman 13:14; Doctrine and Covenants 18:6). It means that a nation or people are ready to be destroyed by the Lord. Leviticus 18 describes many of the behaviors and attitudes that lead a nation to that point. You will see that many of these behaviors have to do with open acceptance of sexual immorality, including homosexuality and other sexual perversions (see heading to chapter 18 in your Bible).

At the time Moses was leading his people toward the promised land—the land of Canaan (Palestine)—it was filled with wickedness and violence. Its inhabitants were "ripe in iniquity," and thus the Lord will have the children of Israel destroy them when they arrive there after their wanderings in the wilderness. As you read the description of their gross wickedness, you will better understand this utter destruction. It is a "type" of the complete destruction of the wicked at the Second Coming.

1 And the LORD spake unto Moses, saying,

2 Speak unto the children of Israel, and say unto them, I am the LORD your God.

3 After the doings of the land of Egypt [*symbolic of wickedness and gross evil*], wherein ye dwelt, **shall ye not do: and after the doings** [*evil and wickedness*] **of the land of Canaan** [*the "promised land" for the Israelites, whose inhabitants were "ripe in iniquity" at this time in history*], **whither I bring you, shall ye not do: neither shall ye walk in their ordinances** [the *deepest evil*

and wickedness in society often makes use of counterfeit or apostate rites, vows, secret combinations, and so forth that copy and mock the true ordinances and covenants of God].

How to avoid becoming wicked and stay alive spiritually

4 **Ye shall do my judgments** [*live My gospel*], **and keep mine ordinances, to walk therein: I** *am* **the LORD your God.**

5 **Ye shall therefore keep my statutes** [*laws*], **and my judgments: which if a man do, he shall live in them** [*will be kept alive spiritually*]: I *am* the LORD.

Abominations that lead to becoming ripe in iniquity
Incest

6 ¶ **None of you shall approach to any that is near of kin to him, to uncover** *their* **nakedness** [*to engage in sexual relations*]: **I am the LORD.**

7 **The nakedness of thy father, or the nakedness of thy mother, shalt thou not uncover:** she *is* thy mother; thou shalt not uncover her nakedness.

8 **The nakedness of thy father's wife** shalt thou not uncover: it *is* thy father's nakedness.

9 **The nakedness of thy sister,** the daughter of thy father, or daughter of thy mother, *whether she be* born

at home, or born abroad, *even* their nakedness thou shalt not uncover.

10 The nakedness of thy son's daughter, or of thy **daughter's daughter**, *even* their nakedness **thou shalt not uncover**: for theirs *is* thine own nakedness.

11 The nakedness of thy father's wife's daughter, begotten of thy father, she *is* **thy sister**, thou shalt not uncover her nakedness.

12 Thou shalt not uncover the nakedness of **thy father's sister**: she *is* thy father's near kinswoman.

13 Thou shalt not uncover the nakedness of **thy mother's sister**: for she *is* thy mother's near kinswoman.

14 Thou shalt not uncover the nakedness of **thy father's brother**, thou shalt not approach to his wife: she *is* **thine aunt**.

15 Thou shalt not uncover the nakedness of **thy daughter in law**: she *is* thy son's wife; thou shalt not uncover her nakedness.

16 Thou shalt not uncover the nakedness of **thy brother's wife**: it *is* thy brother's nakedness.

17 Thou shalt not uncover the nakedness of **a woman and her daughter**, neither shalt thou take **her son's daughter**, or **her daughter's daughter**, to uncover her

nakedness; *for* they *are* her near kinswomen: it *is* wickedness.

18 Neither shalt thou take a wife to her sister, to vex *her*, to uncover her nakedness, beside the other in **her life** *time*.

19 Also thou shalt not approach unto a woman to uncover her nakedness, as long as she is put apart for her uncleanness.

Adultery

20 Moreover **thou shalt not lie carnally** [*commit adultery*] **with thy neighbour's wife**, to defile thyself with her.

Child sacrifice

21 And thou shalt not let any of thy seed [*children*] pass through *the fire* to Molech [*you must not sacrifice your children to the fire god, Molech— see Bible Dictionary, under "Molech"*], neither shalt thou profane the name of thy God: I *am* the LORD.

Homosexuality

22 Thou shalt not lie [*engage in sexual relations*] **with mankind** [*with other men*], as with womankind: it *is* abomination [*see also Leviticus 20:13*].

Bestiality

23 Neither shalt thou lie with any beast to defile thyself therewith [*engage in sexual relations with animals*]: **neither shall any woman**

stand before a beast to lie down thereto: it *is* confusion [*NIV: "perversion"*].

Destruction comes to nations that are ripe in iniquity.

24 Defile not ye yourselves in any of these things: for **in all these** [*sins mentioned above*] **the nations are defiled which I cast out before you:**

25 And the land is defiled: therefore I do visit the iniquity thereof upon it, and **the land itself vomiteth out her inhabitants.**

Laws of the land should prohibit the above-mentioned sins as crimes against society.

26 **Ye shall** therefore keep my statutes [*laws*] and my judgments, and shall **not commit** *any* **of these abominations;** *neither* **any of your own nation, nor any stranger** [*"nonmember"*] **that sojourneth among you:**

27 (For **all these abominations have the men of the land done, which** *were* **before you**, and the land is defiled;)

28 **That the land spue not you out also, when ye defile it, as it spued out the nations that** *were* **before you.**

29 For **whosoever shall commit any of these abominations,** even the souls that commit *them* **shall be**

cut off from among their people.

30 Therefore shall ye keep mine ordinance, that *ye* **commit not** *any* **one of these abominable customs,** which were committed before you, and that ye defile not yourselves therein: I *am* the LORD your God.

Did you notice the word "customs" in verse 30, above? The very use of the word implies that all of the above vile sins had become customary and accepted in the societies that became ripe in iniquity and were destroyed.

LEVITICUS 19

Selection: verses 1–19, 31–37

THESE VERSES POINT out the blessings of being a righteous people. Having warned the children of Israel against the types of sins and behaviors that lead to destruction, in Leviticus 18, the Lord now teaches the wonderful blessings of being in a society of saints. As stated previously, you may be surprised at how many of these attributes and behaviors are part of a Zion society.

1 And the LORD spake unto Moses, saying,

2 Speak unto all the congregation of the children of Israel, and say unto them, **Ye shall be holy:** for I the LORD your God *am* holy.

Keep the Ten Commandments.

3 ¶ Ye shall **fear** [*respect*] **every man his mother, and his father** [*honor your parents*], and keep my Sabbaths [*keep the Sabbath day holy*]: I *am* the LORD your God.

4 ¶ **Turn ye not unto idols, nor make to yourselves molten gods:** I *am* the LORD your God.

5 ¶ And **if ye offer a sacrifice of** peace offerings unto the LORD, **ye shall offer it at your own will** [*obedience is voluntary; in other words, true saints want to be righteous and obedient*].

6 It shall be eaten the same day ye offer it, and on the morrow: and if ought remain until the third day, it shall be burnt in the fire [*be obedient to the details of the laws of God*].

7 And if it be eaten at all on the third day, it *is* abominable; it shall not be accepted.

8 Therefore *every one* that eateth it shall bear his iniquity, because he hath profaned the hallowed thing of the LORD: and that soul shall be cut off from among his people.

Be generous and kind to others.

9 ¶ And **when ye reap the harvest of your land, thou shalt not wholly** [*completely*] **reap the corners** of thy field, **neither shalt thou gather the gleanings** [*grain that is left over after the main harvest*] **of thy harvest.**

10 And **thou shalt not glean thy vineyard, neither shalt thou gather** *every* **grape** of thy vineyard; **thou shalt leave them for the poor and stranger:** I *am* the LORD your God.

Keep the Ten Commandments.

11 ¶ **Ye shall not steal,** neither **deal falsely, neither lie** one to another.

12 ¶ And **ye shall not swear by my name falsely, neither shalt thou profane the name of thy God:** I *am* the LORD.

Complete honesty toward others.

13 ¶ **Thou shalt not defraud thy neighbour, neither rob** *him*: **the wages of him that is hired** [*an employee*] **shall not abide with thee all night** until the morning [*don't withhold wages unfairly*].

Show compassion for those with disabilities.

14 ¶ **Thou shalt not curse the deaf, nor put a stumblingblock before the blind,** but shalt fear thy God: I *am* the LORD.

Don't show favoritism or prejudice.

5 ¶ Ye shall **do no unrighteousness in judgment: thou shalt not respect** [*be prejudiced toward*] **the person of the poor, nor honour the person of the mighty:** *but* in righteousness shalt thou judge thy neighbour.

Don't gossip.

Don't foolishly endanger your neighbor's life.

16 ¶ **Thou shalt not go up and down** *as* **a talebearer** among thy people: **neither shalt thou stand against the blood of thy neighbour** [*don't do things that unnecessarily put your neighbor's life in danger*]; I am the LORD.

Don't be hard-hearted.

17 ¶ **Thou shalt not hate thy brother in thine heart:** thou shalt in any wise rebuke thy neighbour, and not suffer sin upon him [*even though you may have to reprove a neighbor and not ignore his sin, don't hate him—see footnote 17b in your Bible*].

Don't seek revenge; rather, love your neighbor as yourself.

18 ¶ **Thou shalt not avenge, nor bear any grudge** against the children of thy people, but thou shalt **love thy neighbour as thyself:** I am the LORD.

Keep the Church doctrinally pure.

The next verses employ symbolism to teach the importance of not mixing the true religion from God with false doctrines and philosophies from men.

19 ¶ Ye shall **keep my statutes** [*laws, commandments*]. **Thou shalt not let thy cattle gender with a diverse kind** [*don't cross-breed your domestic animals; symbolic of not marrying outside of the covenant people and of not mixing some truth and some falsehood and calling it true religion*]: **thou shalt not sow thy field with mingled seed** [*don't grow different seed crops on the same plot of ground at the same time*]: **neither shall a garment mingled of linen and woolen come upon thee** [*don't wear clothing made of two different kinds of material; symbolic of trying to mix the true gospel with other religions and having a comfortable fit; it doesn't work*].

Additional commandments for a righteous society

Avoid the occult.

31 ¶ **Regard not them that have familiar spirits** [*fortune tellers; people who seek to contact the dead, etc.*]**, neither seek after wizards,** to be defiled by them: I *am* the LORD your God.

Stand up as a show of respect when the elderly come into your presence.

32 ¶ **Thou shalt rise up before the hoary head** [*the white-haired elderly*], and **honour the face of the old man,** and fear [*respect*] thy God: I *am* the LORD.

Don't mistreat people who are not of your "tribe."

33 ¶ And **if a stranger sojourn with thee in your land, ye shall not vex him.**

34 *But* the stranger that dwelleth with you shall be unto you as one born among you, and thou shalt love him as thyself; for ye *were* strangers in the land of Egypt: I *am* the LORD your God.

> Perhaps you've noticed that most of the wars and troubles in the world throughout history have been because people have violated the Law of Moses given in verses 33–34, above.
>
> **Don't use false weights and measures in business dealings (in other words, don't cheat).**

35 ¶ Ye shall **do no unrighteous-ness** in judgment, in **meteyard** [*NIV: "length"*], in **weight,** or in **measure.**

36 Just [*properly calibrated*] **balances, just weights, a just ephah** [*a unit of dry measure*], **and a just hin** [*a unit of liquid measure equal to about 1½ gallons*], **shall ye have:** I *am* the LORD your God, which brought you out of the land of Egypt.

37 Therefore [*in order to be My people*] **shall ye observe all my statutes, and all my judgments, and do them:** I *am* the LORD.

NUMBERS

NUMBERS GETS ITS English name from the census given in the first three chapters (and some of the fourth) and repeated in chapter 26 (see Bible Dictionary, under "Numbers."

Several well-known Bible stories are contained in this book of the Old Testament. Some examples are:

1. Fire from the Lord destroys several Israelites after repeated rebellion and murmuring (Numbers 11:1–3).

2. The people complain again, this time about manna and wish for life back in Egypt (Numbers 11:4–6).

3. A second miracle of quail occurs in which the person who gathered the fewest quail gathered about sixty-five bushels of them (Numbers 11:32).

4. Miriam and Aaron rebel against Moses, and Miriam becomes leprous for a week (Numbers 12).

5. Twelve spies are sent to scout out the land of Canaan. Only two, Joshua and Caleb, bring a favorable report back (Numbers 13–14).

6. Having arrived at the borders of the promised land, the Israelites are commanded to turn back into the wilderness and wander for forty years (Numbers 14:33) because of their constant murmuring and rebellion.

7. The earth swallows up three leaders of rebellion: Korah, Dathan, and

Abiram. Fire consumes 250 other rebel leaders (Numbers 16).

8.   Aaron's rod blossoms and produces almonds (Numbers 17).

9.   Moses smites a rock, and water comes out (Numbers 20:11).

10.   Fiery serpents plague the disobedient Israelites, and Moses makes a brass serpent on a pole. Those who look at it are healed (Numbers 21).

11.   Balaam's donkey speaks to him (Numbers 22).

12.   Joshua is called by the laying on of hands to lead Israel when they enter the promised land (Numbers 27).

At this point in the Bible, it has been several months since Moses and his people left Egypt. As you read Numbers in your Bible, you will see that the children of Israel gradually move from Mount Sinai to Mount Pisgah, which was located east of the Jordan River. From Mount Pisgah, they could see the promised land. But because so many of them still had prideful and rebellious hearts, the Lord turned them back to "wander" in the wilderness for forty years until almost all of the adults had died off.

By the way, "wander" does not mean wander aimlessly every day for forty years. Rather, the people camped for long periods of time at various locations in the wilderness during the forty years of waiting before a new generation was prepared to enter the promised land.

While Numbers does not have many pointed doctrinal sermons, it does carry a number of major messages. For example,

it points out that criticism and rebellion against the Lord and His chosen leaders yield misery and lack of direction for returning to the "promised land" (symbolic of heaven, celestial glory).

Another major message can be found in the fact that the Lord patiently and mercifully provides many obvious proofs of His existence and desire to bless them as invitations for His hard-hearted people to wake up spiritually.

Yet another major message is found in the "good report" given by Joshua and Caleb, who had been sent with ten others to spy out the promised land. Through the eyes of faith, these two men saw the wonderful potential of the promised land, whereas the other ten saw through the eyes of fear and lack of faith, and thus reported the impossibility of carrying out the command of the Lord to enter the promised land.

We will quickly point out a few examples of major messages in the first several chapters of Numbers and then slow down a bit as we get to some of the better-known Bible stories, mentioned above.

NUMBERS 1

Selection: verses 50–53

YOU WILL SEE as you read this chapter in your Bible that the census counted only able-bodied men over twenty years of age (verse 3) and that it excluded the Levites (verse 47), who were to serve as priests in administering the rites and rituals of the Law of Moses to the people. Thus, the census excluded Levites, all females, all children under twenty years of age, old men unable to fight against enemy armies, and any men unable to bear arms.

The census yielded 603,550 able-bodied men (verse 46). We mentioned earlier in this study guide that some Bible scholars suggest that there was a scribal error in copying the earliest Bible manuscripts that resulted in adding an extra 0 to the number of Israelites recorded. If that was the case, there would have been about half a million Israelites total at this time—counting men, women, and children—rather than two to three million. You can read more about this possibility in the *Old Testament Student Manual, Genesis–2 Samuel*, page 194.

As mentioned above, the Levites were in charge of the tabernacle and priesthood rites. We will quote some verses dealing with this:

Numbers 1:50–53

50 But **thou shalt appoint the Levites over the tabernacle of testimony** [*which housed the ark of the covenant, sometimes called the ark of the testimony*], and **over all the vessels thereof,** and **over all things that** *belong* **to it:** they shall **bear the tabernacle** [*transport the tabernacle when the Israelites were traveling*], **and all the vessels thereof; and they shall minister unto it** [*take care of it*], and shall encamp round about the tabernacle [*their tents were to be set up nearest to it, between it*

and the rest of the Israelites].

51 And **when the tabernacle setteth forward** [*when it is time to travel*], **the Levites shall take it down: and when the tabernacle is to be pitched, the Levites shall set it up:** and the stranger that cometh nigh shall be put to death [*one of the very strict "school-master" laws to teach obedience to God's laws*].

52 And **the children of Israel shall pitch their tents, every man by his own camp,** and every man by his own standard [*flag, banner*], throughout their hosts.

53 But the Levites shall pitch round about the tabernacle of testimony, that there be no wrath upon the congregation of the children of Israel: and **the Levites shall keep the charge of the tabernacle** of testimony.

NUMBERS 2

AS YOU READ this chapter in your Bible, you will see that the children of Israel were organized according to which tribe of Israel they belonged to. This allowed things to be done in an orderly manner among this large group of people, including when they traveled.

It may have occurred to you that, in effect, our patriarchal blessings today are organizing us also according to our tribe in the twelve tribes of Israel.

During our patriarchal blessing, our lineage is "declared" by the patriarch. The use of this organizing may yet be future. There is a hint in Doctrine and Covenants 77:11 that each of the twelve tribes will be organized in a major missionary effort in the wind-up scenes of the earth. In the meantime, each worthy member of the twelve tribes is entitled to the blessings of Abraham, Isaac, and Jacob, which are the blessings of exaltation (Abraham 2:9–11).

We will quote from the *Old Testament Student Manual* about the organization of the Israelites by tribes, as they were led by Moses. We will use **bold** for emphasis:

"God's house is a house of order (see Doctrine and Covenants 132:8). In symbolic representation thereof, so was the camp of Israel. **Order was maintained in both their encampments and marches**.

"The tribes were de**ployed in four groups of three tribes**. On the east side of the camp and at the front of the moving column were Issachar and Zebulun with Judah at the head. On the south side in second position were Simeon and Gad under the leadership of Reuben. In the middle were the Levites. On the west and fourth in the line of march were Manasseh and Benjamin, led by Ephraim. On the north and in the rear were Asher and Naphtali, with Dan at the head.

"The places of honor, at the head of the hosts and immediately following the tabernacle, were held by Judah and Ephraim, respectively. Judah camped directly east of the tabernacle entrance" (*Old Testament Student Manual: Genesis–2 Samuel*, page 197).

NUMBERS 3

Selection: verses 3–10, 12, 45–51

AS YOU READ chapter 3 in your Bible, you will see that there was a difference in assignment within the Aaronic Priesthood for the sons of Aaron and the other Levites. All of them were from the tribe of Levi. However, Aaron and his descendants served in the office of priest, performing the actual priesthood rituals of the tabernacle, such as making sacrifice, burning incense, and so forth. The other Levites assisted in maintaining and taking care of the tabernacle but could not perform the actual offerings and rites.

This difference between the descendants of Aaron and the other men in the tribe of Levi is sometimes spoken of as the "Aaronic Priesthood" and the "Levitical Priesthood." A rough comparison in terms we understand in our day might be that the descendants of Aaron were priests, and the rest of the priesthood holders of the tribe of Levi were teachers and deacons.

We will point out the difference in function of the sons of (or descendants of) Aaron as compared to the other Levites.

NUMBERS 3:3–10

3 These *are* the names of **the sons of Aaron**, the **priests** which were anointed, whom he **consecrated to minister in the priest's office.**

4 And Nadab and Abihu died

before the LORD, when they offered strange fire before the LORD [*Leviticus 10:1–2*], in the wilderness of Sinai, and they had no children: and **Eleazar and Ithamar ministered in the priest's office** in the sight of Aaron their father.

5 ¶ And the LORD spake unto Moses, saying,

6 Bring **the tribe of Levi** near, and present them before Aaron the priest, that they may **minister unto him** [*serve under the priests*].

7 And **they shall** keep his charge, and the charge of the whole congregation before the tabernacle of the congregation, to **do the service of the tabernacle** [*in other words, they will maintain the tabernacle—see also verse 8*].

8 And **they shall keep all the instruments of the tabernacle** of the congregation, and the charge of the children of Israel, to do the service of the tabernacle [*to maintain and take care of the tabernacle*].

9 And **thou shalt give the Levites unto Aaron and to his sons:** they *are* wholly given [*consecrated for life to the duties of the Levitical Priesthood*] unto him out of the children of Israel.

10 And **thou shalt appoint Aaron and his sons, and they shall wait on** [*serve in*] **their priest's office:**

and the stranger that cometh nigh shall be put to death.

Joseph Fielding Smith explained the distinction between the Aaronic Priesthood and the Levitical Priesthood. He taught (**bold** added for emphasis):

"The Aaronic Priesthood is divided into the **Aaronic and the Levitical, yet it is but one priesthood. This is merely a matter of designating certain duties within the priesthood.** The sons of Aaron, who presided in the Aaronic order, were spoken of as holding the Aaronic Priesthood; and the sons of Levi, who were not sons of Aaron, were spoken of as the Levites. They held the Aaronic Priesthood but served under, or in a lesser capacity, than the sons of Aaron" (Smith, *Doctrines of Salvation*, 3:86).

The men of the tribe of Levi took the place of the firstborn son of each family among the twelve tribes.

You may recall that the Lord instructed that the firstborn son of each family in Israel be dedicated to Him for full-time service (Exodus 13:2, 12). In Numbers, chapter 3, we see that the Levites were now consecrated to serve in the priesthood duties, in the place of the firstborn son of each family.

Numbers 3:12, 45

12 And I, behold, **I have taken the Levites from among the children of Israel instead of** [*in the place of*] **all the firstborn** that openeth the

matrix [*womb*] among the children of Israel: therefore **the Levites shall be mine;**

45 Take the Levites instead of all the firstborn among the children of Israel, and the cattle of the Levites instead of their cattle; and **the Levites shall be mine:** I *am* the LORD.

> There was a logistical problem that came up in substituting, man for man, a male member of the tribe of Levi for each of the firstborn sons of the tribes in general. At the time this census was taken, there were 273 more firstborn sons (verse 46) than there were Levite males. Knowing this will help you make sense of verses 45–51.

Numbers 3:45–51

45 Take the Levites instead of [*in the place of*] **all the firstborn among the children of Israel,** and the cattle of the Levites instead of their cattle; and the Levites shall be mine: I *am* the LORD.

46 And for those that are to be redeemed of the **two hundred and threescore and thirteen of the firstborn of the children of Israel,** which are **more than the Levites;**

> The solution to the problem was given by the Lord as explained in the next verses. The families of the firstborn sons, where there was no Levite substitute for their sons, were to give a five shekel donation to Aaron in place of their son.

47 Thou shalt even take five shekels [*NIV: "about 2 ounces" of whatever they were using for money*] **apiece** by the poll, after the shekel of the sanctuary shalt thou take *them:* (a shekel *is* twenty gerahs:)

48 And **thou shalt give the money,** wherewith the odd number [*the 273 who didn't have a Levite to substitute for them*] of them is to be redeemed, **unto Aaron and to his sons.**

49 And **Moses took the redemption money** of them [*for the 273*] that were over and above them that were redeemed by the Levites [*those who had a Levite to substitute for them*]:

50 Of the firstborn of the children of Israel took he the money; **a thousand three hundred and threescore and five** *shekels,* after the shekel of the sanctuary:

51 And **Moses gave the money of them that were redeemed unto Aaron and to his sons, according to the word of the LORD,** as the LORD commanded Moses.

> We will move on to chapter 5 and consider some practical and spiritual laws therein.

NUMBERS 5

Selection: verses 1–8

IN VERSES 1-4 of this chapter, you will see laws dealing with preventing the spread of leprosy and infectious diseases. Sanitation and the prevention of the spread of communicable diseases were a very vital and practical part of the Law of Moses.

1 AND the LORD spake unto Moses, saying,

2 Command the children of Israel, that they put out of the camp every leper, and every one that hath an issue [*infectious discharge*], and whosoever is defiled by the dead [*has touched a dead body and is thus ceremonially unclean*]:

3 Both male and female shall ye put out, without [*outside of*] the camp shall ye put them; that they defile not their camps, in the midst whereof I dwell.

4 And the children of Israel did so, and put them out without the camp: as the LORD spake unto Moses, so did the children of Israel.

Confession, restitution, and atonement

We saw much about the aspects of true repentance, including confession and restitution as we studied selected verses in Leviticus (for example, Leviticus 5:5, 16). They are reiterated again in this chapter.

5 ¶ And the LORD spake unto Moses, saying,

6 Speak unto the children of Israel, **When a man or woman shall commit any sin** that men commit, to do **a trespass against the LORD,** and that person be guilty;

7 Then **they shall confess their sin** which they have done: **and** he shall **recompense his trespass** [*make restitution*] with the principal thereof, and add unto it the fifth *part* thereof, and give *it* **unto him against whom he hath trespassed.**

8 But if the man have no kinsman to recompense the trespass unto, let the trespass be recompensed unto the LORD, *even* to the priest; beside the ram of the atonement, whereby **an atonement shall be made for him** [*symbolic of the Atonement of Christ*].

Dealing with a woman whose husband accuses her of adultery.

Before you read verses 11–31 in your Bible, it will be helpful to read the following verse in Leviticus:

Leviticus 20:10

10 ¶ And the man that committeth adultery with *another* man's wife, *even* he that committeth adultery with his neighbour's wife, **the adulterer and the adulteress shall surely be put to death.**

With the above verse from

115

Leviticus stating clearly that the penalty for adultery was the same for both the man and the woman involved, verses 11–31 of Numbers, chapter 5, may be viewed as a way for an innocent wife, accused of adultery by her husband, to be cleared of guilt. As you read these verses in your Bible, you can see that the Lord said, in effect, that He personally would intervene in behalf of an innocent wife, causing the "test" of drinking a certain potion of water to work in her favor. This could perhaps be her only safeguard in cases where emotion and false accusation were running high.

NUMBERS 6

Selection: verses 1–8, 24–26

HERE WE WILL briefly consider the difference between a "Nazarite" and a "Nazarene," and then read a beautiful blessing given in verses 24–26.

First, students sometimes confuse the terms "Nazarite" and "Nazarene." The reason we bring these two terms up here is that some people refer to the Savior as a "Nazarite." He was not. He was a "Nazarene," meaning simply that He came from Nazareth (see Bible Dictionary, under "Nazarene"). In this chapter, we see the terms for being a "Nazarite" spelled out.

The Nazarite vow.

The vow of a Nazarite, which involved consecrating one's self to the Lord,

might be for a lifetime or for a short, finite period of time (see Bible Dictionary, under "Nazarite"). Samson (Judges 13:5) was an example of one who lived under a Nazarite vow.

Let's look in verses 1–8 for some details as to how a man or a woman could thus consecrate himself or herself to the Lord.

1 And the LORD spake unto Moses, saying,

2 Speak unto the children of Israel, and say unto them, **When either man or woman** shall separate *themselves* to **vow a vow of a Nazarite**, to separate [*consecrate*] *themselves* unto the LORD:

FIRST: No wine, strong drink, grape juice, grapes, or raisins.

3 He shall **separate** *himself* **from** [*he shall have no*] **wine and strong drink** [*fermented juice*], and **shall drink no vinegar of wine, or vinegar of strong drink, neither** shall he drink **any liquor** [*juice*] **of grapes,** nor eat **moist grapes, or dried.**

4 All the days of his separation [*all the time he is consecrated to the Lord*] shall he eat nothing that is made of the vine tree [*grape vine*], from the kernels even to the husk.

SECOND: No hair cuts.

5 All the days of the vow of his separation **there shall no razor come upon his head:** until the days be

fulfilled, in the which he separateth *himself* unto the LORD, he shall be holy, *and* shall **let the locks of the hair of his head grow.**

THIRD: No coming near a dead body, including his own family members.

6 All the days that he separateth *himself* unto the LORD he shall **come at no dead body.**

7 He shall not make himself unclean for his father, or for his mother, for his brother, or for his sister, when they die [*he must not come near a parent or sibling if they have died—symbolic of his loyalty to the Lord being stronger than any earthly loyalty*]: because the consecration of his God *is* upon his head.

8 All the days of his separation he *is* holy unto the LORD.

A beautiful blessing for the people.

One of the most beautiful of all the "blessings" given in the scriptures is found in this chapter. The Lord instructed Moses to have Aaron and his sons pronounce it upon the children of Israel:

24 The LORD bless thee, and keep thee:

25 The LORD make his face shine upon thee, and be gracious unto thee:

26 The LORD lift up his countenance upon thee, and give thee peace.

We will now move to chapter 8 and do a quick review of Atonement symbolism in the rituals and sacrifices given the people in the Law of Moses.

NUMBERS 8

Selection: verses 5–26

MORE WASHING, consecrating, and being set apart by the laying on of hands. More Atonement symbolism in the Law of Moses.

IN THESE NEXT verses, we will again see many words that are familiar to active Latter-day Saints. Once again, they are a reminder that the Law of Moses was given to the Israelites by the Savior, and that rather than being a punishment or low law, it was a high law designed to bring them to the point that they could accept the "higher" law, which incorporates all of the gospel of Jesus Christ. We will use **bold** as usual, for teaching emphasis:

Numbers 8:5–21

5 ¶ And the LORD spake unto Moses, saying,

6 Take the Levites from among the children of Israel, and **cleanse them.**

7 And thus shalt thou do unto them, to cleanse them: **Sprinkle water of**

purifying upon them, and let them **shave all their flesh** [*symbolic of being born again, a new person, a new start, cleansed—see Leviticus 14:1–9 in this study guide*], and let them **wash their clothes**, and *so* **make themselves clean.**

8 Then let them take a young bullock with his meat offering, *even* fine flour mingled with **oil** [*symbolic of light, cleansing, healing from the Lord*], and another young bullock shalt thou take for **a sin offering** [*symbolic of Christ's Atonement, His "offering" for our sins*].

9 And thou shalt bring the Levites before the tabernacle of the congregation: and thou shalt gather the whole assembly of the children of Israel together:

10 And thou shalt bring the Levites before the LORD: and the children of Israel shall **put their hands upon the Levites** [*a reminder that blessings and authority were given anciently by the laying on of hands*]:

11 And Aaron shall offer the Levites before the LORD *for* an offering of the children of Israel, that they may execute the service of the LORD.

12 And **the Levites shall lay their hands upon the heads of the bullocks** [*symbolically transferring their own identities to the sacrificial animals, and, in turn, symbolizing that*

our sins were transferred to the Savior who was sacrificed for them]: and thou shalt **offer the one *for* a sin offering**, and the other *for* a burnt offering, unto the LORD, **to make an atonement for the Levites.**

13 And thou shalt set the Levites before Aaron, and before his sons, and offer them *for* an offering [*dedicate and consecrate them*] unto the LORD.

14 Thus shalt thou separate the Levites from among the children of Israel: and the Levites shall be mine [*the Levites were thus consecrated to the service of the Lord*].

15 And after that shall the Levites go in to do the service [*perform the rites and rituals*] of the tabernacle of the congregation: and **thou shalt cleanse them**, and offer them *for* an offering.

16 For they *are* wholly given [*completely dedicated*] unto me from among the children of Israel; instead of such as open every womb, *even instead of* the firstborn of all the children of Israel, have I taken them unto me.

17 For **all the firstborn of the children of Israel *are* mine** [*symbolic of Jesus Christ, the Firstborn of the Father—meaning the firstborn spirit child of the Father—see Colossians 1:13–15*], *both* man and beast: on the day that I smote every firstborn in the land of Egypt I sanctified them for myself.

18 And I have taken the Levites for [*in the place of*] all the firstborn of the children of Israel.

19 And I have given the Levites *as* a gift to Aaron and to his sons from among the children of Israel, to do the service of the children of Israel in the tabernacle of the congregation, and to make an atonement for the children of Israel: that there be no plague among the children of Israel, when the children of Israel come nigh unto the sanctuary.

20 And Moses, and Aaron, and all the congregation of the children of Israel, did to the Levites according unto all that the LORD commanded Moses concerning the Levites, so did the children of Israel unto them.

21 And the Levites were **purified**, and they **washed** their clothes; and Aaron offered them *as* an offering before the LORD; and Aaron made **an atonement for them to cleanse them.**

In verses 23–26, we see that Levites served from age twenty-five to fifty and then were "retired" from daily service.

23 ¶ And the LORD spake unto Moses, saying,

24 This *is it* that *belongeth* unto the **Levites: from twenty and five years old and upward** they **shall go in to wait upon the service of the tabernacle of the congregation:**

25 And **from the age of fifty years they shall cease** waiting upon the service *thereof,* **and shall serve no more:**

26 But shall minister with their brethren in the tabernacle of the congregation, to keep the charge, and **shall do no service** [*will no longer be consecrated to full-time service*]. Thus shalt thou do unto the Levites touching their charge.

NUMBERS 9

Selection: all verses

IN THE FIRST five verses of this chapter, the Lord gives instructions for keeping the Passover. Beginning with verse 6, you will see an interesting problem develop for some men who wanted to keep the Passover but had become ritually unclean because they touched a dead body, probably in the course of carrying it away for burial. They asked Moses what they should do, and he asked the Lord. Let's take a quick look and see what the Lord told them.

1 And **the LORD spake unto Moses** in the wilderness of Sinai, in the **first month** of the second year after they were come out of the land of Egypt, saying,

2 Let the children of Israel also keep the passover at his appointed season.

3 In the fourteenth day of this month, at even [*in the evening*], ye shall keep it in his appointed season: according to all the rites of it, and according to all the ceremonies thereof, shall ye keep it.

4 And Moses spake unto the children of Israel, that they should keep the passover.

5 And they kept the passover on the fourteenth day of the first month at even in the wilderness of Sinai: according to all that the LORD commanded Moses, so did the children of Israel.

6 ¶ And there were certain men, who were defiled by the dead body of a man, that they could not keep the passover on that day: and they came before Moses and before Aaron on that day:

7 And those men said unto him, We *are* defiled by the dead body of a man: wherefore [*why*] are we kept back, that we may not offer an offering of the LORD in his appointed season among the children of Israel [*why can't we participate in Passover*]?

8 And Moses said unto them, Stand still [*wait here*], and I will hear what the LORD will command concerning you.

The Lord's answer:

9 ¶ And the LORD spake unto Moses, saying,

10 Speak unto the children of Israel, saying, If any man of you or of your posterity shall be unclean by reason of a dead body, or *be* in a journey afar off, yet he shall keep the passover unto the LORD.

11 The fourteenth day of the second month [*in other words, you may keep it one month later*] at even they shall keep it, *and* eat it with unleavened bread and bitter *herbs*.

12 They shall leave none of it unto the morning, nor break any bone of it: according to all the ordinances of the passover they shall keep it.

Next, the Lord gives instructions for dealing with a person who is clean but who refuses to participate in Passover at the normal time; in other words, one who wants to change the Lord's commandments for personal convenience.

13 But the man that *is* clean, and is not in a journey, and forbeareth [*refuses*] to keep the passover, even the same soul shall be cut off [*excommunicated*] from among his people: because he brought not the offering of the LORD in his appointed season, that man shall bear his sin.

Next, what about a non-Israelite?

14 And **if a stranger** [*a non-Isra-elite—see Bible Dictionary, under "Stranger"*] **shall sojourn among you** [*is living among you*]**, and will** [*desires to*] **keep the passover** unto the LORD; according to the ordinance of the passover, and according to the manner thereof, **so shall he do**: ye shall have one ordinance, both for the stranger, and for him that was born in the land.

> We mentioned previously that in his mercy and kindness, the Lord gave them witness after witness that He exists, while these often prideful and rebellious people camped and journeyed on their way to the promised land. One of the most significant and obvious proofs of Him and His care for them is pointed out again in verses 15–23. The presence of the Lord was miraculously manifest by day in the form of a cloud that rested on the tabernacle. By night, the tabernacle had "the appearance of fire" all night.
>
> When the cloud lifted from the tabernacle, it was a signal for the Israelites to take down their tents and continue their journey. They followed the cloud until it stopped, and there they pitched their camp. But as long as it rested upon the tabernacle, they were to stay put. As you will see in the next verses, sometimes they remained in one place for a few days, "or a month, or a year" (verse 22).
>
> One of the lessons taught to the children of Israel by these marvelous manifestations was that of following the Lord

thoroughly and completely.

15 ¶ And on the day that the tabernacle was reared up **the cloud covered the tabernacle,** *namely,* the tent of the testimony: and **at even** [*when it began to get dark*] **there was upon the tabernacle as it were the appearance of fire, until the morning.**

16 So it was always [*continuously*]: **the cloud covered it by day, and the appearance of fire by night.**

17 And **when the cloud was taken up from the tabernacle,** then after that **the children of Israel journeyed: and in the place where the cloud abode, there the children of Israel pitched their tents.**

18 At the commandment of the LORD the children of Israel journeyed, and at the commandment of the LORD they pitched** [*set up camp*]**: as long as the cloud abode upon the tabernacle they rested in their tents.**

19 And **when the cloud tarried long upon the tabernacle many days, then the children of Israel** kept the charge of the LORD, and **journeyed not.**

20 And *so it was,* **when the cloud was a few days upon the tabernacle;** according to the commandment of the LORD **they abode** [*stayed*] **in their tents,** and according to the commandment of the LORD they journeyed [*when the cloud lifted and moved*].

21 And *so* it was, **when the cloud** abode from even unto the morning, and *that* the cloud **was taken up** in the morning, **then they journeyed: whether** *it was* **by day or by night** that the cloud was taken up, they journeyed [*thus, they were being taught to obey and follow the Lord (literally) no matter what*].

22 Or **whether it were two days, or a month, or a year, that the cloud tarried upon the tabernacle,** remaining thereon, **the children of Israel** abode in their tents, and **journeyed not:** but **when it was taken up, they journeyed.**

23 **At the commandment of the LORD they rested in the tents, and at the commandment of the LORD they journeyed:** they kept the charge [*instructions*] of the LORD, at the commandment of the LORD by the hand of Moses.

Remember that Moses is the author of the first five books in the Old Testament. In the general background notes to Numbers in this study guide, we pointed out several familiar Bible stories that are contained in this "Fourth Book of Moses," beginning with chapter 11. It is helpful when studying these chapters to look for patterns and lessons that Moses was teaching us as he included these

incidents in his written record.

You may wish to ask yourself the following questions as you study:

1. With the many possible things to include in his record, why did Moses choose to include this one?

2. What lessons did he and the Lord want me to learn from it?

We will point out some possible lessons or major messages as we proceed. You will no doubt see many others.

NUMBERS 11

Selection: verses 1–8, 10–34

THE CHILDREN OF Israel are on their way to the promised land. They have not yet been turned back to "wander" in the wilderness. Many of them are still rebellious and fail to learn obedience in spite of so many opportunities to build testimonies and recognize that the Lord wants to bless them. Several "major messages" contained in this chapter can apply to us in our day.

Major Message

Spiritual and physical destruction await those who develop a lifestyle of rebellion and complaining against the laws of God.

1 And **when the people complained,** it displeased the LORD: and the LORD heard *it;* and his anger was kindled; and **the fire of**

the LORD burnt among them, and consumed *them that were* in the uttermost parts of the camp [*as far away from the tabernacle as possible; as far away from the mercy seat as possible—symbolic of deliberately being far away from God*].

Major Message

We can turn to the Lord's living prophet for help and guidance in times of trouble.

2 And **the people cried unto Moses**; and when Moses prayed unto the LORD, the fire was quenched.

3 And he called the name of the place Taberah: because the fire of the LORD burnt among them.

Major Message

We cannot successfully move forward toward God while at the same time looking back with desire for the ways of the world that we are leaving.

Remember that "manna" can be symbolic of nourishment and blessings from heaven. "Egypt" can be symbolic of wickedness and the ways of the world (Revelation 11:8). Thus, in this chapter, in effect, the Israelites are getting tired of the religious life and desire the lustful ways of the world with the instant gratification that attends them. They have lost their perspective and are valuing appetites of the physical body over being nourished by the Lord.

4 ¶ And **the mixt multitude** [*NIV: "the rabble"*] **that** *was* **among them**

fell a lusting: and the children of Israel also wept again, and said, Who shall give us flesh to eat? [*In other words, they are taking manna for granted and no longer appreciate it. Instead, they want meat to eat.*]

5 **We remember the fish**, which we did eat **in Egypt** freely [*abundantly*]; the **cucumbers**, and the **melons**, and the **leeks**, and the **onions**, and the **garlick:**

6 But **now our soul** *is* **dried away:** *there is* **nothing at all, beside this manna**, *before* our eyes.

Next, we are given a description of manna and how it was used.

7 And the **manna** *was* as coriander seed, and the colour thereof as **the colour of bdellium.**

8 *And* **the people** went about, and gathered *it*, and **ground** *it* in mills, or **beat** *it* **in a mortar,** and **baked** *it* **in pans**, and **made cakes of it:** and the taste of it was as **the taste of fresh oil.**

You may wish to read ahead and see the Lord's response to their complaints about not having meat and lack of gratitude for manna, in verses 18–23 and 31–34. It is a severe lesson. Have you noticed that these people are severely afflicted with the lack of gratitude? Gratitude is one of the most healing and soothing of all desirable human attributes. Its relative importance is given in Doctrine and Covenants 59:21.

Next, we turn to another topic.

Major Message

Everyone, including prophets, can get discouraged and overwhelmed while trying to do the Lord's work.

As you read verses 10–15, you will see that Moses is still learning and that he is discouraged at this point. In fact, he is very open with the Lord about how he feels. First, we will look at verses 10–15, and then we will watch how the Lord responds to Moses's concerns, beginning with verse 16. We have seen somewhat similar situations of discouragement with Nephi (2 Nephi 4:17–19) and with the Prophet Joseph Smith in Liberty Jail (Doctrine and Covenants 121:1–6).

10 ¶ Then Moses heard the people weep throughout their families, every man in the door of his tent [*they all came to Moses's tent to cry and complain*]: and **the anger of the LORD was kindled greatly; Moses also was displeased.**

11 And Moses said unto the LORD, Wherefore [*why*] **hast thou afflicted thy servant?** and **wherefore have I not found favour in thy sight, that thou layest the burden of all this people upon me?** [*In other words, what did I do wrong to have such heavy burdens placed on me and not get the help I need from Thee?*]

In the next two verses, Moses asks, in effect, why the Lord is treating him as if the Israelites were his people instead of the Lord's people. Why is the Lord acting like it is Moses's responsibility to take care of them, rather than the Lord's?

This is a bit touchy, but it is a good reminder that the role of leadership can be hard for prophets too.

Above all, remember that Moses continued to grow and develop and became one of the greatest prophets of all time. In fact, he was translated and appeared to the Savior on the Mount of Transfiguration to minister to Him and comfort Him in preparation for the Atonement six months later (Matthew 17:1–3).

12 Have I conceived all this people? have I begotten them [*in effect, are these my children? No, they are Yours*]**, that thou shouldest say unto me, Carry them** in thy bosom, as a nursing father beareth the sucking child, unto the land which thou swarest [*promised*] unto their fathers [*in other words, why is all the responsibility for these people on my shoulders*]?

13 Whence should I have flesh [*where can I find meat*] **to give unto all this people?** for **they weep unto me** [*instead of crying to the Lord*], saying, Give us flesh, that we may eat.

14 I am not able to bear [*carry*] **all this people alone, because** *it is* **too heavy for me.**

15 And **if thou deal thus with me** [*if this is the way You want it to be*], **kill me, I pray thee** [*please*], **out of hand** [*right now—see footnote 15a in your Bible*], **if I have found favour in thy sight** [*it would be a kindness to me*]; and **let me not see my wretchedness** [*my shortcomings are overwhelming me*].

> Rather than chastising him, the Lord responds with kindness and help for Moses. He appoints seventy men to assist him.

16 ¶ And **the LORD said unto Moses, Gather** unto me **seventy men** of the elders of Israel, whom thou knowest to be the elders of the people, and officers over them; **and bring them unto the tabernacle of the congregation, that they may stand there with thee.**

17 And **I will come down and talk with thee there:** and **I will take of the spirit which** *is* **upon thee, and will put** *it* **upon them; and they shall bear the burden of the people with thee, that thou bear** *it* **not thyself alone.**

> For the rest of this account, you may wish to read verses 24–29 now.
>
> #### Major Message
>
> Bad attitudes and demands that the Lord give us what we want are unwise.
>
> The people had a bad and rebellious attitude. Rather than humbly requesting some meat

to go with the manna, if it had been in harmony with the Lord's will, they demanded meat and complained loudly to Moses, as if he were the Lord. Their prideful and strident approach is answered by the Lord with a severe lesson.

18 And **say thou unto the people, Sanctify yourselves against to morrow** [*brace yourselves against what is coming tomorrow*], **and ye shall eat flesh: for ye have wept in the ears of the LORD, saying, Who shall give us flesh to eat?** for *it was* **well with us in Egypt** [*we were better off in Egypt than we are under the care of the Lord now*]: **therefore the LORD will give you flesh, and ye shall eat.**

19 Ye shall **not** eat **one day,** nor two days, **nor five** days, **neither ten days, nor twenty days;**

20 *But* **even a whole month, until it come out at your nostrils,** and it be loathsome unto you: **because that ye have despised the LORD** which *is* among you, and have wept before him, saying, Why came we forth out of Egypt?

> Next, Moses asks the Lord a logistical question, wondering about possible ways the Israelites could eat meat for a whole month without decimating the herds and flocks they will need for a start in the promised land. He will be mildly chastised for his lack of trust in the Lord's ability to provide (verse 23).

21 And Moses said, The people, among whom I *am,* **are six hundred thousand footmen; and thou hast said, I will give them flesh, that they may eat a whole month.**

22 Shall the flocks and the herds be slain for them, to suffice [*satisfy*] them? or shall all the fish of the sea be gathered together for them, to suffice them?

23 And the LORD said unto Moses, **Is the LORD's hand waxed short** [*have I lost My power*]? **thou shalt see** now whether my word shall come to pass unto thee or not.

You may wish to read the continuation of this account now, in verses 31–34.

In the meantime, verses 24–29, next, are a continuation of the Lord's kind response, in verses 16–17, to Moses's concern about being overwhelmed with his leadership responsibilities.

24 ¶ And Moses went out, and told the people the words of the LORD, and **gathered the seventy men** of the elders of the people [*selected from among the leaders of Israel*], and set them round about the tabernacle.

25 And the LORD came down in a cloud, and spake unto him, and **took of the spirit that** *was* **upon him, and gave** *it* **unto the seventy elders** [*they were now called of God and authorized to function in their*

callings, just as Moses was]: and it came to pass, *that,* when the spirit rested upon them, **they prophesied,** and did not cease.

26 But there remained two *of the* men in the camp [*who had not made it to the installation meeting with the others*], the name of the one *was* Eldad, and the name of the other Medad: and the spirit rested upon them; and they *were* of them that were written [*they were part of the group of seventy which had been called*], but went not out unto the tabernacle: and they prophesied in the camp.

27 And there ran a young man, and told Moses, and said, Eldad and Medad do prophesy in the camp.

Joshua was concerned that the two who had not made it to the meeting were out of line in prophesying like the others of the seventy. Moses teaches him a lesson.

28 And Joshua the son of Nun, the servant of Moses, *one* of his young men, answered and **said, My lord Moses, forbid them.**

29 And Moses said unto him, Enviest thou for my sake [*are you worried about my feelings*]? **would God that** [*I just wish that*] **all the LORD's people were prophets,** *and* **that the LORD would put his spirit upon them** [*I wish that all the Israelites would live worthy to have the*

Spirit of the Lord on them; it would solve all sorts of problems]!

30 And Moses gat him into the camp, he and the elders of Israel.

> Next, hordes of quail fall around the camp of the Israelites, piled about three feet deep and extending about a day's walk in every direction.

31 ¶ And there went forth **a wind from the LORD,** and **brought quails** from the sea, **and let** *them* **fall by the camp,** as it were a day's journey on this side, and as it were a day's journey on the other side, round about the camp, and as it were **two cubits** *high* [*thirty-six inches deep*] upon the face of the earth.

32 And the people stood up **all that day, and all** *that* **night, and all the next day,** and **they gathered** the quails: **he that gathered least gathered ten homers** [*the smallest number of quail gathered was about sixty-five bushels*]: and they spread *them* all abroad for themselves round about the camp.

33 And while the flesh *was* **yet between their teeth, ere it was chewed,** the wrath of the LORD was kindled against the people, and **the LORD smote the people with a very great plague.**

34 And he called the name of that place Kibroth-hattaavah: because **there they buried the people that lusted.**

It may well be that there had been instruction to gather only what was needed (as was the case with manna) and that the people went wild with greed. Whatever the case, the people who "lusted" (verse 34, above) were destroyed by a plague and were buried.

Have you noticed that the most wicked and rebellious people are being weeded out from the children of Israel? The rest are spared until they either make progress toward being righteous or fall deeper into apostasy and transgression.

As we continue with these selections in Numbers, we will see more of this pattern of the Lord, destroying the more wicked while continuing to work with those who still have a tendency to repent and follow the Him.

You may even see a form of this pattern with the early members of the Church after the Restoration. Each time they were driven out of an area, some apostatized, some stayed put, and some followed the Lord's instructions through His prophet and traveled to another gathering place. We see this as they were driven from New York and gathered in Ohio. Then, from Ohio to Missouri and from Missouri to Illinois. By the time they arrived in the Salt Lake Valley, the Lord had a proven and faithful people from whom the gospel could be sent to all the world.

NUMBERS 12

Selection: all verses

IN THIS CHAPTER, Miriam and Aaron grow jealous of their younger brother, Moses, and seek to discredit him. They desire glory for themselves. Moses forgives them and pleads with the Lord to heal Miriam, who was punished with leprosy.

Major Message

One of Satan's well-used tools against us is that of jealousy. While it can be damaging to those against whom it is used, it is far more destructive to those who harbor it within their souls.

In verse 1, Miriam and Aaron seek to discredit Moses by bringing up the fact that he married an Ethiopian woman back when he was a prince and military leader in Egypt.

Even though it was a political marriage only (according to Josephus, *Antiquities of the Jews*, book 2, chapter 10, paragraph 1), contracted to cement a political alliance, Miriam and Aaron still try to make their younger brother look like a hypocrite for marrying someone outside of the covenant people.

We see evidence of their jealousy in verse 2. It appears that Miriam was the instigator of these attacks on Moses since she was the main target of the Lord's anger.

1 And Miriam and Aaron spake against Moses because of the Ethiopian woman whom he had married: for he had married an Ethiopian woman.

2 And they said, Hath the LORD indeed spoken only by Moses? hath he not spoken also by us? And the LORD heard *it.*

Moses was a meek and humble man.

3 (Now the man Moses *was* very meek, above all the men which *were* upon the face of the earth.)

Miriam and Aaron are told in no uncertain terms that Moses is the Lord's prophet. They are told by Jehovah Himself.

4 And the LORD spake suddenly unto Moses, and unto Aaron, and unto Miriam, Come out ye three unto the tabernacle of the congregation. And they three came out.

5 And the LORD came down in the pillar of the cloud, and stood *in* the door of the tabernacle, **and called Aaron and Miriam: and they both came forth.**

The Lord tells them, in effect, that Moses is not only a prophet but also that he stands above most other prophets.

6 And he said, Hear now my words [*get this and get it straight*]: **If there be a prophet among you, I the LORD will make myself known unto him in a vision, *and* will speak** unto him **in a dream.**

**7 My servant Moses *is* not so [*that*

is not how I communicate with Moses], who *is* faithful in all mine house.

8 With him will I speak mouth to mouth, even apparently [*I speak to him openly, in person*], and not in dark speeches; and **the similitude of the LORD shall he behold** [*he will continue to see the Lord in person*]: **wherefore then were ye not afraid to speak against my servant Moses** [*so, why were you two not afraid to criticize him*]?

9 And the anger of the LORD was kindled against them; and he departed.

10 And **the cloud departed** from off the tabernacle; and, behold, **Miriam *became* leprous, *white* as snow:** and Aaron looked upon Miriam, and, behold, *she was* leprous.

Aaron humbly repents and apologizes to Moses for himself and Miriam, asking for his forgiveness.

11 And **Aaron said unto Moses, Alas,** my lord, I beseech thee, lay not the sin upon us, wherein **we have done foolishly,** and wherein **we have sinned.**

12 Let her not be as one dead [*leprosy was considered to be a living death*], of whom the flesh is half consumed when he cometh out of his mother's womb [*like a baby born with leprosy*].

Moses forgives and pleads with the Lord for Miriam.

13 And Moses cried unto the LORD, saying, Heal her now, O God, I beseech thee.

Major Message

Sometimes we want instant forgiveness of sin, but the Lord waits a while so the lesson will sink in.

14 ¶ And the LORD said unto Moses, If her father had but spit in her face [*which caused a person to be disgraced for seven days*], should she not be ashamed seven days? **let her be shut out from the camp seven days, and after that let her be received in** *again.* [*In other words, her sin of criticizing you was serious, far more serious than getting spit on, so let her experience the humiliation of being cut off from the people for seven days so she learns her lesson.*]

15 And **Miriam was shut out from the camp seven days:** and the people journeyed not till Miriam was brought in *again.*

16 And afterward the people removed from Hazeroth, and pitched in the wilderness of Paran.

NUMBERS 13

Selection: all verses

THE TIME FOR entering the promised land is getting close. The Lord instructs Moses to send out twelve spies, one from each tribe, to check out the land of Canaan. They are to return and report what they see. We will pay special attention to the difference in reports given by Caleb and Joshua (called "Oshea" in verse 8), who see through the eyes of faith, as opposed to those given by the other ten spies, who see through the eyes of fear and lack of faith in God.

Keep in mind that the Lord has led them to this location. They have followed the cloud by which He led them. His presence and care for them has been obviously made known in a cloud by day and fire by night. They have seen miracle after miracle, including the ten plagues in Egypt, which plagued the Egyptians but not the Israelites. They came through the Red Sea on dry land, heard the voice of the Lord as He personally spoke the Ten Commandments from Sinai, have had manna, water from a rock, good and bad experiences with quail, deaths by fire because of rebellion, and on and on. In short, they have had many chances to know Jehovah and that they are being led and blessed by Him, and that Moses is indeed His prophet. They have every reason to believe—based on miracles and obvious, tangible proof—that He can bring them into the promised land, regardless of whatever and whoever might stand in the way.

In the list of spies, verses 4–16, we will **bold** the names of the two spies who express faith that the Lord would lead them to successfully occupy the promised land.

Major Message

Some see through the eyes of faith and follow the commandments of God, seeing opportunity in opposition and trials. They see things from the Lord's perspective and truly live life to its fullest. Others see through the eyes of fear and lack of faith. They are generally miserable and spread their misery. They often stop following the prophet.

1 And **the LORD spake unto Moses,** saying,

2 **Send thou men, that they may search the land of Canaan,** which I give unto the children of Israel: of every tribe of their fathers [*one from each of the twelve tribes*] shall ye send a man, every one a ruler [*leader*] among them.

3 And Moses by the commandment of the LORD sent them from the wilderness of Paran: all those men [*the spies*] *were* heads of [*leaders among*] the children of Israel.

4 And these *were* their names: of the tribe of Reuben, Shammua the son of Zaccur.

5 Of the tribe of Simeon, Shaphat the son of Hori.

6 Of the tribe of Judah, **Caleb** the son of Jephunneh.

7 Of the tribe of Issachar, Igal the son of Joseph.

8 Of the tribe of Ephraim, **Oshea** [*Joshua*] the son of Nun.

9 Of the tribe of Benjamin, Palti the son of Raphu.

10 Of the tribe of Zebulun, Gaddiel the son of Sodi.

11 Of the tribe of Joseph, *namely,* of the tribe of Manasseh, Gaddi the son of Susi.

12 Of the tribe of Dan, Ammiel the son of Gemalli.

13 Of the tribe of Asher, Sethur the son of Michael.

14 Of the tribe of Naphtali, Nahbi the son of Vophsi.

15 Of the tribe of Gad, Geuel the son of Machi.

16 These *are* the names of the men which Moses sent to spy out the land. And **Moses called Oshea the son of Nun Jehoshua** [*Joshua*].

17 ¶ And **Moses sent them to spy out the land of Canaan, and said** unto them, Get you up this *way* southward, and go up into the mountain:

18 And **see the land, what it** *is;* **and** the people that dwelleth therein, whether they *be* strong or weak, few or many;

19 And **what the land** *is* **that they dwell in, whether it** *be* **good or bad**; and what cities *they be* that they dwell in, whether in tents, or in strong holds;

20 And **what the land** *is,* **whether it** *be* **fat or lean** [*whether it is productive or poor land*], whether there be wood therein, or not. And be ye of good courage, and bring of the fruit of the land [*bring some samples of what is grown there*]. Now the time *was* the time of the firstripe grapes [*it was the season of the year in which the first crop of grapes was ripening*].

21 ¶ So they went up, and searched the land from the wilderness of Zin unto Rehob, as men come to Hamath.

22 And they ascended by the south, and came unto Hebron; where Ahiman, Sheshai, and Talmai, the children of Anak, *were*. (Now Hebron was built seven years before Zoan in Egypt.)

23 And **they** came unto the brook of Eshcol, and **cut down** from thence a branch with **one cluster of grapes,** and they bare it between two upon a staff [*the cluster of grapes was so big that it took two men to carry it*]; **and**

they brought of the pomegranates, and of the figs.

24 The place was called the brook Eshcol, because of the cluster of grapes which the children of Israel cut down from thence.

25 And **they returned** from searching of the land after forty days.

The spies give their report to Moses, Aaron, and all the people.

26 ¶ And **they went and came to Moses, and to Aaron, and to all the congregation** of the children of Israel, unto the wilderness of Paran, to Kadesh; and brought back word unto them, and unto all the congregation, and shewed [*pronounced "showed"*] them the fruit of the land.

27 And they told him, and said, **We came unto the land whither thou sentest us, and surely it floweth with milk and honey** [*it is a very prosperous and productive land*]; **and this** *is* **the fruit of it.**

Next, the "eyes of fear and lack of faith" warp their report.

28 **Nevertheless** [*however*] **the people** *be* **strong** that dwell in the land, and **the cities** *are* **walled** [*well set up for defense*], *and* **very great** [*huge*]: and moreover **we saw the children of Anak** [*"giants," a race of large people—see verse 33*] **there.**

29 **The Amalekites** dwell in the land of the south: and the **Hittites,** and the **Jebusites,** and the **Amorites,** dwell in the mountains: and the **Canaanites** dwell by the sea, and by the coast of Jordan [*in other words, great and powerful people live there*].

Next, the "eyes of faith."

30 And **Caleb stilled the people** before Moses, **and said, Let us go up at once, and possess it; for we are well able to overcome it** [*Joshua says the same thing as Caleb—see Numbers 14:6–8*].

Again, the "eyes of fear and lack of faith."

31 **But the men that went up with him** [*the other ten spies*] **said, We be not able to go up against the people; for they** *are* **stronger than we.**

32 And **they brought** up an evil [*a negative*] **report of the land** which they had searched **unto the children of Israel, saying** [*they spread their lack of faith and negative report among the Israelites*], **The land,** through which we have gone to search it, *is* **a land that eateth up the inhabitants thereof;** and **all the people** that we saw in it *are* **men of a great stature** [*all the men whom we would have to fight to take over the promised land are huge*].

33 And there we **saw the giants,** the sons of Anak, *which* come of the giants: and **we were in our own sight as grasshoppers, and so we**

were in their sight [*we look like grasshoppers to them*].

NUMBERS 14

Selection: all verses

THE PEOPLE CHOOSE to believe the faithless reports of the ten spies who warned against going into the promised land. In effect, they warned against following the Lord and His prophet.

In what quickly becomes a national tragedy for these Israelites, word of the ten spies' report spreads like wildfire among the children of Israel, camped across the Jordan River east of the land of Palestine, the promised land. With fear and open hostility against Moses and Aaron, they adopt a mob mentality (a major tool of the devil) and cry out in complete abandonment of faith and trust in the Lord. They completely ignore the constant reminders of God's power, demonstrated time and again over the past months

Major Message

Beware of those today, in and out of the Church, who counsel against following the advice of the current living prophets. They are, in effect, counseling against having faith and following the Lord.

In verses 1-3, we again see the "eyes of fear and lack of faith."

1 And **all the congregation lifted up their voice, and cried; and the people wept that night.**

2 And **all the children of Israel murmured against Moses and against Aaron:** and the whole congregation said unto them, **Would God that we had died in the land of Egypt!** or would **God we had died in this wilderness!**

3 And **wherefore** [*why*] **hath the LORD brought us unto this land, to fall by the sword, that our wives and our children should be a prey** [*become victims to the powerful inhabitants of Palestine*]? **were it not better for us to return into Egypt?**

Open rebellion and mutiny against Moses is seen in verses 4-5.

4 And they said one to another, **Let us make a captain** [*choose a leader to replace Moses*], **and let us return into Egypt.**

5 Then Moses and Aaron fell on their faces [*a cultural way of showing great agony and concern*] before all the assembly of the congregation of the children of Israel.

Next, Joshua and Caleb attempt to pacify the crowds and convince them to enter the promised land, but do not succeed even though they, themselves have the "eyes of faith."

6 ¶ And **Joshua** the son of Nun, **and Caleb** the son of Jephunneh, *which were* of them that searched the land, **rent** [*tore*] **their clothes**

[a cultural sign of great distress and concern]:

7 And they spake unto all the company of the children of Israel, saying, The land, which we passed through to search it, is an exceeding good land.

8 If the LORD delight in us [if the Lord helps us], then he will bring us into this land, and give it us; a land which floweth with milk and honey [it is a land in which we would prosper].

9 Only rebel not ye against the LORD, neither fear ye the people of the land; for they are bread for us [we can consume them]: their defence is departed from them [they cannot defend themselves against us], and the LORD is with us: fear them not.

> Through the "eyes of fear and lack of faith," the people incite each other to stone Joshua and Caleb. The Lord intervenes.

10 But all the congregation bade stone them with stones. And the glory of the LORD appeared in the tabernacle of the congregation before all the children of Israel.

> Next, Moses prays for his people, giving an "intercessory prayer." In this sense, he is a type of Christ (a symbolic representation of Christ). He does not seek to excuse their behavior; rather, he pleads for mercy toward them.

11 ¶ And the LORD said unto Moses, How long will this people provoke me? and how long will it be ere they believe me, for [in light of] all the signs which I have shewed among them?

12 I will smite them with the pestilence, and disinherit them, and will make of thee a greater nation and mightier than they [we will start over with a new group].

> In cultures where each nation and community had its own gods, it was commonly believed that when one army overcame another, it was because their gods were more powerful than those of the enemy. This bit of background information helps us understand what Moses says to the Lord next. Obviously, the reputation of Israel's god as being more powerful than the gods of Egypt has preceded the children of Israel into the promised land. And if they fail to successfully enter, or if they are destroyed now, it will look like Israel's god could not overcome the gods of the nations occupying Palestine.

13 ¶ And Moses said unto the LORD, Then the Egyptians shall hear it, (for thou broughtest up this people in thy might from among them;)

14 And they will tell it to the inhabitants of this land [Palestine, the promised land]: for they have heard that thou LORD art among

this people [*that You are our God*], that thou LORD art seen face to face, and *that* thy cloud standeth over them, and *that* thou goest before them, by day time in a pillar of a cloud, and in a pillar of fire by night.

15 ¶ Now *if* thou shalt kill *all* this people as one man, **then the nations which have heard the fame of thee will speak, saying,**

16 Because the LORD [*the god of Israel*] was not able to bring this people into the land which he sware [*promised*] unto them, therefore he hath slain them in the wilderness.

Next, Moses, in a sweet and powerful prayer, reminds the Lord of His mercy and kindness. In a way, this prayer reminds us of the prayer uttered by the brother of Jared in Ether 3:2–5, especially verse 3.

Have you noticed that praying is especially helpful to the person saying the prayer, since God already knows what is going to be said? It is a learning experience for us and allows us to formulate our thoughts and express our feelings. It allows the Spirit of the Lord to inspire and direct our thoughts, in effect, teaching us what the will of the Lord is (compare with Doctrine and Covenants 46:30 and 50:30).

Moses was obviously inspired regarding what to say as he continued pleading for his people.

17 And **now, I beseech thee, let the power of my LORD be great,** according as thou hast spoken, saying [*according to what Thou hast taught us*],

18 The LORD *is* **longsuffering, and of great mercy, forgiving iniquity and transgression,** and by no means clearing *the guilty* [*not violating the law of justice—see Alma 42:25*], visiting the iniquity of the fathers upon the children unto the third and fourth *generation.*

19 **Pardon, I beseech thee, the iniquity of this people according unto the greatness of thy mercy,** and as thou hast forgiven this people, from Egypt even until now.

Next, the Savior approves His prophet's request.

20 And **the LORD said, I have pardoned according to thy word** [*the Israelites will not be destroyed now*]:

21 But *as* truly *as* I live, all the earth shall be filled with the glory of the LORD [*the day will come when all the earth will know that the God of Israel is the true God—during the Millennium and when the earth becomes the celestial kingdom—see Doctrine and Covenants 130:9–11*].

Because of rebellion and lack of faith, the children of Israel must turn around and return to the wilderness until all adults over twenty years of age, except Caleb and Joshua, have died.

Major Message

There are limits to how much mercy can be extended before the law of justice must take effect.

22 Because all those men which have seen my glory, and my miracles, which I did in Egypt and in the wilderness, and **have tempted** [*tested, tried*] **me now these ten times** [*"ten" can mean "well-organized" in biblical numeric symbolism; the beast representing Satan's kingdom—Revelation 13:1—has ten horns, representing Satan's power; thus, "ten times" can possibly mean, "You have worked under Satan's power, rebelling against Me time and time again"*], **and have not hearkened to my voice;**

23 Surely they shall not see the land which I sware [*promised*] **unto their fathers** [*ancestors, including Abraham—see Genesis 12:6–7*], **neither shall any of them that provoked me see it:**

24 But my servant Caleb [*Joshua gets the same blessing—see verse 30; see also Deuteronomy 34*], **because he had another spirit** [*the eye of faith*] **with him, and hath followed me fully, him will I bring into the land** whereinto he went; and his seed shall possess it.

Because of their rebellion, the people must turn around tomorrow and head back into the wilderness.

25 (Now the Amalekites and the Canaanites dwelt in the valley.) To morrow turn you, and get you into the wilderness by the way of the Red sea.

26 ¶ And the LORD spake unto Moses and unto Aaron, saying,

27 How long *shall I bear with* **this evil congregation, which murmur against me?** I have heard the murmurings of the children of Israel, which they murmur against me.

28 Say unto them, *As truly as* I live, saith the LORD, as ye have spoken in mine ears, so will I do to you:

29 Your carcases shall fall in this wilderness; and **all** that were numbered of you, according to your whole number, **from twenty years old and upward, which have murmured against me,**

30 Doubtless ye shall not come into the land, *concerning* which I sware to make you dwell therein, **save** [*except*] **Caleb** the son of Jephunneh, **and Joshua** the son of Nun.

31 But your little ones, which ye said should be a prey [*which you said would be overcome by the current inhabitants of the promised land—see verse 3*], them **will I bring in,** and they shall know the land which ye have despised [rejected].

32 But as for you, your carcases, they shall fall in this wilderness.

33 And your children shall wander in the wilderness forty years, and bear your whoredoms [suffer because of your wickedness], until your carcases be wasted in the wilderness.

34 After the number of the days in which ye searched the land, even forty days, each day for a year, shall ye bear your iniquities, even forty years, and ye shall know my breach of promise [you shall feel My displeasure—see footnote 34a in your Bible; in other words, you will know what it means to release Me from My promise (compare Doctrine and Covenants 82:10) by breaking your part of the bargain].

35 I the LORD have said, I will surely do it unto all this evil congregation, that are gathered together against me: in this wilderness they shall be consumed, and there they shall die.

36 And the men [the ten spies], which Moses sent to search the land, who returned, and made all the congregation to murmur against him, by bringing up a slander upon the land,

37 Even those men that did bring up the evil report upon the land, died by the plague before the LORD.

38 But Joshua the son of Nun, and Caleb the son of Jephunneh, which were of the men that went to search the land, lived still.

Will these people never learn? They refuse to obey God's command to return to the wilderness. Instead, they decide to enter the promised land and take it on their own.

39 And Moses told these sayings unto all the children of Israel: and the people mourned greatly.

40 ¶ And they rose up early in the morning, and gat them up into the top of the mountain, saying, Lo, we be here [we have arrived at the borders of the promised land], and will go up unto the place which the LORD hath promised: for we have sinned.

41 And Moses said, Wherefore [why] now do ye transgress the commandment of the LORD [why are you going against the commandment of the Lord to return to the wilderness]? but it shall not prosper [your plan will not work].

42 Go not up, for the LORD is not among you; that ye be not smitten before your enemies.

43 For the Amalekites and the Canaanites are there before you, and ye shall fall by the sword: because ye are turned away from the LORD,

137

therefore the LORD will not be with you.

44 But **they presumed to go up unto the hill top:** nevertheless the ark of the covenant of the LORD, and Moses, departed not out of the camp.

45 Then **the Amalekites** came down, **and the Canaanites** which dwelt in that hill, and **smote them, and discomfited them** [*slaughtered many of them*], *even* unto Hormah.

NUMBERS 16

Selection: verse 3

WHEN YOU READ this chapter in your Bible, you will see that there is yet another rebellion, led by three men—Korah, Dathan, and Abiram—along with 250 other leaders among the Israelites. These men and those closely associated with them will be swallowed up by the earth, and the 250 will be consumed by fire.

Other events similar to those in previous chapters will also occur.

Another thing: Don't miss what the rebellious leaders claim about the wicked people in Israel. In fact, we will take a moment and quote the verse here:

Numbers 16:3

3 And they gathered themselves together against Moses and against Aaron, and said unto them, *Ye take* too much upon you, seeing **all the congregation** *are* **holy, every one of them, and the LORD is among them:** wherefore then lift ye up yourselves above the congregation of the LORD?

Did you notice what they said to the prophet about the wicked people they were representing? They claimed that the wicked people were righteous! Does that sound familiar?

Major Message

Don't be deceived when the wicked persuade many to believe that wickedness is good and righteousness is evil.

Isaiah prophesied that there would be great deception in the form of calling wickedness good and righteousness evil. He taught:

Isaiah 5:20

20 ¶ Woe unto them that **call evil good, and good evil;** that **put darkness for light, and light for darkness;** that put bitter for sweet, and sweet for bitter!

We see much of this in our day. People who represent moral decay in all forms are honored and upheld by the multitudes. People flock to entertainment that is degrading and perverted, and they mock those who stand up for the right. We see many religious groups claiming to worship God while abandoning the standards set by the Lord in the Bible. They teach, in effect, that the Ten Commandments, and especially the commandments dealing with sexual immorality, are no longer valid. And thus, they endorse that which is evil as being permissible and even good.

As mentioned above, Moses faced this same evil deception in his day.

NUMBERS 20

Selection: verses 7–12

IN THIS CHAPTER, the people have run out of water. In a sense, there is even symbolism in this, since Christ is the "living water" (John 4:10) and the Israelites have rejected Him. Thus, they are "out of water," literally and symbolically.

First, though, we will note the passing of Miriam and Aaron, older siblings of Moses. In verse 1, Miriam dies, and in verse 28, Aaron dies. As you read verses 23–28, you will see that the special priestly clothing worn by Aaron, designating him as the high priest, will be transferred from Aaron to his son, Eleazar, who will take over Aaron's position.

As stated above, the people have run out of water. Pay close attention to what the Lord tells Moses to do in verse 8, and then see if he follows this instruction in verse 11. Watch in verse 10, also, for who is claiming credit for

bringing water out of the rock. Even Moses is still learning.

7 ¶ And the LORD spake unto Moses, saying,

8 Take the rod, and gather thou the assembly together, thou, and Aaron thy brother, and **speak ye unto the rock** before their eyes; and it shall give forth his water, and thou shalt bring forth to them water out of the rock: so thou shalt give the congregation and their beasts drink.

9 And Moses took the rod from before the LORD, as he commanded him.

10 And **Moses** and Aaron gathered the congregation together before the rock, and he **said** unto them, Hear now, ye rebels; **must we fetch you water out of this rock?**

11 And Moses lifted up his hand, and **with his rod he smote the rock twice:** and the water came out abundantly, and the congregation drank, and their beasts *also.*

> Did you notice that Moses was told to "speak" to the rock, but he hit it instead? You may wish to mark footnote 12a in your Bible, which points this out. Also, did you see that, in effect, Moses took credit to himself and Aaron, rather than giving credit to the Lord? Jehovah will confront Moses and Aaron for this, in verse 12, next.

12 ¶ And the LORD spake unto

Moses and Aaron, Because ye believed me not [*didn't obey*], to sanctify me [*build up the Lord*] in the eyes of the children of Israel, therefore ye shall not bring this congregation into the land which I have given them.

Be careful to keep things in perspective as far as Moses's punishment for disobedience is concerned.

While it may have been a punishment for Moses not to be allowed to bring Israel into the promised land, we can look at what did happen to him and perhaps keep things in perspective.

For one thing, Moses will be translated, taken up into heaven without tasting death. This will happen after the children of Israel have completed the forty additional years (actually about thirty-eight more years because the approximately two years they have been in the wilderness already count toward the forty years) of wandering.

If being translated and taken up to heaven after being the prophet-leader of this type of people is punishment, perhaps all of us would like to be so punished.

Another thing. Moses did not lose his position as one of the greatest prophets to ever live. And as previously mentioned, in his translated state he will minister to the Savior on the Mount of Transfiguration six months before the Atonement and Crucifixion (Matthew 17:1–3).

Yet another great blessing and confirmation of the high status of this humble prophet is the fact that Moses appeared to Joseph Smith and Oliver Cowdery in the Kirtland Temple on April 3, 1836, and restored the keys of the gathering of Israel and the bringing back of the lost ten tribes (Doctrine and Covenants 110:11).

In summary, be careful not to be overly critical of Moses as he learns yet another lesson during his mortal instruction as a choice and humble child of God. As long as we are here on earth as mortals, none of us will be through with our mortal lessons either.

In the Doctrine and Covenants, we gain additional insight into this situation:

Doctrine and Covenants 84:21–25

21 And without the ordinances thereof [*of the Melchizedek Priesthood*], and the authority of the priesthood, the power of godliness is not manifest unto men in the flesh;

22 For without this no man can see the face of God, even the Father, and live.

23 Now this Moses plainly taught to the children of Israel in the wilderness, and sought diligently to sanctify his people that they might behold the face of God;

24 But they hardened their hearts and could not endure his presence; therefore, the Lord in his wrath, for his

anger was kindled against them, swore that they should not enter into his rest while in the wilderness, which rest is the fulness of his glory.

25 Therefore, he **took Moses out of their midst, and the Holy Priesthood also;**

NUMBERS 21

Selection: verses 4–9

ONE OF THE well-known events that occurred in the Old Testament was the incident in which fiery serpents were sent to plague rebellious Israel. We understand fiery to mean "fiery, poisonous, stinging" bites.

The serpents came in response to yet another rebellion on the part of the children of Israel. We will pick the story up in verse 4.

Major Message

Continued rebellion brings the punishment of God. Punishment is a requirement of the law of justice.

4 ¶ And they journeyed from mount Hor by the way of the Red sea [*the "Reed Sea"—a marshy area north of the Red Sea; see footnote 4b in your Bible*], to compass [*go around*] the land of Edom: and **the soul of the people was much discouraged** because of the way.

5 And **the people spake against God, and against Moses,**

Wherefore have ye brought us up out of Egypt to die in the wilderness? for *there is* **no bread,** neither *is there any* **water;** and **our soul loatheth this light bread** [*and we can't stand any more manna*].

6 And **the LORD sent fiery serpents among the people, and they bit the people;** and **much people of Israel died.**

Next, the people repent yet again.

7 ¶ Therefore **the people came to Moses, and said, We have sinned,** for we have spoken against the LORD, and against thee; **pray unto the LORD, that he take away the serpents from us.** And Moses prayed for the people.

Next, Jehovah instructs Moses to make a brass serpent and place it on a pole.

Major Messages

• Look to Christ and live. Do not refuse because of the simplicity of the command.

• What the prophet tells us to do is right, regardless of possible other considerations.

• The gospel is actually very simple.

Have you ever thought that this was, in a way, an extra test of obedience for the people to follow instructions given here? Remember that one of the Ten Commandments was not to make any "graven" images. Yet, here the Lord tells Moses to make an image of a serpent, place it on a pole, and request that the people look at it in order to be healed.

8 And the LORD said unto Moses, **Make** thee **a fiery serpent**, and **set it upon a pole**: and it shall come to pass, that **every one that is bitten, when he looketh upon it, shall live.**

9 And **Moses made a serpent of brass, and put it upon a pole**, and it came to pass, that **if a serpent had bitten any man, when he beheld** [*looked at*] **the serpent of brass, he lived** [*he was healed*].

Alma taught about the symbolism involved in the brass serpent. He said:

Alma 33:19–21
19 Behold, **he** [*the Son of God*] **was spoken of by Moses**; yea, and behold **a type** [*something that symbolizes something else; in this case, the brass serpent was a "type" of Christ on the cross*] **was raised up in the wilderness, that whosoever would look upon it might live.** And many did look and live.
20 But **few understood the meaning of those things,** and this **because of the hardness of their hearts. But there were many who were so hardened that they would not look, therefore they perished.** Now the reason they would not look is because **they did not believe that it would heal them.**
21 O my brethren, **if ye could be healed by merely casting**

about your eyes that ye might be healed, would ye not behold quickly, or would ye rather harden your hearts in unbelief, and be slothful, that ye would not cast about your eyes, that ye might perish?

We see additional symbolism taught by Nephi, the son of Helaman, in the Book of Mormon:

Helaman 8:14–15
14 Yea, did he [*Moses*] not bear record that the Son of God should come? And **as he lifted up the brazen serpent in the wilderness, even so shall he** [*Christ*] **be lifted up** [*upon the cross*] who should come.
15 **And as many as should look upon that serpent should live, even so as many as should look upon the Son of God with faith, having a contrite spirit, might live, even unto that life which is eternal.**

Jesus made reference to the symbolism of the brass serpent as he taught Nicodemus about the necessity of baptism. He said:

John 3:14–15
14 ¶ **And as Moses lifted up the serpent in the wilderness, even so must the Son of man be lifted up:**
15 **That whosoever believeth in him should not perish, but have eternal life.**

And finally, we will turn to the teaching of Nephi, son of Lehi, as he instructs about the brass serpent:

1 Nephi 17:41

41 And **he did straiten** [*discipline*] **them** [*the children of Israel*] **in the wilderness** with his rod; for they hardened their hearts, even as ye have; and the Lord straitened them because of their iniquity. **He sent fiery flying serpents among them; and after they were bitten he prepared a way that they might be healed; and the labor which they had to perform was to look; and because of the simpleness of the way, or the easiness of it, there were many who perished.**

We will have to wait for further clarification from an authoritative source as to how and why a brass serpent could be used as a symbol of Christ.

NUMBERS 22

Selection: all verses

WE WILL NOW turn our attention to Balaam and the account of the talking donkey. It is found mainly in Numbers, chapters 22–24 with Balaam's death recorded in chapter 31.

By way of background, at the time of this account, Balaam is a man who lives in Mesopotamia (part of modern Iraq today, near the Euphrates River, according to *The New Compact Bible Dictionary*,

1981; see also *Smith's Bible Dictionary*, 1972, as well as the *Old Testament Student Manual*, page 209). He holds the priesthood of God and apparently has a reputation as one who can successfully curse and bless people. Balak, the king of Moab (the area southeast of the Dead Sea) and his people (who are confederate with the Midianites) are deathly afraid of the Israelites as they approach. It has become clear to them from what they have heard that the god of the children of Israel is more powerful than their god, Baal.

Therefore, King Balak, who has heard of Balaam, attempts to pay him to curse Israel so they can't defeat his armies. It sounds like he figures that since his own god, Baal, can't do the job, it would be smart to use the Israelites own god against them. This basic thinking would be in harmony with the general culture and mentality of the day, among idol worshiping peoples.

It is difficult to know quite what to do with these three chapters and bits of some that follow, which likewise deal with Balaam. While the account seems somewhat out of character for God's dealings with one who holds the Melchizedek Priesthood, the story seems to be treated rather matter-of-factly in the Bible.

We will go ahead and see what messages and lessons we can learn from it. There are many. Certainly, one of the first is that Balaam seems to enjoy living on the edge as far as obeying the Lord is concerned. It will finally catch up with him when he is slain with the Midianites as the Israelites fight them (Numbers 31:8).

1 And the children of Israel set forward [*continued their travels*], and pitched in the plains of Moab on this side Jordan *by* Jericho [*on the east side of the Jordan, across from Jericho*].

2 ¶ And **Balak** [*king of Moab*] the son of Zippor **saw all that Israel had done to the Amorites.**

3 And **Moab was sore afraid** [*terrified*] of the people [*the Israelites*], because they *were* many: and Moab was distressed **because of the children of Israel.**

4 And **Moab said unto the elders** [*leaders*] **of Midian** [*the allies of the Moabites*], **Now shall this company** [*the Israelites*] **lick up** [*gobble up*] **all** *that are* **round about us, as the ox licketh up the grass of the field. And Balak** the son of Zippor *was* king of the Moabites at that time.

5 He **sent messengers therefore unto Balaam** the son of Beor to Pethor [*in Mesopotamia*], which *is* by the river [*probably the Euphrates, according to* Smith's Bible Dictionary, *1972*] of the land of the children of his people, to call him, **saying, Behold, there is a people come out from Egypt: behold, they cover the face of the earth, and they abide over against me:**

6 Come now therefore, I pray thee, **curse me this people** [*curse the Israelites for me*]; for they *are* too mighty for me: peradventure [*perhaps*] I shall prevail, **that we may smite them**, and *that* I may drive them out of the land: for I wot [*know*] that he whom thou blessest *is* blessed, and he whom thou cursest is cursed [*I know you have a reputation for blessing and cursing successfully*].

> King Balak sends a delegation of important leaders from Moab and Midian, carrying money and gifts to help persuade Balaam to fulfill his request.

7 And the elders of Moab and the elders of Midian departed with the rewards of divination in their hand [*with money to pay Balaam for using his powers*]; and they came unto Balaam, and spake unto him the words of Balak.

> To give Balaam the benefit of the doubt, it may be that he did not know that the people Balak wanted cursed were the Israelites, the covenant people of the Lord. However, accepting money to use his priesthood was wrong. We know, from 2 Nephi 26:29 that such would be an example of priestcraft. We will quote this passage here:
>
> <u>2 Nephi 26:29</u>
> 29 He commandeth that there shall be no priestcrafts; for, behold, **priestcrafts are that men preach and set themselves up for a light unto**

the world, that they may get gain and praise of the world; but they seek not the welfare of Zion.

Balaam should have refused immediately, but it appears that he was tempted by the money and thus invited the messengers to stay overnight while he checked with the Lord.

8 And **he said unto them, Lodge here this night, and I will bring you word again, as the LORD shall speak unto me**: and the princes [*leaders*] of Moab abode with Balaam.

9 And **God came unto Balaam, and said, What men** *are* **these with thee?**

10 And **Balaam said unto God, Balak** the son of Zippor, **king of Moab, hath sent unto me,** *saying,*

11 Behold, *there is* **a people come out of Egypt, which covereth the face of the earth** [*Moab's perception of the Israelites*]: **come now, curse me them**; peradventure [*perhaps*] I shall be able to overcome them, and drive them out.

The Lord leaves no doubt as to how Balaam should respond to the offer and request.

12 And **God said** unto Balaam, **Thou shalt not go with them; thou shalt not curse the people: for they** *are* **blessed.**

13 And **Balaam rose up in the morning, and said unto the princes of Balak, Get you into your land: for the LORD refuseth to give me leave** [*permission*] **to go with you.**

14 And **the princes of Moab rose up, and they went unto Balak, and said, Balaam refuseth to come** with us.

15 ¶ And **Balak sent yet again princes**, more, and more honourable than they [*more prestigious leaders than those in the first delegation*].

16 And **they came to Balaam, and said to him, Thus saith Balak** the son of Zippor, **Let nothing, I pray thee, hinder thee from coming unto me:**

Next, Balaam is tempted with power and prestige—in other words, the "honors of men."

17 For **I will promote thee unto very great honour, and I will do whatsoever thou sayest unto me** [*sounds like the devil speaking to Cain—see Moses 5:30*]: **come therefore**, I pray thee, **curse me this people.**

Balaam has the right answer for them. It is the right answer for any of us when tempted to compromise our commitment to God for worldly wealth and honor.

Major Message

Don't compromise your

commitments to God for worldly wealth.

18 And **Balaam answered** and said unto the servants of Balak, **If Balak would give me his house full of silver and gold, I cannot go beyond the word of the LORD my God, to do less or more.**

Balaam would have been far better off if he had dropped the matter right there, but he did not. He opens the door for more temptation. Perhaps he was hoping the Lord would change His mind so he could get rich off the deal. He is living on the edge.

Major Message

It is dangerous to seek personal exceptions to God's counsel and commandments.

19 Now therefore, I pray you, **tarry ye also here this night, that I may know what the LORD will say unto me more.**

20 And God came unto Balaam at night, and **said** unto him, If the men come to call thee, rise up, *and* **go with them; but yet the word which I shall say unto thee, that shalt thou do** [*if you insist on going, then go, but obey strictly what I tell you to do*].

JST Numbers 22:20

20 And God came unto Balaam at night, and said unto him, If the men come to call thee, rise up, **if thou wilt** go with them; but yet the word

which I shall say unto thee, shalt thou speak.

The Joseph Smith Translation for verse 20, above, seems perhaps to imply that the Lord is saying to Balaam, that if he still insists on using his agency to foolishly place himself in temptation, go ahead and go with them.

21 And **Balaam** rose up in the morning, and saddled his ass, and **went with the princes of Moab.**

Judging from the first phrase in verse 22, Balaam must have had unrighteous motives in his heart. Peter indicates that this was the case. He warned:

2 Peter 2:15

15 Which have forsaken the right way, and are gone astray, following the way of **Balaam** *the son* of Bosor, who **loved the wages of unrighteousness;**

22 ¶ And **God's anger was kindled because he went: and the angel of the LORD stood in the way** for an adversary against him. Now he was riding upon his ass, and his two servants *were* with him.

Next, Balaam's donkey sees the angel with a drawn sword blocking the way and turns off the path. Balaam gets angry.

23 And **the ass saw the angel of the LORD standing in the way, and his sword drawn in his hand:** and **the ass turned aside out of the way, and went into the field:** and **Balaam smote the ass, to turn her**

into the way [*to get her back on the path to Moab*].

24 But the angel of the LORD stood in a path of the vineyards, a wall *being* **on this side, and a wall on that side.**

25 And when the ass saw the angel of the LORD, she thrust herself unto the wall, and crushed Balaam's foot against the wall: and he smote her again.

26 And the angel of the LORD went further, and stood in a narrow place, where *was* **no way to turn either to the right hand or to the left.**

27 And when the ass saw the angel of the LORD, she fell down under Balaam: and Balaam's anger was kindled, and **he smote the ass with a staff.**

Next, the donkey talks.

28 And the LORD opened the mouth of the ass, and she said unto Balaam, What have I done unto thee, that thou hast smitten me these three times?

It is surprising that Balaam doesn't act startled when his donkey starts talking to him. Perhaps he was so angry that the uniqueness of the situation didn't penetrate his mind. He answers her question and wishes he could kill her.

Major Message

We often blame others when they stand in the way of our own unrighteous desires. Blaming others is Satan's way.

29 And Balaam said unto the ass, Because thou hast mocked me: I would [*wish*] **there were a sword in mine hand, for now would I kill thee.**

30 And the ass said unto Balaam, *Am* **not I thine ass, upon which thou hast ridden ever since** *I was* **thine unto this day? was I ever wont to do so unto thee** [*did I ever act like this before*]? **And he said, Nay.**

Balaam's eyes are enabled by the Lord to see the angel.

31 Then the LORD opened the eyes of Balaam, and he saw the angel of the LORD standing in the way, and his sword drawn in his hand: and **he bowed down his head, and fell flat on his face** [*Balaam immediately bowed to the ground in humility and remorse*].

32 And the angel of the LORD **said** unto him, Wherefore [*why*] hast thou smitten thine ass these three times? behold, I went out to withstand [*stop*] thee, because *thy* way is perverse before me [*you are doing the wrong thing*]:

33 And the ass saw me, and turned from me these three times: unless she had turned from me, surely

now also I had slain thee, and saved her alive.

34 And **Balaam said** unto the angel of the LORD, **I have sinned**; for I knew not that thou stoodest in the way against me: now therefore, **if it displease thee, I will get me back again.**

> While we might wonder why the angel didn't take Balaam up on his offer to turn around and go home, it seems that continuing the journey to Moab will give him another opportunity to see if he will be obedient in the face of temptation.
>
> **Major Message**
>
> We are given many opportunities to repent and be obedient.

35 And **the angel** of the LORD **said** unto Balaam, **Go with the men: but only the word that I shall speak unto thee, that thou shalt speak.** So Balaam went with the princes of Balak.

36 ¶ And **when Balak heard that Balaam was come, he went out to meet him** unto a city of Moab, which *is* in the border of Arnon, which *is* in the utmost coast [*the outer borders of his country*].

> In verses 37–41, next, Balaam continue to keep himself in a dangerous setting of temptation, seeming to remain true to God, in verse 38, but continuing to live on the edge. We are reminded of the Savior's warning in Matthew 6:24, "Ye cannot serve God and mammon."

37 And Balak said unto Balaam, Did I not earnestly send unto thee to call thee? wherefore camest thou not unto me? am I not able indeed to promote thee to honour?

38 And Balaam said unto Balak, Lo, I am come unto thee: have I now any power at all to say any thing? **the word that God putteth in my mouth, that shall I speak.**

39 And Balaam went with Balak, and they came unto Kirjath-huzoth.

40 And Balak offered oxen and sheep, and sent to Balaam, and to the princes that were with him.

41 And it came to pass on the morrow, that Balak took Balaam, and brought him up into the high places of Baal, that thence he might see the utmost part of the people.

NUMBERS 23

Selection: all verses

NEXT, WE SEE more temptation and additional opportunities to pass the test of being faithful to the Lord. First, it seems that Balaam is stringing Balak along as he continues to flirt with disobedience and evil himself, still thinking that he can straddle the line between obedience and sin successfully.

1 And Balaam said unto Balak,

Build me here seven altars, and prepare me here seven oxen and seven rams.

"Seven," in verse 1, above, symbolically, can represent God's work and the perfection attained through righteous obedience to His commandments.

2 And Balak did as Balaam had spoken; and Balak and Balaam offered on every altar a bullock and a ram.

3 And Balaam said unto Balak, Stand by thy burnt offering, and I will go: peradventure the LORD will come to meet me: and whatsoever he sheweth me I will tell thee. And he went to an high place.

4 And God met Balaam: and he said unto him, I have prepared seven altars, and I have offered upon every altar a bullock and a ram.

5 And the LORD put a word in Balaam's mouth, and said, Return unto Balak, and thus thou shalt speak.

6 And he returned unto him, and, lo, he stood by his burnt sacrifice, he, and all the princes of Moab.

7 And he took up his parable, and said, Balak the king of Moab hath brought me from Aram, out of the mountains of the east, saying, Come, curse me Jacob, and come, defy Israel.

8 How shall I curse, whom God hath not cursed? or how shall I defy, whom the LORD hath not defied?

Next, much to Balak's dismay, Balaam praises and blesses the Israelites.

9 For from the top of the rocks I see him, and from the hills I behold him: lo, the people shall dwell alone, and shall not be reckoned among the nations [will be above all nations].

10 Who can count the dust of Jacob [Israel], and the number of the fourth part of Israel? Let me die the death of the righteous, and let my last end be like his!

11 And Balak said unto Balaam, What hast thou done unto me? I took thee to curse mine enemies, and, behold, thou hast blessed them altogether.

12 And he answered and said, Must I not take heed to speak that which the LORD hath put in my mouth?

Next, we see basically a repeat of the above scenario.

Major Message

God loves even those who live on the edge, and mercifully gives them many chances to change their ways.

13 And Balak said unto him, Come, I pray thee, with me unto another place, from whence thou mayest see them: thou shalt see but the utmost

part of them, and shalt not see them all: and curse me them from thence.

14 ¶ And he brought him into the field of Zophim, to the top of Pisgah, and built seven altars, and offered a bullock and a ram on every altar.

15 And he said unto Balak, Stand here by thy burnt offering, while I meet the LORD yonder.

16 And the LORD met Balaam, and put a word in his mouth, and said, Go again unto Balak, and say thus.

17 And when he came to him, behold, he stood by his burnt offering, and the princes of Moab with him. And Balak said unto him, What hath the LORD spoken?

18 And he took up his parable, and said, Rise up, Balak, and hear; hearken unto me, thou son of Zippor:

19 God is not a man, that he should lie; neither the son of man, that he should repent: hath he said, and shall he not do it? or hath he spoken, and shall he not make it good?

20 Behold, I have received commandment to bless: and he hath blessed; and I cannot reverse it.

Next, Balaam reaffirms that the blessings of the Lord will be with the Israelites.

21 He hath not beheld iniquity in Jacob, neither hath he seen perverseness in Israel: the LORD his God is with him, and the shout of a king is among them.

22 God brought them out of Egypt; he hath as it were the strength of an unicorn.

23 Surely there is no enchantment against Jacob, neither is there any divination against Israel: according to this time it shall be said of Jacob and of Israel, What hath God wrought!

24 Behold, the people shall rise up as a great lion, and lift up himself as a young lion: he shall not lie down until he eat of the prey, and drink the blood of the slain.

Next, in desperation, Balak says, in effect, if you can't curse the Israelites, at least don't bless them!

25 ¶ And Balak said unto Balaam, Neither curse them at all, nor bless them at all.

26 But Balaam answered and said unto Balak, Told not I thee, saying, All that the LORD speaketh, that I must do?

27 ¶ And Balak said unto Balaam, Come, I pray thee, I will bring thee unto another place; peradventure [perhaps] it will please God that thou mayest curse me them from thence.

28 And Balak brought Balaam

unto the top of Peor, that looketh toward Jeshimon.

29 And Balaam said unto Balak, Build me here seven altars, and prepare me here seven bullocks and seven rams.

30 And Balak did as Balaam had said, and offered a bullock and a ram on every altar.

NUMBERS 24

Selection: all verses

IN VERSES 1-9, Balaam seems to finally be coming to his senses. He has a vision about Israel and prophesies concerning them.

1 AND when Balaam saw that it pleased the LORD to bless Israel, he went not, as at other times, to seek for enchantments [*he quit living on the edge with Balak*], but he set his face toward the wilderness.

2 And Balaam lifted up his eyes, and he saw Israel abiding in his tents according to their tribes; and the spirit of God came upon him.

3 And he took up his parable [*prophesied*], and said, Balaam the son of Beor hath said, and the man whose eyes are open hath said:

4 He hath said, which heard the words of God, which saw the vision of the Almighty, falling into a trance [*a vision*], but having his eyes open:

5 How goodly are thy tents, O Jacob, and thy tabernacles, O Israel!

6 As the valleys are they spread forth, as gardens by the river's side, as the trees of lign aloes which the LORD hath planted, and as cedar trees beside the waters.

7 He shall pour the water out of his buckets, and his seed shall be in many waters, and his king shall be higher than Agag [*the Amalekites*], and his kingdom shall be exalted.

Watch the imagery of great strength against enemies depicted in verses 8 and 9, next.

8 God brought him forth out of Egypt; he hath as it were the strength of an unicorn [*a wild ox*]: he shall eat up the nations his enemies, and shall break their bones, and pierce them through with his arrows.

9 He couched, he lay down as a lion, and as a great lion: who shall stir him up? Blessed is he that blesseth thee, and cursed is he that curseth thee.

Next, Balak, king of the Moabites, finally quits trying to get Balaam to curse Israel and lets his anger flare up.

10 ¶ And Balak's anger was kindled against Balaam, and he smote his hands together: and Balak said unto Balaam, I called thee to curse mine enemies, and, behold, thou hast altogether blessed them these three times.

11 Therefore now flee thou to thy place [*go back home*]: I thought to promote thee unto great honour; but, lo, the LORD hath kept thee back from honour.

Balaam defends himself, acting quite innocent, even though he led Balak on and on.

12 And Balaam said unto Balak, Spake I not also to thy messengers which thou sentest unto me, saying,

13 If Balak would give me his house full of silver and gold, I cannot go beyond the commandment of the LORD, to do either good or bad of mine own mind; but what the LORD saith, that will I speak?

14 And now, behold, I go unto my people: come therefore, and I will advertise [*tell*] thee what this people shall do to thy people in the latter days.

15 ¶ And he took up his parable, and said, Balaam the son of Beor hath said, and the man whose eyes are open [*in other words, Balaam, whose eyes have been opened by the Lord to prophesy*] hath said:

16 He hath said, which heard the words of God, and knew the knowledge of the most High, which saw the vision of the Almighty, falling into a trance, but having his eyes open:

Next, Balaam prophesies of the coming of the Messiah.

17 I shall see him [*Christ*], but not now [*the Savior's coming is yet far in the future*]: I shall behold him, but not nigh: there shall come a Star [*Christ*] out of Jacob [*Israel*], and a Sceptre shall rise out of Israel, and shall smite the corners of Moab, and destroy all the children of Sheth [*symbolizing that Christ will ultimately triumph over all His enemies, the enemies of His people*].

Did you notice that the word "sceptre" is capitalized, in verse 17, above. Capitalizing it, in this context, makes it another name for Christ.

18 And Edom shall be a possession, Seir also shall be a possession for his enemies; and Israel shall do valiantly.

19 Out of Jacob [*Israel*] shall come he [*Christ*] that shall have dominion, and shall destroy him that remaineth of the city [*will destroy all who remain wicked, who think they are getting away*].

20 ¶ And when he looked on Amalek, he took up his parable, and said, Amalek was the first of the nations; but his latter end shall be that he perish for ever.

Balaam continues prophesying the destruction of enemies of

the Lord's people and His work.

21 And he looked on the Kenites, and took up his parable, and said, Strong is thy dwellingplace, and thou puttest thy nest in a rock.

22 Nevertheless the Kenite shall be wasted, until Asshur shall carry thee away captive.

23 And he took up his parable, and said, Alas, who shall live when God doeth this!

24 And ships shall come from the coast of Chittim, and shall afflict Asshur, and shall afflict Eber, and he also shall perish for ever.

25 And Balaam rose up, and went and returned to his place: and Balak also went his way.

NUMBERS 25

Selection: verses 1–3

EVEN THOUGH BALAAM successfully followed the Lord's instructions not to curse Israel as King Balak requested, he continued to live on the edge, as you saw in the previous chapters, allowing Balak to take him from place to place, tempting him. It gradually weakened him to the point that he deliberately told the Midianites (Moab's allies) how they could weaken the Israelites without the need to have Balaam curse them. In Numbers 31:16, we discover that he counseled the Midianite leaders to tempt the men of Israel to join in Baal worship, which included sexual immorality.

The Israelites succumbed to this temptation. Thus, they were effectively cursed without being formally cursed by Balaam himself. They lost the help of the Lord because of unworthiness. This fact is summarized in verses 1–3.

Major Message

It is dangerous to deliberately place ourselves in temptation. By living on the edge, we can gradually be weakened.

1 And Israel abode in Shittim, and **the people began to commit whoredom with the daughters of Moab.**

2 And **they** [*the Moabites and Midianites*] **called the people unto the sacrifices of their gods** [*invited the Israelites to worship Baal with them*]: **and the people** [*Israelites*] **did eat** [*participate in Baal worship*]**, and bowed down to their gods.**

The last two phrases of verse 2, above, are an example of deliberate repetition in Old Testament writing. Repetition was a way of providing emphasis and making a strong point. Thus, "and the people did eat" and "bowed down to their gods" both say the same thing, namely, that the Israelites joined the enemy in worshiping Baal.

The first phrase of verse 3, next, also says the same thing. Thus, we have a triple emphasis to the fact that Israel joined in the abominations of Baal worship.

3 And **Israel joined himself unto Baal-peor** [*worshipped Baal*]: and the anger of the LORD was kindled against Israel.

NUMBERS 27

Selection: verses 22–23

BEFORE WE CONCLUDE the account of Balaam, in chapter 31, we will pause for an important doctrinal point. As you know, the Lord's house is a "house of order." As our missionaries teach the gospel throughout the world, the orderly transfer of priesthood and authority is a point they emphasize. A good scripture to use in this teaching is found in this chapter, verses 22-23, where Joshua is called by the laying on of hands.

22 And **Moses** did as the LORD commanded him: and he **took Joshua**, and set him before Eleazar the priest, and before all the congregation:

23 **And he laid his hands upon him,** and gave him a charge, as the LORD commanded by the hand of Moses.

NUMBERS 31

Selection: verses 1–8 and 16

AS MENTIONED PREVIOUSLY, Balaam was the one who suggested that the Moabites and the Midianites could weaken the Israelites by inviting them to come worship Baal and join in the sexual immorality that was a prescribed part of the worship services. We are told this in verse 16. But first, we will read the record of Balaam's being slain. Verses 1-8 tell that the armies of Israel went to war against the Midianites. Balaam is slain in verse 8. Sadly, it appears that Balaam was still content to associate with Israel's enemies, in this case, the Midianites, who were allies of the Moabites.

1 AND the LORD spake unto Moses, saying,

2 **Avenge the children of Israel of the Midianites:** afterward shalt thou be gathered unto thy people.

3 And Moses spake unto the people, saying, **Arm some of yourselves unto the war,** and let them go **against the Midianites,** and avenge the LORD of Midian.

> Moses calls for 1,000 soldiers from each of the twelve tribes to take up arms against the Midianites.

4 Of every tribe a thousand, throughout all the tribes of Israel, shall ye send to the war.

5 So there were delivered out of the thousands of Israel, a thousand of every tribe, **twelve thousand armed for war.**

6 And Moses sent them to the war, a thousand of every tribe, them and Phinehas the son of Eleazar the priest, to the war, with the holy instruments, and the trumpets to blow in his hand.

7 And they warred against the Midianites, as the LORD commanded Moses; and they slew all the males.

8 And they slew the kings of Midian, beside the rest of them that were slain; namely, Evi, and Rekem, and Zur, and Hur, and Reba, five kings of Midian: **Balaam also the son of Beor they slew with the sword.**

As previously mentioned, verse 16 is where we discover Balaam's foolish and wicked counsel as to how the Israelites could be weakened to the point that they would not have the Lord's protection.

16 Behold, these [*Moabites and Midianites*] caused the children of Israel, **through the counsel of Balaam,** to commit trespass against the LORD in the matter of Peor [*by worshiping Baal, which involved sexual immorality*], and there was a plague among the congregation of the LORD [*the Israelites*].

In summary:

Elder Bruce R. McConkie, of the Quorum of the Twelve Apostles, wrote an article in the *New Era* in which he taught about Balaam. We will quote that article here:

"Let me tell you the story of a prophet, in some respects a very great prophet, but one 'who loved the wages of unrighteousness,' who 'was rebuked for his iniquity' in a most strange and unusual way, and whose actions (which included the uttering of great and true prophecies) were described by another prophet in another day as 'madness.'

"This is a true story, a dramatic story; one with a great lesson for all members of the Church; one that involves seeing God, receiving revelation, and facing a destroying angel in whose hand was the sword of vengeance. It includes the account of how the Lord delivered a message to the prophet in a way that, as far as we know, has never been duplicated in the entire history of the world.

"As we study the events involved, suppose we seek answers to these questions: Why did the Lord permit (or did he direct?) the strange series of events? What are "the wages of unrighteousness"? And how could a prophet who sought such remain in tune with "the spirit of God" and proclaim great truths, including one of our most marvelous Messianic prophecies?

"But even more important: What lesson are we expected to learn from the intermixture of both good and bad conduct shown forth by this ancient representative of the Lord?

'Now let us turn to the story, with an open mind, seeking the lesson it teaches us. And as we do so, please keep in mind that everything I have so far or shall hereafter put in quote marks is copied from the Bible, except in one instance where help is sought from a passage of latter-day revelation.

"Our story took place on the plains of Moab near Jericho; the time was 1451 BC; the chief participants were Balak, king of the Moabites, and Balaam, a prophet from the land of Midian. Israel's hosts, numbering in the millions, had just devastated the land of the Amorites and were camped on the borders of Moab. Fear and anxiety filled the hearts of the people of Moab and Balak their king. Would they also be overrun and slaughtered by these warriors of Jehovah?

"So Balak sent the elders and princes of his nation to Balaam, 'with the rewards of divination in their hand,' to hire him to come and curse Israel. In Balak's name they said: 'Behold, there is a people come out from Egypt: behold, they cover the face of the earth, and they abide over against me:

'Come now therefore, I pray thee, curse me this people; for they are too mighty for me: peradventure I shall prevail, that we may smite them, and that I may drive them out of the land: for I wot that he whom thou blessest is blessed, and he whom thou cursest is cursed.'

"Anxious to gain the riches they offered him, Balaam invited them to lodge with him that night while he inquired of the Lord and sought permission to curse Israel. That night 'God came unto Balaam' and said: 'Thou shalt not go with them; thou shalt not curse the people: for they are blessed.'

"Next morning Balaam said to the princes of Balak: 'Get you into your land: for the Lord refuseth to give me leave to go with you.'

"Thereupon Balak sent more honorable and noble princes than the first and they said to Balaam: 'Thus saith Balak the son of Zippor, Let nothing, I pray thee, hinder thee from coming unto me:

"'For I will promote thee unto very great honour, and I will do whatsoever thou sayest unto me: come therefore, I pray thee, curse me this people.

"'And Balaam answered and said unto the servants of Balak, If Balak would give me his house full of silver and gold, I cannot go beyond the word of the Lord my God, to do less or more.'

"And yet, still anxious to receive the riches and honors offered by the king, Balaam lodged his visitors and importuned the Lord for permission to go with them and curse Israel.

"'And God came unto Balaam at night, and said unto him, If the men come to call thee, rise up, and go with them; but yet the word which I shall say unto thee, that shalt thou do.'

"After gaining this permission Balaam 'saddled his ass, and went with the princes of Moab.'

"Now note: The Lord had given Balaam permission to go, and yet the scripture says: 'And God's anger was kindled because he went: and the angel of the Lord stood in the way for an adversary against him.'

"As Balaam rode along, 'the ass saw the angel of the Lord standing in the way, and his sword drawn in his hand.' Three times the dumb beast turned aside, crushing Balaam's foot against a wall and falling down under him. In anger the prophet "smote the ass with a staff.

"'And the Lord opened the mouth of the ass, and she said unto Balaam, What have I done unto thee, that thou hast smitten me these three times?

"'And Balaam said unto the ass, Because thou hast mocked me: I would there were a sword in mine hand, for now would I kill thee.

"'And the ass said unto Balaam, Am not I thine ass, upon which thou hast ridden ever since I was thine unto this day? was I ever wont to do so unto thee? And he said, Nay.

"'Then the Lord opened the eyes of Balaam, and he saw the angel of the Lord standing in the way, and his sword drawn in his hand: and he bowed down his head, and fell flat on his face.'

"After rebuking and counseling Balaam, the angel yet said: 'Go with the men: but only the word that I shall speak unto thee, that thou shalt speak.'

"When they met, Balak renewed his promise 'to promote' Balaam 'to honour,' and the prophet responded: 'Have I now any power at all to say any thing? the word that God putteth in my mouth, that shall I speak.'

"Balak then offered sacrifices, and at the visiting prophet's request built seven altars upon which Balaam also sacrificed, obviously pleading with the Lord for permission to curse Israel and receive the honors offered by the king of the Moabites. But with it all Balaam promised that if 'the Lord will come to meet me,' then 'whatsoever he sheweth me I will tell thee.'

"'And God met Balaam,' and told him what to say, which he then proclaimed in the presence of all the princes of Moab: 'How shall I curse, whom God hath not cursed? or how shall I defy, whom the Lord hath not defied?

"'For from the top of the rocks I see him, and from the hills I behold him: Lo, the people shall dwell alone, and shall not be reckoned among the nations.

"'Who can count the dust of Jacob, and the number of the fourth part of Israel? Let me die the death of the righteous, and let my last end be like his!'

"Balak was angry, but Balaam remained true to his trust, saying, 'Must I not take heed to speak that which the Lord hath put in my mouth?'

"Then they went through the whole process again. Sacrifices were offered; the Lord was importuned; but the result was the same.

"'God is not a man,' Balaam said, 'that he should lie; neither the son of man, that he should repent: hath he said, and shall he not do it? or hath he spoken, and shall he not make it good?

"'Behold, I have received commandment to bless: and he hath blessed; and I cannot reverse it.'

"Then he continued, 'Surely there is no enchantment against Jacob, neither is there any divination against Israel: according to this time it shall be said of Jacob and of Israel, What hath God wrought!'

"When Balak yet complained, Balaam replied: 'Told not I thee, saying, All that the Lord speaketh, that I must do?'

"And yet at the King's request the prophet still sought to curse Israel. Further sacrifices were offered; again pleading entreaties ascended to the Lord; and again the answer was the same. 'The spirit of God came upon him,' and he prophesied with power and force of the greatness of Israel, concluding with the statement, 'Blessed is he that blesseth thee, and cursed is he that curseth thee.

"'And Balak's anger was kindled against Balaam, and he smote his hands together: and Balak said unto Balaam, I called thee to curse mine enemies, and, behold, thou hast altogether blessed them these three times.

"'Therefore now flee thou to thy place: I thought to promote thee unto great honour; but, lo, the Lord hath kept thee back from honour.'

But Balaam, fixed in his purpose to deliver only that message that the Lord revealed to him, said:

'Spake I not also to thy messengers which thou sentest unto me, saying,

"'If Balak would give me his house full of silver and gold, I cannot go beyond the commandment of the Lord, to do either good or bad of mine own mind; but what the Lord saith, that will I speak?'

"Then, while the Spirit still rested upon him, Balaam gave this great Messianic prophecy: 'I shall see him, but not now: I shall behold him, but not nigh: there shall come a Star out of Jacob, and a Sceptre shall rise out of Israel.'

"In spite of all this, the record recites that Balaam 'taught' Balak "to cast a stumblingblock before the children of Israel, to eat things sacrificed unto idols, and to commit fornication,' and shortly thereafter, while aligned against Israel in the camps of the Midianites, he was 'slain with the sword.'

"The full account of these events is found in Numbers 22:23; 24; 25; 31:8; 2 Peter 2:15–16; Jude 1:11; and Revelations 2:14.

"What a story this is! Here is a prophet of God who is firmly committed to declare only what the Lord of heaven directs. There does not seem to be the slightest doubt in his mind about the course he should pursue. He represents the Lord, and neither a house full of gold and silver nor high honors offered by the king can sway him from his determined course, which has been charted for him by that God whom he serves.

"But greed for wealth and lust for honor beckon him. How marvelous it would be to be rich and powerful—as well as having the prophetic powers that already are his.

"Perhaps the Lord would let him compromise his standards and have some worldly prosperity and power as well as a testimony of the gospel. Of course he knew the gospel was true, as it were, but why should he be denied the things his political file leader could confer?

"I wonder how often some of us get our direction from the Church and then, Balaam-like, plead for some worldly rewards and finally receive an answer which says, in effect, If you are determined to be a millionaire or to gain this or that worldly honor, go ahead, with the understanding that you will continue to serve the Lord. Then we wonder why things don't work out for us as well as they would have done if we had put first in our lives the things of God's kingdom?

"What are the rewards of unrighteousness? Do they not include seeking for worldly things when these run counter to the interests of the Church?

"And don't we all know people who, though they were once firm and steadfast in testimony, are now opposing the Lord's purposes and interests on earth because money and power have twisted their judgment of what should or should not be?

"Balaam, the prophet, inspired and mighty as he once was, lost his soul in the end because he set his heart on the things of this world rather than the riches of eternity.

"What a wealth of meaning there is in these inspired words of Joseph Smith, words addressed to people who have testimonies but want to mingle the things of this world with them: 'Behold, there are many called, but few are chosen. And why are they not chosen?

"'Because their hearts are set so much upon the things of this world, and aspire to the honors of men, that they do not learn this one lesson—

"'That the rights of the priesthood are inseparably connected with the powers of heaven, and that the powers of heaven cannot be controlled nor handled only upon the principles of righteousness.

"'That they may be conferred upon us, it is true; but when we undertake to cover our sins, or to gratify our pride, our vain ambition, or to exercise control or dominion or compulsion upon the souls of the children of men, in any degree of unrighteousness, behold, the heavens withdraw themselves; the Spirit of the Lord is grieved; and when it is withdrawn, Amen to the priesthood or the authority of that man.

"'Behold, ere he is aware, he is left unto himself, to kick against the pricks, to persecute the saints, and to fight against God. . . .

"'Hence many are called, but few are chosen.'" (Doctrine and Covenants 121:34-38, 40.) ("The Story of a Prophet's Madness," *New Era*, April 1972, 4-7.)

DEUTERONOMY

THE WORD "DEUT-
ERONOMY" means "rep-
etition of the law" (see Bible
Dictionary, under "Deuteronomy").
Moses is nearing 120 years of age and,
before he departs, he will provide his
people a major review or "repetition" of
the laws the Lord has given them.

The children of Israel have gathered
on the plains of Moab, east, across the
Jordan River from the land of Canaan,
the "promised land," in preparation for
finally entering and occupying it. The
rebellious adults have all died off, and
those of the current generation are
the ones through whom the Lord will
fulfill His promise to Abraham that his
descendants would someday inherit the
land of Canaan (Genesis 12:6-7).

It has now been forty years since the
Israelites left Egypt, and the time has
come for Moses to leave his people.
At the end of Deuteronomy, chapter
34, verse 5-6, the Bible will record his
death and burial. However, we know
from modern revelation that he did
not die; rather, he was translated and
taken up. In the Bible Dictionary, under
"Moses," we read concerning him:

Bible Dictionary
"In company with Elijah,
he came to the Mount of
Transfiguration and bestowed
keys of the priesthood upon
Peter, James, and John. From
this event, which occurred
before the resurrection of

Jesus, we understand that
Moses was a translated being,
and had not died as reported
in Deut. 34 (Alma 45:19)."

At the end of Deuteronomy, we will
see that Joshua will take over as the
prophet and lead the Israelites across
the Jordan River into the promised
land.

Before he is taken up into heaven,
Moses will deliver three last discourses
or sermons to his people. These last
three great discourses are:

1. CHAPTERS 1-4, a summary
of the most important events during
the forty years in the wilderness.

2. CHAPTERS 5-26, a review
of the Law of Moses with expanded
explanations and emphasis on the spiritual aspects of the law, consisting of
two main parts:

A. CHAPTERS 5-11, in
which Moses explains and teaches
about the Ten Commandments and
other laws of spiritual progress.

B. CHAPTERS 12-26, deal-
ing with details and further devel-
opment of a code of law for the
Israelites, including religious, judi-
cial, and political law.

3. CHAPTERS 27-30, con-
taining a renewal of the covenant and
an explanation of the blessings that
attend obedience and the cursings that
accompany disobedience to God's laws
and commandments.

You can read more about these three

discourses in the Bible Dictionary, under "Deuteronomy."

The last four chapters of Deuteronomy, chapters 31–34, serve as a supplement and speak of Joshua's ordination as Moses' successor. Some speculation exists among Bible scholars that these last four chapters may have been written by someone other than Moses.

A hint as to the importance of Deuteronomy is the fact that it is quoted by Old Testament prophets more than any other of the five books that Moses wrote (Genesis, Exodus, Leviticus, Numbers, and Deuteronomy).

DEUTERONOMY 1

Selection: all verses

IN THIS CHAPTER, Moses begins a review of the most important events among the Israelites during their forty years in the wilderness. The review will continue through chapter 4.

Our approach to this review will be to make extensive use of bold to point out the major elements of this first discourse by the 120-year-old prophet, Moses. You may wish to mark several of the bolded words and phrases in your own scriptures. If you go through these chapters just reading the bold print, you will get a quick overview of the inspired words of this great prophet. You might be pleasantly surprised at how easily you understand them. Then you will have the big picture when you go back and read everything.

First Discourse

Deuteronomy 1–4

1 THESE be the words which Moses spake unto all Israel on this side Jordan [*the east side of the Jordan River*] in the wilderness, in the plain over against the Red sea, between Paran, and Tophel, and Laban, and Hazeroth, and Dizahab.

> Be aware that the parentheses in verse 2, next, as well as several other verses in these chapters, are part of the Old Testament text and not a note in this study guide.

2 (There are eleven days' journey from Horeb by the way of mount Seir unto Kadesh-barnea.)

3 And it came to pass in the fortieth year [*since they left Egypt*], in the eleventh month, on the first day of the month, that Moses spake unto the children of Israel, according unto all that the LORD had given him in commandment unto them;

4 After he had slain Sihon the king of the Amorites, which dwelt in Heshbon, and Og the king of Bashan, which dwelt at Astaroth in Edrei:

5 On this side Jordan, in the land of Moab, **began Moses to declare this law, saying,**

6 **The LORD our God spake unto us in Horeb** [*Mount Sinai*]**, saying,**

Ye have dwelt long enough in this mount:

7 Turn you, and **take your journey**, and go to the mount of the Amorites, and unto all *the places* nigh thereunto, in the plain, in the hills, and in the vale, and in the south, and by the sea side, **to the land of the Canaanites, and unto Lebanon, unto the great river, the river Euphrates.**

8 Behold, I have set the land before you: **go in and possess the land** which the LORD sware [*promised, covenanted*] unto your fathers, Abraham, Isaac, and Jacob, to give unto them and to their seed after them.

9 ¶ And I [*Moses*] **spake unto you at that time, saying, I am not able to bear you myself alone:**

10 The LORD your God hath multiplied you, and, behold, ye *are* this day as the stars of heaven for multitude.

11 (The LORD God of your fathers make you a thousand times so many more as ye *are*, and bless you, as he hath promised you!)

12 **How can I myself alone bear your cumbrance, and your burden, and your strife?**

13 **Take you wise men**, and understanding, and known among your

tribes, **and I will make them rulers over you.**

14 And **ye answered me, and said, The thing which thou hast spoken** *is* **good** *for us* **to do.**

15 **So I took the chief of your tribes, wise men**, and known, and made them **heads over you,** captains over thousands, and captains over hundreds, and captains over fifties, and captains over tens, and officers among your tribes.

16 **And I charged** [*explained the duties and responsibilities to*] **your judges at that time, saying,** Hear *the causes* between your brethren, and **judge righteously** between *every* man and his brother, and the stranger [*non-Israelite*] *that is* with him.

17 **Ye shall not respect** [*be prejudiced against*] **persons in judgment;** *but* ye shall hear the small [*hardly known*] as well as the great [*well-known*]; ye shall not be afraid of the face of man; for the judgment *is* God's: **and the cause that is too hard for you, bring** *it* **unto me, and I will hear it.**

18 And I commanded you at that time all the things which ye should do.

19 ¶ **And when we departed from Horeb** [*Sinai*], **we went through all that great and terrible wilderness,**

which ye saw by the way of the mountain of the Amorites, as the LORD our God commanded us; **and we came to Kadesh-barnea** [*on the northeast side of the Sinai Peninsula*].

20 And I said unto you, Ye are come unto the mountain of the Amorites [*inhabitants of southern Palestine—see Bible Dictionary, under "Amorites"*]**, which the LORD our God doth give unto us.**

21 Behold, the LORD thy God hath set the land before thee: **go up** *and* **possess** *it*, as the LORD God of thy fathers hath said unto thee; fear not, neither be discouraged.

22 ¶ And ye came near unto me every one of you, **and said, We will send men** [*spies*] **before us, and they shall search us out the land, and bring us word again** by what way we must go up, and into what cities we shall come.

23 And **the saying pleased me well: and I took twelve men** of you, one of a tribe:

24 And they turned and went up into the mountain, and came unto the valley of Eshcol, and **searched it out.**

25 And they took of the fruit of the land in their hands, and brought *it* down unto us, **and brought us word again, and said, It** *is* **a good land which the LORD our God doth give us.**

26 Notwithstanding [*however*] **ye would not go up, but rebelled** against the commandment of the LORD your God:

27 And ye murmured in your tents, and said, Because the LORD hated us, he hath brought us forth out of the land of Egypt, to deliver us into the hand of the Amorites, to destroy us.

28 Whither shall we go up? our brethren have discouraged our heart, saying, The people *is* greater and taller than we; the cities *are* great and walled up to heaven; and moreover we have seen the sons of the Anakims [*the giants, such as the ancestors of Goliath*] there.

29 Then I said unto you, Dread not, neither be afraid of them.

30 The LORD your God which goeth before you, he **shall fight for you,** according to all that he did for you in Egypt before your eyes;

31 And in the wilderness, where thou hast seen how that the LORD thy God bare thee, as a man doth bear his son, in all the way that ye went, until ye came into this place.

32 Yet in this thing **ye did not believe the LORD** your God,

33 Who went in the way before

you, to search you out a place to pitch your tents *in*, **in fire by night**, to shew you by what way ye should go, **and in a cloud by day.**

34 And the LORD heard the voice of **your words, and was wroth**, and sware [*gave His word*], saying,

35 Surely **there shall not one of these men of this evil generation see that good land**, which I sware to give unto your fathers,

36 Save Caleb the son of Jephunneh; he shall see it, and to him will I give the land that he hath trodden upon, and to his children, because he hath wholly followed the LORD.

37 Also the LORD was angry with me for your sakes, saying, Thou also shalt not go in thither.

38 *But* **Joshua** the son of Nun, which standeth before thee, he **shall go in** thither: encourage him: for he shall cause Israel to inherit it.

39 Moreover your little ones, which ye said should be a prey, and your children, which in that day had no knowledge between good and evil, they **shall go in** thither, and unto them will I give it, **and they shall possess it.**

40 But *as for* **you, turn you, and take your journey into the wilderness** by the way of the Red sea.

41 Then ye answered [*responded*]

and said unto me, **We have sinned against the LORD, we will** [*we have changed our minds and now desire to*] **go up and fight, according to all that the LORD our God commanded us.** And when ye had girded on every man his weapons of war, **ye were ready to go up into the hill.**

42 And **the LORD said** unto me, Say unto them, **Go not up**, neither fight; for I *am* not among you; **lest ye be smitten** before your enemies.

43 So I spake unto you; and ye would not hear, but rebelled against the commandment of the LORD, **and went** presumptuously [*without permission*] **up into the hill.**

44 And **the Amorites**, which dwelt in that mountain, **came out against you, and chased you, as bees do, and destroyed you** in Seir, *even* unto Hormah.

45 And **ye returned and wept** before the LORD; **but the LORD would not hearken to your voice, nor give ear unto you.**

46 So ye abode in Kadesh many days, according unto the days that ye abode *there*.

DEUTERONOMY 2

Selection: all verses

MOSES CONTIN-UES HIS first discourse or sermon, reviewing the history of these Israelites during their 40 years in the wilderness. The review will continue through chapter four. Remember that the children of Israel have now gathered east of the Jordan River and can look across west into the promised land. Verse 1 is a continuation from chapter 1.

1 Then we turned, and took our journey into the wilderness by the way of the Red sea, as the LORD spake unto me [*Moses*]: and we compassed [*went around*] mount Seir many days.

2 And the LORD spake unto me, saying,

3 Ye have compassed this mountain long enough: **turn you northward.**

4 And command thou the people, saying, Ye *are* to **pass through the coast** [*the borders*] **of your brethren** [*distant relatives*] **the children of Esau** [*the descendants of Esau*], which dwell in Seir; and **they shall be afraid of you**: take ye good heed unto yourselves [*behave yourselves*] therefore:

5 Meddle not with them; for I will not give you of their land, no, not so much as a foot breadth; because I

have given mount Seir unto Esau *for* a possession.

6 Ye shall **buy meat** [*food*] of them for money, that ye may eat; and ye shall **also** buy **water** of them for money, that ye may drink.

7 For the LORD thy God hath blessed thee in all the works of thy hand: he knoweth thy walking through this great wilderness: **these forty years the LORD thy God** *hath been* **with thee; thou hast lacked nothing.**

8 And **when we passed** by from our brethren **the children of Esau**, which dwelt in Seir, through the way of the plain from Elath, and from Ezion-gaber, **we turned and passed by the way of the wilderness of Moab.**

9 And the LORD said unto me, **Distress not the Moabites**, neither contend with them in battle: for I will not give thee of their land *for* a possession; because I have given Ar unto the children of Lot *for* a possession.

10 The Emims dwelt therein in times past, a people great, and many, and tall, as the Anakims;

11 Which also were accounted giants, as the Anakims; but the Moabites call them Emims.

12 The Horims also dwelt in Seir

beforetime; but the children of Esau succeeded them, when they had destroyed them from before them, and dwelt in their stead; as Israel did unto the land of his possession, which the LORD gave unto them.

13 Now rise up, *said I,* **and get you over the brook Zered. And we went over the brook Zered.**

14 And the space in which we came **from Kadesh-barnea, until** we were come over **the brook Zered,** *was* **thirty and eight years** [*from the time we were turned back into the wilderness up to now has been thirty-eight years*]; **until all the generation of the men of war were wasted** [*died*] **out** from among the host, as the LORD sware unto them.

15 For indeed the hand of the LORD was against them, to destroy them from among the host, until they were consumed.

16 ¶ So it came to pass, **when all the** [*rebellious*] **men of war were** consumed and **dead** from among the people,

17 That **the LORD spake** unto me, saying,

18 Thou art to **pass over through Ar,** the coast [*border*] of Moab, **this day:**

19 And *when* **thou comest nigh** over against **the children of Ammon, distress them not, nor meddle with them:** for I will not give thee of the land of the children of Ammon *any* possession; because I have given it unto the children of Lot *for* a possession.

20 (That also was accounted [*considered to be*] a land of giants: giants dwelt therein in old time; and the Ammonites call them Zamzummims;

21 A people great, and many, and tall, as the Anakims; but the LORD destroyed them before them; and they succeeded them, and dwelt in their stead:

22 As he did to the children of Esau, which dwelt in Seir, when he destroyed the Horims from before them; and they succeeded them, and dwelt in their stead even unto this day:

23 And the Avims which dwelt in Hazerim, *even* unto Azzah, the Caphtorims, which came forth out of Caphtor, destroyed them, and dwelt in their stead.)

24 ¶ Rise ye up, **take your journey,** and pass **over the river Arnon:** behold, I have given **into** thine hand Sihon the Amorite, king of **Heshbon,** and his land: **begin to possess** *it,* **and contend with him in battle.**

25 This day will I begin to put the

dread of thee and the fear of thee upon the nations *that are* under the whole heaven, who shall hear report of thee, and shall tremble, and be in anguish because of thee.

26 ¶ And **I sent messengers** out of the wilderness of Kedemoth **unto Sihon king of Heshbon with words of peace**, saying,

27 Let me pass through thy land: I will go along by the high way, I will neither turn unto the right hand nor to the left.

28 Thou shalt sell me meat for money, that I may eat; and give me water for money, that I may drink: only I will pass through on my feet;

29 (As the children of Esau which dwell in Seir, and the Moabites which dwell in Ar, did unto me;) until I shall pass over Jordan into the land which the LORD our God giveth us.

30 **But Sihon king of Heshbon would not let us pass by him**: for the LORD thy God hardened his spirit [*we know from many previous JST corrections (example: Exodus 11:10) that the Lord does not harden hearts; rather, individuals use their own agency to become hard-hearted*], and made his heart obstinate, that he might deliver him into thy hand, as *appeareth* this day.

31 And **the LORD said** unto me,

Behold, I have begun to give Sihon and his land before thee: **begin to possess**, that thou mayest inherit **his land**.

32 **Then Sihon came out against us**, he and all his people, **to fight** at Jahaz.

33 **And the LORD** our God **delivered him before us; and we smote him**, and his sons, and all his people.

34 And we took all his cities at that time, and utterly destroyed the men, and the women, and the little ones, of every city, we left none to remain [*while this may seem terribly harsh, remember that these people were "ripe in iniquity," as described in Leviticus 18*]:

35 Only the cattle we took for a prey unto ourselves, and the spoil of the cities which we took.

36 From Aroer, which *is* by the brink of the river of Arnon, and *from* the city that *is* by the river, even unto Gilead, **there was not one city too strong for us: the LORD our God delivered all unto us:**

37 Only unto the land of the children of Ammon thou camest not, *nor* unto any place of the river Jabbok, nor unto the cities in the mountains, nor unto whatsoever the LORD our God forbad us.

DEUTERONOMY 3

Selection: all verses

MOSES CONTINUES HIS first discourse or sermon, reviewing the history of these Israelites during their 40 years in the wilderness. The review will continue through chapter four. Remember that the children of Israel have now gathered east of the Jordan River and can look across west into the promised land. Verse 1 is a continuation from chapter 2.

1 Then we turned, and went up the way **to Bashan: and Og** the king of Bashan [*a "giant" who slept in a 13½-foot bed—see verse 11*] **came out against us, he and all his people,** to battle at Edrei.

> Remember that the ten spies who brought back a negative report said that it was impossible for the Israelites to triumph against the "giants" in the land (Numbers 13:32–33).

2 And the LORD said unto me, **Fear him not:** for I will deliver him, and all his people, and his land, into thy hand; and thou shalt do unto him as thou didst unto Sihon king of the Amorites, which dwelt at Heshbon.

3 So the LORD our God delivered into our hands Og also, the king of Bashan, **and all his people:** and **we smote him until none was left to him remaining.**

4 And **we took all his cities** at that time, there was not a city which we took not from them, threescore cities, all the region of Argob, the kingdom of Og in Bashan.

5 All these cities *were* **fenced with high walls, gates, and bars; beside unwalled towns a great many** [*the negative report of the ten spies said that these cities could not be taken— see Numbers 13:28*].

6 And we utterly destroyed them, as we did unto Sihon king of Heshbon, utterly destroying the men, women, and children, of every city.

7 But all the cattle, and the spoil of the cities, we took for a prey to ourselves.

8 And we took at that time out of the hand of the two kings of the Amorites **the land that** *was* **on this side Jordan,** from the river of Arnon unto mount Hermon;

9 (*Which* Hermon the Sidonians call Sirion; and the Amorites call it Shenir;)

10 All the cities of the plain, and all Gilead, and all Bashan, unto Salchah and Edrei, cities of the kingdom of Og in Bashan.

11 For only Og king of Bashan remained of the remnant of giants; behold, his bedstead *was* a bedstead

of iron; *is* it not in Rabbath of the children of Ammon? nine cubits *was* the length thereof, and four cubits the breadth of it, after the cubit of a man.

12 And this land, *which* we possessed at that time, from Aroer, which *is* by the river Arnon, and half mount Gilead, and the cities thereof, **gave I unto the Reubenites and to the Gadites** [*the tribes of Reuben and Gad*].

13 And the rest of Gilead, and all Bashan, *being* the kingdom of Og, **gave I unto the half tribe of Manasseh;** all the region of Argob, with all Bashan, which was called the land of giants.

14 Jair the son of Manasseh took all the country of Argob unto the coasts of Geshuri and Maachathi; and called them after his own name, Bashan-havoth-jair, unto this day.

15 And I gave Gilead unto Machir.

16 And unto the Reubenites and unto the Gadites I gave from Gilead even unto the river Arnon half the valley, and the border even unto the river Jabbok, *which is* the border of the children of Ammon;

17 The plain also, and Jordan, and the coast *thereof,* from Chinnereth even unto the sea of the plain, *even* the salt sea, under Ashdoth-pisgah eastward.

18 ¶ And I commanded you [*the people of the tribes that had already been given land to settle in*] **at that time,** saying, The LORD your God hath given you this land to possess it: **ye shall pass over armed before** [*ahead of*] **your brethren** [*of the other tribes of*] **the children of Israel,** all *that are* meet for the war [*all able-bodied men from your tribes*].

19 But your wives, and your little ones, and your cattle, (*for* I know that ye have much cattle,) **shall abide in your cities** which I have given you;

20 Until the LORD have given rest unto your brethren, as well as unto you [*until the rest of the twelve tribes are settled in their respective territories*], **and** *until* **they also possess the land which the LORD** your God **hath given them beyond Jordan** [*west of the Jordan River*]: **and** *then* **shall ye return** every man unto his possession, which I have given you.

21 ¶ And I commanded Joshua at that time, saying, Thine eyes have seen all that the LORD your God hath done unto these two kings: so shall the LORD do unto all the kingdoms whither thou passest.

22 Ye shall not fear them: for the LORD your **God** he **shall fight for you.**

Next, Moses explains that he

requested that he be allowed to enter the promised land also. But his request was denied as part of his chastisement for taking credit for bringing water from the rock rather than giving the Lord credit (Numbers 20:7–8, 11–12).

23 And I besought the LORD at that time, saying,

24 O Lord GOD, thou hast begun to shew thy servant thy greatness, and thy mighty hand: for what God *is there* **in heaven or in earth, that can do according to thy works, and according to thy might?**

25 I pray thee, let me go over, and see the good land that *is* **beyond Jordan,** that goodly mountain, and Lebanon.

26 But the LORD was wroth with me for your sakes, **and would not hear me: and** the LORD **said** unto me, Let it suffice thee; **speak no more unto me of this matter.**

27 Get thee up into the top of Pisgah, and lift up thine eyes westward, and northward, and southward, and eastward, and **behold** *it* **with thine eyes: for thou shalt not go over this Jordan.**

28 But charge Joshua, and encourage him, and strengthen him: **for he shall go over** before this people, and he shall cause them to inherit the land which thou shalt see.

29 So we abode in the valley over against Beth-peor.

DEUTERONOMY 4

Selection: all verses

IN THIS CHAPTER, Moses finishes his first discourse or sermon (see Background to Deuteronomy, in this study guide,) reviewing the history of these Israelites during their 40 years in the wilderness. Remember that the children of Israel have now gathered east of the Jordan River and can look across west into the promised land. Verse 1 is a continuation from chapter 3.

1 Now therefore hearken, O Israel, unto the statutes and unto the judgments, which I teach you, for to do *them*, **that ye may live,** and go in and possess the land which the LORD God of your fathers giveth you.

Missionaries and other members of the Church are often confronted by those who do not believe that the Book of Mormon and other scriptures can appropriately be added to the Bible. They cite Revelation 22:18–19 as their scriptural proof that this is the case. We will quote these two verses and then help solve the concern using Deuteronomy 4:2.

Revelation 22:18–19

18 For I testify unto every man that heareth the words

of the prophecy of this book, **If any man shall add unto these things, God shall add unto him the plagues that are written in this book:**

19 And if any man shall take away from the words of the book of this prophecy, God shall take away his part out of the book of life, and out of the holy city, and *from* the things which are written in this book.

As you can see, Deuteronomy 4:2 basically says the same thing.

2 Ye shall not add unto the word which I command you, neither shall ye diminish *ought* [take anything] from it, that ye may keep the commandments of the LORD your God which I command you.

As a young missionary in Austria, having had Revelation 22:18–19 used against us several times, I chose to use a bit of humor the next time it came up. When an investigator objected to the Book of Mormon, using Revelation 22 as his weapon, I asked him if he had a Bible in his apartment, and if so, would he please get it and a pair of scissors. He complied, with a puzzled look on his face. I then asked him to turn to Deuteronomy 4:2 and tell us if it said basically the same thing as Revelation 22:18. He read the verse in Deuteronomy, and then, with a bit of reluctance, agreed that the two references said basically the same thing. I then suggested that he take the scissors and cut out all the pages of his Bible after Deuteronomy

4:2 because they violated the injunction not to add any more scriptures beyond that point.

With a bit of a grin, he concluded that maybe these two references meant something else, to which my companion and I agreed. We then explained that both references meant not to go beyond what the Lord had said by giving personal interpretations that deviate from the word of the Lord. Likewise, we are not to water down or explain away what the Lord says.

We also mentioned that the Book of Revelation was not the last book to be written in the New Testament. In fact, the Gospel of John was written after Revelation.

We will now continue with Moses' review and teachings to his people in his first of three major farewell discourses to them before Joshua led them into the promised land.

3 Your eyes have seen what the LORD did because of Baal-peor [*because many of you participated in Baal worship with its accompanying sexual immorality—see Numbers 25:1–3*]: for **all the men that followed Baal-peor,** the LORD thy **God hath destroyed** them from among you [*about twenty-four thousand—see Numbers 25:9*].

4 But ye that did cleave unto the LORD your God *are* alive every one of you this day.

5 Behold, I have taught you

statutes and judgments, even as the LORD my God commanded me, that ye should do so in the land [*Canaan, the promised land*] whither ye go to possess it.

Major Message

Your good example has the potential to positively influence many others.

6 Keep therefore and do *them*; for this *is* your wisdom and your understanding **in the sight of the nations,** which shall hear all these statutes, and say, Surely this great nation *is* a wise and understanding people [*in other words, your good example will influence many others*].

7 For **what nation** *is* **there so great,** who *hath* God *so* nigh unto them, as the LORD our God *is* in all *things that* we call upon him *for?*

8 And **what nation** *is* **there so great,** that hath statutes and judgments *so* righteous as all this law, which I set before you this day?

9 Only **take heed to thyself,** and keep thy soul diligently, lest thou forget the things which thine eyes have seen, and lest they depart from thy heart all the days of thy life: but **teach them thy sons, and thy sons' sons;**

The miraculous circumstances of the ten commandments.

10 *Specially* the day that thou stoodest before the LORD thy God in Horeb [*Sinai*], when the LORD said unto me, Gather me the people together, and I will make them hear my words, that they may learn to fear [*respect and reverence*] me all the days that they shall live upon the earth, and *that* they may teach their children.

11 And **ye came near and stood under the mountain; and the mountain burned with fire** unto the midst of heaven, with darkness, clouds, and thick darkness.

12 And the LORD spake unto you out of the midst of the fire: **ye heard the voice** of the words, but saw no similitude; only *ye heard* a voice.

13 And **he declared unto you his covenant,** which he commanded you to perform, *even* **ten commandments**; and he wrote them upon two tables of stone.

14 ¶ **And the LORD commanded me at that time to teach you statutes and judgments,** that ye might do them in the land whither ye go over to possess it.

15 Take ye therefore good heed unto yourselves; for ye saw no manner of similitude [*you didn't actually see the Lord*] on the day *that* the LORD spake unto you in Horeb out of the midst of the fire:

16 Lest ye corrupt *yourselves*, and make you a graven image, the similitude of any figure, the likeness of male or female,

17 The likeness of any beast that *is* on the earth, the likeness of any winged fowl that flieth in the air,

18 The likeness of any thing that creepeth on the ground, the likeness of any fish that *is* in the waters beneath the earth:

19 And lest thou lift up thine eyes unto heaven, and when thou seest the sun, and the moon, and the stars, *even* all the host of heaven, shouldest be driven to worship them, and serve them, which the LORD thy God hath divided unto all nations under the whole heaven.

20 But **the LORD hath taken you, and brought you forth** out of the iron furnace, *even* **out of Egypt** [*symbolic of the world*], **to be unto him a people of inheritance** [*a covenant people with the opportunity to inherit exaltation in the "promised land" (heaven)*], as ye are this day.

21 Furthermore the LORD was angry with me for your sakes [*because of how I reacted to you when I hit the rock twice to bring water out rather than speaking to it as instructed—see Numbers 20:7–8, 11–12*], **and sware** [*strongly instructed*] **that I should not go over Jordan** [*cross the*

Jordan River], **and that I should not go in unto that good land** [*the land of Canaan*], which the LORD thy God giveth thee *for* an inheritance:

22 But I must die in this land [*this phrase may not be translated correctly because Moses will be translated— see Bible Dictionary, under "Moses"; however, he may not yet have known that he would be translated*], **I must not go over Jordan: but ye shall go over,** and possess that good land.

23 Take heed unto yourselves, lest ye forget the covenant of the LORD your God, which he made with you, **and make you a graven image** [*in violation of the Ten Commandments*], or the likeness of any *thing*, which the LORD thy God hath forbidden thee.

24 For the LORD thy God *is* a consuming fire, *even* a jealous God [*does not want you worshiping idols or any type of false gods*].

Next, Moses delivers a very strong warning.

25 ¶ When thou shalt beget children, and children's children, and ye shall have remained long in the land, and shall corrupt *yourselves*, and make a graven image, *or* the likeness of any *thing*, and shall do evil in the sight of the LORD thy God, to provoke him to anger:

26 I call heaven and earth to witness

against you this day, that ye shall soon utterly perish from off the land whereunto ye go over Jordan to possess it; ye shall not prolong *your* days upon it, but shall utterly be destroyed.

Moses prophesies the scattering of Israel.

27 And **the LORD shall scatter you among the nations**, and ye shall be left few in number among the heathen, whither the LORD shall lead you.

28 And **there ye shall serve gods, the work of men's hands, wood** and **stone, which neither see**, nor **hear,** nor **eat**, nor **smell** [*in other words, false gods; you will be deceived*].

Next, Moses teaches hope, making use of what we often refer to as an "if...then" clause

29 But **if** from thence [*from the nations into which you are scattered*] **thou shalt seek the LORD** thy God, [*then*] **thou shalt find** *him*, **if thou seek him with all thy heart and with all thy soul.**

Next, Moses prophesies that Israel will be gathered in the last days. We are part of the ongoing fulfillment of this prophecy.

30 When thou art in tribulation, and all these things are come upon thee, *even* **in the latter days**, if thou turn to the LORD thy God, and shalt be obedient unto his voice;

31 (For **the LORD thy God** *is* a **merciful** God;) he will not forsake thee, neither destroy thee, nor forget the covenant of thy fathers which he sware unto them.

Do you remember how Moses reacted to his initial call from the Lord, at the time of the burning bush? He worried, saying "I am not eloquent . . . but I am slow of speech." (Exodus 4:10). Perhaps you have noticed how eloquent and powerful in speech and teaching he now is. There is a great lesson for each of us here as we see what growth can come to one who is willing to accept callings from God.

Next, Moses teaches a course in perspective.

32 For **ask now** of the days that are past, which were before thee, since the day that God created man upon the earth, and *ask* from the one side of heaven unto the other, **whether there hath been** *any such thing* as **this great thing** *is,* **or hath been heard like it?**

33 Did *ever* **people hear the voice of God speaking out of the midst of the fire** [*on Mount Sinai*], **as thou hast heard, and live?**

34 Or hath God assayed to go *and* take him a nation from the midst of *another* nation, by temptations, by signs, and by wonders, and by war, and by a mighty hand, and by a stretched out arm, and by great terrors, **according to all that the LORD your God did for you in Egypt before your eyes** [*has any nation ever had so many obvious signs and wonders as the Lord did for you to free you from Egypt*]?

35 Unto thee it was shewed, that thou mightest know that the LORD he *is* **God;** *there is* **none else beside him.**

As mentioned previously, repetition is one of the techniques used in ancient biblical writing to emphasize something. As you can see, Moses uses it here.

36 Out of heaven he made thee to hear his voice, that he might instruct thee: and upon earth he shewed thee his great fire [*on Sinai*]; **and thou heardest his words out of the midst of the fire.**

37 And because **he** loved thy fathers, therefore he chose their seed after them, and **brought thee** out in his sight **with his mighty power out of Egypt;**

Major Message

With the help of God, we can ultimately triumph over all our enemies.

38 To drive out nations from before thee greater and mightier than thou *art*, to bring thee in, to give thee their land *for* an inheritance, as *it is* this day.

39 Know therefore this day, and consider *it* in thine heart, **that the LORD he** *is* **God in heaven** above, **and upon the earth** beneath: *there is* **none else.**

40 Thou shalt keep therefore his statutes, and his commandments, which I command thee this day, **that it may go well with thee, and with thy children after thee**, and that thou mayest prolong *thy* days upon the earth, which the LORD thy God giveth thee, for ever.

Next, in verses 41-43, three cities are designated by Moses as cities of refuge for temporary asylum and safety for persons who commit involuntary manslaughter. This allows for passions to cool and the justice system to come into play.

41 ¶ Then Moses severed [*set apart, designated*] **three cities** on this side Jordan [*on the east side of the Jordan River*] toward the sunrising;

42 That the slayer might flee thither [*to one of these cities*], **which should kill his neighbour unawares** [*without premeditated intent—in other words, accidentally killed a person*], and hated him not in times past; and that fleeing unto one of these cities he might live [*be saved from retaliation until a fair trial could be held*]:

43 *Namely*, **Bezer** in the wilderness, in the plain country, of the Reubenites; and **Ramoth** in Gilead,

of the Gadites; and **Golan** in Bashan, of the Manassites.

Verses 44–49 are a summary of Moses's first major review of the law to his people, at the end of the forty years since leaving Egypt, as he prepares them to enter the promised land.

44 ¶ And **this** *is* **the law which Moses set before the children of Israel:**

45 **These** *are* **the testimonies, and the statutes, and the judgments, which Moses spake unto the children of Israel, after they came forth out of Egypt,**

46 **On this side Jordan** [*on the east side of the Jordan River*], **in the valley over against Beth-peor, in the land of Sihon king of the Amorites, who dwelt at Heshbon, whom Moses and the children of Israel smote, after they were come forth out of Egypt:**

47 **And they possessed his land, and the land of Og king of Bashan,** two kings of the Amorites, which *were* on this side Jordan toward the sunrising;

48 From Aroer, which *is* by the bank of the river Arnon, even unto mount Sion, which *is* Hermon [*north of the Sea of Galilee*],

49 And all the plain on this side Jordan eastward, even unto the sea of the plain, under the springs of Pisgah.

DEUTERONOMY 5

Selection: all verses

IN THIS SECOND of three final discourses, comprising chapters 5–26 (see Background to Deuteronomy in this study guide), before his translation, Moses explains and teaches about the Ten Commandments and other laws of spiritual progress. You will see the Ten Commandments repeated. In addition, you will see many other teachings that were also given by the Savior during His mortal ministry as He taught the higher law. The existence of such teachings in Moses's review and discourse to his people is a reminder that the Law of Moses was indeed a high law. We will continue now with this first portion of Moses's second discourse to his people in preparation for them to enter the land of Canaan, the promised land. We will continue our use of **bold** to summarize Moses' teachings.

Second Discourse, Part 1

Deuteronomy 5–11

First, in verses 1–5, Moses gives a brief review of the circumstances surrounding the giving of the Ten Commandments.

1 And **Moses called all Israel,** and said unto them, **Hear, O Israel, the statutes** [*commandments—see footnote 1a in your Bible*] **and judgments** [*laws, ordinances—see footnote 1b in your Bible*] **which I speak** in your ears this day, that ye may **learn**

them, and keep, and do them.

2 **The LORD** our God **made a covenant with us in Horeb** [*Sinai, where the Ten Commandments were given—see Exodus 19–20*].

3 The LORD made not this covenant with our fathers [*ancestors*], but with us, *even* us, who *are* all of us here alive this day [*in other words, none of our ancestors as a people had such a direct experience with the Lord as we have had*].

4 **The LORD talked with you** face to face [*you could personally see the fire and smoke that indicated His presence*] in the mount **out of the midst of the fire,**

5 (I stood between the LORD and you at that time, to shew you the work of the LORD: for ye were afraid by reason of [*because of*] the fire, and went not up into the mount;) **saying,**

6 ¶ **I** *am* **the LORD** [*I am Jehovah*] thy God, which brought thee out of the land of Egypt, from the house of bondage.

> In verses 7–21, next, by way of review, Moses repeats the Ten Commandments.

7 Thou shalt have none other gods before me.

8 Thou shalt not make thee *any* **graven image,** *or* any likeness *of any*

thing that *is* in heaven above, or that *is* in the earth beneath, or that *is* in the waters beneath the earth:

9 Thou shalt not bow down thyself unto them, nor serve them: for I the LORD thy God *am* a jealous God, visiting the iniquity of the fathers upon the children unto the third and fourth *generation* of them that hate me,

10 And shewing mercy unto thousands of them that love me and keep my commandments.

11 Thou shalt not take the name of the LORD thy God in vain: for the LORD will not hold *him* guiltless that taketh his name in vain.

12 Keep the sabbath day to sanctify it [*you are to make it a holy day; notice that the wording is just a bit different than in Exodus 20:8*], as the LORD thy God hath commanded thee.

13 Six days thou shalt labour, and do all thy work:

14 But the seventh day *is* the sabbath of the LORD thy God: *in it* thou shalt not do any work, thou, nor thy son, nor thy daughter, nor thy manservant, nor thy maidservant, nor thine ox, nor thine ass, nor any of thy cattle, nor thy stranger that *is* within thy gates; that thy manservant and thy maidservant may rest as well as thou.

15 And remember that thou wast a servant in the land of Egypt, and *that* the LORD thy God brought thee out thence through a mighty hand and by a stretched out arm: therefore the LORD thy God commanded thee to keep the sabbath day.

Major Message

Honoring parents can strengthen the family unit, which is the key to a stable nation.

16 ¶ Honour thy father and thy mother, as the LORD thy God hath commanded thee; that thy days may be prolonged, and **that it may go well with thee, in the land** which the LORD thy God giveth thee.

17 Thou shalt not kill.

18 Neither shalt thou commit adultery.

19 Neither shalt thou steal.

20 Neither shalt thou bear false witness against thy neighbour.

21 Neither shalt thou desire thy neighbour's wife, neither shalt thou **covet** thy neighbour's house, his field, or his manservant, or his maidservant, his ox, or his ass, or any *thing* that *is* thy neighbour's.

In verses 22–27, Moses reminds the people about their reaction to hearing the voice of the Lord as He gave the Ten Commandments from Sinai.

22 ¶ These words the LORD spake unto all your assembly in the mount [*Sinai*] out of the midst of the fire, of the cloud, and of the thick darkness, **with a great voice:** and he added no more. **And he wrote them in two tables of stone, and delivered them unto me.**

23 And it came to pass, **when ye heard the voice** out of the midst of the darkness [*the smoke on Sinai*], (for the mountain did burn with fire,) that **ye came near unto me**, *even* all the heads of your tribes, and your elders;

24 And ye said, Behold, the LORD our **God hath shewed us his glory** and his greatness, and **we have heard his voice** out of the midst of the fire: **we have seen this day that God doth talk with man, and he liveth.**

25 Now therefore why should we die? for this great fire will consume us: **if we hear the voice of the LORD our God any more, then we shall die.**

26 For who *is there of* all flesh, that hath heard the voice of the living God speaking out of the midst of the fire, as we *have*, and lived?

27 Go thou [*Moses*] near, and hear all that the LORD our God shall say: and speak thou unto us all that the LORD our God shall speak unto thee; and we will hear *it*, and do *it*.

Next, Moses reviews the Lord's response to the people's request, as recorded above.

28 And **the LORD heard** the voice of **your words,** when ye spake unto me; **and** the LORD **said** unto me, I have heard the voice of the words of this people, which they have spoken unto thee: they have well said all that they have spoken.

29 O that there were such an heart in them, that they would fear me, and keep all my commandments always, that it might be well with them, and with their children for ever!

30 Go **say to them, Get you into your tents again.**

Next, Moses reviews how he got the "laws of Moses" from the Savior after the people had requested that he be their go-between, fearing that they would be killed by the Lord's glory if He spoke directly to them again.

31 But as for thee, stand thou here by me, and I will speak unto thee all the commandments, and the statutes, and the judgments, [*the laws of Moses, beginning with Deuteronomy 6:1; see also Exodus 21–23*] which thou shalt teach them, that they may do *them* in the land which I give them to possess it.

Major Message

Stay right in the middle of the "strait and narrow path."

32 **Ye shall observe to do** therefore **as** the LORD your God hath **commanded** you: **ye shall not turn aside to the right hand or to the left** [*don't deviate at all from the laws and commandments you have been given*].

33 **Ye shall walk in all the ways which the LORD your God hath commanded** you, that ye may live, and *that it may be* well with you, and *that* ye may prolong *your* days in the land which ye shall possess.

DEUTERONOMY 6

Selection: all verses

MOSES REVIEWS THE "laws of Moses," as mentioned in Deuteronomy 5:31, given him by Jehovah after He personally spoke the Ten Commandments to the people from Sinai.

1 Now these *are* the commandments, the statutes, and the judgments, which the LORD your God commanded to teach you, that ye might do *them* in the land whither ye go to possess it:

Next, in verses 2–3, the purpose of the Law of Moses is pointed out.

2 That thou mightest fear [*respect and reverence*] **the LORD** thy God, to keep all his statutes and his commandments, which I command thee, thou, and thy son, and thy son's son, all the days of thy life; and **that thy days may be prolonged.**

3 ¶ Hear therefore, O Israel, and observe to do *it*; that it may be well with thee, and **that ye may increase mightily,** as the LORD God of thy fathers hath promised thee, in the land that floweth with milk and honey.

Verses 4–9, next, are considered most sacred and are much used among devout Jews today. They go together with Deuteronomy 11:13–21 and Numbers 15:37–41 (in this order). They are repeated twice a day as an evening and a morning prayer.

In addition, devout Jews sometimes wear phylacteries (beautiful tiny leather boxes) tied to their foreheads. Inside the phylacteries are four tiny scrolls, with four passages of scripture in tiny print written on them: Exodus 13:1–10, 11–16, Deuteronomy 6:5–9; 11:13–21. You can read about this in the Bible Dictionary, under "Frontlets."

In biblical symbolism, "forehead" denotes "loyalty." Thus, wearing the phylacteries upon one's forehead symbolizes loyalty to the Lord. And the verses of scripture on scrolls inside the phylactery detail various aspects of loyalty to God.

We will continue now with Moses's second discourse to his people.

4 Hear, O Israel: The LORD our God *is* **one LORD:**

5 And thou shalt love the LORD thy God with all thine heart, and with all thy soul, and with all thy might.

Do you recognize verse 5 above? It is also found in Matthew 22:37. In this part of the New Testament, a Jewish leader had asked the Savior what the most important commandment in the Law of Moses was. We will quote these verses here in order to see the Master's response in context:

<u>Matthew 22:35–40</u>
35 Then one of them, *which was* a lawyer, asked *him a question,* tempting [*testing*] him, and saying,
36 Master, **which** *is* **the great commandment in the law** [*the Law of Moses*]?
37 **Jesus said** unto him, **Thou shalt love the Lord thy God with all thy heart, and with all thy soul, and with all thy mind** [*note that Deuteronomy says "might"*].
38 **This is the first and great commandment.**
39 And the second *is* like unto it, **Thou shalt love thy neighbour as thyself.**
40 On these two commandments hang all the law [*the Law of Moses*] and the prophets [*such as Isaiah, Jeremiah, and so forth; in other words, all the laws of Moses*

and the teachings of other Old Testament prophets are designed to lead to the living of these two commandments].

In effect, if everyone were to live the two commandments given above, we wouldn't need any other commandments, just priesthood ordinances of salvation.

We will now continue with the review of the laws of Moses, which their 120-year-old prophet gives his people in this discourse.

6 And **these words,** which I command thee this day, **shall be in thine heart:**

Next, Moses reminds his people to take every opportunity to teach their children.

7 And thou shalt **teach them diligently unto thy children,** and shalt **talk of them when thou sittest in thine house,** and **when thou walkest** by the way, and **when thou liest down, and when thou risest up.**

8 And thou shalt **bind them for a sign upon thine hand** [*symbolic of actions*], **and they shall be as frontlets** [*phylacteries—see Bible Dictionary, under "Frontlets"*] **between thine eyes** [*symbolic of keeping one's eyes on the Lord for direction*].

9 And **thou shalt write them upon the posts** [*doorposts*] **of thy house, and on thy gates.**

Responding to verse 9, above, devout Jews attach a "mezuzah" on the door frame of their house. It is a tiny, cylindrical box containing parchment with a passage of scripture on it. Each time they enter or leave their home, they touch or kiss the mezuzah, symbolizing that they must do the will of God as they leave to interact with others in the world or as they enter the home to interact with family.

In verses 10–17, we are reminded that we obtain the "promised land" (heaven) through making and keeping covenants with God.

10 And it shall be, **when the LORD thy God shall have brought thee into the land** [*the promised land*] **which he sware unto thy fathers** [*promised to your ancestors by covenant*], to Abraham, to Isaac, and to Jacob, to give thee great and goodly cities, which thou buildedst not,

11 And houses full of all good *things,* which thou filledst not, and wells digged, which thou diggedst not, vineyards and olive trees, which thou plantedst not; when thou shalt have eaten and be full;

12 *Then* **beware lest thou forget the LORD,** which brought thee forth out of the land of Egypt, from the house of bondage.

13 **Thou shalt fear** [*respect and honor*] **the LORD** thy God, and **serve him,** and shalt **swear by** [*make covenants with Him in*] **his name.**

14 Ye shall not go after other gods, of the gods of the people which *are* round about you;

15 (For [*because*] the LORD thy God *is* a jealous God [*a God with tender and sensitive feelings*] among you) lest the anger of the LORD thy God be kindled against thee, and destroy thee from off the face of the earth.

16 ¶ Ye shall not tempt the LORD your God [*push the Lord's patience*], as ye tempted *him* in Massah [*the first incident of obtaining water from a rock, after the people expressed anger at the Lord for letting them get so thirsty—see Exodus 17:1–7*].

17 Ye shall diligently keep the commandments of the LORD your God, and his testimonies [*be loyal to the witnesses He has given you*], and his statutes, which he hath commanded thee.

Verses 18–19, next, contain a simple message.

Major Message
Be good.

18 And thou shalt do *that which is* right and good in the sight of the LORD: that it may be well with thee, and that thou mayest go in and possess the good land which the LORD sware unto thy fathers,

19 To cast out all thine enemies from before thee, as the LORD hath spoken.

In the final verses of this chapter, Moses instructs his people to teach these things to their children and to bear witness to them of the goodness of the Lord to them.

20 *And* when thy son asketh thee in time to come, saying, What *mean* the testimonies, and the statutes, and the judgments, which the LORD our God hath commanded you?

21 Then thou shalt say unto thy son, We were Pharaoh's bondmen in Egypt; and the LORD brought us out of Egypt with a mighty hand:

22 And the LORD shewed signs and wonders, great and sore, upon Egypt, upon Pharaoh, and upon all his household, before our eyes:

23 And he brought us out from thence, that he might bring us in, to give us the land which he sware unto our fathers.

24 And the LORD commanded us to do all these statutes, to fear [*respect, honor*] the LORD our God, for our good always, that he might preserve us alive, as *it is* at this day.

25 And it shall be our righteousness [*it will make us righteous*], if we observe to do all these commandments before the LORD our God, as he hath commanded us.

DEUTERONOMY 7

Selection: all verses

IN THIS CHAPTER, Moses emphasizes the consequences of being "ripe in iniquity." Nephi tells us that the inhabitants of the promised land were indeed "ripe in iniquity" at the time the children of Israel were told to enter Canaan and destroy them (1 Nephi 17:35). We learned from Leviticus 18 that "ripe in iniquity" is a phrase that basically means hopelessly wicked and evil, beyond recovery. You may wish to read the notes and commentary for that chapter in this study guide. If you do, you will see that a nation or people who are ripe in iniquity openly accept all forms of sexual immorality, including incest, homosexuality, and bestiality. The depravity of such societies also includes child sacrifice, which might be cause for concern given the widespread acceptance of voluntary abortion in our day.

The instructions of the Lord to the Israelites as they prepare to enter, are to "utterly destroy" the inhabitants of the land. Several hundred years earlier, Abraham was told that, at that time, the "iniquity of the Amorites [*inhabitants of Canaan*] is not yet full" (Genesis 15:16). Thus, in the approximately four hundred years between the time of Abraham and the time the Israelites were told to utterly destroy the residents of the promised land, those inhabitants had become fully ripe in iniquity.

1 When the LORD thy God shall bring thee into the land whither thou goest to possess it, and hath cast out many nations before thee, the Hittites, and the Girgashites, and the Amorites, and the Canaanites, and the Perizzites, and the Hivites, and the Jebusites, seven nations greater and mightier than thou;

> The Hittites, Hivites, and Jebusites were direct descendants of Canaan, son of Ham and Egypt, and were therefore referred to as Canaanites. The Girgashites, Amorites, and Perizzites were also considered to be Canaanites. We understand that they had intermarried with the descendants of Ham. Anyone else living in that land was also considered to be a Canaanite, regardless of race. All were considered by the Lord to be "ripe for destruction."

2 And when the LORD thy God shall deliver them before thee; **thou shalt smite them,** *and* **utterly destroy them**; thou shalt make no covenant with them, nor shew mercy unto them [*the law of justice must take over completely; "mercy cannot rob justice"—Alma 42:25*]:

Major Message

Do not marry outside the covenant.

3 Neither shalt thou make marriages with them; thy daughter thou shalt not give unto his son, nor his daughter shalt thou take unto thy son.

4 For they will turn away thy son from following me, that they may serve other gods: so will the anger of the LORD be kindled against you, and destroy thee suddenly.

5 But **thus shall ye deal with them**; ye shall **destroy their altars**, and **break down their images** [*idols*], and **cut down their groves**, and **burn their graven images** with fire.

Some Bible students wonder why the Israelites were instructed to "cut down their groves" in verse 5, above. The answer is simple. Sexual immorality accompanied most idol worship of the time. Groves of trees were conveniently located around the idols for such purposes. Thus, destroying the groves was part of getting rid of all things associated with the abomination of worshiping idols.

Major Message

Those who make and keep covenants associated with the gospel receive the highest blessings from God. Thus, they are blessed above any other people. They are covenant Israel, the people of the Lord. All people are ultimately invited.

6 For thou *art* **an holy people** unto the LORD thy God: the LORD thy God hath chosen thee to be **a special people** unto himself, **above all people that** *are* **upon the face of the earth.**

7 The LORD did not set his love upon you, nor **choose you, because** ye were more in number than any people; for ye *were* the fewest of all people:

8 But because the LORD loved you, and **because he would keep the oath** [*covenant*] **which he had sworn** [*covenanted*] **unto your fathers** [*ancestors, including Abraham—see Genesis 12:1–3, 6–7*], hath the LORD brought you out with a mighty hand, and redeemed you out of the house of bondmen, from the hand of Pharaoh king of Egypt.

9 Know therefore that the LORD thy God, **he** *is* God, **the faithful God, which keepeth covenant and mercy with them that love him and keep his commandments** to a thousand generations [*in other words, throughout eternity*];

10 And repayeth them that hate him [*the wicked*] to their face, **to destroy them**: he will not be slack to him that hateth him, he will repay him to his face.

11 Thou shalt therefore keep the commandments, and the statutes, and the judgments, which I command thee this day, to do them.

Major Message

"I, the Lord, am bound when ye do what I say; but when ye do not what I say, ye have no promise" (Doctrine and Covenants 82:10).

12 ¶ Wherefore it shall come to pass, **if ye hearken to these judgments, and keep, and do them, that the LORD thy God shall keep unto thee the covenant and the mercy which he sware unto thy fathers:**

13 And **he will love thee** [*bless you with His highest blessings*], and **bless thee**, and **multiply thee**: he will also **bless the fruit of thy womb** [*your children*], and **the fruit of thy land**, thy corn, and thy wine, and thine oil, the increase of thy kine [*cattle*], and the flocks of thy sheep, in the land which he sware unto thy fathers to give thee.

14 Thou shalt be blessed above all people: there shall not be male or female barren among you, or among your cattle.

15 And **the LORD will take away from thee all sickness**, and will put none of the evil diseases [*plagues*] of Egypt, which thou knowest, upon thee; but will lay them upon all *them* that hate thee.

16 And **thou shalt consume all the people** [*enemies*] which the LORD thy God shall deliver thee; thine eye shall have no pity upon them: **neither shalt thou serve their gods;** for that *will be* a snare unto thee.

17 If thou shalt say in thine heart, These nations *are* more than I; how can I dispossess [*conquer*] them?

Major Message

It is vital to our salvation that we remember past blessings to us from the Lord. It can strengthen our faith for enduring present troubles.

18 Thou shalt not be afraid of them: *but* shalt well **remember what the LORD thy God did unto Pharaoh, and unto all Egypt;**

19 The great temptations [*plagues, troubles—see footnote 19a in your Bible*] which thine eyes saw, and the signs, and the wonders, and the mighty hand, and the stretched out arm, whereby the LORD thy God brought thee out: so shall the LORD thy God do unto all the people of whom thou art afraid.

20 Moreover the LORD thy God will send the hornet among them, until they that are left, and hide themselves from thee, be destroyed.

21 Thou shalt not be affrighted at them: for the LORD thy God *is* **among you,** a mighty God and terrible [*awesome—see footnote 21a in your Bible*].

Next, the Lord tells the Israelites that they are to destroy the inhabitants of Canaan little by little so that the land does not get overrun by animals.

22 And the LORD thy God will put out those nations before thee **by little and little:** thou mayest not consume them at once, **lest the beasts of the field increase upon thee.**

23 But the LORD thy God shall deliver them unto thee, and shall destroy them with a mighty destruction, until they be destroyed.

24 And **he shall deliver their kings into thine hand**, and thou shalt destroy their name from under heaven: **there shall no man be able to stand before thee**, until thou have destroyed them.

25 The graven images of their gods shall ye burn with fire: thou shalt not desire the silver or gold *that is* on them, **nor take it unto thee, lest thou be snared therein:** for it *is* an abomination to the LORD thy God.

Major Message

"Touch not their unclean things" (Alma 5:57).

26 Neither shalt thou bring an abomination [*items such as mentioned in verse 25, above*] **into thine house,** lest thou be a cursed thing like it: *but* **thou shalt utterly detest it,** and thou shalt utterly **abhor it;** for it *is* a cursed thing.

DEUTERONOMY 8

Selection: all verses

THIS CHAPTER IS a continuation of the second discourse or sermon Moses gave his people as they prepared to enter the promised land. He explains many "whys," in other words, reasons for how the Lord deals with us (chapters 5–26—see General Background to Deuteronomy in this study guide).

1 All the commandments which I command thee this day **shall ye observe** to do, **that ye may live, and multiply, and go in and possess the land** which the LORD sware unto your fathers.

2 And thou shalt remember all the way which the LORD thy God led thee these **forty years in the wilderness, to humble thee,** *and* to **prove thee, to know what** *was* **in thine heart, whether thou wouldest keep his commandments, or no** [*compare with Abraham 3:25*].

Major Message

"Man shall not live by bread alone, but by every word that proceedeth out of the mouth of God" (Matthew 4:4).

3 And he **humbled thee, and suffered** [*allowed*] **thee to hunger, and fed thee with manna,** which thou knewest not [*which you had never seen before*], neither did thy fathers [*ancestors*] know; **that he might**

make thee know that man doth not live by bread only, but by every *word* that proceedeth out of the mouth of the LORD doth man live.

In verse 4, next, Moses reminds the people of a wonderful miracle. During the forty years in the wilderness, the Israelites' clothes did not wear out; nor did the people have foot trouble.

4 Thy raiment [*clothing*] waxed not old upon thee, neither did thy foot swell, these forty years.

Next, he points out that it is because of the Lord's love for us that He chastens and disciplines us as needed.

5 Thou shalt also consider in thine heart, that, as a man chasteneth his son, *so* the LORD thy God chasteneth thee.

6 Therefore thou shalt keep the commandments of the LORD thy God, to walk in his ways, and to fear him.

Next comes a promise of prosperity in the promised land.

7 For the LORD thy God bringeth thee into a good land, a land of brooks of water, of fountains and depths that spring out of valleys and hills;

8 A land of wheat, and barley, and vines, and fig trees, and pomegranates; a land of oil olive, and honey;

9 A land wherein thou shalt eat bread without scarceness, thou shalt not lack any *thing* in it; a land whose stones *are* iron, and out of whose hills thou mayest dig brass.

10 When thou hast eaten and art full, then thou shalt bless [*thank, praise, show gratitude*] the LORD thy God for the good land which he hath given thee.

Have you noticed that gratitude is one of the most effective antidotes for pride?

Major Message

Do not forget the Lord during times of prosperity.

11 Beware that thou forget not the LORD thy God, in not keeping his commandments, and his judgments, and his statutes, which I command thee this day:

12 Lest [*for fear that*] when thou hast eaten and art full, and hast built goodly houses, and dwelt *therein*;

13 And when thy herds and thy flocks multiply, and thy silver and thy gold is multiplied, and all that thou hast is multiplied;

Major Message

Pride tends to make us forget past blessings and gratitude.

14 Then thine heart be lifted up [*in pride*], and thou forget the LORD thy God, which brought thee forth out of the land of Egypt, from the house of bondage;

15 Who led thee through that great and terrible wilderness, *wherein were* fiery serpents, and scorpions, and drought, where *there was* no water; who brought thee forth water out of the rock of flint;

16 Who fed thee in the wilderness with manna, which thy fathers knew not, that he might humble thee, and that he might prove thee, to do thee good at thy latter end;

17 And thou say in thine heart, My power and the might of *mine* hand hath gotten me this wealth.

18 But thou shalt **remember the LORD** thy God: for *it is* **he that giveth thee power to get wealth, that he may establish his covenant** which he sware unto thy fathers, as *it is* this day.

Next, Moses gives his people a strong warning.

19 And it shall be, **if thou do at all forget the LORD** thy God, and walk after other gods, and serve them, and worship them, I testify against you this day that **ye shall surely perish.**

20 As the nations which the LORD destroyeth before your face, so shall ye perish; **because ye would not be obedient unto the voice of the LORD your God.**

DEUTERONOMY 9

Selection: all verses

THIS CHAPTER IS a continuation of the first part (chapters 5–11) of Moses's second discourse (chapters 5–26), as explained in the General Background for Deuteronomy, in this study guide. In verses 1–3, the people are reminded that the power of the Lord will enable them to enter into the promised land.

1 HEAR, O Israel: Thou art to pass over Jordan this day, to **go in to possess nations greater and mightier than thyself,** cities great and fenced up to heaven,

2 A people great and tall, the children of the Anakims [*an extraordinarily tall race of people, settled around Hebron in the Holy Land at the time*], whom thou knowest, and of whom thou hast heard say, Who can stand before the children of Anak!

3 Understand therefore this day, that the LORD thy God is he which goeth over before thee; as a consuming fire he shall destroy them, and he shall bring them down before thy face: so shalt thou drive them out, and destroy them quickly, as the LORD hath said unto thee.

For the rest of the chapter, Moses reminds the people that it is not their righteousness that will enable them to take over the land of Canaan. Rather, it is the wickedness of the current inhabitants. It is a warning to the Israelites not to adopt the wickedness of these people.

4 Speak not thou **in thine heart,** after that the LORD thy God hath cast them out from before thee, **saying, For my righteousness the LORD hath brought me in to possess this land: but for the wickedness of these nations the LORD doth drive them out from before thee.**

5 Not for thy righteousness, or for the uprightness of thine heart, dost thou go to possess their land: but for the wickedness of these nations the LORD thy God doth drive them out from before thee, and that he may perform the word which the LORD sware unto thy fathers, Abraham, Isaac, and Jacob.

6 Understand therefore, **that the LORD** thy God **giveth thee not this good land to possess it for** [because of] **thy righteousness;** for thou art a **stiffnecked people.**

7 ¶ Remember, and forget not, **how thou provokedst the LORD thy God to wrath in the wilderness:** from the day that thou didst depart out of the land of Egypt, until ye came unto this place, **ye have been rebellious** against the LORD.

8 Also in Horeb [Sinai] **ye provoked the LORD to wrath,** so that

the LORD was angry with you to have destroyed you.

9 When I was gone up into the mount to receive the tables of stone, even the tables of the covenant which the LORD made with you, then I abode in the mount **forty days and forty nights,** I neither did eat bread nor drink water:

10 And the LORD delivered unto me two tables of stone written with the finger of God; and on them was written according to all the words, which the LORD spake with you in the mount out of the midst of the fire in the day of the assembly.

11 And it came to pass at the end of forty days and forty nights, that the LORD gave me the two tables of stone, even the tables of the covenant.

12 And **the LORD said unto me, Arise, get thee down quickly** from hence; for **thy people** which thou hast brought forth out of Egypt **have corrupted** themselves; they are quickly turned aside out of the way which I commanded them; **they have made them a molten image** [the gold calf].

13 Furthermore the LORD spake unto me, saying, I have seen this people, and, behold, **it** is **a stiffnecked people:**

14 Let me alone, that I may

189

destroy them, and blot out their name from under heaven: and I will make of thee a nation mightier and greater than they.

15 So I turned and came down from the mount, and the mount burned with fire: and the two tables of the covenant *were* in my two hands.

16 And I looked, and, behold, ye had sinned against the LORD your God, *and* had made you a molten calf: ye had turned aside quickly out of the way which the LORD had commanded you.

17 And I took the two tables [*the stone tablets which had the Ten Commandments written on them*], and cast them out of my two hands, and brake them before your eyes.

18 And I fell down [*in utter humility*] before the LORD, as at the first, forty days and forty nights: I did neither eat bread, nor drink water, because of all your sins which ye sinned, in doing wickedly in the sight of the LORD, to provoke him to anger.

19 For I was afraid of the anger and hot displeasure, wherewith the LORD was wroth against you to destroy you. But the LORD hearkened unto me at that time also [*and did not destroy you because of my pleading*].

20 And the LORD was very angry with Aaron [*because he supervised the building of the gold calf*] to have destroyed him: and I prayed for Aaron also the same time.

21 And I took your sin, the calf which ye had made, and burnt it with fire, and stamped it, *and* ground *it* very small, *even* until it was as small as dust: and I cast the dust thereof into the brook that descended out of the mount.

22 And at Taberah, and at Massah [*when they were out of water*], and at Kibroth-hattaavah, ye provoked the LORD to wrath.

23 Likewise when the LORD sent you from Kadesh-barnea, saying, Go up and possess the land which I have given you; then ye rebelled against the commandment of the LORD your God, and ye believed him not, nor hearkened to his voice.

24 Ye have been rebellious against the LORD from the day that I knew you.

25 Thus I fell down before the LORD forty days and forty nights, as I fell down *at the first*; because the LORD had said he would destroy you.

26 I prayed therefore unto the LORD, and said, O Lord GOD, destroy not thy people and thine inheritance, which thou hast

redeemed through thy greatness, which thou hast brought forth out of Egypt with a mighty hand.

27 Remember thy servants, Abraham, Isaac, and Jacob [*remember the covenants You made to Abraham, Isaac, and Jacob to bring their descendants into Canaan*]; **look not unto the stubbornness of this people, nor to their wickedness, nor to their sin:**

> In effect, Moses was saying to the Lord, "Don't ruin Your reputation by not bringing the Israelites into the promised land."

28 Lest the land [*Egypt*] **whence** [*from which*] **thou broughtest us out say, Because the LORD was not able to bring them into the land** which he promised them, and because he hated them, he hath brought them out to slay them in the wilderness.

29 Yet they *are* thy people and thine inheritance, which thou broughtest out by thy mighty power and by thy stretched out arm.

DEUTERONOMY 10

Selection: all verses

AS MOSES CONTINUES reviewing and teaching lessons to be learned from the past wandering in the wilderness, he mentions the second set of stone tablets in verses 1–2. We will need the JST (Joseph Smith Translation of the Bible) to get the correct account.

1 At that time [*after Moses broke the first set of tablets*] **the LORD said unto me, Hew thee two tables of stone like unto the first** [*which the Lord, Himself, had made*], **and come up unto me** into the mount, and make thee an ark [*chest*] of wood.

2 And I will write on the tables the words that were in the first tables which thou brakest, and thou shalt put them in the ark.

JST Deuteronomy 10:1–2
1 At that time the Lord said unto me, Hew thee **two other tables of stone** like unto the first, and come up unto me upon the mount, and make thee an ark of wood.
2 And I will write on the tables the words that were on the first tables, which thou breakest, **save** [*except*] **the words of the everlasting covenant of the holy priesthood**, and thou shalt put them in the ark.

Thus we learn from the JST that the second set of stone tablets did not contain the higher ordinances, the ordinances of the Melchizedek Priesthood.

In verses 3–8, next, Moses continues reviewing this part of the history of the children of Israel in the wilderness.

3 And I made an ark *of* shittim

[acacia] wood, **and hewed** [chiseled] **two tables of stone** like unto the first, **and went up into the mount,** having the two tables in mine hand.

4 And he [Jehovah] **wrote on the tables,** according to the first writing, the ten commandments, which the LORD spake unto you in the mount out of the midst of the fire in the day of the assembly: and the LORD gave them unto me.

5 And I turned myself and **came down from the mount, and put the tables in the ark** which I had made; and there they be [they are still there now, almost forty years later], as the LORD commanded me.

6 ¶ And the children of Israel took their journey from Beeroth of the children of Jaakan to Mosera: **there Aaron died, and there he was buried; and Eleazar his son ministered** in the priest's office **in his stead** [in his place].

7 From thence they journeyed unto Gudgodah; and from Gudgodah to Jotbath, a land of rivers of waters.

8 ¶ At that time the LORD separated [set apart] **the tribe of Levi,** to bear the ark of the covenant of the LORD, to stand before the LORD to minister unto him [to officiate in Aaronic Priesthood ordinances], and to bless in his name, unto this day.

As you can see, in verse 8, above, not all male members of the children of Israel were allowed to hold the priesthood. The men of the tribe of Levi were chosen to hold the Aaronic or Levitical Priesthood. For members of the Church who face criticism because blacks were not allowed to hold the priesthood, until 1978, it can be helpful to point out that other men among the Israelites were likewise denied the priesthood, for the purposes of the Lord.

Next, in verse 10, the tribe of Levi did not get a specific land in which to settle, rather, they were placed in cities throughout the land of promise in order to serve all the people.

9 Wherefore [this is why] **Levi hath no part nor inheritance with his brethren;** the LORD is his inheritance, according as the LORD thy God promised him.

As a master teacher, Moses now asks his people a key question. He then gives the answer. The same question and answer apply to us.

12 ¶ And now, Israel, **what doth the LORD thy God require of thee,** but to **fear** [respect and bring honor to] **the LORD** thy God, to **walk in all his ways,** and to **love him,** and to **serve the LORD thy God with all thy heart and with all thy soul,**

13 To **keep the commandments** of the LORD, **and his statutes,** which I command thee this day for thy good?

14 Behold, the heaven and the heaven of heavens *is* the LORD's thy God, the earth *also*, with all that therein *is*.

15 Only the LORD had a delight in thy fathers to love them, and he chose their seed after them, *even* you above all people, as *it is* this day.

16 Circumcise therefore the foreskin of your heart [*dedicate your heart completely to the Lord*], **and be no more stiffnecked** [*avoid pride and disobedience*].

17 For the LORD your God *is* God of gods, and Lord of lords, a great God, a mighty, and a terrible [*frightening to the wicked*], which regardeth not persons, nor taketh reward:

18 He doth execute the judgment of the fatherless and widow, and loveth the stranger, in giving him food and raiment.

19 Love ye therefore the **stranger** [*nonmembers; foreigners, non-Israelites*]: for ye were strangers in the land of Egypt.

20 Thou shalt **fear the LORD** thy God; **him shalt thou serve**, and **to him shalt thou cleave** [*stay close to Him*], and swear by his name [*make and keep covenants with Him*].

21 He *is* thy praise, and he *is* thy God, that hath done for thee these great and terrible things, which thine eyes have seen.

22 Thy fathers went down into Egypt with threescore and ten [*seventy*] persons; and now the LORD thy God hath made thee as the stars of heaven for multitude.

DEUTERONOMY 11

Selection: all verses

MOSES NOW CONCLUDES the first portion (chapters 5–11) of his second discourse to his people before he is translated and taken up and before they enter the promised land under the leadership of Joshua. First, he reminds them how they can have the blessings of the Lord with them constantly.

1 Therefore [*in order to have the Lord's blessings constantly with you*] thou shalt **love the LORD** thy God, and keep his charge, and his **statutes**, and his **judgments**, and his **commandments**, always.

2 And know ye this day: for *I speak* **not with your children** which have not known, and which have not seen the chastisement of the LORD your God, his greatness, his mighty hand, and his stretched out arm,

3 And his miracles, and his acts, which he did in the midst of Egypt unto Pharaoh the king of Egypt, and unto all his land;

4 And what he did unto the army of Egypt, unto their horses, and to their chariots; how he made the water of the Red sea to overflow them as they pursued after you, and *how* the LORD hath destroyed them unto this day;

5 And what he did unto you in the wilderness, until ye came into this place;

6 And what he did unto Dathan and Abiram, the sons of Eliab, the son of Reuben: how the earth opened her mouth, and swallowed them up, and their households, and their tents, and all the substance that *was* in their possession, in the midst of all Israel:

7 **But your eyes have seen all the great acts of the LORD which he did.**

8 **Therefore shall ye keep all the commandments** which I command you this day, **that ye may be strong, and go in and possess the land,** whither ye go to possess it;

9 And **that ye may prolong *your* days in the land,** which the LORD sware unto your fathers to give unto them and to their seed, a land that floweth with milk and honey.

Next, in verses 10–25, the people are told that the land of Canaan (the "promised land") is not as fertile as Egypt was; therefore, they have more need of the help of the Lord in order to prosper.

10 ¶ **For the land,** whither thou goest in to possess it, **is not as the land of Egypt,** from whence ye came out, where thou sowedst thy seed, and wateredst *it* with thy foot [*with water from the Nile River*], as a garden of herbs:

11 But **the land, whither ye go to possess it, is a land of hills and valleys, *and* drinketh water of the rain of heaven** [*you will need rain*]:

12 A land which the LORD thy God careth for: the eyes of the LORD thy God *are* always upon it, from the beginning of the year even unto the end of the year [*from season to season*].

13 ¶ And it shall come to pass, **if ye shall hearken diligently unto my commandments** which I command you this day, to love the LORD your God, and to serve him with all your heart and with all your soul,

Next, Moses recites the Lord's words to the people.

14 That **I will give *you* the rain** of your land **in** his **due season,** the first rain and the latter rain, that thou mayest gather in thy corn, and thy wine, and thine oil.

15 And **I will send grass in thy fields for thy cattle,** that thou mayest eat and be full.

16 **Take heed to yourselves** [*be*

careful], **that your heart be not deceived**, and ye turn aside, and serve other gods, and worship them;

17 And *then* **the LORD's wrath be kindled against you**, and he shut up the heaven, that there be **no rain**, and that the land yield not her fruit; **and** *lest* **ye perish quickly** from off the good land which the LORD giveth you.

> In order to better understand verses 18–21, next, you may wish to review the notes provided in this study guide for Deuteronomy 6:3–9.

18 ¶ Therefore [*in order to avoid these problems*] shall ye **lay up these my words in your heart and in your soul**, and bind them for a sign upon your hand, that they may be as frontlets between your eyes [*keep these things foremost in your minds*].

19 And ye shall **teach them your children**, speaking of them when thou sittest in thine house, and when thou walkest by the way, when thou liest down, and when thou risest up.

20 And thou shalt write them upon the door posts of thine house, and upon thy gates:

21 That your days may be multiplied, and the days of your children, in the land which the LORD sware unto your fathers to give them, as the days of heaven upon the earth.

22 ¶ For **if ye shall diligently keep all these commandments** which I command you, to do them, to love the LORD your God, to walk in all his ways, and to cleave unto him;

23 Then will the LORD drive out all these nations from before you, and ye shall possess greater nations and mightier than yourselves [*symbolically, you will then overcome all obstacles to salvation*].

24 Every place whereon the soles of your feet shall tread shall be yours: from the wilderness and Lebanon, from the river, the river Euphrates, even unto the uttermost sea shall your coast be.

25 There shall no man be able to stand before you: *for* the LORD your God shall lay the fear of you and the dread of you upon all the land that ye shall tread upon, as he hath said unto you.

> In verses 26–32, next, Moses basically tells his people that they can choose a blessing or a curse—it is up to them.

26 ¶ Behold, **I set before you this day a blessing and a curse** [*I offer you a blessing or a curse—you choose*];

27 A blessing, if ye obey the commandments of the LORD your God, which I command you this day:

28 And **a curse, if ye will not obey**

the commandments of the LORD your God, but turn aside out of the way which I command you this day, to go after other gods, which ye have not known.

Two prominent hills in central Canaan are designated as visual aids, symbols of blessings or cursings, to help the Israelites remember what Moses is teaching here.

29 And it shall come to pass, when the LORD thy God hath brought thee in unto the land whither thou goest to possess it, that thou shalt put the blessing upon **mount Gerizim** [*this mountain will symbolize the blessings from God*], and the curse upon **mount Ebal** [*this one will symbolize the punishments (curses) that will come upon you if you choose disobedience*].

30 *Are* they not on the other side Jordan [*the west side*], by the way where the sun goeth down, in the land of the Canaanites, which dwell in the champaign over against Gilgal, beside the plains of Moreh?

We will quote from a Bible commentary regarding these two prominent hills or mountains:

"The two mountains mentioned were selected for this act, no doubt, because they were opposite to one another, and stood, each about 2500 feet high, in the very centre of the land not only from west to east, but also from north to south. Ebal stands upon the north side, Gerizim upon the south; between the two is Sichem, the present Nabulus, in a tolerably elevated valley, fertile, attractive, and watered by many springs, which run from the south-east to the north-west from the foot of Gerizim to that of Ebal, and is about 1600 feet in breadth. The blessing was to be uttered upon Gerizim, and the curse upon Ebal" (Keil and Delitzsch, Commentary, 1:3:349–50).

31 For ye shall pass over Jordan to go in to possess the land which the LORD your God giveth you, and ye shall possess it, and dwell therein.

32 And **ye shall observe to do all the statutes and judgments which I set before you this day.**

DEUTERONOMY 12

Selection: all verses

THIS CHAPTER IS the beginning of the last portion of Moses' second discourse (given shortly before he was translated and taken up) as contained in chapters 12–26 (see General Background for Deuteronomy in this study guide). This part of his second discourse or sermon is described in the Bible Dictionary, under "Deuteronomy," as follows:

"**The second discourse** (chs. 5–26) consists of two parts: **(1)** 5–11, the Ten Commandments and a practical exposition of them, **(2)** 12–26, **a code of laws**, which forms the nucleus of the whole book. The first group of laws deals with **the ritual of religion** and begins with a command to destroy all idolatrous objects of worship in Canaan; **only one central place for worship** of Jehovah is to be allowed. Then follow special instances of **enticement to false worship** and **rules about food** and about **tithe**. Then we have **the law of debt**, directions about **firstlings**, and a **calendar of festivals**. The next group of laws deals with **the administration of justice**, while **the last group regulates private and social rights**."

In other words, these fifteen chapters deal with day-to-day life among the children of Israel, and the laws, rules, and regulations of the Law of Moses that would provide stability and growth in their society if they would but abide by them.

With the background you have from studying Exodus through Deuteronomy 11 in this study guide, we will invite you to quickly read the **bolded** words and phrases in chapters 12–13. Hopefully, you will be encouraged by how much you understand. The bolded portions will provide a general understanding of the counsel and instruction that Moses gave to his people during this part of his second sermon to them, shortly before they entered the promised land, the land of Canaan.

Second Discourse, Part 2

(Deuteronomy 12–26)

1 These *are* the statutes [*commandments*] **and judgments** [*laws*], **which ye shall observe to do** in the land, which the LORD God of thy fathers giveth thee to possess it, all the days that ye live upon the earth.

2 Ye shall utterly destroy all the places, wherein the nations which ye shall possess served their gods [*worshipped their false gods*], upon the high mountains, and upon the hills, and under every green tree:

3 And ye shall **overthrow their altars**, and **break their pillars**, and **burn their groves** [*where sexual immorality took place in conjunction with idol worship*] with fire; and ye shall **hew down the graven images of their gods**, and **destroy the names of them** out of that place.

4 Ye shall not do so unto the LORD your God [*you must not worship the Lord the way they worshipped their false gods*].

5 But unto the place [*you are to have a central location in which to worship Jehovah; Jerusalem will be the place*] **which the LORD your God shall choose** out of all your tribes to put his name there, *even* unto his habitation shall ye seek, and **thither thou shalt come:**

6 And thither ye shall bring your burnt offerings, and your sacrifices, and your tithes, and heave offerings of your hand, and your vows, and your freewill offerings, and the firstlings of your herds and of your flocks:

7 And there ye shall eat before the LORD your God, and ye shall rejoice in all that ye put your hand unto, ye and your households, wherein the LORD thy God hath blessed thee.

8 Ye shall not do after all *the things* **that we do here this day, every man whatsoever** *is* **right in his own eyes.**

9 For ye are not as yet come to the rest and to the inheritance, which the LORD your God giveth you.

10 But *when* **ye go over Jordan, and dwell in the land which the LORD your God giveth you** to inherit, and *when* he giveth you rest from all your enemies round about, so that ye dwell in safety;

11 Then there shall be a place [*Jerusalem*] **which the LORD your God shall choose** to cause his name to dwell there; thither shall ye bring all that I command you; your burnt offerings, and your sacrifices, your tithes, and the heave offering of your hand, and all your choice vows which ye vow unto the LORD:

12 And ye shall rejoice before the LORD your God, ye, and your sons, and your daughters, and your menservants, and your maidservants, and the Levite that *is* within your gates; forasmuch as he hath no part nor inheritance with you [*the Levites did not have one land in which to settle; rather, they were spread throughout the Holy Land, placed in each city, in order to serve the people with their priesthood*].

Next, you can see that they were to have a "centralized" church.

13 Take heed to thyself that thou offer not thy burnt offerings in every place that thou seest:

14 But in the place [*where the Tabernacle is located, see Leviticus 17:4–5*] **which the LORD shall choose** in one of thy tribes, there thou shalt offer thy burnt offerings, and **there thou shalt do all that I command thee.**

15 Notwithstanding thou mayest kill and eat flesh in all thy gates [*you can slaughter your animals for eating, as long as they are not being used for burnt offerings to the Lord*], whatsoever thy soul lusteth after [*"desires"; in this case, "lust" does not have an evil connotation*], according to the blessing of the LORD thy God which he hath given thee: the unclean and the clean may eat thereof, as of the roebuck [*gazelle*], and as of the hart [*male deer*].

16 Only **ye shall not eat the blood;** ye shall pour it upon the earth as water.

> Next, they are reminded of what they were told above: they are not to eat grain or animals anywhere they want if those things are to be used as offerings to the Lord. Rather, they are to bring them to the centralized worship location.
>
> Perhaps you can see that the Lord is trying to get these people used to a centralized church.

17 ¶ **Thou mayest not eat within thy gates** [*in your own homes and fields*] **the tithe** [*offerings*] of thy corn [*grain*], or of thy wine, or of thy oil, **or the firstlings of thy herds** or of thy flock, **nor any of thy vows** which thou vowest, **nor thy freewill offerings** [*donations and offerings to the Lord*], or heave offering of thine hand:

18 But thou must eat them before the LORD thy God in the place which the LORD thy God shall choose, thou, and thy son, and thy daughter, and thy manservant, and thy maidservant, and the Levite that *is* within thy gates: and thou shalt rejoice before the LORD thy God in all that thou puttest thine hands unto.

19 Take heed to thyself that thou forsake not the Levite as long as thou livest upon the earth [*the Levites received their livelihood from the offerings brought to the Lord by the people; that is how they took care of their families and their own physical needs*].

20 ¶ When the LORD thy God shall enlarge thy border, as he hath promised thee, and thou shalt say, I will eat flesh, because thy soul longeth to eat flesh; thou mayest eat flesh, whatsoever thy soul lusteth after [*whatever you desire; again, the word "lust" as used here by the King James translators, merely denotes desire, whereas the word today carries a negative connotation*].

> Next, provision is made for those who live too far from Jerusalem to bring their sacrifices there.

21 If the place which the LORD thy God hath chosen to put his name there **be too far from thee**, then thou shalt kill of thy herd and of thy flock, which the LORD hath given thee, as I have commanded thee, and **thou shalt eat in thy gates whatsoever thy soul lusteth after.**

22 Even as the roebuck and the hart is eaten, so thou shalt eat them: the unclean and the clean shall eat *of* them alike.

23 Only be sure that thou eat not the blood: for the blood *is* the life; and thou mayest not eat the life with the flesh.

24 Thou shalt not eat it; thou shalt

pour it upon the earth as water.

25 Thou shalt not eat it; that it may go well with thee, and with thy children after thee, when thou shalt do *that which is* right in the sight of the LORD.

26 Only thy holy things [*things to be used for offerings to the Lord*] **which thou hast**, and thy vows, **thou shalt take, and go unto the place which the LORD shall choose:**

27 And **thou shalt offer thy burnt offerings, the flesh and the blood, upon the altar of the LORD** thy God: and the blood of thy sacrifices shall be poured out upon the altar of the LORD thy God, and thou shalt eat the flesh.

28 Observe and hear all these words which I command thee, that it may go well with thee, and with thy children after thee for ever, when thou doest *that which is* good and right in the sight of the LORD thy God.

Major Message

Don't get trapped in the wicked ways of the world.

29 ¶ When the LORD thy God shall cut off the nations from before thee, whither thou goest to possess them, and thou succeedest them, and dwellest in their land;

30 Take heed to thyself that thou be not snared by following them, after that they be destroyed from before thee; and that thou enquire not after their gods, saying, How did these nations serve their gods? even so will I do likewise.

31 Thou shalt not do so unto the LORD thy God: for **every abomination to the LORD, which he hateth, have they done** unto their gods; for even their sons and their daughters they have burnt in the fire to their gods.

Major Message

Don't "edit" the word of the Lord, adding to it or taking from it according to your own whims or desires.

32 What thing soever I command you, observe to do it: thou shalt not add thereto, nor diminish from it.

DEUTERONOMY 13

Selection: all verses

AS MOSES CONTINUES this second of three "farewell" sermons to his people, he points out the dangers of following false prophets, worshiping false gods, and giving in to people who persuade us to do so.

If it were not such a dangerous thing to our eternal souls to follow unrighteous peer pressure, in whatever form, the instructions given in chapter 13 to the children of Israel would sound too harsh. But the eternal worth of a soul is of highest concern to the Lord.

1 If there arise among you a prophet [*a false prophet*], or a dreamer of dreams, and **giveth thee a sign or a wonder,**

2 And the sign or the wonder come to pass, whereof he spake unto thee, **saying, Let us go after other gods**, which thou hast not known, and let us serve them;

3 **Thou shalt not hearken unto the words of that prophet, or that dreamer** of dreams: for the LORD your God proveth [*is testing*] you, to know whether ye love the LORD your God with all your heart and with all your soul.

4 **Ye shall walk after the LORD your God**, and fear him, and keep his commandments, and obey his voice, and ye shall serve him, and cleave unto him.

5 **And that prophet, or that dreamer of dreams, shall be put to death; because he hath spoken to turn *you* away from the LORD your God**, which brought you out of the land of Egypt, and redeemed you out of the house of bondage, to thrust thee out of the way which the LORD thy God commanded thee to walk in. **So shalt thou put the evil away from the midst of thee.**

6 ¶ **If thy brother, the son of thy mother, or thy son, or thy daughter, or the wife of thy bosom, or thy friend,** which *is* as thine own soul, **entice thee secretly, saying, Let us go and serve other gods,** which thou hast not known, thou, nor thy fathers;

7 *Namely,* of the gods of the people which *are* round about you, nigh unto thee, or far off from thee, from the *one* end of the earth even unto the *other* end of the earth;

8 **Thou shalt not consent unto him,** nor hearken unto him; neither shall thine eye pity him, neither shalt thou spare, neither shalt thou conceal him:

9 But **thou shalt surely kill him;** thine hand shall be first upon him to put him to death, and afterwards the hand of all the people.

10 And **thou shalt stone him with stones, that he die; because he hath sought to thrust thee away from the LORD** thy God, which brought thee out of the land of Egypt, from the house of bondage.

11 **And all Israel shall hear, and fear, and shall do no more any such wickedness as this is among you.**

12 ¶ **If thou shalt** hear *say* in one of thy cities, which the LORD thy God hath given thee to dwell there, saying,

13 *Certain* men, the children of Belial [*a general term for the wicked*], are gone out from among you, and have withdrawn the inhabitants of their city, saying, **Let us go and serve other gods**, which ye have not known;

14 Then shalt thou enquire, and make search, and ask diligently; and, behold, *if it be* truth, *and* the thing certain, *that* such abomination is wrought among you;

15 Thou shalt surely smite the inhabitants of that city with the edge of the sword, destroying it utterly, and all that *is* therein, and the cattle thereof, with the edge of the sword.

16 And thou shalt gather all the spoil [*loot, their goods and belongings*] **of it into the midst of the street thereof, and shalt burn with fire the city, and all the spoil thereof** every whit, for the LORD thy God: and it shall be an heap for ever; it shall not be built again.

> Did you notice that they were also to burn all the stuff of the inhabitants rather than keep it for themselves? This protected against falsely accusing and destroying of people for personal gain.

17 And there shall cleave nought of the cursed thing to thine hand [*none of their possessions are to be found in your possession*]: that the LORD may turn from the fierceness of his anger, and shew thee mercy, and have compassion upon thee, and multiply thee, as he hath sworn unto thy fathers;

18 When thou shalt hearken to the voice of the LORD thy God, to keep all his commandments which I command thee this day, to do *that which is* right in the eyes of the LORD thy God.

DEUTERONOMY 14–26

Selections: 14:21; 18:10–12, 15; 23:17–18; 24:5; 25:2–3

BECAUSE OF SPACE limitations for this study guide, we will point out just a few selections between here and Moses' third discourse, which will begin in chapter 27. You are invited to read chapters 14–26 in your own Bible, paying attention to the helps given in footnotes. You will see many laws and rules given by the Lord in order to help and educate these people to separate themselves from the wicked ways of the world. As indicated previously, many of these laws may seem harsh and unreasonable to modern readers. But with an understanding of the background of the children of Israel at this time in history, one can see that the Lord worked with them as they were, culturally as well as religiously. He began at that point to bring them to the point that they could accept the higher laws of the gospel of Jesus Christ, which is the "great plan of happiness" (Alma 42:8).

The JST makes a big difference for chapter 14, verse 21 (footnotes 21a and b in your LDS Bible), which, as it stands in the Bible, sounds like the Lord was giving the Israelites permission to give poisonous carcass meat to unsuspecting victims.

Deuteronomy 14:21

21 ¶ Ye shall not eat *of* any thing that dieth of itself: **thou shalt give it unto the stranger** that *is* in thy gates, that he may eat it; **or thou mayest sell it unto an alien** [*foreigner*]: for thou *art* an holy people unto the LORD thy God. Thou shalt not seethe a kid in his mother's milk.

> #### JST Deuteronomy 14:21
> 21 Ye shall not eat of any thing that dieth of itself; thou shalt **not** give it unto the stranger that is in thy gates, that he may eat it; or thou mayest **not** sell it unto an alien; for thou art a holy people unto the Lord thy God. Thou shalt not seethe a kid in his mother's milk.

In the next selection, we see Moses giving strict instructions against child sacrifice and engaging in the occult. The fact that he has to give such laws reminds us of the low spiritual condition of many of these people.

Deuteronomy 18:10–12

10 There shall not be found among you *any one* that maketh his son or his daughter to pass through the fire [*none of you should sacrifice your children to fire gods, such as Molech—see Bible Dictionary, under "Molech"*], or that useth divination, or an observer of times, or an enchanter, or a witch,

11 Or a charmer, or a consulter with familiar spirits [*such as fortune tellers consulting with the dead*], or a wizard, or a necromancer [*you are commanded to stay away from the occult and black magic*].

12 For all that do these things *are* an abomination unto the LORD: and because of these abominations the LORD thy God doth drive them out from before thee.

> In the next selection, Moses prophesies of Christ. If the Jews at the time of the Savior's mortal mission had been willing to understand this prophecy of Christ given by Moses, they would have accepted Jesus as the Messiah. Instead, they claimed that Jesus was going against their greatest prophet, Moses, and sought every possible way to destroy Him.

Deuteronomy 18:15

15 ¶ The LORD thy God will raise up unto thee a Prophet [*Christ*] from the midst of thee, of thy brethren, like unto me; unto him ye shall hearken;

> The next two verses we will mention give you an idea of how depraved the nations in Canaan had become. When a nation or society accepts these sins, they are approaching the point of being ripe for destruction—in other words, "ripe in iniquity."

Deuteronomy 23:17–18

17 ¶ There shall be no whore [*prostitute*] of the daughters of Israel, **nor** a **sodomite** [*homosexual*] of the sons of Israel.

> In verse 18 Moses tells his people, in effect, that they may not pay tithing on wages earned as prostitutes.

18 **Thou shalt not bring the hire** [*wages*] **of a whore, or the price of a dog** [*the wages earned by a male homosexual prostitute—see Luther A. Weigle,* The Living Word, *page 54*], **into the house of the LORD** thy God **for any vow:** for even both these *are* abomination unto the LORD thy God.

> One of the laws Moses gave to his people was that newlyweds were to be given time off for a one-year honeymoon.

Deuteronomy 24:5

5 ¶ **When a man hath taken a new wife**, he shall not go out to war, neither shall he be charged with any business: but **he shall be free at home one year**, and shall cheer up his wife which he hath taken.

> Perhaps you recall that the Apostle Paul recounted that he had been flogged five times by the Jews, and that each whipping involved "forty stripes save one" (see 2 Corinthians 11:24). In other words, he had been beaten five times with thirty-nine lashes each time. Why thirty-nine? The answer needs to include the following verses in Deuteronomy:

Deuteronomy 25:2–3

2 And it shall be, **if the wicked man** *be* **worthy to be beaten**, that the judge shall cause him to lie down, and to be beaten before his face [*in the presence of the judge*], according to his fault, by a certain number.

3 **Forty stripes he may give him,** *and* **not exceed:** lest, *if* he should exceed, and beat him above these with many stripes, then thy brother should seem vile unto thee.

> One of the laws developed by the Jewish elders over the years was that a person could only receive thirty-nine lashes for fear that they might miscount and go over the forty prescribed in the Law of Moses.

Third Discourse

Deuteronomy 27–30

WE WILL NOW look at the third and final discourse given by Moses before he was translated (in other words, taken up into heaven without dying—see 3 Nephi 28 for details about the Three Nephites, who were likewise translated). After he is taken up, Joshua will lead the Israelites across the Jordan River into the promised land, the land of Canaan.

Moses is now 120 years old. As a translated being, he will minister to the Savior about six months before His crucifixion (Matthew 17:1–3). He will be resurrected with the Savior (Doctrine and Covenants 133:54–55) and will appear to Joseph Smith and Oliver Cowdery in the Kirtland Temple as a resurrected being (Doctrine and Covenants 110:11).

DEUTERONOMY 27

Selection: all verses

IN THIS DISCOURSE, consisting of chapters 27–30, Moses will invite his people to renew their covenants with the Lord and warn them of the consequences of failing to do so. As you will see, he does this in the format of blessings and cursings—blessings for keeping the commandments and cursings (or punishments) for failing to do so. Blessings come through the law of mercy and the Atonement of Christ. Cursings come through the law of justice, which demands that the penalties

for unrepented sin be placed upon the sinner, as explained in Doctrine and Covenants 19:15–17.

1 And **Moses** with the elders of Israel **commanded** the people, saying, **Keep all the commandments** which I command you this day.

Next, Moses instructs the Israelites to build a large altar of uncut stones (symbolizing the hand of the Lord rather than the hand of man) when they cross the Jordan River into the land of Canaan. They are to plaster it and write the words of the Lord given to him upon it.

2 And it shall be on the day **when** ye shall **pass over Jordan unto the land** [*the promised land*] which the LORD thy God giveth thee, that thou shalt **set** thee **up great stones** [*big rocks*], **and plaister them** with plaister:

3 And thou shalt **write upon them all the words of this law**, when thou art passed over, that thou mayest go in unto the land which the LORD thy God giveth thee, a land that floweth with milk and honey; as the LORD God of thy fathers hath promised thee.

4 Therefore it shall be **when ye be gone over Jordan**, *that* ye shall **set up these stones**, which I command you this day, in mount Ebal, **and** thou shalt **plaister them** with plaister.

5 And there shalt thou **build an altar** unto the LORD thy God, an altar of stones: thou shalt not lift up *any* iron *tool* upon them [*the stones used to build the altar must be completely natural, not hand-cut or chiseled*].

6 Thou shalt build the altar of the LORD thy God **of whole stones: and** thou shalt **offer burnt offerings thereon unto the LORD** thy God:

7 And thou shalt **offer peace offerings, and** shalt **eat** there, **and rejoice** before the LORD thy God.

8 And thou shalt **write upon the stones all the words of this law very plainly.**

Next, the people are specifically invited to renew their covenants with the Lord. You will once again be reminded that the Israelite society is riddled with evil and perversion.

9 ¶ And **Moses and the priests** the Levites **spake unto all Israel,** saying, Take heed, and hearken, O Israel; **this day thou art become the people of the LORD thy God** [*today you are renewing your covenant to be the Lord's covenant Israel*].

10 Thou shalt **therefore obey the voice of the LORD** thy God, and **do his commandments and his statutes,** which I command thee this day.

Next, beginning with verse 11, Moses instructs six of the tribes of Israel, after they cross the Jordan, to gather on Mount Gerizim. He instructs the other six tribes to gather on Mount Ebal. (Refer to the note following Deuteronomy 11:30 in this study guide for more about these two mountains and the symbolism involved here). Imagine the excitement and drama as Moses tells them what they are to say in this ceremony as they dramatize the principle of blessings and cursings from the Lord!

11 ¶ And **Moses charged** [*commanded*] **the people** the same day, **saying,**

12 These [*the people who belong to these tribes*] **shall stand upon mount Gerizim to bless** [*to symbolize the many blessings which will come through obedience to the Lord's commandments*] **the people,** when ye are come over Jordan; **Simeon,** and **Levi,** and **Judah,** and **Issachar,** and **Joseph,** and **Benjamin:**

13 And these [*tribes*] **shall stand upon mount Ebal to curse** [*to represent the many cursings or punishments that will come if you are disobedient*]; **Reuben, Gad,** and **Asher,** and **Zebulun, Dan,** and **Naphtali.**

Next, we see the script for the ceremony. Notice how dramatic and forceful it would be, at the end of each commitment, to hear all the people in unison say "amen," which means, "we agree."

14 ¶ And the Levites shall speak, and say unto all the men of Israel with a loud voice,

15 Cursed *be* the man that maketh *any* graven or molten image [*in other words, who makes and worships idols*], an abomination unto the LORD, the work of the hands of the craftsman, and putteth *it* in *a* secret *place*. And all the people shall answer and say, Amen.

16 Cursed *be* he that setteth light by his father or his mother [*in other words, who dishonors or disgraces his parents—see footnote 16a in your Bible*]. And all the people shall say, Amen.

17 Cursed *be* he that removeth his neighbour's landmark [*boundary markers for his property*]. And all the people shall say, Amen.

18 Cursed *be* he that maketh the blind to wander out of the way [*who deliberately torments a blind person by leading him astray from his intended destination*]. And all the people shall say, Amen.

19 Cursed *be* he that perverteth the judgment of the stranger, fatherless, and widow [*who deliberately preys upon the weak and defenseless*]. And all the people shall say, Amen.

20 Cursed *be* he that lieth with his father's wife [*who commits incest*]; because he uncovereth his father's skirt. And all the people shall say, Amen.

21 Cursed *be* he that lieth with any manner of beast [*who commits sexual acts with animals*]. And all the people shall say, Amen.

22 Cursed *be* he that lieth with his sister, the daughter of his father, or the daughter of his mother [*in other words, incest*]. And all the people shall say, Amen.

23 Cursed *be* he that lieth with his mother in law [*another form of incest*]. And all the people shall say, Amen.

24 Cursed *be* he that smiteth his neighbour secretly [*commits terrorist acts*]. And all the people shall say, Amen.

25 Cursed *be* he that taketh reward [*accepts bribes or payment*] to slay an innocent person. And all the people shall say, Amen.

26 Cursed *be* he that confirmeth not *all* the words of this law to do them [*who fails to keep this covenant with the Lord*]. And all the people shall say, Amen.

Moses uses comparison and contrast to teach more about blessings and cursings.

You may wish to put "blessings and cursings" at the beginning of chapter 28 or at the top of that page in your Bible.

DEUTERONOMY 28

Selection: all verses

THIS CHAPTER IS a continuation of chapter 27 and is the second of four chapters recording Moses's final discourse or sermon to his people before he was translated and taken up. See Background to chapter 27 for more details. This chapter can be divided into two main topics, "blessings" for obedience to the laws and commandments of the Lord and "cursings" for disobedience and rebellion.

BLESSINGS

1 And it shall come to pass, **if thou shalt hearken diligently unto the voice of the LORD** thy God, to observe *and* to **do all his commandments** which I command thee this day, that the LORD thy **God will set thee on high above all nations of the earth** [*you will be the most highly blessed of all people on earth*]:

2 And all these blessings shall come on thee, and overtake thee, if thou shalt hearken unto the voice of the LORD thy God.

3 Blessed *shalt* thou *be* in the city, and **blessed** *shalt* thou *be* in the field.

4 Blessed *shall be* the fruit of thy body [*your children*], and the fruit of thy ground, and the fruit of thy cattle, the increase of thy kine, and the flocks of thy sheep.

5 Blessed *shall be* thy basket and thy store.

6 Blessed *shalt* thou *be* when thou comest in, and **blessed** *shalt* thou *be* when thou goest out.

7 The LORD shall cause thine enemies that rise up against thee to be smitten** before thy face: they shall come out against thee one way, and flee before thee seven ways.

8 The LORD shall command the **blessing** upon thee in thy storehouses, and in all that thou settest thine hand unto; and he shall **bless** thee in the land which the LORD thy God giveth thee.

9 The LORD shall establish thee an holy people unto himself, as he hath sworn unto thee, if thou shalt keep the commandments of the LORD thy God, and walk in his ways.

10 And **all people of the earth** shall see that thou art called by the name of the LORD; and they **shall be afraid of thee.**

11 And the LORD shall make thee **plenteous in goods,** in the **fruit of thy body,** and in the fruit of thy **cattle,** and in the fruit of thy **ground,** in the land which the LORD sware unto thy fathers to give thee.

12 The LORD shall open unto thee

his good treasure, the heaven to give the **rain** unto thy land in his season, and to bless all the work of thine hand: and **thou shalt lend unto many nations, and thou shalt not borrow.**

13 And the LORD shall make thee the head, and not the tail; and thou shalt be above only, and thou shalt not be beneath; if that thou hearken unto the commandments of the LORD thy God, which I command thee this day, to observe and to do *them*:

14 And thou shalt not go aside from any of the words which I command thee this day, *to the* **right hand, or** *to* **the left**, to go after other gods to serve them.

CURSINGS

15 ¶ But it shall come to pass, **if thou wilt not hearken unto the voice of the LORD** thy God, to observe to do all his commandments and his statutes which I command thee this day; that all these curses shall come upon thee, and overtake thee:

16 Cursed *shalt* thou *be* in the city, and **cursed** *shalt* thou *be* in the field.

17 Cursed *shall be* thy basket and thy store.

18 Cursed *shall be* the fruit of thy body, and the fruit of thy land, the increase of thy kine, and the flocks of thy sheep.

19 Cursed *shalt* thou *be* when thou comest in, and **cursed** *shalt* thou *be* when thou goest out.

20 The LORD shall send upon thee **cursing**, **vexation**, and **rebuke**, in all that thou settest thine hand unto for to do, **until thou be destroyed**, and until thou perish quickly; **because of** the **wickedness** of thy doings, whereby thou hast forsaken me.

21 The LORD shall make the **pestilence** cleave unto thee, until he have consumed thee from off the land, whither thou goest to possess it.

22 The LORD shall smite thee with a **consumption** [*devastating disease*], and with a **fever**, and with an **inflammation**, and with an **extreme burning** [*heat and drought*], and with the **sword** [*military conquest*], and with **blasting** [*crop blight*], and with **mildew**; and they shall pursue thee until thou perish.

23 And thy **heaven** that *is* over thy head **shall be brass** [*your prayers and cries will not get the response you desire from heaven; also can mean no rain, just heat and drought*], and the **earth** that *is* under thee *shall be* **iron** [*unyielding to your needs; the ground will be too hard to plow*].

24 The LORD shall make the rain of **thy land powder and dust**: from heaven shall it come down upon thee, **until thou be destroyed.**

25 The LORD shall cause thee to be **smitten before thine enemies:** thou shalt go out one way against them, and flee seven ways before them: and shalt be removed into all the kingdoms of the earth.

26 And **thy carcase shall be meat** [*food*] **unto all fowls of the air, and unto the beasts of the earth,** and no man shall fray [*frighten*] *them* away.

27 The LORD will smite thee with the botch [*boils*] of Egypt, and with the **emerods** [*hemorrhoids or tumors*], and with the **scab**, and with the **itch**, whereof thou canst not be healed.

28 The LORD shall smite thee with **madness,** and **blindness,** and **astonishment of heart** [*you will be amazed at how bad it can get if you desert the Lord*]:

29 And **thou shalt grope at noon-day, as the blind gropeth in darkness,** and thou shalt **not prosper** in thy ways: and **thou shalt be only oppressed** and **spoiled** [*ravished, decimated*] evermore, and no man shall save *thee*.

30 Thou shalt betroth a wife, and another man shall lie with her: thou shalt **build an house, and** thou shalt **not dwell therein** [*because*

someone else will take it from you by force*]: thou shalt **plant a vineyard, and** shalt **not gather the grapes thereof.**

31 Thine ox *shall be* **slain** before thine eyes, and thou shalt not eat thereof: thine **ass** *shall be* **violently taken away** from before thy face, and shall not be restored to thee: thy **sheep** *shall be* **given unto thine enemies,** and thou shalt have none to rescue *them*.

32 Thy sons and thy daughters *shall be* **given unto another people** [*slavery*], and thine eyes shall look, and fail *with longing* for them all the day long: and **there** *shall be* **no might in thine hand** [*you will be powerless to stop all this*].

33 The fruit of thy land, and all thy labours, shall a nation which thou knowest not eat up [*enemies from far away will invade and take your resources*]; and thou shalt be only oppressed and crushed alway:

34 So that **thou shalt be mad for the sight of thine eyes which thou shalt see** [*you will be driven crazy by what you see but cannot remedy*].

35 The LORD shall smite thee in the knees, and in the legs, with a sore botch that cannot be healed, **from the sole of thy foot unto the top of thy head** [*in other words, everything that can go wrong will go wrong*].

In verses 36–48, next, Moses prophesies that, if Israel chooses disobedience, a major cursing will come in the form of being scattered throughout the world. This will be accompanied by economic disaster.

36 The LORD shall bring thee, and thy king which thou shalt set over thee, **unto a nation which neither thou nor thy fathers have known;** and there shalt thou serve other gods, wood and stone.

37 And **thou shalt become an astonishment** [*an object of pity and horror*], **a proverb** [*an object of scorn*], and **a byword** [*an object of ridicule*], **among all nations whither the LORD shall lead thee.**

38 Thou shalt carry much seed out into the field, and shalt gather *but* **little in** [*you will have crop failure*]; **for the locust shall consume it.**

39 Thou shalt plant vineyards, and dress [*take care of*] *them,* **but shalt neither drink** *of* **the wine, nor gather** *the* **grapes;** for the worms shall eat them.

40 Thou shalt have olive trees throughout all thy coasts [*the borders of your land*], **but thou shalt not anoint** *thyself* **with the oil** [*you won't have olive oil to use*]; for thine olive shall cast [*prematurely drop*] *his fruit.*

41 Thou shalt beget sons and daughters, but thou shalt not enjoy them; for they shall go into captivity.

42 All thy trees and fruit of thy land shall the locust consume.

43 The stranger that *is* **within thee shall get up above thee very high** [*invading armies will succeed against you*]; **and thou shalt come down very low** [*you will be conquered*].

44 He shall lend to thee, and thou shalt not lend to him: **he shall be the head, and thou shalt be the tail** [*foreigners will control your finances and politics*].

45 Moreover **all these curses shall come upon thee, and shall pursue thee, and overtake thee, till thou be destroyed; because thou hearkenedst not unto the voice of the LORD thy God, to keep his commandments and his statutes which he commanded thee:**

46 And they shall be upon thee for a sign and for a wonder, and upon thy seed for ever.

47 Because thou servedst not the LORD thy God with joyfulness, and with **gladness of heart,** for the abundance of all *things* [*when things were going well for you*];

48 Therefore shalt thou serve thine enemies which the LORD shall send against thee, **in hunger,**

and in **thirst**, and in **nakedness**, and in **want** of all *things*: and **he shall put a yoke of iron** [*bondage*] **upon thy neck, until he have destroyed thee.**

> If the children of Israel choose disobedience to the Lord, they will be conquered by invading armies. Among these invaders, historically, were the Assyrians, Babylonians, and Romans. Verses 49–52 prophesy of invaders and terrible conditions that will come upon the people because of apostasy.

49 The LORD shall bring a nation against thee from far, from the end of the earth, *as swift as the eagle flieth* [*they will come swooping down on you like an eagle upon its prey*]; a nation **whose tongue** [*language*] **thou shalt not understand;**

50 A nation of fierce countenance [*which will appear very frightening*], **which shall not regard** [*have sympathy for*] the person of **the old, nor** shew favour to **the young:**

51 And he shall eat the fruit of thy cattle [*will destroy your herds*], **and the fruit of thy land** [*your crops*], **until thou be destroyed**: which *also* shall not leave thee *either* corn, wine, or oil, *or* the increase of thy kine, or flocks of thy sheep, until he have destroyed thee.

52 And he shall besiege thee in all thy gates [*everywhere you live*], until thy high and fenced walls

come down, wherein thou trustedst, **throughout all thy land**: and he shall besiege thee in all thy gates throughout all thy land, which the LORD thy God hath given thee.

> In verses 53–57, the people are warned that if they choose disobedience and apostasy, they will be brought down so low that they will ultimately resort to cannibalism. These verses are terribly unpleasant, to say the least.

53 And thou shalt eat the fruit of thine own body, the flesh of thy sons and of thy daughters, which the LORD thy God hath given thee, **in the siege**, and in the straitness [*dire straits*], wherewith thine enemies shall distress thee [*this happened during the Roman siege of Jerusalem—see Josephus, Wars of the Jews, book 5, chapter 10, paragraphs 1–5; chapter 13, paragraph 7, book 6, chapter 3, paragraph 2*]:

54 So that the man *that is* **tender among you, and very delicate** [*even the most sensitive and compassionate man among you*], **his eye shall be evil toward his brother,** and toward the **wife** of his bosom, and toward the remnant of his **children** which he shall leave:

55 So that he will not give to any of them of the flesh of his children whom he shall eat: because he hath nothing left him in the siege, and in the straitness, wherewith thine enemies shall distress thee in all thy gates.

56 The tender and delicate woman among you, which would not adventure to set the sole of her foot upon the ground for delicateness and tenderness, **her eye shall be evil toward the husband** of her bosom, and toward her **son,** and toward her **daughter,**

57 And toward her young one that cometh out from between her feet [*her newborn baby*], and toward her children which she shall bear: for **she shall eat them for want of all** *things* **secretly in the siege** and straitness [*the terrible circumstances*], wherewith thine enemy shall distress thee in thy gates.

Major Message

Although wickedness may have its initial appeal, the end results of violating God's commandments are vile, repulsive, and devastating.

Verses 58–68 give a strong message that the ultimate end of gross wickedness is extreme misery.

58 If thou wilt not observe to do all the words of this law that are written in this book, that [*given so that*] **thou mayest fear this glorious and fearful name, THE LORD THY GOD** [*the purpose of God's laws are to enable you to respect and honor the Lord, for your benefit and good*];

59 Then the LORD will make thy plagues wonderful [*extraordinary; beyond your ability to comprehend—see footnote 59b in your Bible*], **and the plagues of thy seed** [*the punishments upon your descendants who continue in your evil ways*], *even* **great plagues,** and **of long continuance,** and **sore** [*terrible*] **sicknesses,** and of long continuance.

60 Moreover **he will bring upon thee all the diseases** [*the ten plagues*] **of** Egypt, which thou wast afraid of; and they shall cleave unto thee [*stick to you*].

61 Also every sickness, and every plague, which *is* **not written in the book of this law,** them will the LORD bring upon thee, **until thou be destroyed.**

62 And ye shall be left few in number, whereas ye were as the stars of heaven for multitude; because thou wouldest not obey the voice of the LORD thy God.

63 And it shall come to pass, *that* **as the LORD rejoiced over you** [*just as it pleased the Lord*] **to do you good** [*to bless you*], and to multiply you; **so the LORD will rejoice over you** [*will be pleased to honor the law of justice, which will obligate Him*] **to destroy you,** and to bring you to nought; and ye shall be plucked from off the land whither thou goest to possess it.

The scattering of Israel.

64 And the LORD shall scatter thee among all people, from the one end of the earth even unto the other; and there thou shalt serve other gods, which neither thou nor thy fathers have known, *even* wood and stone.

65 And among these nations shalt thou find no ease, neither shall the sole of thy foot have rest [*you will not be at ease nor find a permanent home*]: but the LORD shall give thee there a trembling heart [*you will live in anxiousness and fear*], and failing of eyes [*your eyes will look for a permanent home, but you will not find it*], and sorrow of mind [*you will live with much despair*]:

66 And thy life shall hang in doubt before thee; and thou shalt fear day and night, and shalt have none assurance of thy life [*you will not know from one day to the next whether or not you will survive*]:

67 In the morning thou shalt say, Would God it were even [*evening*]! and at even thou shalt say, Would God it were morning! [*In other words you will dread the coming of daylight, and you will dread the coming of night*] for [*because of*] the fear of [*terror in*] thine heart wherewith thou shalt fear, and for the sight of thine eyes which thou shalt see [*and because of the things that you will see*].

68 And the LORD shall bring thee into Egypt [*symbolic of the wicked nations of the world*] again with ships [*symbolizing that they would be taken by force and could not escape*], by the way whereof I spake unto thee, Thou shalt see it no more again [*which the Lord promised would not happen again if you would be obedient*]: and there ye shall be sold unto your enemies for bondmen and bondwomen [*you will be in bondage in those nations*], and no man shall buy *you* [*no one will want you*].

DEUTERONOMY 29

Selection: all verses

THIS IS A continuation of Moses's final sermon to his people, before he is taken up. In verses 1–9, he reviews the obvious miracles and evidences that the Lord is with the Israelites, but they still don't get it. They don't recognize that they must be obedient in order to receive the Lord's blessings.

1 These *are* the words of the covenant, which the LORD commanded Moses to make with the children of Israel in the land of Moab, beside [*in addition to*] the covenant which he made with them in Horeb [*Sinai*].

2 ¶ And Moses called unto all Israel, and said unto them, Ye have seen all that the LORD did before your

eyes [*you are witnesses of the things the Lord did for you*] in the land of Egypt unto Pharaoh, and unto all his servants, and unto all his land;

3 The great temptations [*trials, troubles, plagues*] which thine eyes have seen, the signs, and those great miracles:

4 Yet the LORD hath not given you an heart to perceive, and eyes to see, and ears to hear, unto this day [*in other words, you still don't get it; you still are not spiritually perceptive enough to understand the importance of keeping the commandments*].

5 And I have led you forty years in the wilderness: your clothes are not waxen old [*have not grown old nor worn out*] upon you, and thy shoe is not waxen old upon thy foot [*you are still wearing the same clothes and shoes you wore forty years ago and they have not worn out—you have that obvious miracle but still don't understand what is going on*].

6 Ye have not eaten bread, neither have ye drunk wine or strong drink [*the Lord has fed you all these years with manna*]: that [*so that*] ye might know that I *am* the LORD your God.

7 And when ye came unto this place, Sihon the king of Heshbon, and Og the king of Bashan, came

out against us unto battle, and we smote them:

8 And we took their land, and gave it for an inheritance unto the Reubenites, and to the Gadites, and to the half tribe of Manasseh.

9 Keep therefore the words of this covenant [*this is why you should keep your covenant*], and do them, that ye may prosper in all that ye do.

> In verses 10–29, Moses explains the covenant his people must keep in order to prosper.

10 ¶ Ye stand this day all of you before the LORD your God; your captains of your tribes, your elders, and your officers, *with* all the men of Israel,

11 Your little ones, your wives, and thy stranger [*foreigner; non-Israelite*] that *is* in thy camp, from the hewer of thy wood unto the drawer of thy water:

12 That thou shouldest enter into covenant with the LORD thy God, and into his oath [*the Lord's part of the bargain; His promise to you*], which the LORD thy God maketh with thee this day:

> Moses explains the purpose of the covenant.

13 That he may establish thee to day for a people unto himself, and *that* he may be unto thee a God, as he hath said unto thee, and as

he hath sworn unto thy fathers, to Abraham, to Isaac, and to Jacob [*so that you can have the same blessings as Abraham, Isaac, and Jacob—they have become gods—see Doctrine and Covenants 132:37*].

A most important doctrine is seen in verses 14–15, namely that the covenant is available to all.

14 Neither with you only do I make this covenant and this oath;

15 But with *him* that standeth here with us this day before the LORD our God, **and also with *him* that *is* not here with us this day** [*it will ultimately be available to all people*]:

Next, Moses explains that the children of Israel should be wise enough to know that the lifestyles of wicked nations are to be avoided.

16 (For ye know how we have dwelt in the land of Egypt; and how we came through the nations which ye passed by;

17 And ye have seen their abominations, and their idols, wood and stone, silver and gold, which *were* among them:)

18 Lest there should be among you man, or woman, or family, or tribe, whose heart turneth away this day from the LORD our God [*the Lord has shown you all these other lifestyles as a warning*], to go *and*

serve the gods of these nations; lest there should be among you a root that beareth gall and wormwood [*a terribly bitter-tasting substance; in other words, lest you foolishly turn away from God and to the bitterness of wickedness*];

Major Message

The wicked do not think straight.

19 And it come to pass, when he heareth the words of this curse, that he bless himself in his heart, saying, I shall have peace, though I walk in the imagination of mine heart, to add drunkenness to thirst [*I can have peace even though I am wicked*]:

20 The LORD will not spare him, but then the anger of the LORD and his jealousy shall smoke against that man, and **all the curses that are written in this book shall lie upon him,** and the LORD shall blot out his name from under heaven [*he will be cut off from the people of the Lord on Judgment Day*].

21 And the LORD shall separate him unto evil out of all the tribes of Israel [*he will be cut off from covenant Israel*], according to all the curses of the covenant that are written in this book of the law:

After Israel is conquered and scattered, future nations will say that they were destroyed by the Lord because they were as wicked as Sodom and Gomorrah.

22 So that the generation to come of your children that shall rise up after you, **and the stranger** that shall come from a far land, **shall say,** when they see the plagues of that land, and the sicknesses which the LORD hath laid upon it;

23 *And that* the whole land thereof is brimstone, and salt, *and* burning, *that* it is not sown, nor beareth, nor any grass groweth therein, like the overthrow of Sodom, and Gomorrah, Admah, and Zeboim, which the LORD overthrew in his anger, and in his wrath:

24 Even all nations shall say, **Wherefore** [*why*] **hath the LORD done thus unto this land?** what *meaneth* the heat of this great anger?

25 Then men shall say [*the answer will be*], **Because they have forsaken the covenant of the LORD God** of their fathers, **which he made with them** when he brought them forth out of the land of Egypt:

26 For **they went and served other gods, and worshipped them**, gods whom they knew not, and *whom* he had not given unto them:

27 And **the anger of the LORD was kindled against this land**, to bring upon it all the curses that are written in this book:

28 And **the LORD rooted them out of their land** in anger, and in wrath, and in great indignation, and cast them into another land, as *it is* this day.

Major Message

There are plenty of mysteries that only the Lord knows, but He has given us plenty of evidence to convince us to keep His commandments.

29 The secret *things belong* **unto the LORD** our God: **but those** *things which are* revealed *belong* **unto us and to our children for ever, that** *we* **may do all the words of this law.**

DEUTERONOMY 30

Selection: all verses

IN THIS LAST chapter of his final sermon to the Israelites, Moses prophesies the gathering of Israel in the last days. We are part of its fulfillment and are watching its fulfillment accelerate in our day.

It is significant to note that Moses was the one to restore the keys to the gathering of Israel in these last days. He conferred them upon Joseph Smith and Oliver Cowdery in the Kirtland Temple on April 3, 1836 (Doctrine and Covenants 110:11).

1 And **it shall come to pass, when all these things are come upon thee** [*when you have been scattered* into all nations of the earth], the blessing and the curse, which I have set before thee, **and thou shalt call** them **to mind among all the nations, whither the LORD thy God hath driven thee,**

2 And shalt return unto the LORD thy God [*a major purpose of missionary work today*], and shalt obey his voice according to all that I command thee this day, thou and thy children, **with all thine heart, and with all thy soul;**

3 That **then the LORD thy God will turn** [*reverse, cancel, revoke*] **thy captivity,** and have compassion upon thee, **and will** return and **gather thee from all** the **nations,** whither the LORD thy God hath scattered thee.

4 If any **of thine be driven out unto the outmost** parts **of heaven** [*the farthest place on earth under the heavens*], **from thence will the LORD thy God gather thee,** and from thence will he fetch thee:

5 And **the LORD thy God will bring thee into the land which thy fathers possessed, and thou shalt possess it**; and he will do thee good, and multiply thee above thy fathers.

6 And the LORD thy God will circumcise thine heart [*bless you with a righteous heart; in other words, you will desire personal righteousness*],

and the heart of thy seed [*your children will also desire righteousness*], **to love the LORD thy God with all thine heart, and with all thy soul,** that thou mayest live.

7 And the LORD thy God will put all these curses upon thine enemies, and on them that hate thee, which persecuted thee.

8 And thou shalt return and obey the voice of the LORD, and do all his commandments which I command thee this day.

> In the last days, the Lord's covenant Israel (The Church of Jesus Christ of Latter-day Saints) will grow and prosper.

9 And the LORD thy God will make thee plenteous [*prosperous*] in every work of thine hand, in the fruit of thy body, and in the fruit of thy cattle, and in the fruit of thy land, for good: for the LORD will again rejoice over thee for good, as he rejoiced over thy fathers:

10 If thou shalt hearken unto the voice of the LORD thy God, **to keep his commandments and his statutes** which are written in this book of the law, **and if thou turn unto the LORD thy God with all thine heart, and with all thy soul.**

> Moses reminds his people that the commandments and words of the Lord are open, obvious, and readily available to them.

11 ¶ For **this commandment** which I command thee this day, it *is* **not hidden from thee**, neither *is* it far off.

12 **It** *is* **not in heaven, that thou shouldest say, Who shall go up for us to heaven, and bring it unto us, that we may hear it, and do it?**

13 **Neither** *is* **it beyond the sea**, that thou shouldest say, Who shall go over the sea for us, and bring it unto us, that we may hear it, and do it?

14 **But the word** *is* **very nigh** [*near*] unto thee, in thy mouth, and in thy heart, that thou mayest do it.

> Moses tells the people that the obvious and clear pros and cons of living the gospel are right in front of them.

15 ¶ **See, I have set before thee this day life and good, and death and evil** [*the blessings and cursings of living the gospel or rejecting it*];

16 **In that I command thee this day to love the LORD thy God, to walk in his ways,** and to keep his commandments and his statutes and his judgments, that thou mayest live and multiply: and the LORD thy God shall bless thee in the land whither thou goest to possess it.

17 **But if thine heart turn away,** so that thou wilt not hear, but shalt be drawn away, and worship other gods, and serve them;

18 **I denounce** unto **you** this day, that ye shall surely perish, *and that* ye shall not prolong *your* days upon the land, whither thou passest over Jordan to go to possess it.

> Moses stands as a witness that he has taught his people the word of God. They are now accountable.

19 **I call heaven and earth to record this day against you,** *that* **I have set before you life and death, blessing and cursing: therefore choose life, that both thou and thy seed may live:**

20 **That thou mayest love the LORD** thy God, *and* that thou mayest **obey his voice,** and that thou mayest **cleave unto him:** for **he** *is* **thy life** [*eternal life*], and the length of thy days: that thou mayest dwell in the land which the LORD sware unto thy fathers, to Abraham, to Isaac, and to Jacob, to give them.

DEUTERONOMY 31

Selection: all verses

SEVERAL THINGS HAPPEN in this chapter. Moses tells us that he is now 120 years old. Joshua is formally presented to succeed him as the leader of the children of Israel. Moses writes what is known as the "Song of Moses." He also writes the words of the law that he has been given and instructs that these writings be placed in the ark of the covenant.

One of the things in this chapter that stands out to those who are familiar with the Book of Mormon is the beginning phase of the cycle of apostasy. It is the cycle emphasized in the Book of Mormon in which **prosperity** leads to **pride**, which leads to **apostasy**, which leads to **destruction**. The next steps of the cycle (not mentioned in this chapter but which you have seen time and time again among these Israelites) are **humility**, **repentance**, **righteousness**, the **blessings** of the Lord, and then **prosperity** again, and the cycle starts all over.

Our opportunity and responsibility is to avoid the cycle ourselves by remaining humble and avoiding pride when we become prosperous.

1 And **Moses** went and **spake** these words unto all Israel.

2 And he said unto them, **I** *am* **an hundred and twenty years old** this day; I can no more go out and come in [*I can no longer be your leader*]: also the LORD hath said unto me, Thou shalt not go over this Jordan.

3 **The LORD** thy God, he **will go over before thee**, *and* he will destroy these nations from before thee, and thou shalt possess them: *and* **Joshua, he shall go over before thee** [*Joshua will now be your leader*], **as the LORD hath said.**

4 And the LORD shall do unto them as he did to Sihon and to Og, kings of the Amorites, and unto the land of them, whom he destroyed.

5 And the LORD shall give them up before your face, that ye may do unto them according unto all the commandments which I have commanded you.

6 **Be strong and of a good courage, fear not,** nor be afraid of them: **for the LORD thy God, he** *it is* **that doth go with thee; he will not fail thee, nor forsake thee.**

7 ¶ And **Moses called** unto **Joshua**, and said unto him in the sight of all Israel [*in front of all the people*], **Be strong and of a good courage:** for thou must go with this people unto the land which the LORD hath sworn unto their fathers to give them; and thou shalt cause them to inherit it.

8 And **the LORD**, he *it is* that doth go before thee; he **will be with thee**, he will not fail thee, neither forsake thee: fear not, neither be dismayed.

Moses writes down the laws, to be put in the ark of the covenant.

9 ¶ And **Moses wrote this law**, and delivered it unto the priests the sons of Levi, which bare the ark of the covenant of the LORD, and unto all the elders of Israel.

10 And Moses commanded them, saying, **At the end of** *every* **seven years**, in the solemnity of the year of release, in the feast of tabernacles,

11 When all Israel is come to appear before the LORD thy God in the place which he shall choose, **thou shalt read this law before all Israel in their hearing.**

12 Gather the people together, men, and women, and children, and thy stranger that *is* within thy gates, that they may hear, and **that they may learn, and fear the LORD your God, and observe to do all the words of this law:**

13 And *that* **their children, which have not known** *any thing,* **may hear, and learn to fear the LORD** your God, as long as ye live in the land whither ye go over Jordan to possess it.

Next, the Lord appears in a cloud to Moses and Joshua. Regarding the statement in verse 14, next, as well as elsewhere, that Moses will die, you may wish to read the note following Deuteronomy 34:6 in this study guide regarding the fact that he didn't die, rather was translated. One common speculation is that, at this point, it had not yet been revealed to Moses that he was to be translated. But it is mere speculation. Perhaps he can give us the facts when we see him during the Millennium.

14 ¶ And the LORD said unto Moses, Behold, thy days approach that thou must die [*he will be translated and taken up without tasting death—see Bible Dictionary, under "Moses"*]: **call Joshua, and present yourselves in the tabernacle** of the congregation, **that I may give him a charge** [*issue the call to him to lead Israel*]. And **Moses and Joshua went**, and presented themselves in the tabernacle of the congregation.

15 And **the LORD appeared** in the tabernacle **in a pillar of a cloud**: and the pillar of the cloud stood over the door of the tabernacle.

Next, Jehovah prophesies about Israel's behavior after Moses is taken from them.

16 ¶ And **the LORD said unto** Moses, Behold, thou shalt sleep with thy fathers; and **this people will rise up, and go a whoring after the gods of the strangers of the land** [*the Israelites will adopt the evil ways of the people they drive out of the promised land*], whither they go *to* be among them, **and will forsake me**, and **break my covenant** which I have made with them.

17 Then my anger shall be kindled against them in that day, and **I will forsake them** [*withdraw from them*], and I will **hide my face** from them, and **they shall be devoured,** and **many evils and troubles shall befall them**; so that **they will say** in that day, **Are not these evils come**

upon us, because our God *is* not among us?

Major Message

Wickedness drives the blessings of the Lord away.

18 And **I will surely hide my face** in that day **for** [*because of*] **all the evils which they shall have wrought,** in that they are turned unto other gods.

Next, Moses is instructed to write what is known as "the Song of Moses." A "song," in this context is a poetic or stylized rendition of emotions, feelings, facts, and doctrines praising God. The Song of Moses is recorded in Deuteronomy 32:1–43.

19 **Now therefore** [*because the Israelites will apostatize*] **write ye this song** for you, **and teach it the children of Israel:** put it in their mouths, that this song may be a witness for me against the children of Israel.

THE "CYCLE OF APOSTASY"

One of the messages of this "song" is that the cycle of apostasy will begin anew among the Israelites.

20 **For when I shall have brought them into the land** which I sware unto their fathers, that floweth with milk and honey [*which will bring prosperity*]; **and they shall have eaten and filled themselves, and waxen fat** [*will have grown prosperous*]; **then**

will they turn unto other gods, and serve them, and provoke me, **and break my covenant.**

21 **And it shall come to pass, when many evils and troubles are befallen them** [*destruction*], that **this song shall testify against them as a witness;** for it shall not be forgotten out of the mouths of their seed [*descendants*]: for I know their imagination [*the evils in their imaginations*] which they go about, even now, before I have brought them into the land which I sware.

22 ¶ **Moses therefore wrote this song** [*see chapter 32, verses 1–43*] **the same day, and taught it the children of Israel.**

Next, the Lord gives counsel to Joshua.

23 And he gave Joshua the son of Nun a charge, and said, **Be strong and of a good courage:** for thou shalt bring the children of Israel into the land which I sware [*promised*] unto them: and **I will be with thee.**

Next, in verses 24–26, Moses instructs the Levites to place the record that he has written into the ark of the covenant.

24 ¶ And it came to pass, **when Moses had made an end of writing the words of this law in a book,** until they were finished,

25 That **Moses commanded the Levites,** which bare [*who were*

assigned to carry] the ark of the covenant of the LORD, saying,

26 Take this book of the law, and put it in the side of the **ark of the covenant** of the LORD your God, that it may be there **for a witness against thee.**

> Next, Moses expresses his concern about pride among the people.

27 For I know thy rebellion, and thy stiff neck [*pride*]: **behold, while I am yet alive with you this day, ye have been rebellious against the LORD;** and **how much more after my death?**

> Next, we see that all the Israelites were to be warned against apostasy and that the heaven and earth were called to witness that they were duly warned.

28 ¶ Gather unto me all the elders [*leaders*] of your tribes, and your officers, **that I may speak these words in their ears, and call heaven and earth to record against them.**

29 For I know that after my death ye will utterly corrupt *yourselves*, and turn aside from the way which I have commanded you; **and evil will befall you** in the latter days [*later on*]; **because ye will do evil in the sight of the LORD,** to provoke him to anger through the work of your hands.

30 And Moses spake in the ears of all the congregation of Israel **the words of this song**, until they were ended [*until he had finished reciting the whole thing*].

DEUTERONOMY 32

Selection: all verses

IN DEUTERONOMY 31:19 Moses was instructed to write a "song." A "song," in this context, is a literary structure, in a sense a poetic structure, in which an author presents the thoughts of his or her heart, portraying feelings, emotions, hopes, and dreams, praising God, instructing, expressing concerns, and so forth.

The Song of Moses is recorded in verses 1–43 of this chapter. It is to be recited by the children of Israel often to remind them of their worth and the opportunities that the Lord has given them. It is also to warn them of impending doom if they reject the Lord.

In a very real sense, Moses is bearing his testimony to his people for the last time during his life on earth.

THE SONG OF MOSES

Verses 1–43

1 Give ear, O ye heavens, and I will speak; and hear, O earth, the words of my mouth.

2 My doctrine shall drop as the rain, my speech shall distil as the dew, as the small rain upon the tender herb, and as the showers upon the grass:

3 Because **I will publish the name of the LORD**: ascribe ye greatness unto our God.

4 *He is* **the Rock**, his work *is* perfect: for all his ways *are* judgment [*fair*]: a God of truth and without iniquity, just and right *is* he.

5 They have corrupted themselves [*the wicked Israelites are accountable*], their spot *is* not *the spot* of his children: *they are* a perverse and crooked generation.

6 Do ye thus requite the LORD [*is this how your repay the Lord for His blessings?*], O foolish people and unwise? *is* not he thy father *that* hath bought [*ransomed, redeemed*] thee? hath he not made thee, and established thee?

7 ¶ Remember the days of old, consider the years of many generations: ask thy father, and he will shew thee; thy elders, and they will tell thee.

Next, Moses teaches that Israel was organized in premortality.

8 When the most High divided to the nations their inheritance [*in premortality—see footnote 8c in your Bible*], when he separated the sons of Adam [*when people were foreordained for their missions on earth*], he set the bounds of the people according to the number of the children of Israel.

9 For the LORD's portion *is* his people; Jacob [*Israel*] *is* the lot of his inheritance.

Next, Moses reminds us that the Lord loves to nourish His people with tenderness and watchful care.

10 He [*the Lord*] found him [*covenant Israel*] in a desert land, and in the waste howling wilderness; he led him about, he instructed him, he kept him as the apple of his eye.

11 As an eagle stirreth up her nest, fluttereth over her young, spreadeth abroad her wings, taketh them, beareth them on her wings:

12 *So* the LORD alone did lead him [*Israel*], and *there was* no strange god with him.

13 He made him ride on the high places of the earth [*the Lord provides the best for His people*], that he might eat the increase of the fields; and he made him to suck honey out of the rock, and oil [*olive oil*] out of the flinty rock;

14 Butter of kine [*milk cows*], and milk of sheep, with fat of lambs, and rams of the breed of Bashan, and goats, with the fat of kidneys of wheat; and thou didst drink the pure blood [*juice*] of the grape.

Next, we see major elements of the cycle of apostasy.

THE CYCLE OF APOSTASY

Prosperity and Pride

Wickedness

15 ¶ But Jeshurun [*righteous Israel*] **waxed fat** [*grew prosperous*], and kicked [*rebelled*]: thou art waxen fat, thou art grown thick, thou art covered *with fatness*; **then he forsook God** *which* made him, and lightly esteemed the Rock of his salvation [*Jesus Christ*].

16 They provoked him to jealousy with strange *gods* [*idol worship; apostasy*], with abominations provoked they him to anger.

17 They sacrificed unto devils, not to God; to gods whom they knew not, to new *gods that* came newly up, whom your fathers feared not [*did not worship*].

18 Of the Rock *that* begat thee thou art unmindful [*you don't even think about your Creator anymore*], and hast forgotten God that formed thee.

Withdrawal of the Lord's Blessings

19 And when the LORD saw *it*, he abhorred *them*, because of the provoking of his sons, and of his daughters.

20 And he [*the Lord*] said, I will hide my face from them, I will see what their end *shall be*: for they *are* a very froward generation, children in whom *is* no faith.

21 They have moved me to jealousy with *that which is* not God; they have provoked me to anger with their vanities [*pride*]: and I will move them to jealousy with *those which are* not a people; I will provoke them to anger with a foolish nation.

Destruction

22 For a fire is kindled in mine anger, and shall burn unto the lowest hell, and shall consume the earth with her increase, and set on fire the foundations of the mountains.

23 I will heap mischiefs [*destructions*] **upon them**; I will spend mine arrows upon them.

24 *They shall be* burnt with **hunger**, and devoured with burning **heat**, and with **bitter destruction**: I will also send the teeth of beasts upon them, with the poison of serpents of the dust.

25 The sword without [*from outside enemies*], and terror within, shall destroy both the young man and the virgin, the suckling [*nursing baby*] *also* with the man of gray hairs.

Scattering of Israel

26 I said, I would scatter them into corners [*throughout the earth*], I would make the remembrance of them to cease from among men:

27 Were it not that I feared the wrath of the enemy, lest their adversaries should behave themselves strangely, *and* lest they should say, Our hand *is* high, and the LORD hath not done all this.

28 For they *are* a nation void of counsel, neither *is there any* understanding in them.

29 O that they were wise, *that they* understood this, *that* they would consider their latter end [*if they would only look ahead and consider what the end result of their behavior will be*]!

30 How should one chase a thousand, and two put ten thousand to flight, except their Rock had sold them, and the LORD had shut them up? [*In other words, the only way Israel could be terrorized and scattered so completely, often by only a few, is if they reject their God and He withdraws His power from them.*]

31 For their rock [*the false gods of other cultures*] *is* not as our Rock [*Jesus Christ*], even our enemies themselves *being* judges.

32 For their vine *is* of the vine of Sodom [*they pattern their lives after the sins of Sodom*], and of the fields of Gomorrah: their grapes *are* grapes of gall [*they feed on the poison of wickedness*], their clusters *are* bitter:

33 Their wine *is* the poison of dragons [*serpents*], and the cruel venom of asps [*cobras*].

34 Is not this laid up in store with me, *and* sealed up among my treasures?

> Next, Moses teaches that the wicked will be destroyed in the Lord's due time.

35 To me *belongeth* vengeance, and recompence; **their foot shall slide in** *due* **time**: for the day of their calamity *is* at hand, and the things that shall come upon them make haste [*the punishments for their wickedness are hurrying toward them*].

36 For the LORD shall judge his people, and repent himself [*feel sorry, weep*] for his servants, when he seeth that *their* power is gone, and *there is* none shut up, or left.

Major Message

> False gods and lifestyles have no power to rescue or save from the results of intentional wickedness.

37 And he shall say, **Where** *are* **their gods** [*their false gods*], *their* rock **in whom they trusted,**

38 Which did eat the fat of their sacrifices [*to whom they sacrificed*], *and* drank the wine of their drink offerings? **let them rise up and help you,** *and* **be your protection.**

> The true God is all powerful. Idols have no power. The Lord has all power to save or destroy.

39 See now that I, *even* I, *am* he, and *there is* no god with me: I kill, and I make alive; I wound, and I heal: neither *is there any* that can deliver out of my hand.

40 For I lift up my hand to heaven, and say, I live for ever.

41 If I whet [*sharpen*] my glittering sword, and mine hand take hold on judgment; I will render vengeance to mine enemies, and will reward them that hate me.

42 I will make mine arrows drunk with blood, and my sword shall devour flesh; *and that* with the blood of the slain and of the captives, from the beginning of revenges upon the enemy.

Major Message

There is yet a bright future in store for Israel.

43 Rejoice, O ye nations, *with* his people: for **he** will avenge the blood of his servants, and will render vengeance to his adversaries, and **will be merciful unto his land, *and* to his people.**

This is the End of Moses' song. Having written it, as instructed in Deuteronomy 31:19, Moses now recites it to the people, with the help of Joshua.

44 ¶ And **Moses came and spake all the words of this song in the ears of the people,** he, and Hoshea [*Joshua*] the son of Nun.

45 And **Moses made an end of speaking** all these words to all Israel:

Next, Moses counsels the people to tune their hearts to the words he has just spoken to them.

46 And he said unto them, **Set your hearts unto all the words which** [*tune your hearts to the words which*] **I testify among you this day,** which ye shall **command your children to observe to do,** all the words of this law.

Next, Moses uses understatement to emphasize his point.

47 For **it *is* not a vain** [*useless*] **thing for you; because it *is* your life:** and through this thing ye shall prolong *your* days in the land, whither ye go over Jordan to possess it.

In verses 48–49, Jesus instructs Moses to come up on Mount Nebo (a mountain east of the Jordan River from which one can see the Holy Land across the river).

48 And **the LORD spake unto Moses** that selfsame day, saying,

49 **Get thee up into this mountain Abarim, *unto* mount Nebo,** which *is* in the land of Moab, that *is* over against Jericho [*opposite Jericho, and east, across the Jordan River*]; and behold [*take a look at*] the land of Canaan, which I give unto the children of Israel for a possession:

50 **And die** in the mount whither

thou goest up, **and be gathered unto thy people** [*go to the spirit world and meet your departed ancestors*]; as Aaron thy brother died in mount Hor, and was gathered unto his people:

> As you have probably noticed, several verses in the Bible here in these last chapters keep saying that Moses will die on Nebo. Whoever wrote these last four chapters of Deuteronomy apparently was not aware that Moses was translated. Thus, whoever it was filled in with his opinion that Moses died. You may wish to look ahead to the note after Deuteronomy 34:6 in this study guide for a quote from the 2001 Gospel Doctrine Teacher's Manual regarding this.
>
> Mormon verified that Moses was translated. He said:

Alma 45:18–19

18 And when Alma had done this he departed out of the land of Zarahemla, as if to go into the land of Melek. And it came to pass that he was never heard of more; as to his death or burial we know not of.

19 Behold, this we know, that he was a righteous man; and the saying went abroad in the church that he was taken up by the Spirit, or buried by the hand of the Lord, even as Moses. But behold, **the scriptures saith the Lord took Moses unto himself**; and **we suppose that he has also received Alma in the spirit, unto himself; therefore, for this cause we know nothing**

concerning his death and burial.

> We will quote a statement from the Bible Dictionary to the effect that Moses was translated:

Bible Dictionary

"As was the case with many of the ancient prophets, Moses' ministry extended beyond the limits of his own mortal lifetime. In company with Elijah, he came to the Mount of Transfiguration and bestowed keys of the priesthood upon Peter, James, and John (Matt. 17:3–4; Mark 9:4–9; Luke 9:30; Doctrine and Covenants 63:21; HC 3:387). From this event, which occurred before the resurrection of Jesus, **we understand that Moses was a translated being, and had not died as reported in Deut. 34** (Alma 45:19). It was necessary that he be translated, in order to have a body of flesh and bones at the time of the transfiguration, since the resurrection had not yet taken place. Had he been a spirit only, he could not have performed the work on the mount of giving the keys to the mortal Peter, James, and John (cf. Doctrine and Covenants 129)."

> We will now finish this chapter. You may wish to review the notes in this study guide for Numbers 20:7–12, for a softening of verse 51, next.

51 Because ye trespassed against

me among the children of Israel at the waters of Meribah-Kadesh, in the wilderness of Zin; because ye sanctified me not in the midst of the children of Israel.

52 Yet thou shalt see the land before *thee*; but thou shalt not go thither unto the land which I give the children of Israel.

DEUTERONOMY 33

Selection: all verses

IN THIS CHAPTER, Moses leaves his final blessing upon his people. It is contained in verses 1–25. We don't know who the writer was who finished the book of Deuteronomy (see note after 34:6, in this study guide).

1 And **this** *is* **the blessing, wherewith Moses the man of God** [*a reaffirmation by the writer of this chapter that Moses was a righteous man*] **blessed the children of Israel before his death.**

2 And **he said,** The LORD came from Sinai, and rose up from Seir unto them; he shined forth from mount Paran, and he came with ten thousands of saints: from his right hand *went* a fiery law for them.

3 Yea, he loved the people; all his saints *are* in thy hand: and they sat down at thy feet; *every one* shall receive of thy words.

4 Moses commanded us a law, *even* the inheritance of the congregation of Jacob.

5 And he was king in Jeshurun [*NIV: the upright one, that is, Israel*], when the heads of the people *and* the tribes of Israel were gathered together.

As you will see, Moses leaves a final blessing upon each tribe of Israel. It is interesting to note that about 450 years ago, from this time in history, Jacob had given his final blessings to his twelve sons (Genesis 49). By the time of Moses' final blessing to them here, each tribe had grown to consist of thousands of members.

Note that the tribe of Joseph, with the descendants of Ephraim and Manasseh, his sons (treated as two tribes in land inheritances) received the foremost blessing. They have the main initial responsibility of getting things going in the last days, as the gospel is restored and taken to all the earth. They will bring it to the other tribes (see Doctrine and Covenants 133:32–34).

A blessing for the tribe of Reuben

6 ¶ Let **Reuben** live, and not die; and let *not* his men be few.

A blessing for the tribe of Judah

7 ¶ And this *is the blessing* of **Judah:**

and he said, Hear, LORD, the voice of Judah, and bring him unto his people: let his hands be sufficient for him; and be thou an help *to him* from his enemies.

A blessing for the tribe of Levi

8 ¶ And of **Levi** he said, *Let* thy Thummim and thy Urim *be* with thy holy one, whom thou didst prove at Massah, *and with* whom thou didst strive at the waters of Meribah;

9 Who said unto his father and to his mother, I have not seen him; neither did he acknowledge his brethren, nor knew his own children: for they have observed thy word, and kept thy covenant.

10 They [*the Levites*] shall teach Jacob [*all of Israel*] thy judgments, and Israel thy law: they shall put incense before thee, and whole burnt sacrifice upon thine altar.

11 Bless, LORD, his substance, and accept the work of his hands: smite through the loins of them that rise against him, and of them that hate him, that they rise not again.

A blessing for the tribe of Benjamin

12 ¶ *And* of **Benjamin** he said, The beloved of the LORD shall dwell in safety by him; *and the LORD* shall cover him all the day long, and he shall dwell between his shoulders.

A blessing for the tribe of Joseph

13 ¶ And of **Joseph** he said, Blessed of the LORD *be* his land, for the precious things of heaven, for the dew, and for the deep that coucheth beneath,

14 And for the precious fruits *brought forth* by the sun, and for the precious things put forth by the moon,

15 And for the chief things of the ancient mountains, and for the precious things of the lasting hills,

16 And for the precious things of the earth and fulness thereof, and *for* the good will of him that dwelt in the bush: let *the blessing* come upon the head of Joseph, and upon the top of the head of him *that was* separated from his brethren.

17 His glory *is like* the firstling of his bullock, and his horns *are like* the horns of unicorns [*wild oxen*]: with them **he shall push the people together** [*the gathering of Israel*] **to the ends of the earth**: and they *are* the ten thousands of **Ephraim**, and they *are* the thousands of **Manasseh**.

Did you notice that the tribes of Ephraim and Manasseh are to work together in the last days and will be a powerful force in gathering Israel?

A blessing for the tribes of Zebulun and Issachar

18 ¶ And of **Zebulun** he said, Rejoice, Zebulun, in thy going out; and, **Issachar**, in thy tents.

19 They shall call the people unto the mountain; there they shall offer sacrifices of righteousness: for they shall suck *of* the abundance of the seas, and *of* treasures hid in the sand.

A blessing for the tribe of Gad

20 ¶ And of **Gad** he said, Blessed *be* he that enlargeth Gad: he dwelleth as a lion, and teareth the arm with the crown of the head.

21 And he provided the first part for himself, because there, *in* a portion of the lawgiver, *was* he seated; and he came with the heads of the people, he executed the justice of the LORD, and his judgments with Israel.

A blessing for the tribe of Dan

22 ¶ And of **Dan** he said, Dan *is* a lion's whelp: he shall leap from Bashan.

A blessing for the tribe of Naphtali

23 ¶ And of **Naphtali** he said, O Naphtali, satisfied with favour, and full with the blessing of the LORD: possess thou the west and the south.

A blessing for the tribe of Asher

24 ¶ And of **Asher** he said, Let Asher *be* blessed with children; let him be acceptable to his brethren, and let him dip his foot in oil.

25 Thy shoes *shall be* iron and brass; and as thy days, *so shall* thy strength *be.*

Did you notice that the tribe of Simeon is not mentioned here? We have no answer to the question as to why this tribe was left out. Perhaps it is one of the frequent missing scriptures in the Bible (see Bible Dictionary, under "Lost Books").

Major Message

Nothing can compare with the blessings poured down upon the righteous by the true God.

Next, in verses 26–29, we are again reminded how wonderfully worthwhile it is to do our best to qualify for God's blessings.

26 ¶ *There is* none like unto the God of Jeshurun [*the righteous*], *who* rideth upon the heaven in thy help, and in his excellency on the sky.

27 The eternal God *is thy* refuge, and underneath *are* the everlasting arms: and he shall thrust out the enemy from before thee; and shall say, Destroy *them.*

28 Israel then shall dwell in safety alone: the fountain of Jacob *shall be* upon a land of corn and wine; also his heavens shall drop down dew.

29 Happy *art thou, O Israel*: who *is* like unto thee, O people saved by the LORD, the shield of thy help, and who *is* the sword of thy excellency! and thine enemies shall be found liars unto thee; and thou shalt tread upon their high places.

DEUTERONOMY 34

Selection: all verses

IN THIS CHAPTER, the writer records that Moses goes up into Mount Nebo, as instructed by the Lord.

1 And Moses went up from the plains of Moab **unto the mountain of Nebo, to the top of Pisgah,** that *is* over against Jericho. **And the LORD shewed him all the land** of Gilead, unto Dan [*north of the Sea of Galilee*],

2 And all Naphtali, and the land of Ephraim, and Manasseh, and all the land of Judah, unto the utmost sea,

3 And the south, and the plain of the valley of Jericho, the city of palm trees, unto Zoar.

4 And the LORD said unto him, This *is* the land which I sware [*covenanted*] **unto Abraham, unto Isaac, and unto Jacob**, saying, I will give it unto thy seed [*descendants*]: I have caused thee to see *it* with thine eyes, but thou shalt not go over thither.

5 ¶ So Moses the servant of the LORD died there [*not so—he was translated—see notes following verse 50 in chapter 32 as well as verse 6, next*] in the land of Moab, according to the word of the LORD.

6 And he buried him in a valley in the land of Moab, over against Beth-peor: but no man knoweth of his sepulchre unto this day.

The *Old Testament Gospel Doctrine Teacher's Manual*, 2001, p 81, comments on verse 6, above.

"The writer who finished the book of Deuteronomy knew only that Moses was gone and so assumed that he had died, that the Lord had buried him, and that no one knew where his grave was. However, we know that Moses was translated. (For an explanation of the state of translated beings, see 3 Nephi 28:7–9, 37–40.)" The manual then refers to the Bible Dictionary, under "Moses," for additional commentary.

Moses was still healthy at age 120.

7 ¶ And **Moses** *was* **an hundred and twenty years old when he died: his eye was not dim, nor his natural force abated.**

Next, we see that the children of Israel mourned for Moses for thirty days.

8 ¶ And the children of Israel wept [*mourned*] **for Moses** in the plains of Moab [*on the east side of the Jordan River*] **thirty days:** so the days of weeping *and* mourning for Moses were ended.

In verse 9, next, we see another example of the orderly transfer of priesthood keys and authority as the mantel of leadership is transferred to Joshua.

9 ¶ And **Joshua** the son of Nun **was full of the spirit of wisdom; for Moses had laid his hands upon him:** and the children of Israel hearkened unto him, and did as the LORD commanded Moses.

Moses was one of the greatest prophets.

10 ¶ And **there arose not a prophet since in Israel like unto Moses**, whom the LORD knew face to face,

11 In all the signs and the wonders, which the LORD sent him to do in the land of Egypt to Pharaoh, and to all his servants, and to all his land,

12 And in all that mighty hand, and in all the great terror which Moses shewed in the sight of all Israel.

JOSHUA

WE DO NOT know who wrote the book of Joshua. The book is the account of the establishment of the Israelites in the promised land, which is often referred to in the scriptures as the "land of Canaan." It has twenty-four chapters that can conveniently be divided into two groups:

1. CHAPTERS 1-12: the conquest of Canaan by the children of Israel.

2. CHAPTERS 13-24: the division of the promised land among the twelve tribes of Israel.

The book of Joshua can easily be considered to be a continuation of the five books of Moses (Genesis, Exodus, Leviticus, Numbers, and Deuteronomy) since, in effect, it finishes the story begun in Genesis. The six books go together as a unit.

As the book of Joshua begins, Moses has been taken up—in other words, translated (see Bible Dictionary, under "Moses")—by the Lord without tasting death. The Israelites have completed 30 days of mourning the departure and presumed death of Moses and are now to enter the promised land.

SYMBOLISM

As you read Joshua, watch for symbolism. For example, the book of Joshua can be symbolic of the children of Heavenly Father (having been sent to earth), striving to overcome opposition and trials (symbolized by the battles encountered upon entering Canaan) in order to enter the promised land (symbolic of heaven). They have come from Egypt (symbolic of worldliness) and will be required to go through the Jordan River (symbolic of baptism) in order to obtain the promised land.

Continuing with symbolism, it will take repenting of their rebellious attitudes in order for them to head in the direction of the promised land. Furthermore, they will have to exercise faith to pass through the Jordan on dry land (faith leads to baptism and obedience to God's commandments).

There is yet more symbolism. For example, the people must covenant to follow the Lord. "Joshua" is another Old Testament name for "Jesus." Thus, as they faithfully follow Joshua (a "type" or symbol of Christ), they will be taken home to the promised land (the celestial kingdom). Also, Joshua had twelve tribes to help with organizing and governing the covenant people. The Savior had twelve apostles to assist Him in organizing and governing the covenant people. Moses had chosen seventy men to help with the work among the Israelites (Numbers 11:16). Jesus Christ chose seventy to help with His work (Luke 10:1).

JOSHUA 1

Selection: all verses

JOSHUA IS NOW the prophet who will lead the children of Israel across the Jordan River into the promised land. He is given encouragement and counsel by the Lord, as he takes over from Moses. You can no doubt imagine the need for encouragement, since he was assuming the reins of leadership from one of the greatest prophets ever who had been the prophet for 40 years! Such big shoes to fill! The advice given to him can apply to any member called to a leadership position.

You can see that the first two verses here indicate that Moses died. Apparently, whoever wrote Joshua was not aware that Moses had been translated.

1 NOW after the death of Moses the servant of the LORD it came to pass, that the LORD spake unto Joshua the son of Nun, Moses' minister, saying,

> Joshua is told that the time has come for Israel to cross the Jordan River and enter the land of Canaan.

2 Moses my servant is dead [*not so; see Bible Dictionary, under "Moses"*]; now therefore arise, go over this Jordan, thou, and all this people, unto the land which I do give to them, even to the children of Israel.

3 Every place that the sole of your

foot shall tread upon, that have I given unto you, as I said unto Moses.

Next, we see a geographical description of the promised land.

4 From the wilderness and this Lebanon [NIV: "from the desert to Lebanon"] even unto the great river, the river Euphrates, all the land of the Hittites, and unto the great sea [NIV: "the Mediterranean Sea"] toward the going down of the sun, shall be your coast [your borders].

5 There shall not any man be able to stand before thee all the days of thy life: as I was with Moses, so I will be with thee: I will not fail thee, nor forsake thee.

Next, in addition to encouragement, Joshua is instructed to give an inheritance in the holy land to each of the tribes of Israel.

6 Be strong and of a good courage: for unto this people shalt thou divide for an inheritance the land, which I sware unto their fathers to give them.

7 Only be thou strong and very courageous, that thou mayest observe to do according to all the law [stick to the scriptures], which Moses my servant commanded thee: turn not from it to the right hand or to the left [don't make your own rules that deviate from what the Lord told

Moses; similar to the standard works and the counsel of Church leaders today], that thou mayest prosper whithersoever thou goest.

8 This book of the law shall not depart out of thy mouth [stick to the scriptures in everything you say and teach]; but thou shalt meditate therein day and night [use the scriptures to guide your decisions and actions constantly], that thou mayest observe to do according to all that is written therein: for then thou shalt make thy way prosperous, and then thou shalt have good success.

9 Have not I commanded thee? [Remember, this is the work of the Lord.] Be strong and of a good courage; be not afraid, neither be thou dismayed: for the LORD thy God is with thee whithersoever thou goest.

Does the phrase "be not afraid, neither be thou dismayed" in verse 9, sound familiar? It is similar to the first line of the third verse of the hymn, "How Firm a Foundation," which reads:

"Fear not, I am with thee; oh, be not dismayed" (Hymns, no. 85).

Next, in verses 10-11, Joshua instructs the leaders among the Israelites to tell their people to prepare to enter the promised land within three days. Imagine the excitement, after 40 years of waiting while the older, rebellious generation was purged out, to finally be going into Canaan!

10 ¶ Then Joshua commanded the officers of the people, saying,

11 Pass through the host, and command the people, saying, **Prepare you victuals** [*food and provisions*]; for **within three days ye shall pass over this Jordan**, to go in to possess the land, which the LORD your God giveth you to possess it.

> In verses 12-15, the men of the tribes of Reuben and Gad, along with half the tribe of Manasseh, are told to help the other tribes enter the promised land, but to plan on settling permanently on the east side of the Jordan River. They are to leave their families, cattle, etc., east of the Jordan River while they help the other tribes.

12 ¶ And to the **Reubenites**, and to the **Gadites**, and to **half the tribe of Manasseh**, spake Joshua, saying,

13 Remember the word which Moses the servant of the LORD commanded you, saying, **The LORD your God hath given you** rest, and hath given you **this land.**

14 **Your wives, your little ones, and your cattle, shall remain** in the land which Moses gave you **on this side Jordan; but ye shall pass before your brethren armed, all the mighty men of valour, and help them;**

15 Until the LORD have given your brethren rest, as he hath given you, and they also have possessed the land which the LORD your God giveth them: **then ye shall return unto the land of your possession, and enjoy it,** which Moses the LORD's servant gave you on this side Jordan toward the sunrising [*the rising sun, in other words, to the east of the river*].

> As the children of Israel prepared to follow Joshua across the Jordan River and into the promised land, they made a commitment to follow Joshua with the same faithfulness with which they followed Moses. While they were no doubt sincere at the moment, their past track record gives us some cause for concern.

16 ¶ And they answered Joshua, saying, **All that thou commandest us we will do**, and whithersoever thou sendest us, we will go.

17 **According as we hearkened unto Moses in all things** [*just like we obeyed Moses in everything*], **so will we hearken unto thee:** only [*all we ask is that*] the LORD thy God be with thee, as he was with Moses.

18 **Whosoever he be that doth rebel against thy commandment,** and will not hearken unto thy words in all that thou commandest him, he **shall be put to death:** only be strong and of a good courage [*you can count on us*].

JOSHUA 2

Selection: all verses

IN THIS CHAPTER, Joshua sends two spies to scout out Jericho. Rahab, the harlot, a resident of Jericho, hides Joshua's two spies in the city, which is the first major city standing in the way of the Israelites as they make plans to cross the Jordan and begin the conquest of Canaan.

The idea that Joshua's two spies, sent to scout out Jericho, would associate with a harlot and hide out in her apartment bothers some readers. Some Bible scholars suggest that rather than being a harlot (prostitute), she was an innkeeper. Others theorize that she was indeed a harlot and that entering a harlot's house was the only way outsiders such as the spies could have gained access to the city without causing undue attention because it was common practice for men from outside the city to enter for such purposes. It appears that she was in the process of being converted or was already converted to the Lord, because of what she said in verses 9–13.

Either way, you will see that Joshua sent two spies to scout out Jericho. They stayed with Rahab. She hid them successfully, and they promised her that when the Israelites conquered Jericho, she and her family would be spared if she followed their instructions. We read about this agreement in the following verses:

1 AND **Joshua the son of Nun sent** out of Shittim [*a city east across the Jordan River from Jericho*] **two men to spy** secretly, saying, Go view the land, even Jericho. And they went, and came into an harlot's house, named Rahab, and lodged there.

2 **And it was told the king** of Jericho, saying, Behold, there came men in hither to night of the children of Israel to search out the country.

3 And the king of Jericho sent unto Rahab, saying, Bring forth the men that are come to thee, which are entered into thine house: for they be come to search out all the country.

4 And **the woman took the two men, and hid them**, and said thus, There came men unto me, but I wist not whence they were:

5 And it came to pass about the time of shutting of the gate, when it was dark, that the men went out: whither the men went I wot [*knew*] not: pursue after them quickly; for ye shall overtake them.

6 But she had brought them up to the roof of the house, and hid them with the stalks of flax, which she had laid in order upon the roof.

7 And the men pursued after them the way to Jordan unto the fords: and as soon as they which pursued after them were gone out, they shut the gate.

8 ¶ And before they were laid down, she came up unto them upon the roof;

> In verses 9–11, next, we see that the reputation of the Israelites preceded them as they approached the land of Canaan.

9 And she said unto the men, I know that the LORD hath given you the land, and that **your terror is fallen upon us, and that all the inhabitants of the land faint** [*are already cowering and trembling*] **because of you.**

10 For we have heard how the LORD dried up the water of the Red sea for you, when ye came out of Egypt; and what ye did unto the two kings of the Amorites, that were on the other side Jordan, Sihon and Og, whom ye utterly destroyed.

11 And as soon as we had heard these things, our hearts did melt [*our courage fled*], neither did there remain any more courage in any man, because of you: for the LORD your God, he is God in heaven above, and in earth beneath.

> In verses 12–13, next, Rahab asks the two Israelite spies to swear the strongest possible oath (promise) in their culture that they will protect her and her father's household when they conquer Jericho. To swear by the Lord was the strongest way of covenanting.

12 Now therefore, I pray you, **swear unto me by the LORD,** since I have shewed you kindness, that ye will also shew kindness unto my father's house, and **give me a true token:**

> The "true token," spoken of at the end of verse 12, above, appears to be given by the spies when they say "our life for yours" in verse 14, meaning that we will promise by our lives that your life and that of your family will be protected.

13 And that ye will save alive my father, and my mother, and my brethren, and my sisters, and all that they have, and deliver our lives from death.

14 And the men answered her, **Our life for yours, if ye utter not this our business** [*we promise by our own lives that we will keep this oath if you do not disclose our plans*]. And it shall be, **when the LORD hath given us the land, that we will deal kindly and truly with thee.**

15 **Then she let them down by a cord through the window:** for her house was upon the town wall, and she dwelt upon the wall.

16 And she said unto them, **Get you to the mountain, lest the pursuers meet you; and hide yourselves there three days,** until the pursuers be returned: and afterward may ye go your way.

> Having given their word by way

of a solemn oath, the spies next, in verses 17–20, make sure she understands her part of the bargain. Otherwise, they are free of their promise.

17 And the men said unto her, **We will be blameless of this** thine **oath** which thou hast made us swear [*we will be free of this agreement, unless . . .*].

Among other things, Rahab is to tie a scarlet thread in the same window through which she helped the spies escape the city, so they and Israel's armies will recognize her living quarters when they return to conquer. She is also to make sure all her family members are gathered home when the armies come.

18 Behold, *when* we come into the land, **thou shalt bind** [*tie*] **this line of scarlet thread in the window** which thou didst let us down by: **and thou shalt bring thy father, and thy mother, and thy brethren, and all thy father's household, home unto thee.**

19 And it shall be, *that* **whosoever shall go out of the doors of thy house into the street, his blood** *shall be* **upon his head** [*if any of your family members leave your home during the siege, they are on their own*], **and we** *will be* **guiltless: and whosoever shall be with thee in the house,** his blood *shall be* on our head, if *any* hand be upon him [*it will be our responsibility if our men harm him*].

20 And **if thou utter this our business** [*if you say one thing to anyone about this*], **then we will be quit** [*freed*] **of thine oath** which thou hast made us to swear.

21 **And she said,** According unto your words, **so** *be* **it. And she sent them away,** and they departed: and **she bound the scarlet line in the window.**

Rahab and her family kept their part of the bargain and were spared when the children of Israel conquered Jericho (see Joshua 6:17, 25).

Both Paul and James in the New Testament taught that Rahab was a woman of faith in the Lord (see Hebrews 11:31; James 2:5).

22 And **they went, and came unto the mountain, and abode there three days,** until the pursuers were returned: and the pursuers sought them throughout all the way, but found them not.

23 ¶ So **the two men returned,** and descended from the mountain, and passed over, **and came to Joshua the son of Nun, and told him all things that befell them:**

24 And they said unto Joshua, Truly the LORD hath delivered into our hands all the land; for even all the inhabitants of the country do faint because of us.

JOSHUA 3

Selection: all verses

IN THIS CHAPTER, the Israelites cross the Jordan River on dry land. As you will see, the Lord bore strong witness to the people that Joshua was indeed the one He had called to succeed Moses. He has him perform a miracle similar to the crossing of the Red Sea on dry ground.

1 AND Joshua rose early in the morning; and they removed from Shittim [*a city east of the Jordan River*], and came to Jordan, he and all the children of Israel, and lodged there before they passed over.

2 And it came to pass after three days, that the officers went through the host [*the Israelites*];

3 And they commanded the people, saying, **When ye see the ark of the covenant** of the LORD your God, and the priests the Levites bearing it, then ye shall remove from your place, and **go after it.**

4 Yet there shall be a space between you and it, about two thousand cubits [*about 3,000 feet*]by measure: come not near unto it, that ye may know the way by which ye must go: for ye have not passed this way heretofore.

Next, Joshua instructs the people to prepare themselves spiritually for a wonderful miracle. Imagine the drama and sense of excitement and anticipation among these people at this point!

5 And Joshua said unto the people, **Sanctify yourselves: for to morrow the LORD will do wonders among you.**

6 And **Joshua spake unto the priests, saying, Take up the ark of the covenant, and pass over before the people** [*go ahead of the people*]. And they took up the ark of the covenant, and went before the people.

7 ¶ And the LORD said unto Joshua, **This day will I begin to magnify thee in the sight of all Israel, that they may know that, as I was with Moses, *so* I will be with thee.**

8 And thou shalt command the priests that bear the ark of the covenant, saying, When ye are come to the brink of the water of Jordan, ye shall stand still in Jordan [*NIV: "go and stand in the river"*].

Next, Joshua alerts the people that they are going to witness a miracle that should give them great faith and confidence that the Lord will indeed help them conquer the land of Canaan.

The Lord loves these yet fickle and often rebellious people and, as you can see, is giving them yet another significant opportunity to mend their ways and follow Him to salvation. He does the same for us.

9 ¶ And Joshua said unto the children of Israel, Come hither, and hear the words of the LORD your God.

10 And Joshua said, **Hereby ye shall know that the living God is among you**, and that he will without fail drive out from before you the Canaanites, and the Hittites, and the Hivites, and the Perizzites, and the Girgashites, and the Amorites, and the Jebusites.

11 Behold [*look*], the ark of the covenant of the LORD of all the earth passeth over before you into Jordan.

12 Now therefore take you twelve men out of the tribes of Israel, out of every tribe a man.

Next, Joshua prophesies that, when the feet of the priests who are carrying the ark of the covenant touch the water of the river, it will part.

13 And it shall come to pass, as soon as the soles of the feet of the priests that bear the ark of the LORD, the Lord of all the earth, shall rest in the waters of Jordan, that the waters of Jordan shall be cut off from the waters that come down from above; and they shall **stand upon an heap** [*the water coming down river to this point will back up*].

One definition of faith is to move ahead without verification, believing that the Lord will answer your prayers and provide the blessing you have requested. The children of Israel were involved in such a test of faith. The priests who carried the ark of the covenant had to walk down into the Jordan River, which was in flood stage (see verse 15), and actually enter the water with their feet before it parted, allowing them and all the Israelites who followed, to walk through on dry ground.

Major Message

There are times in our lives when we must move forward with faith, and actually take some steps into the dark, before the promised blessings come.

14 ¶ And **it came to pass, when** the people removed from their tents, to pass over Jordan, and the priests bearing the ark of the covenant before the people;

15 And as they [*the priests*] that bare the ark were come unto Jordan, and **the feet of the priests that bare the ark were dipped in the brim of the water**, (for Jordan overfloweth all his banks all the time of harvest,)

16 **That the waters** which came down from above [*coming down river*] **stood and rose up** [*backed*

241

up] upon an heap very far from the city Adam, that *is* beside Zaretan: and those that came down toward the sea of the plain, *even* the salt sea [*the Dead Sea*], failed [*stopped*], *and* were cut off: **and the people passed over** right against [*right across from*] Jericho.

> As mentioned previously, now these Israelites had experienced the miracle of walking through a parted river on dry ground, just as the previous generation had done in crossing the Red Sea.

17 And the priests that bare the ark of the covenant of the LORD stood firm on dry ground in the midst of Jordan, **and all the Israelites passed over on dry ground**, until all the people were passed clean over Jordan.

JOSHUA 4

Selection: all verses

AS THE CHILDREN of Israel crossed the Jordan River, Joshua instructed that one man from each tribe select a large rock from the river and carry it with him beyond the river. The twelve stones were to form a memorial for future generations. It was to become a teaching tool, causing their children to ask about it and thus opening up the opportunity to teach about the miracle the Lord performed for the Israelites in crossing the Jordan.

Here we have an excellent example of the order that exists in the Lord's kingdom. In verses 1–3, the Lord tells Joshua what to do and then, in verses 4–5, he tells the people what the Lord said for them to do. So it is for us. God instructs our living prophet and he instructs us.

1 AND it came to pass, when all the people were clean passed over Jordan, that **the LORD spake unto Joshua**, saying,

2 Take you twelve men out of the people, out of every tribe a man,

3 And command ye them, saying, Take you hence out of the midst of Jordan, out of the place where the priests' feet stood firm, twelve stones, and ye shall carry them over with you, and leave them in the lodging place, where ye shall lodge this night.

4 Then Joshua called the twelve men, whom he had prepared of the children of Israel, out of every tribe a man:

5 **And Joshua said unto them,** Pass over before the ark of the LORD your God into the midst of Jordan, and **take ye up every man of you a stone upon his shoulder,** according unto the number of the tribes of the children of Israel [*in other words, twelve men, one from each of the twelve tribes*]:

Major Message
It is important to preserve family

history for future generations.

6 That this may be a sign among you, *that* **when your children ask** *their fathers* in time to come, saying, **What** *mean* **ye by these stones** [*why did you put these rocks here*]?

7 Then **ye shall answer** them, That **the waters of Jordan were cut off before the ark of the covenant** of the LORD; **when it passed over Jordan**, the waters of Jordan were cut off: and **these stones shall be for a memorial unto the children of Israel for ever.**

> Next, we see that the children of Israel were obedient. Notice also that there is quite a bit of repetition for emphasis through-out the rest of the chapter. Such repetition is typical of biblical culture and teaching.

8 And the children of Israel did so as Joshua commanded, and took up twelve stones out of the midst of Jordan, as the LORD spake unto Joshua, according to the number of the tribes of the children of Israel, and carried them over with them unto the place where they lodged, and laid them down there.

9 And Joshua set up twelve stones in the midst of Jordan, in the place where the feet of the priests which bare the ark of the covenant stood: and they are there unto this day.

> There could be some confusion as to where Joshua had the men build the monument because of the wording in verse 9, above. However, verses 19–20 make it clear that the stones were set up in Gilgal, east of Jericho.
>
> In verses 10–13, we learn that the priests who carried the ark of the covenant and who were first to enter the water, waited in the dry riverbed until all the people had crossed over. We also see that the tribes of Reuben and Gad, along with half of Manasseh, supplied about forty thousand armed men for the coming conflict.

10 ¶ For the priests which bare the ark stood in the midst of Jordan, until every thing was finished that the LORD commanded Joshua to speak unto the people, according to all that Moses commanded Joshua: and the people hasted and passed over.

> Did you notice, at the end of verse 10, above, that the people hurried through the dry river-bed? We would have probably done the same!

11 And it came to pass, when all the people were clean passed over, that the ark of the LORD passed over, and the priests, in the presence of the people.

12 And the children of Reuben, and the children of Gad, and half the tribe of Manasseh, passed over armed before the children of Israel, as Moses spake unto them:

13 About forty thousand prepared

for war passed over before the LORD unto battle, to the plains of Jericho.

Next, the fact that Joshua was magnified as the prophet is emphasized.

14 ¶ On that day the LORD magnified Joshua in the sight of all Israel; and they feared him, as they feared Moses, all the days of his life.

Have you ever stopped to realize that we have an ongoing and obvious miracle before our eyes daily as we see the Lord sustain and magnify our First Presidency and Apostles? They continue functioning with high energy and health way beyond what would normally be seen in men of their age. This is a beautiful witness and testimony from the Lord to us as members.

Next, in verses 15–18, we again see the pattern where the Lord instructs the prophet and the prophet instructs the people.

15 And the LORD spake unto Joshua, saying,

16 Command the priests that bear the ark of the testimony, that they come up out of Jordan.

17 Joshua therefore commanded the priests, saying, Come ye up out of Jordan.

18 And it came to pass, when the priests that bare the ark of the covenant of the LORD were come up out of the midst of Jordan, and

the soles of the priests' feet were lifted up unto the dry land, that the waters of Jordan returned unto their place, and flowed over all his banks, as they did before.

19 ¶ And the people came up out of Jordan on the tenth day of the first month, and encamped in Gilgal, in the east border of Jericho.

20 And those twelve stones, which they took out of Jordan, did Joshua pitch in Gilgal.

Once again we see emphasis on the importance of teaching and bearing testimony of our own spiritual experiences to our children and grandchildren.

21 And he spake unto the children of Israel, saying, When your children shall ask their fathers in time to come, saying, What mean these stones?

22 Then ye shall let your children know, saying, Israel came over this Jordan on dry land.

23 For the LORD your God dried up the waters of Jordan from before you, until ye were passed over, as the LORD your God did to the Red sea, which he dried up from before us, until we were gone over:

24 That all the people of the earth might know the hand of the LORD, that it is mighty: that ye might fear the LORD your God for ever.

JOSHUA 5

Selection: all verses

THE ISRAELITES HAVE traveled west on dry ground through the Jordan River, and are now in the land of Canaan, a spectacular miracle indeed! The inhabitants of Canaan, who are ripe in iniquity as described in Leviticus 18, have heard of their miraculous entry into the land and are terrified.

1 AND it came to pass, when all the kings of the Amorites, which were on the side of Jordan westward [*on the west side of the Jordan River*], and all the kings of the Canaanites, which were by the sea [*along the western borders of the Dead Sea*], heard that the LORD had dried up the waters of Jordan from before the children of Israel, until we were passed over, that their heart melted [*their courage left them*], neither was there spirit in them any more [*they are terrified*], because of the children of Israel.

In verses 2–8, next, we are informed that, during the 40 years in the wilderness, the Israelites had ignored one of the most basic requirements for being the covenant people of the Lord. They had failed to circumcise newborn males of Israel when they were eight days old, which at the time was the token of the covenant the Lord made with Abraham (Genesis 17:9–14). This is a very serious omission and the Lord requires that it be resolved immediately.

2 ¶ At that time the LORD said unto Joshua, Make thee sharp knives [*flint knives, see footnote 2a in your LDS Bible*], and circumcise again the children of Israel the second time.

3 And Joshua made him sharp knives, and circumcised the children of Israel at the hill of the foreskins.

Next, we have an explanation as to why this was necessary.

4 And this is the cause why Joshua did circumcise: **All the people that came out of Egypt, that were males, even all the men of war, died in the wilderness** by the way, after they came out of Egypt.

5 Now all the people that came out were circumcised: but **all the people that were born in the wilderness by the way as they came forth out of Egypt, them they had not circumcised.**

6 For the children of Israel walked forty years in the wilderness, till all the people that were men of war, which came out of Egypt, were consumed, because they obeyed not the voice of the LORD: unto whom the LORD sware that he would not shew them the land, which the LORD sware unto their fathers that he would give us, a land that floweth with milk and honey.

7 And their children, whom he raised up in their stead, them Joshua circumcised: for **they were uncircumcised, because they had not circumcised them by the way.**

8 And it came to pass, when they had done circumcising all the people, that they abode in their places in the camp, till they were whole [*the Israelites stayed put until the men had healed up from the surgery*].

9 And the LORD said unto Joshua, This day have **I rolled away the reproach** of Egypt from off you [*the sins of Egypt that rubbed off on you*]. Wherefore the name of the place is called Gilgal [*the Hebrew word for "roll" or "rolling"*] unto this day.

Next, these people who have just renewed their covenant with the Lord will keep the Passover.

10 ¶ And the children of Israel encamped in Gilgal, and **kept the passover** on the fourteenth day of the month at even in the plains of Jericho.

11 And they did eat of the old corn of the land [*last year's harvest of grain in Canaan*] on the mor-row after the passover, unleavened cakes, and parched corn in the self-same day.

Next, we see that the daily gift of manna from heaven stops. The children of Israel had been fed by manna for just over forty years. But now that they have entered the land of Canaan, where last year's grain was available and new crops could be planted and harvested, the manna was stopped by the Lord.

12 ¶ And **the manna ceased** on the morrow after they had eaten of the old corn of the land; neither had the children of Israel manna any more; but they did eat of the fruit of the land [*crops*] of Canaan that year.

Next, Joshua has another sacred experience, closely paralleling that of Moses. After the Israelites had crossed the Jordan River and were coming near Jericho, Joshua saw a heavenly being. Based on the account and the similarity in language with the "burning bush" that Moses saw (Exodus 3:2–6), there is cause to believe that it may actually have been Jehovah whom he saw.

13 ¶ And it came to pass, **when Joshua was by Jericho, that he lifted up his eyes and looked, and,** behold, **there stood a man** over against him with his sword drawn in his hand: **and Joshua went unto him**, and said unto him, *Art* thou for us, or for our adversaries?

14 And he said, Nay; but *as* captain of the host of the LORD

[*possibly meaning that he is the leader of the righteous*] am I now come. **And Joshua fell on his face to the earth, and did worship**, and said unto him, **What saith my lord unto his servant?**

If it had been an angel of the Lord, we might expect that he would instruct Joshua to stand back up and stop worshiping him (as was the case with the angel who appeared to John in Revelation—see Revelation 19:10 and 22:8–9), because only the Lord is to be worshipped by bowing down. But the heavenly personage to whom Joshua bowed down said no such thing. Rather, He gave him the same instruction as the premortal Jesus Christ gave Moses (Exodus 3:5).

15 And the captain of the LORD's host said unto Joshua, **Loose thy shoe from off thy foot; for the place whereon thou standest *is* holy.** And Joshua did so.

JOSHUA 6

Selection: all verses

IN THIS CHAPTER, the wall of Jericho falls down. The fact that it "came tumbling down" has been made famous by song. It is a well-known Bible story and was a demonstration of the power of the Lord.

The inhabitants of Jericho had heard of the conquest of the Amorites (east of the Jordan) by the children of Israel and of their miraculous crossing of the Jordan River. As a result, as seen in verse 1, they shut the gates of their walled city.

1 NOW Jericho was straitly shut up because of the children of Israel: none went out, and none came in.

Beginning with verse 2, the Lord gives very specific instructions as to what to do to get the city wall to fall down so they can take the city. As you read, you will see that the number "seven" comes up numerous times. This is not accidental. We will say more about this after verse 15.

2 And the LORD said unto Joshua, See, I have given into thine hand Jericho, and the king thereof, and the mighty men of valour.

3 And ye shall compass [*march around*] the city, all ye men of war, and go round about the city once. Thus shalt thou do six days.

4 And **seven** priests shall bear before the ark **seven** trumpets of rams' horns: and the **seventh** day ye shall compass the city **seven** times, and the priests shall blow with the trumpets.

5 And it shall come to pass, that when they make a long blast with the ram's horn, and when ye hear the sound of the trumpet, all the people shall shout with a great shout; and the wall of the city shall fall down flat, and the people shall ascend up every man straight before him.

6 ¶ And Joshua the son of Nun called the priests, and said unto them, Take up the ark of the covenant, and let **seven** priests bear **seven** trumpets of rams' horns before the ark of the LORD.

7 And he said unto the people, Pass on, and compass the city, and let him that is armed pass on before the ark of the LORD.

8 ¶ And it came to pass, when Joshua had spoken unto the people, that the **seven** priests bearing the **seven** trumpets of rams' horns passed on before the LORD, and blew with the trumpets: and the ark of the covenant of the LORD followed them.

9 ¶ And the armed men went before the priests that blew with the trumpets, and the rereward [*those following*] came after the ark, the priests going on, and blowing with the trumpets.

> Notice the requirement for strict obedience to the commandment not to utter a word, in verse 10. Such self-control and strict obedience is often required for specific help from the Lord.

10 And Joshua had commanded the people, saying, **Ye shall not shout, nor make any noise with your voice, neither shall any word proceed out of your mouth, until the day I bid you shout;** then shall ye shout.

11 So the ark of the LORD compassed the city, going about it once: and they came into the camp, and lodged in the camp.

12 ¶ And Joshua rose early in the morning, and the priests took up the ark of the LORD.

13 And **seven** priests bearing **seven** trumpets of rams' horns before the ark of the LORD went on continually, and blew with the trumpets: and the armed men went before them; but the rereward came after the ark of the LORD, the priests going on, and blowing with the trumpets.

14 And the second day they compassed the city once, and returned into the camp: so they did six days.

15 And it came to pass on the **seventh** day, that they rose early about the dawning of the day, and compassed the city after the same manner **seven** times: only on that day they compassed the city **seven** times.

> "Seven" was used numerous times in the Law of Moses to symbolize the covenant. This number means "completeness," "perfection," "wholeness," as used in the scriptures. Perfection comes eventually through the help of the Savior, through making and keeping

covenants. Through strict obedience to the Lord's instructions for conquering Jericho, the Israelites succeeded because of the "perfect" power of the Lord, represented by the number "seven."

We will briefly mention some other numbers that have symbolic meaning in the scriptures and elsewhere, and then draw some conclusions:

Numerical Symbolism

1 Unity; God.

3 God; Godhead.

4 Man; earth (see *Smith's Bible Dictionary,* page 456).

7 Completeness; perfection.

10 Numerical perfection; well-organized.

12 God's divine organization, government of God.

40 days Can be literal. Sometimes means "a long time," as in 1 Samuel 17:16.

Forever Endless; can sometimes be a specific period or age, not endless (see BYU Religious Studies Center Newsletter, vol. 8, no. 3, May 1994).

Using the above numerical symbolism, you can see that when people (4) allow the Godhead (3) to work with them, they can become perfect (7). In other words, 4 + 3 = 7. So also, as the Israelites followed the instructions of the Lord (whose presence was represented by the ark of the covenant, carried with them as they walked around the wall of Jericho each day for six days, and then, seven times on the seventh day), they were able to conquer the obstacles in their way and "perfectly" complete the task He assigned them. This "perfect" work of the Lord is shown especially in verse 20 where "the wall fell down flat."

16 And it came to pass at the **seventh** time, when the priests blew with the trumpets, Joshua said unto the people, Shout; for the LORD hath given you the city.

In verses 17–18, next, the word "accursed" is used several times. One meaning is things in Jericho that are off limits for the Israelites to take for their own use, including things that are to be dedicated to the Lord for sacrifices or to be added to the Lord's treasury. Another meaning is to bring upon yourself condemnation, as in the second use of the word in verse 18.

Note also, in verse 17, that Joshua gave strict instructions that Rahab and her family should be saved from destruction, as promised in Joshua chapter 2.

17 ¶ And **the city shall be accursed,** even it, and all that are therein, to the LORD: **only Rahab the harlot shall live, she and all that are with her in the house,** because she hid the messengers that we sent.

18 And ye, in any wise **keep yourselves from the accursed thing, lest ye make yourselves accursed** [*bring a curse upon yourself*], when ye take of the accursed thing, and make the camp of Israel a curse, and trouble it.

19 But **all the silver, and gold, and vessels of brass and iron, are consecrated unto the LORD**: they shall come into the treasury of the LORD.

20 So the people shouted when the priests blew with the trumpets: and it came to pass, when the people heard the sound of the trumpet, and the people shouted with a great shout, that **the wall fell down flat**, so that the people went up into the city, every man straight before him, **and they took the city.**

21 And they utterly destroyed all that was in the city, both man and woman, young and old, and ox, and sheep, and ass, with the edge of the sword.

Verses 22–23, next, emphasize yet again that the promise made to Rahab and her household was kept.

22 But Joshua had said unto the two men that had spied out the country, **Go into the harlot's house, and bring out thence the woman, and all that she hath**, as ye sware [*promised*] unto her.

23 And the young men that were spies went in, and brought out Rahab, and her father, and her mother, and her brethren, and all that she had; and they brought out

all her kindred, and left them without the camp of Israel.

Did you notice, in verses 22–23, above, that it was the same spies protected by Rahab who got to go to her before the wall fell and fulfill the promise they made to save her and her family? Imagine the sweet emotions in their hearts and hers as the promise was kept! She and her household were welcomed and, according to verse 25, were still alive at the time of the writing of the book of Joshua.

Next, we see that, as instructed, the material wealth of Jericho was added to the Lord's treasury.

24 And they burnt the city with fire, and all that was therein: only **the silver, and the gold, and the vessels of brass and of iron, they put into the treasury of the house of the LORD.**

25 And Joshua saved **Rahab** the harlot alive, **and her father's household, and all that she had**; and she **dwelleth in Israel even unto this day**; because she hid the messengers, which Joshua sent to spy out Jericho.

Next, Joshua swears an oath that whoever rebuilds Jericho will do so at the peril of his own posterity.

26 ¶ And Joshua adjured them [*gave a strong charge or oath*] at that time, saying, **Cursed be the man before the LORD, that riseth up and buildeth this city Jericho: he**

shall lay the foundation thereof in his firstborn [*NIV: "at the cost of his firstborn"*], and in his youngest son [*NIV: "at the cost of his youngest"*] shall he set up the gates of it.

27 So the LORD was with Joshua; and his fame was noised throughout all the country.

JOSHUA 7

Selection: all verses

IN THIS CHAPTER, you will see that the Israelites suffered a humiliating defeat in what should have been an easy victory in the battle for Ai, a city about 10 miles west of Jericho. The Lord's help was not with them. In a sort of reverse order, we will be told why, in verse 1, and then verses 2-5 will provide an account of the stunning defeat.

1 BUT the children of Israel committed a trespass in the accursed thing: for **Achan**, the son of Carmi, the son of Zabdi, the son of Zerah, of the tribe of Judah, **took of the accursed thing**: and the anger of the LORD was kindled against the children of Israel.

2 And Joshua sent men from Jericho to Ai, which is beside Beth-aven, on the east side of Beth-el, and spake unto them, saying, **Go up and view the country**. And the men went up and viewed Ai.

The scouts sent out by Joshua reported back that Ai would be easy to take and there was no need for all the fighting men of Israel to go against the city. Rather, a relatively small contingent of about 2,000-3,000 men could easily do the job.

3 And they returned to Joshua, and said unto him, **Let not all the people go up; but let about two or three thousand men go up and smite Ai**; and make not all the people to labour thither; for they are but few.

4 So there went up thither of the people about three thousand men: and **they fled before the men of Ai.**

The Israelite contingent lost 36 men and the defeat caused the children of Israel to lose all courage and faith.

5 And t**he men of Ai smote of them about thirty and six men**: for they chased them from before the gate even unto Shebarim, and smote them in the going down: wherefore **the hearts** [*courage*] **of the people melted, and became as water.**

As is the case with all who are called to leadership in the Lord's work, the lessons of leadership continue to accrue throughout the duration of the calling. And sometimes, the learning curve is steep. We see this with Joshua in verses 6-12, next. First though, in verses 6-9, he is very open with his concern and complaint.

6 ¶ And **Joshua rent** [*tore*] **his**

clothes [*a sign of great distress in his culture*], and **fell to the earth upon his face before the ark of the LORD** [*the ark of the covenant, where he went to commune with Jehovah*] until the eventide [*evening time*], he and the elders of Israel, and put dust upon their heads [*a sign of great remorse, humility, and mourning*].

7 And **Joshua said**, Alas, O Lord GOD, **wherefore** [*why*] **hast thou at all brought this people over Jordan** [*what is the sense of bringing us across the Jordan River*], to deliver us into the hand of the Amorites, **to destroy us?** Would to God we had been content, and dwelt on the other side Jordan. [*I wish we had stayed on the east side of the river!*]

8 O Lord, **what shall I say**, when Israel turneth their backs before [*retreats from*] their enemies! [*What can I say after my men had to retreat like that from the men of Ai?*]

9 For **the Canaanites and all the inhabitants of the land shall hear of it** [*in other words, when word gets around, our enemies will be encouraged*], and shall **environ** [*surround*] **us** round, and **cut off our name** from the earth [*destroy us completely*]: and **what wilt thou do unto thy great name?** [*how will the Lord move His work forward then?*]

Next, the Lord responds strictly and in no uncertain terms to His complaining prophet. There is no doubt a lesson in parenting here for parents today.

10 ¶ And the LORD said unto Joshua, Get thee up; wherefore [*why*] liest thou thus upon thy face?

No doubt Joshua was startled to learn why the Lord had not helped them easily defeat Ai, as explained in verses 11–12, next.

11 Israel hath sinned, and they have also transgressed my covenant which I commanded them: for they have even taken of the accursed thing, and have also stolen, and dissembled [*deceived*] also, and they have put *it* even among their own stuff.

12 Therefore [*this is the reason*] the children of Israel could not stand before their enemies, *but* turned *their* backs before their enemies, because they were accursed: neither will I be with you any more, except ye destroy the accursed from among you.

As you saw in verses 10–12, above, the Lord, in effect, told Joshua that this is not a time for mourning but rather a time for definite, strict action to root out the evil that is at the bottom of the problem.

Thus far, a man named Achan took some things that were forbidden by the Lord, during the conquest of Jericho, and hid them in the ground under his tent (verses 1, 11, 21, and elsewhere—see also Joshua 6:18, footnote a).

Symbolically, these forbidden things can represent anything we take into our lives that violates the commitments and covenants we have made with the Lord. It is perhaps reasonable to suppose that all of Achan's family had supported him in this attempted deception, and were thus destroyed with him (verses 24–25). Symbolically, their complete destruction can represent the complete destruction of the wicked by fire, at the Second Coming of the Savior.

The Lord's instructions to Joshua continue, in which he is told how Israel can once again become worthy for the Lord's help against their enemies.

13 Up [*get moving*], sanctify [*purify, make clean and worthy before the Lord*] the people, and say, Sanctify yourselves against to morrow: for thus saith the LORD God of Israel, **There is an accursed thing in the midst of thee, O Israel: thou canst not stand before thine enemies, until ye take away the accursed thing from among you.**

There is to be an organized search until the guilty parties are exposed.

14 In the morning therefore **ye shall be brought according to your tribes**: and it shall be, that the tribe which the LORD taketh shall come according to the families thereof; and the family which the LORD shall take shall come by households; and the household which the LORD shall take shall come man by man.

15 And it shall be, that he that is taken with the accursed thing shall be burnt with fire, he and all that he hath: because he hath transgressed the covenant of the LORD, and because he hath wrought folly in Israel.

Joshua is quick to implement the Lord's instructions. Under inspiration, Joshua is to select which tribe is to come forth, then which family group, then which family, then which individual. In verses 16, next, we see that he selected the tribe of Judah.

16 ¶ So Joshua rose up early in the morning, and brought Israel by their tribes; and **the tribe of Judah was taken:**

17 And he brought the family of Judah; and he took the family of the Zarhites: and he brought the family of the Zarhites man by man; and Zabdi was taken:

Next, Achan, who took the forbidden items, is called to come forth. Imagine the feelings and fear in his guilty heart!

18 And he brought his household man by man; and **Achan**, the son of Carmi, the son of Zabdi, the son of Zerah, of the tribe of Judah, **was taken.**

19 And Joshua said unto Achan, My son, give, I pray thee, glory to the LORD God of Israel [*NIV: "tell* *the truth*"], and make confession unto him; and tell me now what thou hast done; hide it not from me.

> Next, Achan confesses, explaining his motives for his disobedience. One of the clear messages here to all of us is that, when it comes to willful disobedience of God's commandments, no excuse will do.

20 And **Achan answered Joshua,** and said, Indeed **I have sinned** against the LORD God of Israel, and thus and thus have I done:

21 When I saw among the spoils a goodly Babylonish garment, and two hundred shekels of silver, and a wedge of gold of fifty shekels weight, then **I coveted them, and took them**; and, behold, they are hid in the earth in the midst of my tent, and the silver under it.

> Finally, the ill-gotten spoils of war are retrieved and laid in front of all the people. It was clear evidence against Achan and his family, who had apparently co-conspired with him to deceive (see verse 11).

22 ¶ **So Joshua sent messengers, and they ran unto the tent**; and, behold, it was hid in his tent, and the silver under it.

23 And they took them out of the midst of the tent, and **brought them unto Joshua, and unto all the children of Israel, and laid them out** before the LORD.

24 And Joshua, and all Israel with him, took Achan the son of Zerah, and the silver, and the garment, and the wedge of gold, and his sons, and his daughters, and his oxen, and his asses, and his sheep, and his tent, and all that he had: and they brought them unto the valley of Achor.

25 And Joshua said, Why hast thou troubled us? the LORD shall trouble thee this day. **And all Israel stoned him with stones, and burned them with fire, after they had stoned them with stones.**

26 And they raised over him a great heap of stones unto this day. So the LORD turned from the fierceness of his anger. Wherefore the name of that place was called, The valley of Achor [*NIV: "trouble"*], unto this day.

Major Message

One of the lessons we can learn from the account of Achan is the importance of not taking the evil things of an unrighteous society into our lives and homes. It can result in spiritual death. Alma reminds us of this. He taught:

Alma 5:57

57 And now I say unto you, all you that are desirous to follow the voice of the good shepherd, come ye out from the wicked, and be ye separate, and **touch not their unclean things**; and behold, their

names shall be blotted out, that the names of the wicked shall not be numbered among the names of the righteous, that the word of God may be fulfilled, which saith: The names of the wicked shall not be mingled with the names of my people;

NOTE

For our study of the remainder of the book of Joshua, we will be limited to a few selections.

As you read the next several chapters of Joshua in your Bible, you will see that the Israelites continue conquering enemy nations who occupy the promised land. When that is close to completion, Joshua divides the land up among the tribes of Israel.

One of the unfortunate problems you will see as you read is that the children of Israel failed to entirely destroy the previous cultures as commanded. As a result, some of the wickedness and evil practices of the former inhabitants are still around to pollute the covenant people.

First, a selection from Joshua 10 in which miraculous help is provided for Israel's armies.

JOSHUA 10

Selection: verses 12–13

ONE OF THE better-known accounts in the Old Testament is that which tells of the sun and the moon standing still during a battle fought by Israel as they entered the promised land. This miraculous event occurred after a terrible hailstorm had been sent by the Lord to destroy another enemy army (Joshua 10:11). In this next battle, the Israelites needed more daylight in order to defeat the enemy. Joshua commanded both the sun and the moon to remain where they were until the victory was attained. It appears that they were given another day's worth of daylight.

12 ¶ Then spake Joshua to the LORD in the day when the LORD delivered up the Amorites before the children of Israel, and he said in the sight of Israel, **Sun, stand thou still** upon Gibeon; **and thou, Moon,** in the valley of Ajalon.

13 **And the sun stood still, and the moon stayed,** until the people had avenged themselves upon their enemies [*until they had won the battle*]. *Is not this written in the book of Jasher [a book that is missing from the Old Testament]?* **So the sun stood still** in the midst of heaven, and hasted not to go down **about a whole day.**

Mormon reminds us that it is the earth that stopped, not the sun and moon (Helaman 12:15). It is interesting that such knowledge was had back then. In fact, we know that Abraham was taught much about astronomy by direct revelation (Abraham 3) and understand that he taught the Egyptians much about it during his stay in Egypt (see Facsimile No. 3, last line). Thus, considerable correct knowledge about astronomy was available in ancient times. It was eliminated by apostasy and ignorance of the Lord's revelations to mankind.

JOSHUA 11

Selection: verse 20

AS YOU READ this chapter in your Bible, you will see that the Lord gives Israel victory over a large coalition of enemy forces. Israel goes on to conquer and destroy city after city. Verse 20 contains an explanation as to why these enemies of Israel were destroyed completely, but we need the JST to understand it correctly. Otherwise, one could come to the false conclusion that the Lord sometimes hardens people's hearts in order to be justified in punishing them. This could be very confusing to a sincere seeker of truth.

Verse 20 is an example of what Joseph Smith meant as he penned the eighth Article of Faith which states: "We believe the Bible to be the word of God as far as it is translated correctly; we also believe the Book of Mormon to be the word of God."

Now, to verse 20, which speaks of those destroyed by the Israelites.

20 For it was of the LORD to harden their hearts, that they should come against Israel in battle, that he might destroy them utterly, and that they might have no favour, but that he might destroy them, as the LORD commanded Moses.

JST Joshua 11:20

20 For it was of the Lord to destroy them utterly, because they hardened their hearts, that they should come against Israel in battle; that they might have no favor, that they might destroy them in battle, as the Lord commanded Moses.

As you can see, in the JST above, the inhabitants used their agency to choose to be wicked and have hard hearts. God never violates people's agency by hardening their hearts. Such a belief could easily lead one to believe in the false doctrine of predestination.

JOSHUA 14

Selection: verses 6–14

AS MENTIONED IN the General background to the book of Joshua in this study guide, chapters 13–24 report the dividing up of the promised land, the land of Canaan, among the twelve tribes of Israel. The next selection we have chosen provides a brief review of both the faithfulness and the faith of Caleb, who will be given the area of Hebron for an inheritance as a reward.

A bit of specific background is helpful to understand Caleb's reward as mentioned in Joshua 14. In Numbers 13, the children of Israel were getting close to the promised land. Moses sent 12 spies to check out the possibility of entering it (Numbers 13:17-20). Two of the spies, Caleb and Joshua, returned and reported that, with the help of the Lord, Israel could enter and conquer the land of Canaan (Numbers 13:30, 14:6-8). The other ten spies showed lack of faith and gave negative reports (Numbers 13:31-33). The people believed the negative reports and rebelled against Moses and Aaron (Numbers 14). As a result, the Lord sent the children of Israel back into the wilderness to wander until all of the rebellious twenty years old and up had died off (Numbers 14:25-34). They were in the wilderness for a total of 40 years and now have entered and conquered sufficiently for inheritances to be given out.

In Joshua 14, the process of dividing up Canaan is underway. As we get to verses 6, next, faithful Caleb, who is now 85 years old, has approached Joshua to request that he be given the area of Hebron as an inheritance, as promised him by Moses.

6 ¶ Then the children of Judah came unto Joshua in Gilgal: and **Caleb** the son of Jephunneh the Kenezite **said unto him,** Thou knowest the thing that the LORD said unto Moses the man of God concerning me and thee in Kadesh-barnea.

7 Forty years old was I when Moses the servant of the LORD sent me from Kadesh-barnea to espy out the land; and I brought him word again as it was in mine heart.

8 Nevertheless my brethren [*the other spies, except Joshua*] that went up with me made the heart of the people melt [*used their negative report to completely discourage the people*]: but **I wholly followed the LORD my God.**

Next, we see that Moses promised Caleb an inheritance in Hebron. This promise is not specifically recorded elsewhere.

9 And **Moses sware on that day, saying, Surely the land whereon thy feet have trodden** [*the area around Hebron, see Numbers 13:22*] **shall be thine inheritance,** and thy children's for ever, **because thou hast wholly followed the LORD my God.**

Next, Caleb expresses gratitude for the Lord's kindness in keeping him alive and healthy to this day.

10 And now, behold, **the LORD hath kept me alive,** as he said, these forty and five years, even since the LORD spake this word unto Moses, while the children of Israel wandered in the wilderness: and now, lo, **I am this day fourscore and five years old** [*85 years old*].

11 As yet **I am as strong this day as I was in the day that Moses sent me:** as my strength was then, even so is my strength now, for war, both to go out, and to come in.

> Next, Caleb specifically requests the land of Hebron, if it be the will of the Lord.

12 **Now therefore give me this mountain,** whereof the LORD spake in that day; for thou heardest in that day how the Anakims were there, and that the cities were great and fenced: **if so be the LORD will be with me,** then I shall be able to drive them out, as the LORD said.

13 **And Joshua blessed him, and gave unto Caleb** the son of Jephunneh **Hebron for an inheritance.**

14 **Hebron therefore became the inheritance of Caleb** the son of Jephunneh the Kenezite unto this day, **because that he wholly followed the LORD God of Israel.**

> Did you notice the emphasis on the fact that Joshua "wholly followed the Lord" in verses 8, 9, and 14? Did you also notice that it took a whole lot of work and commitment for him to achieve that degree of faithfulness?

JOSHUA 21

Selection: verse 41

YOU MAY HAVE noticed in your Bible that Joshua 13:33 indicated that the tribe of Levi was not to be given a large section of land as were the other tribes. Here in chapter 21, we are informed that the Levites, the tribe whose male members held the Aaronic Priesthood and who were assigned to carry out the daily rites and rituals of the Law of Moses for the people, were given forty-eight cities, and thus spread throughout the land. They and their families lived in these cities and the suburbs around them. In this way, the priesthood ceremonies associated with sacrifices and offerings were made easily available to all Israelites.

41 All the cities of the Levites within the possession of the children of Israel *were* **forty and eight cities with their suburbs.**

In a way, the same thing is happening throughout the world today, through the establishment of stakes and temples. Perhaps you have noticed that wherever a stake is organized, the members of the Church in that area then have the full organization of the Church available to them, including patriarchal blessings. And as temples spread throughout the world, the blessings of temple work are likewise made available within much easier reach of all members.

We will spend some time now in the last two chapters of Joshua. In the first part of chapter 23, we see that Joshua is getting quite old. He will die at age 110.

JOSHUA 23

Selection: all verses

THE ISRAELITES HAVE long since been settled in the lands of their inheritance. Joshua is now about 110 years old and his age is showing. Chapters 23 and 24 contain his final messages to his people. There is much valuable counsel and admonition for each of us in his departing words.

As mentioned often in this study guide, repetition is frequently used by Old Testament writers for emphasis. Sometimes, students of the scriptures begin looking for other meanings in the repeated phrases and verses. They think that because there is so much repetition, it must not be repetition, rather, the author must be saying something other than what it looks like he is saying. Such is generally not the case. This chapter has many important teachings and, consequently, much repetition for purposes of emphasis.

1 And it came to pass a long time after that **the LORD had given rest unto Israel from all their enemies** round about [*in other words, a long time after the twelve tribes had settled down on their lands*], that **Joshua waxed** [*grew*] **old** and stricken in age [*his age was showing*].

2 And Joshua called for all Israel, *and* for their elders, and for their heads, and for their judges, and for their officers, **and said unto them, I am old** *and* **stricken in age:**

3 And ye have seen [*you are eye-witnesses to*] **all that the LORD your God hath done unto all these nations** [*the wicked nations which they had destroyed*] **because of you** [*for your sake*]; for the LORD your **God** *is* **he that hath fought for you.**

Under Joshua's leadership, as instructed by Jehovah, the Israelites had destroyed a total of thirty-one city-states (generally referred to in the Bible as "nations") up to this point. However, the job was not yet complete. In verse 4, next, Joshua reminds his people that there were yet wicked cultures to be destroyed. He had assigned the task by the use of lots, to the various tribes.

Don't forget that the nations destroyed and yet to be destroyed were "ripe in iniquity" as described in Leviticus 18. You may wish to review the notes and commentary for that chapter in this study guide, in order to grasp why it was essential that they not be allowed to remain where they could pollute the Lord's covenant people with their gross evils.

4 Behold, I have divided unto you [*assigned to you*] **by lot these nations that remain** [*the city-states that were yet to be destroyed*], **to be an inheritance for your tribes**

[whose lands you will occupy], from Jordan [the Jordan River], with all the nations that I have cut off [with all the nations already destroyed], even unto the great sea westward [the Mediterranean Sea].

5 And the LORD your God, he shall expel them from before you, and drive them from out of your sight; and ye shall possess their land, as the LORD your God hath promised unto you.

> In order to qualify for the help of the Lord, as promised in verse 5, Joshua reminds the people that they must do their part.

6 Be ye therefore very courageous to keep and to do all that is written in the book of the law of Moses, that ye turn not aside therefrom to the right hand or to the left [do not deviate from the commandments of God];

7 That ye come not among these nations [don't associate with them and thus take chances on being polluted by their evils], these that remain among you; neither make mention of the name of their gods, nor cause to swear by them [nor make covenants with their evil], neither serve them, nor bow yourselves unto them:

8 But cleave unto the LORD your God, as ye have done unto this day.

Major Message

None can stop the work of the Lord if the members, as a whole, live the gospel.

9 For the LORD hath driven out from before you great nations and strong: but as for you, no man hath been able to stand before you [stop you] unto this day.

Major Message

Do not underestimate the amount of good one righteous person can do with the help of the Lord.

10 One man of you shall chase a thousand [enemies]: for the LORD your God, he it is that fighteth for you, as he hath promised you.

11 Take good heed therefore unto yourselves, that ye love the LORD your God.

> Next, in verses 12–13, Joshua warns of the consequences if Israel gets involved with the evils of the nations they were to drive out.

12 Else if ye do in any wise go back, and cleave unto the remnant of these nations, even these that remain among you, and shall make marriages with them, and go in unto them [have children by them], and they to you:

13 Know for a certainty that the LORD your God will no more drive out any of these nations from before you; but they shall be snares and

traps unto you, and scourges in your sides, and thorns in your eyes, until ye perish from off this good land which the LORD your God hath given you.

> Next, Joshua reminds his people that he will soon die.

14 And, behold, **this day I *am* going the way of all the earth:** and ye know in all your hearts and in all your souls, that **not one thing hath failed of all the good things which the LORD your God spake concerning you** [*the Lord has kept His word in every one of His promises to you*]; all are come to pass unto you [*repetition*], *and* not one thing hath failed thereof [*repetition*].

Major Message

Just as all of the blessings promised by the Lord will come to you if you keep the commandments, so also will all the promised punishments come upon you if you leave Him.

15 Therefore it shall come to pass, *that* **as all good things are come upon you, which the LORD your God promised you; so shall the LORD bring upon you all evil things, until he have destroyed you** from off this good land which the LORD your God hath given you.

16 When ye have transgressed the covenant of the LORD your God, which he commanded you, and

have gone and served other gods, and bowed yourselves to them; **then shall the anger of the LORD be kindled against you, and ye shall perish quickly from off the good land which he hath given unto you.**

JOSHUA 24

Selection: all verses

AS WAS THE case with Moses, Joshua gathered his people together for his final blessing and farewell. This took place in Shechem, which is about 35 miles north of Jerusalem. Imagine what a great event this must have been, with tens of thousands of people gathering to bid farewell to their prophet leader who had brought them into the promised land.

1 And **Joshua gathered all the tribes of Israel to Shechem,** and called for the elders of Israel, and for their heads, and for their judges, and for their officers; and they presented themselves before God.

> In verses 2-13, Jehovah bears His personal testimony to the Israelites, bearing witness of things reaching back to Abraham and his father, Terah. He reminds these people that they have been eyewitnesses to His blessings and help to them.
>
> You may wish to circle "I" each time it appears in these twelve verses. You will find it at least seventeen times. Thus, Christ

bears specific testimony to the Israelites at least seventeen times. In a way, this is similar to the testimony that the Savior bore in 3 Nephi 9, that He was the one who had destroyed the wicked Nephites. In effect, He said "I did it" at least eleven times in that chapter.

We will bold and underline "I" each time it occurs in these verses.

2 And Joshua said unto all the people, **Thus saith the LORD God** of Israel, Your fathers [*ancestors*] dwelt on the other side of the flood [*lived after the Flood*] in old time [*in ancient times*], *even* Terah, the father of Abraham, and the father of Nachor ["*Nahor*"—*see Genesis 11:26*]: and they served other gods [*Terah and Nahor worshipped idols—see Abraham 1:5*].

3 And **I took your father** [*ancestor*] **Abraham** from the other side of the flood [*who lived after the Flood*], **and led him** throughout all the land of Canaan, and multiplied his seed [*gave him many descendants*], and **gave him Isaac.**

4 And **I gave unto Isaac Jacob and Esau:** and **I gave unto Esau mount Seir**, to possess it; but Jacob [*whose name was changed to Israel— see Genesis 32:28*] **and his children went down into Egypt.**

5 **I sent Moses** also and Aaron, and **I plagued Egypt**, according to that which **I did** among them: and afterward **I brought you out.**

6 And **I brought your fathers out of Egypt**: and ye came unto the sea [*the Red Sea*]; and the Egyptians pursued after your fathers with chariots and horsemen unto the Red sea.

7 And when they cried unto the LORD, he put darkness between you and the Egyptians, and brought the sea upon them [*the Egyptian army*], and covered them; and **your eyes have seen what I have done in Egypt** [*you are eyewitnesses*]: and ye dwelt in the wilderness a long season.

8 And **I brought you into the land of the Amorites**, which dwelt on the other side Jordan [*on the east side of the Jordan River*]; and they fought with you: and **I gave them into your hand**, that ye might possess their land; and **I destroyed them** from before you.

9 **Then Balak** the son of Zippor, **king of Moab**, arose and **warred against Israel**, and sent **and called Balaam** [*the man whose donkey talked to him—see Numbers 22:28–30*] the son of Beor **to curse you:**

10 But **I would not hearken unto Balaam;** therefore he blessed you still: so **I delivered you out of his hand.**

11 And ye went over Jordan, and

came unto Jericho: and the men of Jericho fought against you, the Amorites, and the Perizzites, and the Canaanites, and the Hittites, and the Girgashites, the Hivites, and the Jebusites; and **I delivered them into your hand.**

12 And **I sent the hornet** [*Exodus 23:27–28*] before you, which drave [*drove*] them out from before you, *even* the two kings of the Amorites; *but* not with thy sword, nor with thy bow.

13 And **I have given you a land** for which ye did not labour, and cities which ye built not, and ye dwell in them; of the vineyards and oliveyards which ye planted not do ye eat.

> Having delivered the Savior's personal testimony to the people, Joshua next, beginning with verse 14, speaks as the leader of the Israelites and counsels them to serve the Lord. Verse 15, which follows, is a very well-known verse, likely quite familiar to you.

14 ¶ Now **therefore fear** [*respect and honor*] **the LORD, and serve him in sincerity and in truth:** and **put away the gods** [*do away with false gods, evil practices, wickedness, wrong priorities, and so forth*] **which your fathers served** on the other side of the flood [*since the Flood*], and in Egypt; and **serve ye the LORD.**

Major Message

Intentionally choose to serve the Lord.

15 And if it seem evil [*undesirable*] unto you to serve the LORD, **choose you this day whom ye will serve;** whether the gods [*idols*] which your fathers served that *were* on the other side of the flood [*since the flood*], or the gods of the Amorites, in whose land ye dwell: **but as for me and my house, we will serve the LORD.**

> The Israelites affirm their desire to be loyal to the true God and to renew their covenant to do so.

> Notice that as the people confirm their desire to be faithful to Jehovah, they basically repeat the words of the testimony the Savior bore to them in verses 2–13 of this chapter.

16 And **the people answered** and said, **God forbid that we should forsake the LORD, to serve other gods;**

17 For the LORD our God, **he** *it is* **that brought us up and our fathers out of the land of Egypt,** from the house of bondage, **and which did those great signs in our sight, and preserved us** in all the way wherein we went, and among all the people through whom we passed:

18 And **the LORD drave** [*drove*] **out from before us all the people,** even the Amorites which dwelt in the land: *therefore* will we also serve the LORD; for he *is* our God.

Notice the teaching psychology Joshua is using in verses 19–21, next. He challenges the people, saying, in effect, that in their present state, they are not capable of truly serving the Lord ("Ye cannot serve the Lord"), verse 19.) The people respond with energy, in verse 21, saying, in effect, "You are wrong! We will indeed serve the Lord!"

19 And **Joshua said unto the people, Ye cannot serve the LORD:** for he *is* an holy God [*in other words, He must have a holy people*]; he *is* a jealous God [*He requires your exclusive devotion*]; he will not forgive your transgressions nor your sins.

20 If ye forsake the LORD, and serve strange gods, then he will turn and do you hurt, and consume you, after that he hath done you good. [*In other words, if you apostatize after He has blessed you so abundantly, with such obvious help, you will be destroyed.*]

21 And the people said unto Joshua, **Nay; but we will serve the LORD.**

Next, in verse 22, Joshua says, in effect, that if the people go ahead and make (renew) a covenant to serve the Lord, their own words will serve as a witness against them if they violate the covenant. The people agree to these terms.

22 And **Joshua said** unto the people, **Ye** *are* **witnesses against yourselves** that ye have chosen you the LORD, to serve him. And **they said,** *We* **are witnesses.**

Major Message
One effective way to remain close to the Lord is to "incline" our hearts toward Him constantly.

23 Now therefore put away, *said he,* the strange gods which *are* among you, and **incline your heart unto the LORD** God of Israel [*let the Lord constantly be the center focus of your loyalties, thoughts, and feelings*].

The people willingly enter into a covenant with the Lord.

24 And **the people said unto Joshua, The LORD our God will we serve, and his voice will we obey.**

25 **So Joshua made a covenant with the people that day,** and set them a statute and an ordinance in Shechem.

A monument is erected to commemorate the making of this covenant. The stone is to serve as a reminder or token of the covenant made.

26 ¶ And **Joshua wrote these words** in the book of the law of God, **and took a great** [*large*] **stone, and set it up there under an oak,** that *was* by the sanctuary of the LORD.

27 And Joshua said unto all the people, Behold, **this stone shall be**

a witness unto us; for it hath heard all the words of the LORD which he spake unto us: it shall be therefore a witness unto you, lest ye deny your God.

28 So Joshua let the people depart, every man unto his inheritance.

Joshua dies at age 110.

29 ¶ And it came to pass after these things, that **Joshua** the son of Nun, the servant of the LORD, **died,** *being* **an hundred and ten years old.**

30 And they buried him in the border of his inheritance in Timnath-serah, which *is* in mount Ephraim, on the north side of the hill of Gaash.

31 And Israel served the LORD all the days of Joshua, and all the days of the elders that overlived [*outlived*] Joshua, and which had known all the works of the LORD, that he had done for Israel.

Lastly, the writer of the book of Joshua informs us that Joseph's remains were moved to Shechem.

Just before he died, at age 110, Joseph prophesied that the children of Israel would someday be brought out of Egypt by the Lord. In conjunction with that prophecy, he requested that his mortal remains be taken with the Israelites to the promised land at that time (Genesis 50:24–26). As a result, Moses brought Joseph's remains with the children of Israel as they left Egypt (Exodus 13:19). Now, Joseph's embalmed body was given a final resting place in Shechem.

32 ¶ And **the bones of Joseph, which the children of Israel brought up out of Egypt, buried they in Shechem**, in a parcel of ground which Jacob bought of [*from*] the sons of Hamor the father of Shechem for an hundred pieces of silver: and it became the inheritance of the children of Joseph.

33 And Eleazar the son of Aaron died; and they buried him in a hill that pertained [*was near*] to Phinehas his son, which was given him in mount Ephraim.

JUDGES

THE PERIOD OF Judges in the Old Testament lasted for about two hundred years, from the death of Joshua to the birth of Samuel. Some Bible chronologies place this era roughly between 1300 BC and 1100 BC. It was a time when there was no strong central leadership for the tribes of Israel.

Generally, the judges were successful military leaders rather than political judges or rulers. The tribes tended to do things as individual groups, although some of them occasionally banded together against common enemies. As you read Judges in your Bible, you will quite often come across a phrase to the effect that a certain judge "judged Israel six years" or "seven years" or that this judge judged Israel "ten years" (example: Judges 12:7, 9, 11, 14). As mentioned above, this generally meant that they had been successful in military endeavors and were considered to be heroes by the people of Israel but it does not mean that there was a strong central government.

However, you will also see that the Lord, in His mercy, often inspired and called these judges to serve and help the Israelites. Thus, even though they did not seem to have a strong central church or national government, as was the case under Moses and Joshua, the Lord still offered them much help and preserved them as His covenant people.

This period of Old Testament history was quite similar to the situation in Third Nephi, preceding the coming of Christ to America. The people in America at that time basically broke up into tribes and had no strong central government (3 Nephi 7:2).

When Joshua gave his farewell address to his people, one of the things he stressed was the importance of driving the rest of the Canaanites and their wicked ("ripe-in-iniquity") culture out of the land. He had already given each tribe a specific assignment to finish driving them out (Joshua 23:4–5). Tragically for them, they failed in this and ended up adopting the evil practices of these people into their own lives. One of these wicked practices was idol worship.

QUESTION: Why was idolatry so popular? Why did the Israelites so willingly join their non-Israelite neighbors in idol worship?

ANSWER: A prominent part of the answer is found in the fact that sexual immorality was widely used as a part of the worship of idols. In fact, temple prostitutes, both men and women, were provided at worship sites as a common part of idolatry. The worship of Baal and Ashtaroth (referred to in Judges 2:13) was notoriously licentious. We will read some quotes explaining this.

S. KENT BROWN

> "The material culture and international trade of the Canaanites was highly advanced, but their religious ways stood diametrically opposed to Israel's. **Based on the fertility cults led by the god Baal, the Canaanite religion**

was an extraordinarily immoral form of paganism, including . . . prostitution, homosexuality, and other orgiastic rites" ("I Have a Question," Ensign, October 1973, page 58).

BIBLE ENCYCLOPEDIA

"The general rites of idolatrous worship consist in burning incense; in offering bloodless sacrifices, as the dough-cakes and libations in [Jeremiah 7:18], and the raisin-cake in [Hosea 3:1]: in sacrificing victims [1 Kings 18:26]; and especially in human sacrifices. . . . These offerings were made on high places, hills, and roofs of houses, or in shady groves and valleys. Some forms of idolatrous worship had libidinous [sexual] orgies. . . . Divinations, oracles [2 Kings 1:2], and rabdomancy [Hosea 4:12] form a part of many of these false religions. The priesthood was generally a numerous body; and where **persons of both sexes were attached to the service of any god** (like that of Ashtoreth), **that service was infamously immoral**" (Fallows, Bible Encyclopedia, s.v. "idolatry," 2:850; quoted in the Old Testament Student Manual, page 246).

SMITH'S BIBLE DICTIONARY

"Many have wondered why the Israelites were so easily led away from the true God, into the worship of idols. (1) Visible, outward signs, with shows, pageants, parades, have an attraction to the natural heart, which often fails to perceive the unseen spiritual realities. (2) But **the greatest attraction seems**

to have been in licentious revelries and obscene orgies with which the worship of the Oriental idols was observed. This worship, appealing to every sensual passion, joined with the attractions of wealth and fashion and luxury, naturally was a great temptation to a simple, restrained, agricultural people, whose worship and laws demanded the greatest purity of heart and of life" (Smith, Dictionary of the Bible, s.v. "Idolatry," page 264).

You may wish to read a summary of idol worship under "Idol" in the Bible Dictionary in your LDS Bible. You might underline the phrase "which encouraged as a rule immoral practices."

One other thing before we begin our study of selections from Judges. Have you noticed that the Lord did not appoint a successor to Joshua? Abraham was succeeded by Isaac, then Jacob, then Joseph, then a period of two hundred to three hundred years at least with no central prophet-leader while the children of Israel languished in Egyptian bondage. Moses was called by the Lord to be the prophet-leader of Israel, then Joshua. But there was no prophet called to follow Joshua. This is a sad commentary on the lack of obedience and loyalty to God on the part of the children of Israel at this point in history. They had rejected the Lord and His prophets over and over, claiming loyalty but quickly reverting again to apostasy. Thus, they were left basically on their own after Joshua.

The next strong central church government for Israel, with a prophet at the head, was not established again until the

Savior established His Church at the time of His mortal ministry. It died out via the Great Apostasy after the first century AD and was not established again until Joseph Smith.

We are blessed to live at a time when the Church will be led by prophets, seers, and revelators right up to the Second Coming, when the keys of leadership will be turned over to the Savior, who will be "King of kings" and "Lord of lords" (Revelation 17:14; 19:16) over the whole earth during the Millennium. We are guaranteed by the Lord in prophetic declarations that the restored Church will continue (Daniel 2:35, 44–45, for example). Thus, we are privileged to have a strong central church headquarters from which the word of the Lord goes out constantly to the whole world.

JUDGES 1

Selection: verses 17–36

AS YOU READ this chapter, you will see that some of the tribes of Israel worked with each other and drove many of the Canaanites out of their territories. However, several tribes allowed a number of the inhabitants of the land to remain, contrary to strict instructions given by Moses in Exodus 23:33 and elsewhere. Consequently, they began intermingling with the remaining Canaanites and adopting their wicked practices. We will point these things out with **bold** in selected verses.

17 And **Judah went with Simeon** his brother [*the tribe of Judah worked with the tribe of Simeon*], and they slew the Canaanites that inhabited Zephath, and **utterly destroyed it.** And the name of the city was called Hormah.

18 Also **Judah took Gaza** with the coast thereof, and **Askelon** with the coast thereof, and **Ekron** with the coast thereof.

19 And the LORD was with Judah; and he drave out the inhabitants of the mountain; but **could not drive out the inhabitants of the valley,** because they had chariots of iron.

20 And they gave Hebron unto **Caleb,** as Moses said: and he **expelled thence the three sons of Anak** [*the "giant race—see Bible Dictionary under "Anak"— who lived in the Hebron area*].

21 And the children of **Benjamin did not drive out the Jebusites that inhabited Jerusalem; but the Jebusites dwell with the children of Benjamin in Jerusalem unto this day.**

22 ¶ And the house of Joseph, they also went up against Beth-el: and the LORD was with them.

23 And the house of Joseph sent to descry [*spy*] out Beth-el. (Now the name of the city before was Luz.)

24 And the spies saw a man come

forth out of the city, and they said unto him, Shew us, we pray thee, the entrance into the city, and we will shew thee mercy.

25 And when he shewed them the entrance into the city, they smote the city with the edge of the sword; but they let go the man and all his family.

26 And the man went into the land of the Hittites, and built a city, and called the name thereof Luz: which is the name thereof unto this day.

27 ¶ Neither did Manasseh drive out the inhabitants of Beth-shean and her towns, nor Taanach and her towns, nor the inhabitants of Dor and her towns, nor the inhabitants of Ibleam and her towns, nor the inhabitants of Megiddo and her towns: but the Canaanites would dwell in that land.

28 And it came to pass, when Israel was strong, that they put the Canaanites to tribute, and did not utterly drive them out.

29 ¶ Neither did Ephraim drive out the Canaanites that dwelt in Gezer; but the Canaanites dwelt in Gezer among them.

30 ¶ Neither did Zebulun drive out the inhabitants of Kitron, nor the inhabitants of Nahalol; but the Canaanites dwelt among them, and became tributaries [paid tribute to the tribe of Zebulun as part of the agreement for them to remain in the land].

31 ¶ Neither did Asher drive out the inhabitants of Accho, nor the inhabitants of Zidon, nor of Ahlab, nor of Achzib, nor of Helbah, nor of Aphik, nor of Rehob:

32 But the Asherites dwelt among the Canaanites, the inhabitants of the land: for they did not drive them out.

33 ¶ Neither did Naphtali drive out the inhabitants of Beth-shemesh, nor the inhabitants of Beth-anath; but he dwelt among the Canaanites, the inhabitants of the land: nevertheless the inhabitants of Beth-shemesh and of Beth-anath became tributaries unto them.

34 And the Amorites forced the children of Dan [the tribe of Dan, who were given the northernmost inheritance in the holy land] into the mountain: for they would not suffer them to come down to the valley:

35 But the Amorites would dwell in mount Heres in Aijalon, and in Shaalbim: yet the hand of the house of Joseph prevailed, so that they became tributaries.

36 And the coast of the Amorites was from the going up to Akrabbim, from the rock, and upward.

Major Message

If we allow the inappropriate and wicked practices of people among whom we live to enter into our lives and homes, we are, in effect, following these Israelites who were led into apostasy.

A quote from the *Old Testament Student Manual* shows why it was such a serious matter for the Israelites to be sloppy in following the command to destroy the Canaanites completely or drive them from the land.

"The book of Judges makes clear that **Israel did not conquer all of Canaan when first she entered it**. . . . For a long time during the days of the Judges many of the Israelites were essentially 'hillbillies' [see Judges 6:2], hemmed in by their enemies on every side. After the generations of Israelites who had been acquainted with Joshua passed away, **the effects of Canaanite morals and religion began to be apparent upon the younger generation**. For long periods of time the Canaanites conquered Israel and this fact alone would tend to disrupt her settled religious life and practice. Times were rough and banditry was rampant. As the record itself states: '**In those days there was no king in Israel; every man did that which was right in his own eyes**' [Judges 17:6]. **All of this seems to have taken place because Israel did not drive the Canaanites completely out**. The Lord said to the Israelites: 'Ye have not hearkened to My voice; what is this ye have done? Wherefore I also said: I will not drive them out before you; but

they shall be unto you as snares, and their gods shall be a trap unto you.' [Judges 2:2–3.] . . . Israel's conduct during this period had a lasting effect upon her religion and morals. For centuries Israel's prophets and wise men referred to it and denounced her allegiance to old Canaanite practices. **It is plain that Israel, during the period of the Judges, compromised her relatively high religious ideals with Canaanite practices** and certain elements in her population must have apostatized completely" (Sperry, "Spirit of the Old Testament," pages 51–52; in the *Old Testament Student Manual*, page 252).

JUDGES 2

Selection: all verses

ONE THING YOU will see much of in Judges is the cycle of apostasy. In this chapter, we see it especially in verses 6–23. This cycle, well-known also in the Book of Mormon, basically begins with **prosperity**. When things go well, the people become **prideful** and begin to forget the Lord. The ensuing **apostasy** leads to **destruction**, which leads to **humility** in the hearts of the survivors. When humbled, the people **repent** and return to the Lord. As a result, they are **blessed** and delivered from their enemies. With the blessings of the Lord and their kind treatment of each other, they **prosper**, and the cycle starts all over again.

The cycle does not need to continue. By remaining humble and keeping covenants, individuals and society can remain prosperous (such as was the case with the Nephites for two hundred years after the Savior's visit to them) without forgetting the Lord. Many have succeeded. The Book of Mormon contains a key for being prosperous but not succumbing to this cycle.

Jacob 2:16–19

16 O that he would rid you from this iniquity and abomination. And, O that ye would listen unto the word of his commands, and **let not this pride** of your hearts **destroy your souls!**

17 **Think of your brethren like unto yourselves,** and **be familiar** [*generous*] **with all** and free with your substance, that they may be rich like unto you.

18 But **before ye seek for riches, seek ye for the kingdom of God.**

19 And after ye have obtained a hope in Christ ye shall obtain riches, if ye seek them; and ye will seek them for the intent to do good—to clothe the naked, and to feed the hungry, and to liberate the captive, and administer relief to the sick and the afflicted.

As this chapter begins, an angel speaks to the people for Jehovah. When an angel speaks for the Lord (or the Savior speaks for His Father, example: Doctrine & Covenants 29:1, 42 and 46) without specifically announcing that he is so doing, it is called "divine investiture." We don't know who the angel here in verse 1 is, but his message reminds us of

an often-quoted passage in the Doctrine and Covenants:

Doctrine & Covenants 82:10

10 **I, the Lord, am bound when ye do what I say; but when ye do not what I say, ye have no promise.**

1 And **an angel of the LORD came** up from Gilgal to Bochim, and said, I made you to go up out of Egypt, and have brought you unto the land which I sware unto your fathers; and I said, **I will never break my covenant with you.**

Next, we see the cycle of apostasy beginning among these Israelites with pride and disobedience.

THE CYCLE OF APOSTASY

2 And ye shall make no league with the inhabitants of this land; ye shall throw down their altars: **but ye have not obeyed my voice:** why have ye done this?

In verse 3, next, the angel continues speaking for the Lord, warning of the consequences of their disobedience.

3 Wherefore I also said, **I will not drive them out from before you; but they shall be as thorns in your sides, and their gods shall be a snare unto you.**

4 And it came to pass, when the angel of the LORD spake these words unto all the children of Israel, that the people lifted up their voice, and wept.

5 And they called the name of that place Bochim [*a place of weeping*]: and they sacrificed there unto the LORD.

> Verses 6–9 are basically a review going back to Joshua 24:28–30, which gives an account of Joshua's death.

6 ¶ And when Joshua had let the people go, the children of Israel went every man unto his inheritance to possess the land.

7 And the people served the LORD all the days of Joshua, and all the days of the elders that outlived Joshua, who had seen all the great works of the LORD, that he did for Israel.

8 And **Joshua** the son of Nun, the servant of the LORD, **died**, being an hundred and ten years old.

9 And they buried him in the border of his inheritance in Timnath-heres, in the mount of Ephraim, on the north side of the hill Gaash.

> Next, we encounter the same problem that Alma and Mosiah faced in the Book of Mormon. The rising generation among the Israelites did not know the Lord.

10 And also all that generation were gathered unto their fathers [*they had all died*]: and **there arose another generation after them, which knew not the LORD**, nor yet the works which he had done for Israel.

We will quote verses from the Book of Mormon, which set the stage for the account of Alma the younger and the sons of Mosiah, who rebelled against the Church:

Mosiah 26:1–3
1 Now it came to pass that there were **many of the rising generation that could not understand the words of king Benjamin**, being little children at the time he spake unto his people; **and they did not believe the tradition of their fathers.**
2 **They did not believe** what had been said concerning the resurrection of the dead, neither did they believe **concerning the coming of Christ.**
3 And now because of their unbelief they could not understand the word of God; and **their hearts were hardened.**

Similarly, here in Judges, the Israelites apostatized and began worshiping Baal (Baalim is the plural of Baal), thus activating the law of justice against themselves. The cycle of apostasy continues as the people intentionally engage in gross wickedness.

11 ¶ And **the children of Israel did evil in the sight of the LORD, and served Baalim** [*statues of Baal in many locations*]:

12 And **they forsook the LORD** God of their fathers, which brought them out of the land of Egypt, **and followed other gods**, of the gods of the people that *were* round about them, and bowed themselves unto them, **and provoked the LORD to anger.**

13 And **they forsook the LORD, and served Baal and Ashtaroth** [*the female counterpart of Baal*].

Two quotes from Elder Bruce R. McConkie, of the Twelve, are helpful here:

"Numerous Old Testament references recite apostate Israel's worship of Baal and Baalim (plural of Baal). It was the priest of Baal, for instance, with whom Elijah had his dramatic contest in the days of Ahab and Jezebel. (1 Kings 18.) Baal was the supreme male deity of the Phoenician and Canaanitish nation. It is likely that there were, in practice, many Baals or gods of particular places, the worship of whom was licentious [*involved sexual immorality*] in nature, Baalzebub (the same name as Beelzebub or Satan) was the name of the god of one particular group. (2 Kings 1:3.)" (McConkie, *Mormon Doctrine*, page 68).

"As Baal was the supreme male deity of the Phoenician and Canaanitish nations, so Ashtoreth (Ashtaroth) was their supreme female deity. She was the so-called goddess of love and fertility, whose licentious worship pleased Israel in her apostate periods. (Judges 2:13, 10:6; 1 Sam. 7:3-4; 12:10.)" (McConkie, *Mormon Doctrine*, page 55).

The cycle of apostasy continues now with punishment and destruction, which can lead to humility and repentance.

14 ¶ And the anger of the LORD was hot against Israel, and he delivered them into the hands of spoilers [*enemies who plundered them*] that spoiled them, and he sold them into the hands of their enemies round about, so that **they could not any longer stand before their enemies.**

15 Whithersoever they went out, the hand of the LORD was against them for evil, as the LORD had said, and as the LORD had sworn unto them: **and they were greatly distressed.**

As stated in the general background to Judges in this study guide, the "judges" were basically military heroes who led their people to victory. They sometimes were looked to give counsel and advice in addition to leading military expeditions.

16 ¶ Nevertheless **the LORD raised up judges, which delivered them out of the hand of those that spoiled them.**

Unfortunately the Israelites refuse to humble themselves and repent, at this stage of their cycle of apostasy. Consequently, they will remain for a season at the bottom of the cycle, where punishment and destruction prevail.

17 And yet they would not hearken unto their judges, but they went

273

a **whoring after other gods**, and bowed themselves unto them: they turned quickly out of the way which their fathers walked in, obeying the commandments of the LORD; *but* they did not so.

JUDGES 3

Selection: verses 5–31

THIS CHAPTER CONTAINS several examples that illustrate the message near the end of the previous chapter (Judges 2:16), namely, that many "judges" succeeded in delivering some of the Israelites temporarily from their enemies.

First, though, verses 5-7 speak of the problem of widespread marrying outside the faith, which led to large scale apostasy among the children of Israel.

5 ¶ And the children of Israel dwelt among the Canaanites, Hittites, and Amorites, and Perizzites, and Hivites, and Jebusites [*non-Israelites who were "ripe in iniquity" and whom they had been commanded to drive out of the promised land*]:

6 And **they took their daughters to be their wives, and gave their daughters to their sons, and served their gods.**

7 And the children of Israel did evil in the sight of the LORD, **and forgat the LORD their God, and served**

Baalim and the groves [*Asheroth— in other words, fertility cult goddesses— see footnote 7d in your Bible*].

Verses 8-31 are illustrations of judges or bold military leaders who led the Israelites to temporary victories and periods of peace and supremacy over their enemies.

8 ¶ Therefore the anger of the LORD was hot against Israel, and **he sold them** [*punished them by giving them*] into the hand of Chushanrishathaim king of Mesopotamia: and **the children of Israel served Chushan-rishathaim eight years.**

Next, in verses 9-11, righteous Caleb's younger brother rescues Israel from the king of Mesopotamia and they have 40 years of independence and peace.

The next phase of the cycle of apostasy is seen here as the Israelites repent and turn to the Lord.

9 And **when the children of Israel cried unto the LORD, the LORD raised up a deliverer** to the children of Israel, who delivered them, even **Othniel** the son of Kenaz, **Caleb's younger brother.**

10 And the Spirit of the LORD came upon him, and he judged Israel, and went out to war: and the LORD delivered Chushanrishathaim king of Mesopotamia into his hand; and his hand prevailed against Chushan-rishathaim.

11 And **the land had rest forty years**. And Othniel the son of Kenaz died.

> The 40 years of relative peace and prosperity lead once again to wickedness and then to devastation and destruction, this time by Moab and other nations. As they repent again and turn to the Lord, He will send a left-handed leader to redeem them from Eglon, king of Moab, and his allies.

12 ¶ And **the children of Israel did evil again in the sight of the LORD:** and the LORD strengthened **Eglon the king of Moab against Israel**, because they had done evil in the sight of the LORD.

13 And **he gathered unto him the children of Ammon and Amalek, and went and smote Israel**, and possessed the city of palm trees [NIV: "Jericho"].

14 So **the children of Israel served Eglon the king of Moab eighteen years.**

15 But when **the children of Israel cried unto the LORD, the LORD raised them up a deliverer, Ehud** the son of Gera, a Benjamite, a man lefthanded: and by him the children of Israel sent a present unto Eglon the king of Moab.

16 But Ehud made him a dagger which had two edges, of a cubit [about 18 inches] length; and he did gird it under his raiment [clothing] upon his right thigh.

17 And he brought the present unto Eglon king of Moab: and Eglon was a very fat man.

18 And when he had made an end to offer the present [when he had finished delivering the gift], he sent away the people that bare the present [he dismissed his fellow Israelites who had carried the gift to Eglon].

> Next, Ehud turns around near Gilgal (about 2 miles northeast of Jericho), goes back to Jericho and meets King Eglon again, informing him that he has a secret errand for him. Apparently delighted, the king falls for the trap and dismisses his servants in order to meet privately with Ehud.

19 But he himself turned again from the quarries that were by Gilgal, and said, I have a secret errand unto thee, O king: who said, Keep silence. And all that stood by him went out from him.

20 And **Ehud came unto him; and he was sitting in a summer parlour**, which he had for himself alone. And **Ehud said, I have a message from God unto thee. And he arose out of his seat.**

21 And **Ehud put forth his left hand, and took the dagger** from his right thigh, **and thrust it into his belly:**

22 And the haft also went in after the blade; and the fat closed upon the blade, so that he could not draw the dagger out of his belly; and the dirt came out.

23 Then Ehud went forth through the porch, and shut the doors of the parlour upon him, and locked them.

24 When he was gone out, **his servants came; and when they saw that, behold, the doors of the parlour were locked, they said, Surely he covereth his feet** [*NIV: "is relieving himself"*] in his summer chamber.

> In verse 25, next, we see that the king's servants were nervous about how long the king was aparently requiring to take care of his bathrooming needs but reluctant to disturb him during such a private time. Finally, they decide to wait no longer. In the meantime, Ehud's strategy has worked and he has had time to escape.

25 And **they tarried till they were ashamed**: and, behold, **he opened not the doors of the parlour; therefore they took a key, and opened them**: and, behold, **their lord was fallen down dead on the earth.**

26 And **Ehud escaped while they tarried**, and passed beyond the quarries, and escaped unto Seirath.

Ehud announces his triumph and rallies the armies of Israel

to follow him to the attack on Moab, resulting in 80 years of peace.

27 And it came to pass, when he was come, that **he blew a trumpet** in the mountain of Ephraim, **and the children of Israel went down with him from the mount, and he before them.**

28 And **he said unto them, Follow after me: for the LORD hath delivered your enemies the Moabites into your hand.** And they went down after him, and took the fords of Jordan toward Moab, and suffered not a man to pass over.

29 And **they slew of Moab at that time about ten thousand men**, all lusty, and all men of valour; and there escaped not a man.

30 **So Moab was subdued** that day under the hand of Israel. And the land had rest fourscore years [*80 years*].

31 ¶ And after him was **Shamgar** the son of Anath, which slew of the Philistines six hundred men with an ox goad: and he **also delivered Israel.**

JUDGES 4

Selection: all verses

DEBORAH IS ONE of the better-known judges. She is an example of personal righteousness, courage, and faith in God. Furthermore, she encouraged others to do the will of the Lord. People came from far and wide to get counsel from her. In verses 6–7, 9, and 14, you will see that she was given the gift of prophecy (listed as a gift of the Spirit in Doctrine & Covenants 46:22). Apostle James E. Talmage spoke of Deborah in conjunction with the gift of prophecy. He taught:

"No special ordination in the Priesthood is essential to man's receiving the gift of prophecy; bearers of the Melchizedek Priesthood, Adam, Noah, Moses, and a multitude of others were prophets, but not more truly so than others who were specifically called to the Aaronic order, as exemplified in the instance of John the Baptist. **The ministrations of Miriam and Deborah show that this gift may be possessed by women also**" (James E. Talmage, *Articles of Faith*, pages 228–29).

Once again, in verses 1–3, the Israelites find themselves at the bottom of the cycle of apostasy, facing 20 years of punishment and destruction at the hands of Sisera, chief captain of King Jabin's Canaanite armies.

1 AND the children of Israel again did evil in the sight of the LORD, when Ehud was dead.

The word, "sold," in verse 2, next, means, in effect, "turned them over to" or "refused to protect them from."

2 And the LORD sold them into the hand of Jabin king of Canaan, that reigned in Hazor; the captain of whose host was Sisera, which dwelt in Harosheth of the Gentiles.

3 And the children of Israel cried unto the LORD: for he had nine hundred chariots of iron; and **twenty years he mightily oppressed the children of Israel.**

In verses 4–5, next, we see that Deborah held court to arbitrate disputes between the people of Israel.

4 ¶ And Deborah, a prophetess [*see comments in the background to this chapter*], the wife of Lapidoth, she **judged Israel at that time.**

5 And she dwelt [*held court*] under the palm tree of Deborah between Ramah and Beth-el in mount Ephraim: **and the children of Israel came up to her for judgment.**

In verses 6–7, Deborah prophesies victory in battle against Sisera if Barak will gather a large contingent from the tribes of Naphtali and Zebulun and face the Canaananite armies at the Kishon River.

6 And she sent and called Barak the son of Abinoam out of Kedeshnaphtali, and said unto him, **Hath not the LORD God of Israel**

commanded, saying, Go and draw toward mount Tabor, and **take with thee ten thousand men of the children of Naphtali and of the children of Zebulun?**

7 And I [*the Lord*] **will draw unto thee to the river Kishon Sisera,** the captain of Jabin's army, **with his chariots and his multitude; and I will deliver him into thine hand.**

> We see Deborah's courage and willingness to encourage others in their God-given tasks, in the following verses:

8 And Barak said unto her, If thou wilt go with me, then I will go: but if thou wilt not go with me, *then* **I will not go.**

> We see another specific prophecy of Deborah in verse 9, as to how Sisera will die.

9 And she said, I will surely go with thee: notwithstanding the journey that thou takest shall not be for thine honour [*even though you will not have the honor of killing Sisera yourself*]; for **the LORD shall sell** [*deliver*] **Sisera into the hand of a woman.** And Deborah arose, and went with Barak to Kedesh.

> As previously mentioned, Sisera was the leader of the armies of Jabin, King of Canaan, whose armies had been troubling the Israelites for twenty years (verse 3). Through Deborah's prophecies and Barak's obeying her inspired counsel, Sisera and his soldiers were defeated.

Barak, a powerful and capable man, is a good example of humble obedience to inspired counsel.

10 ¶ And Barak called Zebulun and Naphtali to Kedesh [*called fighting men from the tribes of Zebulun and Naphtali to meet at the river Kedesh*]; **and he went up with ten thousand men at his feet: and Deborah went up with him.**

> In verse 11, we are told that a man by the name of Heber, who was a descendant of Jethro, father-in-law of Moses, lived with his wife, Jael, not far from Kedesh, where this battle took place.

11 Now **Heber the Kenite**, which was of the children of Hobab [*a descendant of Jethro*] the father in law of Moses, had severed himself from the Kenites, and **pitched his tent** unto the plain of Zaanaim, which is **by Kedesh.**

> Next, Sisera gets word that an Israelite army is camped on Mount Tabor, not far from the Kedesh River.

12 And **they shewed Sisera that Barak** the son of Abinoam **was gone up to mount Tabor.**

13 And **Sisera gathered together all his chariots,** even nine hundred chariots of iron, and all the people that were with him, from Harosheth of the Gentiles **unto the river of Kishon.**

Deborah alerts Barak that the time is right to attack the Canaananite armies.

14 And **Deborah said unto Barak, Up; for this is the day in which the LORD hath delivered Sisera into thine hand:** is not the LORD gone out before thee? **So Barak went down from mount Tabor, and ten thousand men after him.**

The Canaananite soldiers panic and begin fleeing as Barak leads his men to battle. Sisera deserts his chariot and flees on foot.

15 And **the LORD discomfited** [*put fear and panic into*] Sisera, and all his chariots, **and all his host,** with the edge of the sword before Barak; so that **Sisera lighted down off his chariot, and fled away on his feet.**

Barak and his forces pursue the fleeing chariots and enemy soldiers. Meanwhile, Sisera gets away and seeks refuge in Jael's tent, seemingly safe ground.

16 But **Barak pursued after the chariots, and after the host,** unto Harosheth of the Gentiles: and all the host of Sisera fell upon the edge of the sword; **and there was not a man left.**

17 Howbeit [*however*] **Sisera fled away on his feet to the tent of Jael the wife of Heber** the Kenite: for there was peace between Jabin the king of Hazor [*the Canaananites*] and the house of Heber the Kenite.

18 ¶ And **Jael went out to meet Sisera, and said unto him, Turn in, my lord, turn in to me; fear not.** And when he had turned in unto her into the tent, she covered him with a mantle.

19 And he said unto her, Give me, I pray thee, a little water to drink; for I am thirsty. And she opened a bottle of milk, and gave him drink, and covered him.

The exhausted Sisera falls into a deep sleep, thinking he is safe and totally unaware of Deborah's prophecy that he will die at the hands of a woman.

20 Again he said unto her, Stand in the door of the tent, and it shall be, when any man doth come and enquire of thee, and say, Is there any man here? that thou shalt say, No.

21 **Then Jael Heber's wife took a nail of the tent** [*a tent peg*]**, and took an hammer in her hand, and went softly unto him, and smote the nail into his temples,** and fastened it **into the ground:** for he was fast asleep and weary. **So he died.**

Having destroyed Sisera's forces, Barak pursues Sisera, and finds Deborah's prophecy fulfilled to the last detail.

22 And, behold, as Barak pursued Sisera, Jael came out to meet him, and said unto him, Come, and I will shew thee the man whom thou seekest. And when he came into her tent, behold, Sisera lay dead, and the nail was in his temples.

23 So God subdued on that day Jabin the king of Canaan before the children of Israel.

24 And the hand of the children of Israel prospered, and prevailed against Jabin the king of Canaan, until they had destroyed Jabin king of Canaan.

Major Message

Women can be given the gift of prophecy. Certainly, one of the most valuable uses of this gift, in addition to fulfilling callings in the Church, would be within the family, knowing by the power of the Spirit what the needs of family members are and will be. We understand that woman's intuition is a form of this gift of the Spirit.

JUDGES 6

Selection: all verses

CHAPTERS 6-8 GIVE an account of Gideon, who belonged to the tribe of Manasseh (see Bible Dictionary, under "Gideon"). The story of Gideon is also one of the better-known accounts in the Bible. He became famous for defeating the enemy armies with the help of the Lord and only three hundred men (chapter 7).

The Midianites and Amalekites had been causing grief for Israel for seven years (verse 1). They had driven many Israelites into the hills, to live in caves (verse 2) and had destroyed their crops repeatedly (verse 4).

An angel appeared to Gideon and told him that the Lord had called him to deliver Israel from her enemies (verses 11–12). Gideon is a bit reluctant and hard to convince. Furthermore, he is rather direct with the angel, as indicated in verse 13.

1 AND the children of Israel did evil in the sight of the LORD: and **the LORD delivered them into the hand of Midian seven years.**2 And the hand of Midian prevailed against Israel: and because of the Midianites **the children of Israel made them the dens which are in the mountains, and caves, and strong holds.**

3 And so it was, when Israel had sown, that the Midianites came up, and the Amalekites, and the children of the east, even they came up against them;

4 And **they encamped against them, and destroyed the increase of the earth,** till thou come unto Gaza, and left no sustenance for Israel, neither sheep, nor ox, nor ass.

5 For they came up with their cattle and their tents, and they came as grasshoppers for multitude; for both they and their camels were without number: and they entered into the land to destroy it.

As we get to verses 6–7, next, we see that the children of Israel were once again to the "repent" phase of the cycle of apostasy. They have humbled themselves and are crying to the Lord for help.

6 And **Israel was greatly impoverished because of the Midianites;** and **the children of Israel cried unto the LORD.**

7 ¶ And it came to pass, when **the children of Israel cried unto the LORD** because of the Midianites,

We do not know who the prophet was, mentioned in verses 8–10, but it is clear that the Lord is scolding Israel through him.

8 That **the LORD sent a prophet** unto the children of Israel, which said unto them, **Thus saith the LORD God of Israel, I brought you up from Egypt,** and brought you forth out of the house of bondage;

9 And **I delivered you out of the hand of the Egyptians,** and out of the hand of all that oppressed you, and drave them out from before you, and gave you their land;

10 And I said unto you, I am the LORD your God; fear not the gods of the Amorites, in whose land ye dwell: **but ye have not obeyed my voice.**

In verses 11–12, an angel appeared to Gideon and told him that the Lord had called him to deliver Israel from her enemies. Gideon

is a bit reluctant and hard to convince. Furthermore, he is rather direct with the angel, as indicated in verse 13.

11 ¶ And **there came an angel of the LORD,** and sat under an oak which was in Ophrah, that pertained unto [*belonged to*] Joash the Abi-ezrite: and his son **Gideon threshed wheat by the winepress, to hide it from the Midianites.**

12 And the angel of the LORD appeared unto him, **and said unto him, The LORD is with thee, thou mighty man of valour.**

13 And Gideon said unto him, Oh my Lord [*addressing the angel*], **if the LORD be with us, why then is all this befallen us? And where** *be* **all his miracles** which our fathers told us of, saying, Did not the LORD bring us up from Egypt? **but now the LORD hath forsaken us,** and delivered us into the hands of the Midianites.

The angel, speaking for the Lord, encourages him in verse 14, next, by reminding him whose work this is.

14 And the LORD looked upon him, and said, Go in this thy might, and thou shalt save Israel from the hand of the Midianites: **have not I sent thee?**

As the account continues, you will see that Gideon feels very inadequate and tries to decline the calling. The Lord, represented by the angel, patiently gives Gideon several signs that are designed to convince him that, with the help of the Lord, he can fulfill his calling to defeat the Midianites.

15 And he said unto him, Oh my Lord, **wherewith shall I save Israel?** behold, **my family is poor** in Manasseh, and **I am the least in my father's house.**

16 And **the LORD said** unto him, **Surely I will be with thee,** and thou shalt smite the Midianites as one man.

Have you noticed that when an angel speaks directly for the Lord (known as "divine investiture"), the scriptures don't generally differentiate between the angel and the Lord, as evidenced in these verses?

17 And he said unto him, If now I have found grace in thy sight, then **shew me a sign** that thou talkest with me.

18 Depart not hence, I pray thee [*please stay here*], **until I come unto thee, and bring forth my present** [*hospitality offering for you*], and set it before thee. And he said, I will tarry until thou come again.

Next, Gideon prepares a meal for the angel. Remember that the Israelites are struggling through very poor times, so offering this meal is a real sacrifice for Gideon.

19 ¶ And **Gideon went in, and**

made ready a kid [*a young goat*], and **unleavened cakes** of an ephah of flour: the flesh he put in a basket, and he put the broth in a pot, and brought it out unto him under the oak, and presented it.

Imagine Gideon's curiosity and surprise as he follows the angel's instructions, next.

20 And the angel of God said unto him, **Take the flesh and the unleavened cakes, and lay them upon this rock, and pour out the broth.** And he did so.

21 ¶ Then **the angel of the LORD put forth the end of the staff that was in his hand, and touched the flesh and the unleavened cakes; and there rose up fire out of the rock, and consumed the flesh and the unleavened cakes.** Then the angel of the LORD departed out of his sight.

By the way, verses 22–23 show evidence of a fear of seeing an angel, which was part of Gideon's culture. The fear came from a false belief that one could not see an angel of the Lord without dying as a result.

22 And **when Gideon perceived** that he *was* an angel of the LORD, Gideon said, Alas, O Lord GOD! for because I have seen an angel of the LORD face to face.

23 And the LORD said unto him, Peace *be* unto thee; **fear not: thou shalt not die.**

24 **Then Gideon built an altar there unto the LORD, and called it** Jehovah-shalom [*the Lord is peace*]: unto this day it is yet in Ophrah of the Abi-ezrites.

Sadly, Gideon's father, Joash, was an idol worshiper who even had his own altar built in order to worship Baal. In this difficult situation, Gideon was like Abraham, whose father, Terah, was also an idol worshiper (Abraham 2:5).

The fact that Joash was an idolater becomes important background for what happens in verses 25–32. The Lord commands Gideon to destroy his father's Baal-worshiping facilities, along with the grove of trees that surrounded them. We previously mentioned the role that groves of trees played in Baal worship. We will include a brief quote here from the *Old Testament Student Manual* by way of review:

"Gideon's father, Joash, owned a grove and an altar dedicated to the false god Baal. Groves of trees played a prominent part in ancient heathen worship. Since it was thought wrong to shut up the gods with walls, groves of trees were often used as natural temples. Within the groves the immoral rites [*sexual immorality*] of the heathen religions were performed" (*Old Testament Student Manual*, page 255).

25 ¶ **And it came to pass the same night, that the LORD said unto him, Take thy father's young bullock,** even the second bullock of seven years old, and **throw down the altar of Baal that thy father hath, and cut down the grove that is by it:**

26 **And build an altar unto the LORD** thy God upon the top of this rock, in the ordered place, and take the second bullock, and offer a burnt sacrifice with the wood of the grove which thou shalt cut down.

27 Then **Gideon took ten men of his servants, and did as the LORD had said unto him:** and so it was, because he feared his father's household, and the men of the city, that he could not do it by day, that **he did it by night.**

In verses 28–30, we see that the Israelite men of the city are furious in the morning, and, upon discovering that Gideon is responsibile, demand that his father turn him over to be executed.

28 ¶ **And when the men of the city arose early in the morning, behold, the altar of Baal was cast down, and the grove was cut down that was by it, and the second bullock was offered upon the altar that was built.**

29 And they said one to another, **Who hath done this thing?** And when they enquired and asked, they said, **Gideon the son of Joash hath done this thing.**

30 Then the men of the city said unto Joash, Bring out thy son, that he may die: because he hath cast down the altar of Baal, and because he hath cut down the grove that was by it.

Joash's response is very interesting—even somewhat humorous:

31 And Joash said unto all that stood against him, **Will ye plead for Baal?** will ye save him [*can't Baal handle his own problems*]? **he that will plead for him, let him be put to death** whilst *it is yet* morning [*he who dares to imply that Baal doesn't have power to handle his own problems should be put to death right this morning*]: **if he be a god, let him plead for himself** [*let him handle it himself, if he is really a god*], because one hath cast down his altar.

32 Therefore on that day he [*Gideon's father*] called him **Jerubbaal**, saying, **Let Baal plead against him** [*in other words, Jerubbaal means, "let Baal handle his own problems"*], because he hath thrown down his altar.

In the rest of this chapter, you will see that enemies from the south (Amalekites) and east (Midianites) came across the Jordan River and camped in the valley of Jezreel (roughly sixty miles North of Jerusalem) where they set up to attack the Israelites. Gideon was told by the Spirit of the Lord to gather an army and lead them in defense of Israel. He blew a trumpet that signaled men to gather in defense, and he gathered a large army of volunteers from four tribes. He asked for additional assurance from the Lord that He would bless him in this effort, and he received it.

33 ¶ Then all **the Midianites and the Amalekites** and the children of the east were gathered together, and went over, and **pitched in the valley of Jezreel.**

34 But **the Spirit of the LORD came upon Gideon, and he blew a trumpet;** and Abi-ezer was gathered after him [*a grandson of Manesseh, whose descendants now gather in response to Gideon's signal*].

Next, Gideon gathers large numbers of fighting men from the tribes of Asher, Zebulun, and Naphtali, as well as more from Manesseh.

35 And **he sent messengers throughout all Manasseh;** who also was gathered after him: and he sent messengers unto **Asher,** and unto **Zebulun,** and unto **Naphtali;** and they came up to meet them.

Next, in verses 36–40, Gideon asks for additional reassurances from the Lord that he has truly been called to do this.

36 ¶ And Gideon said unto God, **If thou wilt save Israel by mine hand, as thou hast said,**

37 Behold, **I will put a fleece of wool in the floor; and if the dew**

be on the fleece only, and it be dry upon all the earth beside, then shall I know that thou wilt save Israel by mine hand, as thou hast said.

His request was answered in an amazing way. The fleece was soaked with dew while all around it was dry!

38 And it was so: for he rose up early on the morrow, and thrust [*folded*] the fleece together, and **wringed the dew out of the fleece, a bowl full of water.**

Gideon asks for yet one more sign, only this time that things be reversed.

39 And Gideon said unto God, Let not thine anger be hot against me, and I will speak but this once: **let me prove, I pray thee, but this once with the fleece; let it now be dry only upon the fleece, and upon all the ground let there be dew.**

40 And God did so that night: for it was dry upon the fleece only, and there was dew on all the ground.

JUDGES 7

Selection: all verses

IN THIS CHAPTER, the well-known battle takes place where Gideon and three hundred men, with the help of the Lord, scatter and defeat the large Midianite army, joined by Amalakites and numerous other marauding tribes of the east, whose numbers were as hordes of grasshoppers and whose camels were "without number, as the sand by the sea" (verse 12). Watch as the Lord tells Gideon to reduce his army from at least thirty-two thousand soldiers to only three hundred. This is a dramatic way to show the Israelites that the Lord was indeed behind their success.

Major Message
You and the Lord outnumber all your enemies.

In verse 1, you will see that Gideon is also now known as "Jerubbaal." You may wish to read the notes for Judges 6:31–32 in this study guide to remind you why this is so. Verse 1 goes on to set the stage for a great battle between the Israelites and the Midianites.

1 THEN Jerubbaal, who is **Gideon, and all the people that were with him, rose up early, and pitched** [*camped*] **beside the well of Harod: so that the host** [*armies*] **of the Midianites were on the north side of them,** by the hill of Moreh, in the valley.

2 And the LORD said unto Gideon, **The people that** *are* with **thee** *are* **too many** for me to give the Midianites into their hands, **lest Israel vaunt** [*boast*] **themselves against me, saying, Mine own hand hath saved me** [*in other words,* *you have so many soldiers that they may not recognize My help].*

As a result of the offer made in verse 3, twenty-two thousand of Gideon's soldiers went home, leaving ten thousand fighting men for Gideon.

3 Now therefore go to, proclaim in the ears of the people, saying, **Whosoever is fearful and afraid, let him return** and depart early from mount Gilead. **And there returned of the people twenty and two thousand; and there remained ten thousand.**

Imagine Gideon's suprise and perhaps, concern, at what the Lord says next!

4 And the LORD said unto Gideon, **The people are yet too many;** bring them down unto the water, and **I will try** [*filter out, select some of*] **them for thee there:** and it shall be, that of whom I say unto thee, This shall go with thee, the same shall go with thee; and of whomsoever I say unto thee, This shall not go with thee, the same shall not go.

5 So he brought down the people unto the water; and the LORD said unto Gideon, **Every one that lappeth of the water with his tongue, as a dog lappeth, him shalt thou set by himself** [*put in one group*]; **likewise every one that boweth down upon his knees to drink.**

After this filtering out, only

three hundred remain with Gideon.

6 And the number of them that lapped, putting their hand to their mouth, were **three hundred men:** but all the rest of the people bowed down upon their knees to drink water.

From a logical standpoint, it may well be that those who bowed down on their knees to drink were far more vulnerable to being killed by the enemy because they could not see well around them and thus remain ever-vigilant. Whereas, those who kept their heads up and brought water to their mouths with their hand could remain much more alert to enemy movement.

7 And **the LORD said unto Gideon, By the three hundred men that lapped will I save you,** and deliver the Midianites into thine hand: and **let all the other people go every man unto his place.**

8 So the people took victuals [*provisions*] in their hand, and their trumpets: and **he sent all the rest of Israel every man unto his tent, and retained those three hundred men:** and the host of Midian was beneath him in the valley.

In verses 9–14, next, the Lord instructs Gideon to sneak down and get close to the enemy lines. And if he prefers, take his servant, Phurah, and listen to the conversations among the enemy. What he hears will encourage him to go forth to carry out his battle strategy.

9 ¶ And it came to pass **the same night, that the LORD said unto him, Arise, get thee down unto the host** [enemy soldiers]; for I have delivered it into thine hand.

10 But **if thou fear to go down, go thou with Phurah** thy servant down to the host:

11 And **thou shalt hear what they say** [listen in on their conversations in camp]; and **afterward shall thine hands be strengthened to go down unto the host** [what you hear will encourage you to go ahead with your attack strategy]. **Then went he down** with Phurah his servant unto the outside of the armed men that were in the host.

12 And the **Midianites** and the **Amalekites** and **all the children of the east** [other enemy combatants from eastern lands] **lay along in the valley like grasshoppers for multitude; and their camels were without number,** as the sand by the sea side for multitude.

Next, Gideon overhears an enemy soldier telling one of his fellow soldiers of a disturbing dream he had in which disaster for the Midianite troops was foretold.

13 And when Gideon was come, **behold, there was a man that told**

a dream unto his fellow, and said, Behold, I dreamed a dream, and, lo, a cake [loaf] of barley bread tumbled into the host of Midian, and came unto a tent, and smote it that it fell, and overturned it, that the tent lay along [collapsed].

Next, his frightened colleague interprets the dream correctly.

14 And his fellow answered and said, **This is nothing else save the sword of Gideon the son of Joash, a man of Israel: for into his hand hath God delivered Midian, and all the host** [the God of Israel will deliver us into their hands].

Gideon returns to his three hundred men and goes into action to carry out his inspired strategy.

15 ¶ And it was so, **when Gideon heard the telling of the dream, and the interpretation thereof, that he worshipped** [expressed gratitude to God], **and returned into the host of Israel, and said, Arise; for the LORD hath delivered into your hand the host of Midian.**

16 And **he divided the three hundred men into three companies, and he put a trumpet in every man's hand,** with **empty pitchers, and lamps within the pitchers.**

Next, Gideon shows his men exactly what he wants them to do.

17 And he said unto them, **Look**

on me [*watch my example*], **and do likewise**: and, behold, when I come to the outside of the camp, it shall be that, as I do, so shall ye do.

18 When I blow with a trumpet, I and all that are with me, then blow ye the trumpets also on every side of all the camp, and say [*shout*], **The sword of the LORD, and of Gideon.**

No doubt, the instruction to shout "The sword of the Lord and of Gideon," above, was to thoroughly instill in the hearts of his men that it was the Lord who was fighting this battle for them.

As the account continues, you will see that Gideon placed his group of one hundred men, as well as the other two groups of one hundred each, in strategic locations all around the perimeter of the enemy armies. This took place during the middle watch, verse 19, next, which was between 10 P.M. and 2 A.M. He had each man equipped with a lantern, a pitcher with which to shroud the lantern temporarily so its light would not show as they moved into place, and a trumpet to blow at a given signal. Trumpets were a well-known sound used to rally soldiers to battle.

19 ¶ So Gideon, and the hundred men that were with him, came unto the outside of the camp in the beginning of the middle watch; and they had but newly set the watch [*the enemy had just changed*

their night guards]: and **they blew the trumpets, and brake the pitchers** that were in their hands [*to expose the flames of their lamps*].

20 And the three companies blew the trumpets, and brake the pitchers, and held the lamps in their left hands, and the trumpets in their right hands to blow withal: and they cried, The sword of the LORD, and of Gideon.

When Gideon and his three hundred men sprang their surprise, the startled enemies stumbled around in the confusion and darkness, fighting against each other, eventually fleeing.

21 And they [*Gideon's men*] stood every man in his place round about the camp: and **all the host ran, and cried, and fled.**

22 And the three hundred blew the trumpets, and **the LORD set every man's sword against his fellow,** even **throughout all the host** [*in their confusion in the night, the enemy soldiers fought against each other*]: **and the host fled** to Beth-shittah in Zererath, and to the border of Abel-meholah, unto Tabbath.

Next, Gideon called for additional men from the tribes of Israel to pursue the enemy.

23 And **the men of Israel gathered themselves together out of Naphtali,** and out of **Asher,** and out of all **Manasseh, and pursued after the Midianites.**

24 ¶ And **Gideon sent messengers throughout all mount Ephraim, saying, Come down against the Midianites**, and take before them the waters unto Beth-barah and Jordan. Then all the men of Ephraim gathered themselves together, and took the waters unto Beth-barah and Jordan.

25 And they took two princes of the Midianites, Oreb and Zeeb; and they slew Oreb upon the rock Oreb, and Zeeb they slew at the wine-press of Zeeb, and pursued Midian, and brought the heads of Oreb and Zeeb to Gideon on the other side Jordan.

JUDGES 8

Selection: all verses

THIS IS A sad chapter. The Lord has just blessed the Israelites to prosper against their enemies, who are still fleeing from the pursuit of Gideon and reinforcements from several tribes of Israel.

First, in verses 1–3, men from the tribe of Ephraim complain because they were not invited to join in the defeat of the Midianites. It appears that they are more interested in glory for themselves than in the blessing of the Lord to other tribes.

1 AND the men of Ephraim said unto him, Why hast thou served us thus, that thou calledst us not, when thou wentest to fight with the Midianites? And they did chide with [*scold*] him sharply.

Gideon responds with diplomacy rather than anger and sooths their feelings.

2 And he said unto them, **What have I done now in comparison of you?** Is not the gleaning of the grapes of Ephraim better than the vintage of Abi-ezer [*aren't the left over grapes for gleaning of your fields far more than my full harvest; in other words, the least of your Ephraimites is far more significant than I am*]?

3 God hath delivered into your hands the princes of Midian, Oreb and Zeeb: and what was I able to do in comparison of you? **Then their anger was abated toward him, when he had said that.**

Next, you will see that Gideon and his weary, hungry, valiant little band of three hundred are still pursuing the Midianites and their kings. He and his three hundred have continued east, across the Jordan River in hot pursuit. They come to Succoth, a town of the tribe of Gad, located east across the Jordan from the site of Jericho. There they ask for food, but the leaders of Succoth turn them down because they have not yet caught up with and slain the kings of the Midianites. Perhaps they were afraid that if Gideon failed to capture and destroy the kings and their armies, those enemies would return to Succoth and exact vengeance upon them. Whatever the case, these citizens of the tribe of Gad cruelly refused to feed Gideon and his men.

4 ¶ And Gideon came to Jordan, and passed over, he, and the three hundred men that were with him, faint [*tired and hungry*], yet pursuing them.

5 And **he said unto the men of Succoth, Give, I pray you, loaves of bread unto the people that follow me; for they be faint**, and I am pursuing after Zebah and Zalmunna, kings of Midian.

6 ¶ And the princes of Succoth said, Are the hands of Zebah and Zalmunna now in thine hand, that we should give bread unto thine army?

7 And Gideon said, Therefore when the LORD hath delivered Zebah and Zalmunna into mine hand, then I will tear your flesh with the thorns of the wilderness and with briers [*you will get a deserved punishment*].

The same thing happens as Gideon and his little army come to Penuel (verse 8, where Jacob had wrestled with a messenger of the Lord—Genesis 32:31—so many years ago). The men of Penuel likewise refuse their request for food.

8 ¶ And **he went up thence to Penuel, and spake unto them likewise: and the men of Penuel answered him as the men of Succoth had answered him.**

9 And he spake also unto the men of Penuel, saying, When I come again in peace, I will break down this tower.

Major Message

Apostasy causes the fragmentation of national unity.

We can see that apostasy has caused tragic fragmentation and selfishness on the part of the citizens of Israel at this time in history. It does the same to any nation or people, and often does the same thing to families.

You have seen, in verses 7 and 9, that Gideon promises to return when he and those who have joined him in the cause of freedom have finished with the Midianites, and then he will deal with the Israelite traitors. It was high treason to refuse to assist Gideon and his men, who were indeed fighting for their own freedom as well as that of the traitors themselves. This reminds us of Captain Moroni's response to the King Men in the Book of Mormon (Alma 59–61).

In verses 10–12, next, Gideon and his men successfully complete their mission, capturing the two kings of the Midianites and routing their armies.

10 ¶ Now Zebah and Zalmunna were in Karkor, and their hosts with them, about fifteen thousand men,

all that were left of all the hosts of the children of the east: for there fell an hundred and twenty thousand men that drew sword.

11 ¶ And Gideon went up by the way of them that dwelt in tents on the east of Nobah and Jogbehah, and smote the host: for the host was secure [*felt they were safe*].

12 And when Zebah and Zalmunna fled, he pursued after them, and took the two kings of Midian, Zebah and Zalmunna, and discomfited all the host.

> In verses 13–17, Gideon returns to face the Israelite traitors in Succoth and Penuel who previously refused to feed him and his exhausted army. He meets out punishment for their cowardly refusal to help the cause of Israel.

13 ¶ And **Gideon** the son of Joash **returned from battle** before the sun was up.

14 **And caught a young man of the men of Succoth, and enquired of him** [*questioned him*]: and he described unto him [*wrote down the names of*] the princes [*leaders*] of Succoth, and the elders thereof, even threescore and seventeen men [*77 men*].

15 And he came unto the men of Succoth, and said, Behold Zebah and Zalmunna [*the two kings of Midian*], with whom ye did upbraid

me [*scold me, in verse 6*], saying, Are the hands of Zebah and Zalmunna now in thine hand, that we should give bread unto thy men that are weary?

16 And he took the elders [*leaders*] of the city, and thorns of the wilderness and briers, and with them he taught [*tore, punished, see verse 7*] the men of Succoth.

17 And **he beat down the tower of Penuel, and slew the men of the city.**

> In verses 18–21, Gideon interrogates his two captive Midianite kings and determines that they were involved in killing his own brothers at Tabor. Consequently, he executes them.

18 ¶ Then said he unto Zebah and Zalmunna, **What manner of men were they whom ye slew at Tabor?** And they answered, As thou art, so were they; each one resembled the children of a king.

19 And he said, **They were my brethren, even the sons of my mother**: as the LORD liveth, if ye had saved them alive, I would not slay you.

20 And he said unto Jether his firstborn, Up, and slay them. But the youth drew not his sword: for he feared, because he was yet a youth [*he was just a boy*].

21 Then Zebah and Zalmunna

said, Rise thou, and fall upon us: for as the man is, so is his strength [*in other words, we want the honor of dying at the hands of a warrior equal to us*]. And Gideon arose, and slew Zebah and Zalmunna, and took away the ornaments that were on their camels' necks.

Next, Gideon refuses to be king. He gives wise counsel regarding kings.

22 ¶ Then the men of Israel said unto Gideon, Rule thou over us [*be our king*], both thou, and thy son, and thy son's son also: for thou hast delivered us from the hand of Midian.

23 And Gideon said unto them, I will not rule over you, neither shall my son rule over you: **the LORD shall rule over you.**

Next, the gold, plundered from the Midianites, is made into an ephod and subsequently turned into an object of idol worship by apostate Israel.

We are sadly reminded how fickle and unstable the Israelites were at this time. It sounds like Gideon had honorable intentions in making a gold ephod to honor the Lord, but the people began worshiping it. The ephod was part of the high priest's attire, worn when he officiated in his office. You can read more about it in Bible Dictionary, under "Ephod."

24 ¶ And **Gideon said unto them, I would desire a request of you, that ye would give me every man the earrings of his prey.** (For they had golden earrings, because they were Ishmaelites.)

25 And they answered, We will willingly give them. And they spread a garment, and did cast therein every man the earrings of his prey.

26 And the weight of the golden earrings that he requested was a thousand and seven hundred shekels [*NIV: "about 43 pounds"*] of gold; beside ornaments, and collars, and purple raiment that was on the kings of Midian, and beside the chains that were about their camels' necks.

27 And **Gideon made an ephod thereof, and put it in his city, even in Ophrah:** and all Israel went thither a whoring after it [*started worshiping it*]: which thing became a snare unto Gideon, and to his house.

28 ¶ Thus was Midian [*the Midianites*] subdued before the children of Israel, so that they lifted up their heads no more. And the country was in quietness forty years in the days of Gideon [*they had 40 years of peace because of Gideon's leadership*].

29 ¶ And Jerubbaal [*Gideon*] the son of Joash went and dwelt in his own house.

30 And Gideon had threescore and ten [70] sons of his body begotten: for he had many wives.

31 And his concubine [*second class, servant wife*] that was in Shechem, she also bare him a son, whose name he called Abimelech.

32 ¶ And **Gideon the son of Joash died** in a good old age, and was buried in the sepulchre of Joash his father, in Ophrah of the Abi-ezrites.

In verses 33–35, next, the children of Israel enter yet again into the downward spiral of the cycle of apostasy, substituting Baal (idol worship) for Jehovah, thus setting themselves and their society for destruction and humbling.

33 And it came to pass, **as soon as Gideon was dead, that the children of Israel turned again, and went a whoring after Baalim**, and made Baal-berith their god.

34 And **the children of Israel remembered not the LORD their God, who had delivered them out of the hands of all their enemies on every side:**

35 **Neither shewed they kindness to the house of Jerubbaal**, namely, Gideon, according to all the goodness which he had shewed unto Israel.

Did you notice which very necessary attribute or personal characteristic the children of Israel lacked, as shown by verses 34–35, above? It is a serious and devastating lack. It is gratitude (see Doctrine & Covenants 59:21).

JUDGES 9

Selection: verses 56–57

APOSTASY CONTINUES TO devastate the Israelites during this segment of Judges. In chapter 9 in your Bible, you will see the tragic results of apostasy, which include murder and political intrigue. We will use just two verses from this chapter to summarize the following important message. It is often called the law of the harvest.

Major Message

We reap what we sow; we harvest what we plant. When we plant wickedness in our lives and refuse to repent, the law of justice determines our harvest.

56 ¶ **Thus God rendered** [*repaid*] **the wickedness of Abimelech,** which he did unto his father, in slaying his seventy brethren:

57 And **all the evil of the men of Shechem did God render upon their heads:** and upon them came the curse of Jotham the son of Jerubbaal.

JUDGES 10

Selection: verses 6–16

CHAPTERS 10-11 PRO-VIDE a good look at the cycle of apostasy in action. In verses 1-5, the Israelites appear to have had forty-five years of relative freedom, attended by considerable peace and prosperity.

THE CYCLE OF APOSTASY

Prosperity and freedom

1 AND after Abimelech there arose to defend Israel Tola the son of Puah, the son of Dodo, a man of Issachar; and he dwelt in Shamir in mount Ephraim.

2 And he judged Israel **twenty and three years**, and died, and was buried in Shamir.

3 ¶ And after him arose Jair, a Gileadite, and judged Israel **twenty and two years.**

4 And he had thirty sons that rode on thirty ass colts, and they had thirty cities, which are called Havoth-jair unto this day, which are in the land of Gilead.

5 And Jair died, and was buried in Camon.

Apostasy

6 ¶ **And the children of Israel did evil again in the sight of the LORD,** and served Baalim, and Ashtaroth [*idol worship which included rites involving sexual immorality*], and the gods of Syria, and the gods of Zidon, and the gods of Moab, and the gods of the children of Ammon, and the gods of the Philistines, and forsook the LORD, and served not him.

Destruction and bondage

7 And **the anger of the LORD was hot against Israel**, and **he sold them** [*turned them over to their enemies, refused to bless them, such that they fell*] **into the hands of the Philistines** [*Israel's enemies to the southwest*], and into the hands of the children of Ammon [*the Ammonites, enemies of Israel who lived east of the Jordan River*].

8 And that year **they vexed and oppressed the children of Israel: eighteen years**, all the children of Israel that *were* on the other side Jordan [*the east side of the Jordan River*] in the land of the Amorites, which *is* in Gilead.

9 Moreover [*in addition*], the children of Ammon passed over Jordan [*to the west side*] to fight also against Judah, and against Benjamin, and against the house of Ephraim; so that **Israel was sore distressed.**

Humility and repentance

10 ¶ And **the children of Israel cried unto the LORD, saying, We**

have sinned against thee, both because we have forsaken our God [*sins of omission*], and also served Baalim [*sins of commission*].

11 And the LORD said unto the children of Israel, *Did* not *I deliver you* from the Egyptians, and from the Amorites, from the children of Ammon, and from the Philistines?

12 The Zidonians also, and the Amalekites, and the Maonites, did oppress you; and ye cried to me, and I delivered you out of their hand.

13 Yet **ye have forsaken me, and served other gods: wherefore I will deliver you no more.**

14 Go and cry unto the gods which ye have chosen; let them deliver you in the time of your tribulation.

15 ¶ And the children of Israel said unto the LORD, We have sinned: **do thou unto us whatsoever seemeth good unto thee** [*true humility*]; deliver us only, we pray thee, this day.

16 And they put away the strange gods from among them, and served the LORD: and his soul was grieved for the misery of Israel.

JUDGES 11

Selection: verses 29–40

IN THIS CHAPTER the children of Israel reach the point in the cycle where they are delivered from their enemies by the hand of the Lord and attain the freedoms that come with loyalty to God. In verses 29, 32, and 33, the Lord calls Jephthah, of the tribe of Manasseh, to lead the armies of Israel into battle against their enemies, the Ammonites. Israel is once more set free by the hand of the Lord. (We will return to verses 30-31 in a moment.)

Deliverance and freedom

29 ¶ Then the Spirit of the LORD came upon Jephthah, and he passed over Gilead, and Manasseh, and passed over Mizpeh of Gilead, and from Mizpeh of Gilead he passed over *unto* the children of Ammon [*fought the Ammonites*].

30 And **Jephthah vowed a vow** unto the LORD, and said, If thou shalt without fail deliver the children of Ammon into mine hands,

31 Then it shall be, that **whatsoever cometh forth of the doors of my house to meet me, when I return** in peace from the children of Ammon [*when I return after successfully subduing the Ammonites*], shall surely be the LORD's, and **I will offer it up for a burnt offering.**

32 ¶ So Jephthah passed over unto the children of Ammon to fight against them; and the LORD delivered them into his hands.

33 And he smote them from Aroer, even till thou come to Minnith, *even* twenty cities, and unto the plain of the vineyards, with a very great slaughter. **Thus the children** [*descendants*] **of Ammon were subdued before the children of Israel.**

> Going back to verses 30–31, you see a rather disturbing and foolish vow made by Jephthah where he promised the Lord that if He gave him and his armies success in defeating the Ammonites, he would offer whatever he first saw coming out of his house when he came home after the war as a burnt offering. It turned out to be his daughter, his only child, in verse 34, next.

34 ¶ And Jephthah came to Mizpeh unto his house, and, **behold, his daughter came out to meet him** with timbrels and with dances: and she was his only child; beside her he had neither son nor daughter.

35 And it came to pass, **when he saw her, that he rent his clothes** [*tore his clothes, a sign of extreme anguish in his culture*], and said, Alas, my daughter! thou hast brought me very low, and thou art one of them that trouble me: for **I have opened my mouth unto the LORD, and I cannot go back** [*I made a vow that I have to keep*].

One thing we can learn from this is not to make unwise vows to the Lord. Several years ago when I was serving as a stake president, a member of my stake called from out of town and told me he had decided to make a vow with the Lord. He had been having troubles with unclean thoughts and decided that a vow would solve the problem. His plan was to covenant with the Lord in a prayer that he would never have an unclean thought again. Obviously, this was an impossible vow to keep, and I counseled him not to do it. He accepted the counsel and sought to overcome the problem through more reasonable means.

Jephthah's daughter's response demonstrates deep spiritual maturity and respect for her father, in verse 36, next.

36 And she said unto him, **My father, if thou hast opened thy mouth unto the LORD, do to me according to that which hath proceeded out of thy mouth;** forasmuch as the LORD hath taken vengeance for thee of thine enemies, even of the children of Ammon [*since the Lord kept His part of the bargain, you must keep yours*].

She requested two months in which to prepare for honoring her father's vow.

37 And she said unto her father, Let this thing be done for me: **let me alone two months,** that I may go up and down upon the mountains, and bewail my virginity, I and my fellows.

38 And he said, Go. And he sent her away for two months: and she went with her companions, and bewailed her virginity upon the mountains [*apparently mourning the fact that part of her offering to fulfill her father's vow would be a lifetime without marrying*].

39 And it came to pass **at the end of two months, that she returned unto her father, who did with her according to his vow** which he had vowed: and she knew no man [*implies a lifetime without marrying*]. And it was a custom in Israel,

40 That the daughters of Israel went yearly to lament the daughter of Jephthah the Gileadite four days in a year.

A simple reading of this account in chapter 11 leads the reader to the horrible conclusion that Jephthah ended up offering his daughter as a burnt offering. This cannot be the case. Jephthah was a righteous man (see Hebrews 11:32–35, where Paul mentions him among other mighty servants of God), and it was absolutely and strictly against the laws of God to offer human sacrifices. In fact, human sacrifice is the ultimate blasphemy and mockery of the supreme voluntary sacrifice of the Son of God! It is a Satan-sponsored forced counterfeit of the voluntary Atonement of Jesus Christ.

So, what do we conclude? A more careful reading of these verses leads to the conclusion that he kept his vow and did offer his daughter to the Lord, with her consent, much the same as Hannah did with Samuel in 1 Samuel 1:11, 20. It was a spiritual offering, an offering of lifetime service, exclusively to the Lord. It was, in effect, a spiritual "burnt offering," in which the efforts of the daughter throughout her life were to "rise up to heaven" as the smoke from a burnt offering did literally, a "sweet savor" (Exodus 29:18) rising toward heaven as a symbol of praising and glorifying the Lord. You can read more about this possible interpretation in the *Old Testament Student Manual, Genesis–2 Samuel*, pp 256–257.

It also appears that the daughter's offering, in that culture, included remaining a virgin and not marrying throughout her life. This would be a cultural thing and not a proper part of the true gospel of Jesus Christ.

JUDGES 12

Selection: verses 5–6

AMONG OTHER THINGS in this chapter, we see a pronunciation test to decide between life or death.

Men from the tribe of Ephraim complained to Jephthah, as they had done to Gideon (Judges 8:1–3) that they hadn't been included in the victory against the people of Ammon. It looks suspiciously as if they wanted the glory of victory but not the sacrifice to gain it. They sort of hung back until the battle was won, and then stepped forward complaining that they had been left out. Whereas Gideon had done his best to appease them, Jephthah bluntly rejected their complaints, telling them that he had indeed asked them for help but they had sent no men to assist.

As a result, there was a civil war of sorts between the men of the tribe of Ephraim and the men of Gilead, located east of the River Jordan, which had been divided between the tribe of Gad and the tribe of Manasseh. The men of Gilead were primarily of the tribe of Gad.

When the men of Ephraim tried to escape back across the Jordan to safety, the men of Gilead got ahead of them and took over the steep canyons and escape routes attempted by the Ephraimites. As the escapees approached, the men of Gad stopped them and asked them if they were Ephraimites. If the answer was no, then they asked them to pronounce "Shibboleth," a word that only men of Gilead could pronounce correctly. As the Ephraimites attempted to pronounce it, they said "Sibboleth" (without an "h" sound), thus mispronouncing it and exposing themselves as Ephraimites. At this, they were executed as enemy soldiers. Verses 5–6 explain this.

5 And **the Gileadites took the passages of Jordan before the Ephraimites** [*got ahead of the retreating soldiers of the tribe of Ephraim and occupied the canyons leading west to the Jordan River*]: **and** it was *so,* that **when those Ephraimites which were escaped said, Let me go over** [*in other words, "I'm not an Ephraimite"*]; **that the men of Gilead said unto him,** *Art* **thou an Ephraimite? If he said, Nay;**

6 **Then said they** unto him, **Say** now **Shibboleth: and he said Sibboleth:** for **he could not frame to pronounce** *it* **right** [*he could not pronounce the word properly*]. Then **they took him, and slew him** at the passages of Jordan [*the canyons leading down to the Jordan River*]: and there fell at that time of the Ephraimites **forty and two thousand.**

JUDGES 13

Selection: all verses

CHAPTERS 13-16 CONTAIN the story of Samson. We can learn many lessons from this account. We will point out several, and you will no doubt see others.

One message is that a person who is foreordained in premortality to play a major role in the Lord's work on earth still has agency. Samson should have become one of the greatest servants of the Lord in scripture, revered, respected, and appreciate by his people and used as a favorite example of righteousness and redeeming his people from bondage. But instead he chose to satisfy his own lusts and ego. He was self-centered, immoral, bent on revenge, put his own interests above those of his nation, and intentionally lived on the edge of temptation. His life was wasted in service of self, disappointing his parents and his nation.

As we begin the study of his life here in chapter 13, verse 1 informs us that the Israelites have once again turned away from God and have consequently now been under Philistine oppression for forty years. The Philistines are Israel's enemies to the southwest.

1 AND the children of Israel did evil again in the sight of the LORD; and the LORD delivered them into the hand of the Philistines forty years.

> Samson's parents lived in Zorah, twenty to twenty-five miles west of Jerusalem, and were of the tribe of Dan. They had not been able to have children.

2 ¶ And there was a certain man of Zorah, of the family of the Danites, whose name was Manoah; and his wife was barren, and bare not.

> In verse 3, next, we see that an angel of the Lord appeared to Manoah's wife and announced that she was to have a son, who was to play a role in redeeming Israel from the Philistines. This could be considered a "type" of (symbolic of) the annunciation to Mary that she was to be the mother of Jesus, who would redeem us from the bondage of sin (Luke 1:26–38).
>
> Indeed, the experience that Manoah and his wife have in the next several verses ranks as one

of the most remarkable angelic visitations in all the scriptures.

3 And the angel of the LORD appeared unto the woman, and said unto her, Behold now, thou art barren, and bearest not: but thou shalt conceive, and bear a son.

> The angel gives instructions to her regarding her diet and about Samson's upbringing and mission. She is, in effect, given a "word of wisdom" which will better enable her to carry out her mission. As members of the Church in the last days, we, too, have been given a law of health, known in our case as the Word of Wisdom, to bless our lives physically and spiritually and to better enable us to fulfill our mission to spread the gospel.
>
> If sincere people think we are a bit strange or weird for having our Word of Wisdom, we can point out Manoah's wife to them as an example of such a thing in the Bible.

4 Now therefore beware, I pray thee, and drink not wine nor strong drink, and eat not any unclean thing [*as described in Leviticus 11*]:

> As we continue, you will see that the child was to be dedicated to the work of the Lord and was to live the life of a Nazarite, which included never cutting his hair (see Bible Dictionary, under "Nazarite"). The vow of a Nazarite here should not be confused with "Nazarene," meaning "a person from Nazareth" (Jesus was from Nazareth).

5 For, lo, **thou shalt conceive, and bear a son**; and **no razor shall come on his head** [*don't cut his hair*]: for the child shall be a Nazarite unto God from the womb: and **he shall begin to deliver Israel out of the hand of the Philistines.**

In verses 6–21, Manoah's wife tells him what she has experienced with the angel and they are both privileged to interact with the angel. Among other things, we see here that being on angel duty can have its enjoyable and interesting moments.

6 ¶ **Then the woman came and told her husband**, saying, A man of God came unto me, and his countenance was like the countenance of an angel of God, very terrible: but I asked him not whence he was, neither told he me his name:

7 But he said unto me, Behold, thou shalt conceive, and bear a son; and now drink no wine nor strong drink, neither eat any unclean thing: for the child shall be a Nazarite to God from the womb to the day of his death.

Next, Manoah humbly prays that the angel might come again and instruct them about raising Samson.

8 **Then Manoah intreated** [*prayed to*] **the LORD**, and said, O my Lord, let the man of God which thou didst send come again unto us, and teach us what we shall do unto the child that shall be born.

9 And God hearkened to the voice of Manoah; and **the angel of God came again** unto the woman as she sat in the field: but Manoah her husband was not with her.

10 And the woman made haste, and ran, and shewed her husband, and said unto him, Behold, the man hath appeared unto me, that came unto me the other day.

11 And **Manoah arose, and went after his wife, and came to the man**, and said unto him, Art thou the man that spakest unto the woman? And he said, I am.

12 And Manoah said, Now let thy words come to pass. **How shall we order the child, and how shall we do unto him** [*how shall we raise him*]?

13 And the angel of the LORD said unto Manoah, **Of all that I said unto the woman let her beware** [*obey*].

14 She may not eat of any thing that cometh of the vine, neither let her drink wine or strong drink, nor eat any unclean thing: all that I commanded her let her observe.

15 ¶ And Manoah said unto the angel of the LORD, I pray thee, let us detain thee, until we shall have made ready a kid for thee [*let us kill*

a young goat and prepare a meal for you].

From verse 16, next, it appears that it has not yet completely registered in Manoah's mind that this is truly an angel.

16 And the angel of the LORD said unto Manoah, Though thou detain me, I will not eat of thy bread: and if thou wilt offer a burnt offering, thou must offer it unto the LORD. For **Manoah knew not that he was an angel of the LORD.**

17 And **Manoah said unto the angel of the LORD, What is thy name,** that when thy sayings come to pass we may do thee honour [*what is your name so that when your prophecies come true, we may know to whom to give credit*]?

18 And the angel of the LORD said unto him, Why askest thou thus after my name, seeing it is secret [*NIV: "beyond understanding; wonderful"*]?

With the NIV (New International Version of the Bible) rendering "secret" in verse 18, above, as being more accurately translated "wonderful," we would be safe to suggest that this angel is indeed speaking for the Savior and appearing as though he were Jehovah, through what is known as "divine investiture." In Isaiah 9:6, we see that "Wonderful" is another name for the Savior. This angel would be like the angel who appeared for and spoke for Jesus to John

in the book of Revelation (for example, Revelation 22:1–9).

Next, in verses 19–20, the angel was kind enough to provide clear proof that he was indeed an angel of the Lord.

19 So Manoah took a kid with a meat offering, and offered it upon a rock unto the LORD: and **the angel did wondrously; and Manoah and his wife looked on.**

20 For it came to pass, **when the flame went up toward heaven from off the altar,** that **the angel of the LORD ascended in the flame of the altar.** And Manoah and his wife looked on it, and fell on their faces to the ground.

21 But the angel of the LORD did no more appear to Manoah and to his wife. **Then Manoah knew that he was an angel of the LORD.**

In verses 22–23, we see that Samson's parents feared that they would die because they had seen God (probably the angel—see verse 22). Be aware that there was an incorrect belief among these people at that time that a person would die if he or she were to see God.

22 And **Manoah said unto his wife, We shall surely die, because we have seen God.**

23 But his wife said unto him, If the LORD were pleased to kill us, he would not have received a burnt offering and a meat offering at our hands, neither would he have shewed us all these things, nor would as at this time have told us such things as these.

24 ¶ And **the woman bare a son, and called his name Samson: and the child grew, and the LORD blessed him.**

25 And the Spirit of the LORD began to move him at times in the camp of Dan [*among the people of the tribe of Dan who lived there*] between Zorah [*Samson's home town*] and Eshtaol [*a village a few miles west of Zorah*].

JUDGES 14

Selection: all verses

IN A SENSE, Samson, who had the potential to be a "type" (symbolic of) of Christ, ended up being a "type" of covenant-breaking Israel. He had all the potential and special gifts from God to be a great savior for his people, covenant Israel. But he yielded instead to passion and instant gratification, to unbridled selfishness and pride. He openly defied the laws of Moses by marrying outside of the covenant. He had no shame in violating the law of chastity. He foolishly flirted with obvious danger, until he lost his God-given strength. Even at the end, one of his main motivations for destroying the Philistines was to get personal revenge for the loss of his eyes (Judges 16:28).

In chapter 14, one of the first things Samson does as a young man is to show disregard for the word of the Lord and marry outside of covenant Israel. He marries a young Philistine woman.

1 And **Samson** went down to Timnath, and **saw a woman** in Timnath of the daughters **of the Philistines** [*non-Israelites, who were enemies of Israel*].

2 And he came up, and **told his father and his mother,** and said, I have seen a woman in Timnath of the daughters of the Philistines: now therefore **get her for me to wife.**

3 Then **his father and his mother said** unto him, *Is there* **never a woman among** the daughters of **thy brethren**, or among all my people [*the Israelites*], that thou goest to take a wife of the uncircumcised [*non-Israelite*] Philistines? And **Samson said** unto his father, **Get her for me;** for she pleaseth me well.

> Whenever we come to a verse, such as verse 4, next, we would do well to ask ourselves if the translation is correct. We can ask if it fits within the correct doctrines contained in the gospel of Jesus Christ. Let's read it and then talk about it a bit more.

4 But **his father and his mother knew not that it** *was* **of the LORD,** that he sought an occasion against the Philistines [*wanted to justify* *going to war against the Philistines]:* for at that time the Philistines had dominion over Israel.

> The problem is that the Lord does not inspire and direct us to get involved in breaking commandments that give satisfaction to lustful desires and that go against His laws and commandments. Furthermore, the Lord had already commanded the Israelites to take over and posses the land of the Philistines (Joshua 13:1–2).

> **Major Message**

> Whenever you run across a passage of scripture in the Bible that does not fit within the larger context of correct doctrine given in modern scripture, you would do well to wonder if it is a correct translation (see the eighth article of faith).

> In verses 5–14, you will see that Samson visited the young Philistine lady, and that he used his gift of strength to kill a young lion (considered by the inhabitants of Palestine to be the most dangerous beast). He marries the lady and then proposes a riddle to thirty young Philistine men who are attending the customary wedding feast. The agreement is that if they can solve the riddle, he will give them each a new set of clothing. If they can't, then they owe him thirty outfits of clothing.

5 ¶ Then went Samson down, and his father and his mother, to Timnath, and came to the vineyards of Timnath: and, behold, **a young lion roared against him.**

> Some people wonder why the Lord still allows Samson to retain his gift of physical strength at this point. Have you noticed that God is very patient and allows His children many chances to repent and change their ways before taking away their special gifts from Him?

6 And the Spirit of the LORD came mightily upon him, and he rent him as he would have rent a kid, and he had nothing in his hand [*he tore the lion apart with his bare hands*]: but he told not his father or his mother what he had done.

7 And he went down, and talked with the woman; and she pleased Samson well.

8 ¶ And after a time he returned to take [*NIV: "marry"*] her, and he turned aside to see the carcase of the lion: and, behold, **there was a swarm of bees and honey in the carcase of the lion.**

9 And he took thereof in his hands, and went on eating, and came to his father and mother, and he gave them, and they did eat: but he told not them that he had taken the honey out of the carcase of the lion.

10 ¶ So his father went down unto the woman: and Samson made there **a feast;** for so used the young men to do.

303

11 And it came to pass, when they saw him, that they brought thirty companions [*young Philistines*] to be with him.

12 ¶ And Samson said unto them, **I will now put forth a riddle** unto you: if ye can certainly declare [*solve*] it me within the seven days of the feast, and find it out, then I will give you thirty sheets and thirty change of garments:

13 But if ye cannot declare it me, then shall ye give me thirty sheets and thirty change of garments. And they said unto him, Put forth thy riddle, that we may hear it.

14 And he said unto them, **Out of the eater came forth meat, and out of the strong came forth sweetness.** And they could not in three days expound the riddle.

Unable to solve the riddle given in verse 14, above, they pressure his new wife (threaten her life and her family) to get the solution to the riddle out of Samson and tell them before the time is up. She pries the secret out of him, using her womanly wiles, tells the men, and Samson loses the wager. Furious, Samson goes to Ashkelon (another Philistine city), kills thirty men, and takes their clothing to pay off the wager. He then leaves, and his wife's father gives her to the man who was best man at Samson's wedding (verse 20). Watch now as this unfolds.

15 And it came to pass on the seventh day, that **they said unto Samson's wife, Entice thy husband, that he may declare unto us the riddle, lest we burn thee and thy father's house with fire**: have ye called us to take that we have? is it not so?

Next, Samson's new wife applies persuasive methods that have yielded results over the ages.

16 And **Samson's wife wept** before him, and said, **Thou dost but hate me, and lovest me not**: thou hast put forth a riddle unto the children of my people [*the 30 young Philistine men*], and **hast not told it me**. And he said unto her, Behold, I have not told it my father nor my mother, and shall I tell it thee?

His wife persisted, finally getting her husband to reveal the solution to the riddle just in time. She quickly tells the young men.

17 And **she wept before him the seven days, while their feast lasted**: and it came to pass **on the seventh day, that he told her**, because she lay sore upon him: **and she told the riddle to the children of her people.**

18 And **the men of the city said unto him on the seventh day before the sun went down, What is sweeter than honey? and what is stronger than a lion?** And he said unto them, If ye had not plowed with my heifer [*pressured my young wife*], ye had not found out my riddle.

> Enraged, Samson goes to the Philistine city of Ashkelon, kills thirty men and brings back their suits of clothing to pay off his debt (see verse 12, above).

19 ¶ And the Spirit of the LORD came upon him, and **he went down to Ashkelon, and slew thirty men of them, and took their spoil, and gave change of garments unto them which expounded the riddle.** And his anger was kindled, and he went up to his father's house.

> Next, we see that after Samson's rampage, his wife was given by her father to another man.

20 But **Samson's wife was given to his companion,** whom he had used as his friend [*best man at the wedding*].

JUDGES 15

Selection: all verses

CHAPTER 15 IS a continuation of Samson's use of his special gift of strength to get personal revenge. Perhaps you've noticed that, in general, the Lord gives us many chances to make correct choices before He withdraws His blessings from us and allows full consequences to descend upon us. Samson, who was called of God to use his special gifts from the Lord to redeem his people from the Philistines,

has so far used them only for selfish purposes.

In verses 1–2, it appears that Samson has now decided to reconcile with his wife, but, since her father has already given her to another, he offers Samson her younger sister as a wife.

1 BUT it came to pass within a while after, in the time of wheat harvest [*in the fall*], that **Samson visited his wife with a kid** [*a gift of a young goat*]; and he said, I will go in to my wife into the chamber. **But her father would not suffer** [*allow*] **him to go in.**

2 And **her father said, I verily thought that thou hadst utterly hated her; therefore I gave her to thy companion: is not her younger sister fairer than she? take her, I pray thee, instead of her.**

3 ¶ And Samson said concerning them, Now shall I be more blameless than the Philistines, though I do them a displeasure [*now I'm more justified than ever in getting revenge on the Philistines*].

> Next, Samson causes a disaster to the Philistine harvest by tying foxes tail to tail in pairs and tying torches to their tails, setting them loose to flee in terror through the dry fields of grain. The fires also spread to vineyards and olive groves.

4 And Samson went and **caught three hundred foxes,** and took firebrands [*torches*], and turned tail to tail, and **put a firebrand in the midst between two tails.**

5 And when he had set the brands on fire, **he let them go into the standing corn** [*grain fields*] of the Philistines, and **burnt up both the shocks, and also the standing corn, with the vineyards and olives.**

Samson's vicious self-centered revenge brings tragedy to his wife and father-in-law.

6 ¶ **Then the Philistines said, Who hath done this? And they** answered, **Samson**, the son in law of the Timnite [*Samson's father-in-law*], because he had taken his wife, and given her to his companion. And **the Philistines came up, and burnt her and her father with fire.**

In verses 7–8, next, Samson vows to get revenge for the deaths of his former wife and father-in-law. His continuing vendetta will cause trouble for the tribe of Judah. Remember that, at this time in the history of Israel, the Israelites are in subjection to the Philistines. Samson was foreordained and called by the Lord to set Israel free from this bondage, but, instead, he causes more trouble for his fellow Israelites by killing a large number of the men who had burned his ex-wife and her father.

7 ¶ And Samson said unto them, Though ye have done this, **yet will I be avenged of you**, and after that I will cease [*I'm going to get even with you, then I will leave you alone*].

8 **And he smote them hip and thigh with a great slaughter:** and he went down and dwelt in the top of the rock Etam [*NIV: "stayed in a cave in the rock of Etam"*].

The slaughter of their men in verse 8, above, infuriated the Philistines and, consequently, they went up to the territory occupied by the tribe of Judah and spread out, putting pressure on those of Judah to turn Samson over to them.

9 ¶ Then **the Philistines went up, and pitched in Judah, and spread themselves in Lehi.**

10 **And the men of Judah said, Why are ye come up against us?** And **they answered, To bind Samson** are we come up, to do to him as he hath done to us.

The Jews send a large delegation to Samson to tie him up and turn him over to the Philistines.

11 Then **three thousand men of Judah went** to the top of the rock Etam, **and said to Samson, Knowest thou not that the Philistines are rulers over us** [*don't you realize we are in subjection to the Philistines and you are putting us in jeopardy with them*]? **what is this that thou hast done unto us? And he said unto them, As they did unto me, so have I done unto them.**

Did you notice Samson's selfish lack of concern about what his egocentric actions are doing to his countrymen, at the end of verse 11, above? His concern is still only for himself.

Next, in verses 12–13, Samson exacts a promise from his people that they will not kill him themselves if he surrenders to them to be tied up and turned over to the Philistines.

12 And **they said unto him, We are come down to bind thee, that we may deliver thee into the hand of the Philistines.** And Samson said unto them, **Swear unto me, that ye will not fall upon** [*kill*] **me yourselves.**

13 And they spake unto him, saying, No; but we will bind thee fast, and deliver thee into their hand: but **surely we will not kill thee.** And they bound him with two new cords [*ropes*], and brought him up from the rock [*cave*].

It is interesting to see the name Lehi in verses 9, 14, and 19, in light of the fact that Nephi's father, Lehi, was a great prophet from the Jerusalem area at the beginning of the Book of Mormon. Lehi was a city located in some foothills just a few miles southwest of Jerusalem (see *Old Testament Student Manual,* page 260). While there is no definite evidence that Lehi lived in this area or came from it, it is interesting to wonder.

Next, in verses 14–17, he receives strength, bursts the ropes, and kills 1,000 Philistines.

14 ¶ And when he came unto **Lehi,** the Philistines shouted against him: and the Spirit of the LORD came mightily upon him, and the cords that were upon his arms became as flax that was burnt with fire, and **his bands loosed from off his hands.**

15 And **he found a new jawbone of an ass, and put forth his hand, and took it, and slew a thousand men therewith.**

16 And Samson said, With the jawbone of an ass, heaps upon heaps, with the jaw of an ass have I slain a thousand men.

17 And it came to pass, when he had made an end of speaking, that he cast away the jawbone out of his hand, and called that place Ramath-lehi [*NIV: "jawbone hill"*].

In verses 18–19, next, Samson complains of thirst and the Lord patiently provides water for him with an amazing miracle. No doubt this was yet another opportunity for Samson to rethink his selfish, evil ways and turn to the Lord.

18 ¶ And **he was sore athirst, and called on the LORD, and said, Thou hast given this great deliverance into the hand of thy servant: and now shall I die for thirst, and fall into the hand of the uncircumcised** [*the Philistine Gentiles*]?

19 But **God clave an hollow place that was in the jaw, and there came water thereout;** and when he had drunk, his spirit came again [*his strength returned*], and **he revived:** wherefore he called the name thereof En-hakkore, which is in **Lehi** unto this day.

20 And he judged Israel in the days of the Philistines twenty years.

JUDGES 16

Selection: all verses

IN THIS FINAL chapter chronicling Samson's life, we see the continuing moral decline of this man who had the potential to be a great force for good. In verse 1, he commits adultery with a harlot in Gaza.

1 **THEN** went **Samson** to Gaza, and **saw there an harlot, and went in unto her.**

2 And it was told the Gazites [*the people of Gaza*], saying, Samson is come hither. And **they compassed him in** [*surrounded her place*], and laid wait for him all night in the gate of the city, and were quiet all the night, **saying, In the morning, when it is day, we shall kill him.**

Next, he uses his gift of strength as he carries the gates of the city up onto a hill.

3 And **Samson** lay till midnight, and **arose at midnight, and took the doors of the gate of the city, and the two posts, and went away with them, bar and all, and put them upon his shoulders, and carried them up to the top of an hill** that is before Hebron.

His downward spiral of self-indulgence continues as he violates the Law of Moses and again seeks romance with a woman outside of covenant Israel, a Philistine woman named Delilah.

Major Message

Wickedness does not promote rational thought.

Perhaps the best-known story about Samson is his love affair with Delilah and his subsequent capture by the Philistines. Watch now as Samson deliberately goes against common sense and remains in an environment of danger, spiritually as well as physically. It appears that his constant wickedness has dulled his ability to think wisely and rationally.

4 ¶ And it came to pass afterward, that **he loved a woman** in the valley of Sorek, **whose name was Delilah.**

Next, the leaders of the Philistines offer Delilah a huge bribe to find out how Samson gets his strength and to find out how they can successfully capture and punish him.

5 And the lords [*leaders*] of the Philistines came up unto her, and said unto her, Entice him, and see

wherein his great strength lieth, and by what means we may prevail against him, that we may bind him to afflict him: and **we will give thee every one of us eleven hundred pieces of silver** [NIV: "about 28 pounds"].

> Depending how many leaders were involved in offering her the bribe in verse 5, above, she could be a very rich woman!

> In verses 6–20, Samson's selfish lifestyle collapses. Having agreed, Delilah goes to work trying to pry the secret out of Samson. No doubt he knows what she is attempting, but he has an appetite for living on the edge and remains, teasing her in return. He soon becomes aware of the plot of the Philistine leaders but foolishly continues playing with fire. His ability to think straight is now badly compromised.

6 ¶ And **Delilah said to Samson,** Tell me, I pray thee, wherein thy great strength lieth, and wherewith thou mightest be bound to afflict thee [*how you could be taken captive and tormented*].

7 And **Samson said unto her, If they bind me with seven green withs** [*lengths of fresh sinews from animals, often used for bow strings*] that were never dried, **then shall I be weak, and be as another man.**

8 Then the lords of the Philistines brought up to her seven green withs which had not been dried, and **she**

bound him with them.

> Imagine the surprise and terror of his would-be captors in verse 9, next!

9 Now there were men lying in wait, abiding with her in the chamber. And **she said unto him, The Philistines be upon thee, Samson. And he brake the withs, as a thread** of tow [*yarn*] is broken when it toucheth the fire. So his strength was not known [*the secret of his strength was not discovered*].

10 And **Delilah said unto Samson, Behold, thou hast mocked me, and told me lies:** now tell me, I pray thee, wherewith thou mightest be bound.

11 And **he said unto her, If they bind me fast with new ropes that never were occupied, then shall I be weak**, and be as another man.

12 **Delilah therefore took new ropes, and bound him** therewith, **and said unto him, The Philistines be upon thee, Samson.** And there were liers in wait [*men lying in wait*] abiding in the chamber. **And he brake them from off his arms like a thread.**

> The dangerous game of deception continues.

13 And Delilah said unto Samson, Hitherto **thou hast mocked me, and told me lies: tell me wherewith thou mightest be bound. And**

he said unto her, If thou weavest the seven locks of my head with the web [*if you weave my seven locks of hair into the web on the loom*].

14 And **she fastened it with the pin, and said unto him, The Philistines be upon thee, Samson.** And **he awaked** out of his sleep, **and went away with the pin of the beam, and with the web.**

15 ¶ And she said unto him, **How canst thou say, I love thee, when thine heart is not with me? thou hast mocked me these three times,** and hast not told me wherein thy great strength lieth.

> One of Satan's effective tools is to wear us down with daily temptation, especially when we deliberately remain close to it. We see this same pattern in verses 16–20, next.

16 And it came to pass, when **she pressed him daily** with her words, and urged him, so that his soul was vexed unto death [*he was getting tired to death of it*];

17 That **he told her all his heart** [*he told her the truth*], and said unto her, There hath not come a razor upon mine head; for I have been a Nazarite unto God from my mother's womb: **if I be shaven, then my strength will go from me,** and I shall become weak, and be like any other man.

18 And when **Delilah** saw that he had told her all his heart, she **sent and called for the lords of the Philistines**, saying, Come up this once [*one more time*], for he hath shewed me all his heart. Then the lords of the Philistines came up unto her, and brought money in their hand [*as promised in verse 5*].

19 And **she made him sleep** upon her knees; and **she called for a man, and she caused him to shave off the seven locks of his head;** and she began to afflict him, and his strength went from him.

20 And she said, The Philistines be upon thee, Samson. And **he awoke** out of his sleep, **and said, I will go out as at other times** before, and shake myself. And **he wist** [*knew*] **not that the LORD was departed from him.**

> In telling Delilah that if his hair was cut, he would lose his strength, he showed total disregard for the Lord and foolishly subjected himself to captivity.
>
> The question is sometimes asked whether or not Samson's strength came from his long hair. The answer is obviously no. His great strength was a gift from God, and the violation of his Nazarite vow, which included not cutting his hair, as well as loyalty to God, was his final act of rebellion and conceit before the Lord took away his strength.
>
> Think of the awful reality that

must have settled into Samson's soul as he realized that he now had to face the consequences for a lifetime of intentional sin. His captors put out his eyes, take him to Gaza, and chain him up to a grinding wheel in a mill where he trudges around and around like a lowly beast of burden, day in and day out.

21 ¶ But **the Philistines** took him, and **put out his eyes,** and **brought him down to Gaza, and bound him with fetters of brass; and he did grind in the prison house.**

Over time, Samson's hair grows long again.

22 Howbeit [*however*] **the hair of his head began to grow again** after he was shaven.

Finally, in verses 23–30, Samson was brought from prison into the temple of the Philistine god, Dagon, where the Philistines were celebrating his capture some time ago. They sent for him to be brought in for their amusement. Since he was blind, he asked the young man who was guiding him to place him between the key pillars of the structure. Having been thus positioned, Samson prayed for the return of his great strength, received it, and used it to bring the pillars down, causing a portion of the building to fall on him and many of the revelers.

23 Then the lords of the Philistines gathered them together for to offer a great sacrifice unto Dagon their god, and to rejoice: for they said, Our god hath delivered Samson our enemy into our hand.

24 And when the people saw him, they praised their god: for they said, Our god hath delivered into our hands our enemy, and the destroyer of our country, which slew many of us.

25 And it came to pass, when their hearts were merry, that **they said, Call for Samson, that he may make us sport** [*entertain us*]. And they called for Samson out of the prison house; and he made them sport: and **they set him between the pillars.**

26 And Samson said unto the lad that held him by the hand, **Suffer me** [*allow, help me*] **that I may feel the pillars** whereupon the house standeth, that I may lean upon them.

27 Now **the house was full of men and women**; and all the lords of the Philistines were there; and **there were upon the roof about three thousand men and women**, that beheld while Samson made sport.

28 And **Samson called unto the LORD**, and said, O Lord GOD, remember me, I pray thee, and strengthen me, I pray thee, only this once [*just one more time*], O God, that I may be at once avenged of the Philistines for my two eyes.

29 And **Samson took hold of the two middle pillars upon which the house stood**, and on which it was borne up, of the one with his right hand, and of the other with his left.

30 And **Samson said, Let me die with the Philistines. And he bowed himself with all his might; and the house fell** upon the lords, and upon all the people that were therein. So the dead which he slew at his death were more than they which he slew in his life.

Archeological discoveries shed interesting light on the temple of the Philistine god, Dagon, that Samson brought down:

"The character of [this] building is illustrated by discoveries at Gezer and Gaza. The roof was supported by wooden pillars set on stone bases. It was flat, consisting of logs of wood stretching from one wall to beams supported by the pillars and from these beams to other beams or to the opposite wall. The temple at Gezer had a forecourt leading into a paved inner chamber, separated from it by four circular stones, on which the wooden pillars stood. Samson probably stood between the two central pillars, if there were more than two. The Philistine lords and ladies were in the inner chamber; the crowd watched from the roof. Samson made sport, in the forecourt, and then asked the boy to lead him to the central pillars to rest against them. Then, putting an arm round each, and bending forward so as to force them out of the perpendicular, he brought the roof down. The weight of people on the roof may have made the feat all the easier" (Guthrie, *New Bible Commentary*, page 272).

In verse 31, next, Samson's family had the sad task of laying their wayward relative to rest in the graveyard of his father.

31 Then his brethren and all the house of his father [*all his relatives*] came down, and took him, and brought him up, and **buried him between Zorah and Eshtaol in the buryingplace of Manoah his father**. And he judged Israel twenty years.

Referring to him as one of the judges of Israel, at the end of verse 31, above, is almost a contradiction in terms. About all he did was cause trouble for his people throughout his twenty years of influence.

Thus ended the life of a man with great potential who chose self indulgence over honoring his calling from the Lord.

JUDGES 17

Selection: all verses

IN THIS POINT of their history, the Israelites continue in a state of deep apostasy. In this chapter, we see that idol worship had made deep inroads into the Lord's covenant people. We also see a blatant example of priestcraft, which is described in the Book of Mormon by Nephi as follows: ". . . priestcrafts are that men preach and set themselves up for a light unto the world, **that they may get gain and praise of the world**; but they seek not the welfare of Zion" (2 Nephi 26:29).

Beginning with verse 1, an apostate man from the tribe of Ephraim, named Micah, hires and offers a yearly salary to an apostate Levite to help set up a counterfeit of the Aaronic Priesthood rites and ordinances (established by Moses) to go along with his idol worship. Micah's mother is, herself, deeply involved in idolatry and encourages her son in this false worship. Micah consecrates his own priests, has his own gallery of idols, and, in a strange twist, gives the Lord credit for his good fortune.

In verses 1–5, we are introduced to Micah and his mother.

1 AND there was a man of mount Ephraim [*the mountainous, lushly forested region of central Israel, originally given to the tribe of Ephraim*], whose name was **Micah.**

Apparently, Micah had stolen about 28 pounds of silver from his mother. Next, in verses 2–4, he confesses to her, after hearing her complaints about the missing silver. They work it out and she hires a silversmith to make two idols.

2 And **he said unto his mother, The eleven hundred shekels of silver that were taken from thee, about which thou cursedst,** and

spakest of also in mine ears, behold, the silver is with me; **I took it.** And his mother said, Blessed be thou of the LORD, my son.

Notice, in verse 3, next, how warped his mother's thinking has become because of apostasy. She has dedicated the silver to Jehovah for making idols to heathen gods!

Perhaps you know someone who used to be active in the Church but is not now, whose thinking has gone far astray from the gospel and who is no longer able to carry on a rational conversation in context of the Church. I have had such experiences and it is not only disconcerting but also somewhat startling.

3 And when he had restored the eleven hundred shekels of silver to his mother, **his mother said, I had wholly dedicated the silver unto the LORD** [*Jehovah*] **from my hand for my son, to make a graven image and a molten image**: now therefore I will restore it unto thee.

4 Yet he restored the money unto his mother; and **his mother took two hundred shekels of silver, and gave them to the founder** [*silversmith*], **who made thereof a graven image and a molten image**: and they were in the house of Micah.

Next, in verse 5, we see that Micah had set up his own church, as a replacement for the religious practices established by Jehovah through Moses under the Law of Moses.

5 And **the man Micah had an house of gods** [*a special shrine or room for his idols*], and **made an ephod** [*a counterfeit of the true Aaronic Priesthood high priest's vest or apron—see Exodus 28:2–6*], **and teraphim** [*domestic idols, perhaps in the size and shape of a man—see footnote 5b in your LDS Bible*], **and consecrated one of his sons, who became his priest** [*a counterfeit of Aaron and his sons, who served as priests*].

> Verse 6, next, (repeated in Judges 21:25) explains one of the root causes of the decline of Israelite society during this period of Judges.

6 In those days there was no king in Israel, but **every man did that which was right in his own eyes.**

> In the last five chapters of the book of Judges, you can see the effect upon society of everyone making their own rules and substituting the laws of God for those rules. People usually do this in the name of freedom, not realizing that by leaving God, they leave freedom. The results are devastating.
>
> This same theme is reflected in the Lord's preface to the Doctrine and Covenants:
>
> **Doctrine & Covenants 1:16**
> 16 They seek not the Lord to establish his righteousness, but **every man walketh in his own way,** and after the image of his own god, whose image is in the likeness of the world, and whose substance is that of an idol, which waxeth old and shall perish in Babylon, even Babylon the great, which shall fall.

> Beginning with verse 7, Micah, hires an apostate Levite from Bethlehem to help set up a counterfeit of the Aaronic Priesthood rites and ordinances (established by Moses) to go along with his idol worship, and offers him a yearly salary to remain and become his permanent priest.

7 ¶ And **there was a young man out of Beth-lehem-judah** of the family of Judah, who was a Levite, and he sojourned there [*had been living in Bethlehem among the tribe of Judah*].

8 And **the man departed out of the city** from Beth-lehem-judah [*Bethlehem in Judah*] **to sojourn where he could find a place** [*to find another place to live*]: and he came to mount Ephraim to the house of Micah, as he journeyed.

9 And Micah said unto him, Whence comest thou? And he said unto him, I am a Levite of Beth-lehem-judah, and I go to sojourn where I may find a place [*I'm looking for a place to live*].

> In verses 10–13, we see priestcraft in action, where an unauthorized man is hired by an apostate or nonmember with no priesthood authority himself to perform priesthood functions.

10 And Micah said unto him, Dwell with me, and **be unto me a father and a priest, and I will give thee ten** *shekels* **of silver by the year,** and a suit of apparel, and thy victuals [*meals*]. So the Levite went in.

11 And the Levite was content to dwell with the man; and the young man was unto him as one of his sons.

12 And **Micah consecrated the Levite; and the young man became his priest,** and was in the house of Micah.

> One of Satan's traps is to get people to falsely attribute prosperity in wickedness to be blessings from the Lord and tacit approval of their improper lifestyle. An example of this is found in verse 13, next.

13 Then said Micah, **Now know I that the LORD will do me good, seeing I have a Levite to my priest** [*now I know that I am approved of God because He has helped me find and hire my own personal priest*].

JUDGES 18

Selection: all verses

IN THIS CHAPTER we see the corruption and apostasy of Micah (chapter 17) transferred to an entire tribe of Israel, the tribe of Dan. At this time in history, the tribe of Dan has not yet acquired a permanent inheritance in the land of Canaan. Several members of the tribe of Dan are temporarily living west of Jerusalem. By the way, Samson was a Danite from that region, which put him close to the Philistines (see chapters 13–16).

In verses 1–3, leaders of the tribe of Dan send out some spies to look for a permanent area in the Holy Land in which their people might settle. In their travels, the spies stop at Micah's place in Mount Ephraim.

1 In those days there was no king in Israel: and in those days **the tribe of the Danites sought them an inheritance to dwell in;** for unto that day all their inheritance had not fallen unto them among the tribes of Israel.

2 And **the children of Dan sent** of their family **five men** from their coasts, men of valour, from Zorah [*Samson's home town*], and from Eshtaol, **to spy out the land, and to search it;** and they said unto them, Go, search the land: who **when they came to mount Ephraim, to the house of Micah, they lodged there.**

> In verses 3–6, next, the five men from the tribe of Dan ask Micah's young hired Levite false priest what he is doing there and then ask him whether or not they will be successful in finding an inheritance for their people.

3 When they were by the house of Micah, they knew [*recognized*] the voice of the young man the Levite: and they turned in thither, and said unto him, **Who brought thee hither? and what makest thou in this place? and what hast thou here?**

4 And he said unto them, Thus and thus dealeth Micah with me, and hath hired me, and I am his priest.

5 And they said unto him, **Ask counsel, we pray thee, of God,** that we may know whether our way which we go shall be prosperous [*whether or not we will be successful in our quest for a permanent inheritance for our tribe*].

6 And the priest said unto them, Go in peace: before the LORD is your way wherein ye go [*the Lord approves your quest*].

7 ¶ Then **the five men** departed, and **came to Laish** [*located in the far northern region of the promised land, north of the Sea of Galilee*], **and saw the people that were therein, how they dwelt careless** [*peaceful and secure*], after the manner of the Zidonians [*people to the west, along the Mediterranean Sea coast*], quiet and secure; and there was no magistrate [*central government*] in the land, that might put them to shame in any thing; and they were far from the Zidonians, and had no business with any man.

Next, in verses 8–11, the five spies returned and reported their findings to their leaders, urging them to muster a small army and easily take the land around Laish for an inheritance.

8 And **they came unto their brethren** to Zorah and Eshtaol: **and their brethren said unto them, What say ye?**

9 And they said, Arise, that we may go up against them [*don't waste time, get up and go!*]: for we have seen the land, and, behold, it is very good: and are ye still [*why are you still sitting around*]? be not slothful [*don't miss this opportunity*] to go, and to enter to possess the land.

10 When ye go, ye shall come unto a people secure, and to a large land: for God hath given it into your hands; a place where there is no want of any thing that is in the earth.

11 ¶ **And there went from thence of the family of the Danites** [*the tribe of Dan*], out of Zorah and out of Eshtaol, **six hundred men appointed with weapons of war.**

12 And they went up, and pitched [*camped*] in Kirjath-jearim [*about 10–15 miles northwest of Jerusalem*], in Judah: wherefore they called that place Mahaneh-dan unto this day: behold, it is behind Kirjath-jearim.

As the 600 soldiers continue traveling north, they stop at Micah's residence and the five spies tell them what they discovered previously when they lodged with Micah. Among other things, they mention a golden opportunity here to steal a ready-made religion, complete with ephod (high priest's vest or apron), idols and a Levite priest, to use for themselves when they conquer Laish and move their tribe of Dan to that region.

13 And they passed thence unto mount Ephraim, and **came unto the house of Micah.**

14 ¶ Then answered the five men that went to spy out the country of Laish, and said unto their brethren, Do ye know that there is in these houses an **ephod**, and **teraphim** [*life-sized idols*], and a **graven image** [*a carved idol*], and a **molten image** [*a cast idol of molten silver, see 17:4*]? now therefore consider what ye have to do [*so what do you think you should do, hint, hint*].

15 And they turned thitherward, and came to the house of the young man the Levite, even unto the house of Micah, and saluted [*greeted*] him [*the young Levite*].

With 600 armed men watching, the Levite false priest is forced to stand by helplessly and watch as his and Micah's precious mockery of true religion is appropriated by the men of Dan for their own use and the use of their people.

16 And the six hundred men appointed [*armed*] with their weapons of war, which were of the children of Dan, stood by the entering of the gate.

17 And **the five men** that went to spy out the land went up, and came in thither, and **took the graven image, and the ephod, and the teraphim, and the molten image**: and the priest stood in the entering of the gate with the six hundred men that were appointed with weapons of war.

Verse 18, next, repeats for emphases what is written in verse 17, above. It is an example of typical repetition in the Bible during this period.

18 And **these went into Micah's house, and fetched the carved image, the ephod, and the teraphim, and the molten image**. Then said the priest unto them, What do ye?

When the young Levite begins to protest (end of verse 18, above), he is quickly brought up short and then invited to have a much expanded career with these Danites.

19 And they said unto him, **Hold thy peace,** lay thine hand upon thy mouth [*stop talking*], and **go with us, and be to us a father and a priest: is it better for thee to be a priest unto the house of one man, or that thou be a priest unto a tribe and a family in Israel?**

The young priest is quick to see a better business opportunity and rejoices in his good fortune.

20 And **the priest's heart was glad,** and he took the ephod, and the teraphim, and the graven image, and went in the midst of the people.

21 So they turned and departed, and put the little ones and the cattle [*their little children and livestock*] and the carriage before them.

Next, in verses 22–26, Micah gathers his neighbors and they angrily pursue the Danites.

22 ¶ And when they were a good way from the house of Micah, **the men that were in the houses near to Micah's house** were gathered together, and **overtook the children of Dan.**

23 And **they cried unto the children of Dan. And they turned their faces, and said unto Micah, What aileth thee** [*are you crazy*], that thou comest with such a company [*such a pitifully small group against us*]?

24 And he said, Ye have taken away my gods which I made, and the priest, and ye are gone away: and what have I more? and **what is this that ye say unto me, What aileth thee** [*why do you ask such a foolish question*]?

The Danite warriors threaten Micah in no uncertain terms to stop his foolish pursuit or face annihilation with his family.

25 And the children of Dan said

unto him, Let not thy voice be heard among us [*hold your tongue*], **lest angry fellows run upon thee, and thou lose thy life, with the lives of thy household.**

26 And the children of Dan went their way: and **when Micah saw that they were too strong for him, he turned and went back unto his house.**

In verses 27–31, the six hundred Danite soldiers destroy Laish, build their own city, which they name Dan, then set up their ready-made apostate religion with all the trappings they stole from Micah. Satan is successfully achieving his goals for them. He "cheateth their souls and leadeth them carefully down to hell" (2 Nephi 28:21).

27 And **they took the things which Micah had made, and the priest which he had, and came unto Laish,** unto a people that were at quiet and secure: and they smote them with the edge of the sword, and burnt the city with fire.

28 And there was no deliverer, because it was far from Zidon, and they had no business with any man; and it was in the valley that lieth by Beth-rehob. And they built a city, and dwelt therein.

29 And **they called the name of the city Dan,** after the name of Dan their father [*ancestor*], who was born unto Israel [*Jacob*]: howbeit the name of the city was Laish at the first.

30 ¶ And the children of Dan set up the graven image: and Jonathan, the son of Gershom, the son of Manasseh, he and his sons were priests to the tribe of Dan until the day of the captivity of the land [until about 400 years in the future, when the Assyrians captured the northern ten tribes in about 722 BC, and the tribe of Dan became part of the lost ten tribes].

31 And they set them up Micah's graven image, which he made, all the time that the house of God was in Shiloh [they ran their own religion all the time the Tabernacle built by Moses was centered in Shiloh, about 25 miles north, northeast of Jerusalem].

JUDGES 19

Selection: all verses

IN THE LAST three chapters of Judges, you will get an idea of how depraved Israelite society had become by this time in their history.

The first part of verse 1 of chapter 19 emphasizes again that there was no central government for the tribes of Israel. They had neither a prophet nor a king.

1 AND it came to pass in those days, when there was no king in Israel, that there was a certain Levite sojourning on the side of mount Ephraim, who took to him a concubine out of Beth-lehem-judah.

The rest of verse 1, above, sets the stage for the rest of the chapter. A man of the tribe of Levi who lives in the mountain country of Ephraim acquires a second class, servant wife, known as a "concubine," from Bethlehem.

Verse 2 informs us that, in the course of time, she stepped out on her husband and worked as a prostitute. Eventually, she left him and went back to her father's home in Bethlehem.

2 And his concubine played the whore against him, and went away from him unto her father's house to Beth-lehem-judah, and was there four whole months.

In verses 3–8, we see that, at the end of four months, the Levite traveled to Bethlehem with his servant and successfully attempted to reconcile with his estranged concubine wife.

3 And her husband arose, and went after her, to speak friendly unto her, and to bring her again, having his servant with him, and a couple of asses: and she brought him [invited him] into her father's house: and when the father of the damsel saw him, he rejoiced to meet him.

4 And his father in law, the damsel's father, retained him [begged

him to stay and visit a while]; and he abode with him three days: so they did eat and drink, and lodged there.

5 ¶ And it came to pass **on the fourth day**, when they arose early in the morning, that **he rose up to depart**: and **the damsel's father said unto his son in law, Comfort thine heart with a morsel of bread, and afterward go your way.**

6 And they sat down, and did eat and drink both of them together: for the damsel's father had said unto the man, **Be content, I pray thee, and tarry all night**, and let thine heart be merry.

7 And when the man rose up to depart, his father in law urged him: therefore **he lodged there again.**

8 And **he arose early in the morning on the fifth day to depart**: and the damsel's father said, Comfort thine heart, I pray thee. And they tarried until afternoon, and they did eat both of them.

9 And when the man rose up to depart, he, and his concubine, and his servant, **his father in law, the damsel's father, said unto him, Behold, now the day draweth toward evening, I pray you tarry all night**: behold, the day groweth to an end, lodge here, that thine heart may be merry; and to morrow get you early on your way, that thou mayest go home.

Perhaps the father did not want his daughter to leave home again or possibly he simply wanted to delay their leaving a little longer. Whatever the case, the Levite is determined to start for home, even though the hour is late.

10 **But the man would not tarry that night**, but he rose up and **departed, and came over against** [*toward*] **Jebus**, which is Jerusalem [*Jerusalem used to be called Jebus, until King David conquered it and it became part of Israelite territory*]; and there were with him two asses saddled, his concubine also was with him.

11 And when they were by Jebus, the day was far spent; and **the servant said unto his master, Come, I pray thee, and let us turn in into this city of the Jebusites** [*non-Israelites*], and lodge in it.

12 And **his master said** unto him, **We will not turn aside hither into the city of a stranger** [*non-Israelites*], that is not of the children of Israel; we will pass over to Gibeah [*a city a few miles northwest of Jebus or Jerusalem, inhabited by members of the tribe of Benjamin*].

13 And he said unto his servant, Come, and let us draw near to one of these places to lodge all night, in Gibeah, or in Ramah.

14 And they passed on and went their way; and the sun went down upon them when they were by Gibeah, which belongeth to Benjamin.

As the account continues, the man, his servant, and his concubine could find no lodging for the night and have decided to sleep on the street.

15 And they turned aside thither, to go in and to lodge in Gibeah: and when he went in, he sat him down in a street of the city: for there was no man that took them into his house to lodging.

At this point, an elderly man comes along.

16 ¶ And, behold, **there came an old man from his work** out of the field at even [in the evening], **which was also of mount Ephraim** [he was an Ephraimite]; **and he sojourned** [lived] **in Gibeah:** but the men of the place were Benjamites [Gibeah was a city settled by people from the tribe of Benjamin].

17 And when he [the elderly man] had lifted up his eyes, **he saw a wayfaring man** [a traveler] **in the street** of the city: **and the old man said,** Whither goest thou [where are you going]? and whence comest thou [where have you come from]?

18 And he [the Levite] said unto him, We are passing from Beth-lehem-judah [Bethlehem in Judea] toward the side [hill country] of mount Ephraim; from thence am I: and I went to Beth-lehem-judah, but I am now going to the house of the LORD; and there is no man that receiveth me to house [no one was willing to provide lodging for us].

Next, in verse 19, the traveler assures the old man that they have everything they need to sleep on the street that night.

19 Yet there is both straw and provender [hay, grain] for our asses; and there is bread and wine also for me, and for thy handmaid [the concubine], and for the young man [the servant] which is with thy servants: there is no want of any thing [we don't lack anything].

20 **And the old man said,** Peace be with thee; howsoever **let all thy wants lie upon me** [let me provide for your needs]; **only lodge not in the street.**

21 **So he brought him into his house,** and gave provender unto the asses [fed his donkeys]: and they washed their feet, and did eat and drink.

Next, we see the rampant wickedness, including widespread homosexuality, that has permeated the tribe of Benjamin by now.

22 ¶ *Now* **as they were making their hearts merry** [while they were enjoying the evening together], behold,

the men of the city, **certain sons of Belial** [*evil, wicked men; troublemakers*], beset the house round about, *and* **beat at the door**, and **spake** to the master of the house, **the old man**, saying, **Bring forth the man that came into thine house** [*the traveler*], **that we may know him** [*so that we can have sexual relations with him—see Genesis 19:5, footnote a in your Bible*].

23 And the man, the master of the house, went out unto them, and **said** unto them, **Nay**, my brethren, *nay*, I pray you [*please*], **do not *so* wickedly;** seeing that this man is come into mine house [*this traveler is my guest*], do not this folly.

> Next, the owner of the home offers the rabble his virgin daughter and the guest's concubine (servant wife) in place of the guest.

24 Behold, *here is* **my daughter a maiden** [*a virgin*], **and his concubine;** them I will bring out now, and **humble ye them** [*humiliate them*], and **do with them what seemeth good unto you** [*do what you want with them*]: **but unto this man** [*his Levite guest*] **do not so vile a thing.**

25 But the men would not hearken to him [*the homeowner*]: **so the man** [*the Levite guest*] **took his concubine, and brought her forth unto them; and they knew her** [*raped her*], **and abused her all the night**

until the morning: **and when the day began to spring, they let her go.**

26 Then came the woman [*the concubine*] in the dawning of the day, **and fell down at the door of the man's house** where her lord [*husband, master*] was, till it was light.

27 And her lord [*her husband*] **rose up in the morning, and opened the doors of the house, and went out** to go his way [*to continue his journey home*]: **and,** behold, the woman **his concubine was fallen down** *at the* **door of the house,** and her hands *were* upon the threshold [*she had barely worked her way up to the door and died at the threshold from the brutal abuse*].

28 And he said unto her, Up, and let us be going. But **none answered** [*there was no answer from her*]. Then the man took her *up* upon an ass, and the man rose up, and gat him unto his place [*went home*].

> The concubine had died because of the abuse, and the enraged husband (who had given her to the mob in the first place) decided to send a graphic message to all the tribes of Israel to inform them what the men of the tribe of Benjamin had done.

29 ¶ And when he was come into his house, he took a knife, and laid hold on his concubine, **and divided**

her, *together* with her bones, **into twelve pieces, and sent her into all the coasts of Israel.**

30 And it was so, that **all that saw it said, There was no such deed done nor seen from the day that the children of Israel came up out of the land of Egypt unto this day** [*this is the worst thing we have ever seen*]: **consider of it, take advice, and speak** *your minds* [*in other words, what do you suggest we do about it?*].

JUDGES 20

Selection: verses 1–13, 46–48

THE OTHER ELEVEN tribes of Israel are horrified and outraged at the atrocity committed in Gibeah against the Levite's concubine by men of the tribe of Benjamin, as recorded in chapter 20. The ensuing public outcry results in the uniting of the other tribes against the tribe of Benjamin, which was the smallest tribe of Israel.

In verses 1-3, we see that large numbers of fighting men and citizens from the other tribes gathered at Mizpah, a city about 10 miles north of Jerusalem and only about 3 or 4 miles northeast of Gibeah, where the guilty Benjamites resided.

1 THEN **all the children of Israel** went out, and the congregation was **gathered together as one man,** **from Dan even to Beer-sheba** [*from the far north to the far south, in other words, from throughout Israel*], **with the land of Gilead, unto the LORD in Mizpeh.**

2 And the chief of all the people, even of all the tribes of Israel, presented themselves in the assembly of the people of God, **four hundred thousand footmen that drew sword.**

3 (Now the children of Benjamin heard that **the children of Israel were gone up to Mizpeh.**) Then said the children of Israel, Tell us, how was this wickedness?

In verses 4-6, the murdered concubine's husband tells the excited throngs what the men of the tribe of Benjamin did to his wife.

4 And the Levite, the husband of the woman that was slain, answered [*responded*] and said, I came into Gibeah that belongeth to Benjamin, I and my concubine, to lodge.

5 And the men of Gibeah rose against me, and beset the house round about upon me by night, and thought to have slain me: and **my concubine have they forced** [*raped*], **that she is dead** [*she died from their brutal abuse*].

6 And I took my concubine, and cut her in pieces, and sent her throughout all the country of the inheritance

of Israel: for they have committed lewdness and folly in Israel [*the
Benjamites have brought shame and
scorn upon all of us Israelites*].

7 Behold, ye are all children of
Israel; give here your advice and
counsel [*advise what course of action
we should take*].

In verses 8–11, next, they all
resolve to take immediate
action. But since there are so
many more men capable of
bearing arms among the 11
tribes as compared to the tribe
of Benjamin, they determine to
draw lots to see which tribe
carries out the agreed upon
punishment. Judah will be the
first tribe sent (see verse 18).

8 ¶ And all the people arose as one
man, saying, **We will not any of us
go to his tent, neither will we any
of us turn into his house.**

9 But now **this shall be the thing
which we will do to Gibeah; we
will go up by lot against it;**

10 And we will take ten men of an
hundred throughout all the tribes
of Israel, and an hundred of a thousand, and a thousand out of ten
thousand, to fetch victual for the
people, that they may do, when
they come to Gibeah of Benjamin,
according to all the folly that they
have wrought in Israel.

11 So **all the men of Israel were
gathered against the city, knit**
together as one man [*completely
united in the cause*].

The first option agreed upon is
to demand that the people of
Benjamin deliver the perpetra-
tors up to be executed. They
refuse.

12 ¶ And **the tribes of Israel
sent men through all the tribe of
Benjamin**, saying, What wickedness is this that is done among you?

13 Now therefore **deliver us the
men, the children of Belial** [*the
wicked men who did this horrible
thing*]**, which are in Gibeah, that
we may put them to death, and
put away evil from Israel. But the
children of Benjamin would not**
hearken to the voice of their brethren the children of Israel:

Beginning with verse 14, the
people of the tribe of Benjamin
gather their fighting men to
Gibeah and a tragic civil war
ensues, with eleven tribes
fighting against the tribe of
Benjamin. We will invite you to
read the account in verses 11–45
in your Bible and we will pick up
the account in verse 46.

As you read, you will see that
the Benjamites fought mightily and that the rest of the
nation humbled themselves,
fasting and praying, and that
they consulted with Phinehas
(Aaron's grandson) who was the
Aaronic Priesthood high priest
at the time (verses 26–28) for
direction from the Lord. You
will also see that the Israelites
used the strategy of ambushing

to finally get the upper hand. In the end, only about six hundred men of the tribe of Benjamin were left alive and they escaped to a location in the wilderness.

46 So that **all which fell that day of Benjamin were twenty and five thousand men** that drew the sword; all these were men of valour.

47 But **six hundred men turned and fled to the wilderness** unto the rock Rimmon, and abode in the rock Rimmon four months.

48 And **the men of Israel turned again upon the children of Benjamin**, and smote them with the edge of the sword, as well the men of every city, as the beast, and all that came to hand: also they set on fire all the cities that they came to.

JUDGES 21

Selection: all verses

ONE SAD RESULT of the civil war between the tribe of Benjamin and the other tribes of Israel, chronicled in chapter 20, was that it began to look like one of the twelve tribes was about to become extinct.

By now, there were only about six hundred Benjamite men left (Judges 20:47). To complicate things further, before the fighting had begun, the other eleven tribes had made a pact that they would not allow any of their daughters to marry a man from the tribe of Benjamin. This agreement was made at Mizpeh (Mizpah), where they organized to fight against Benjamin, as stated in verse 1, next.

1 NOW **the men of Israel had sworn in Mizpeh, saying, There shall not any of us give his daughter unto Benjamin** [*any men from the tribe of Benjamin*] **to wife.**

Now, in great sorrow, having almost annihilated the tribe of Benjamin, the Israelites mourn the potential dying out of one of their tribes. If there are no Israelite girls for the few remaining Benjamite men to marry, and since they are not to marry outside of covenant Israel, the end is in sight for the tribe of Benjamin.

2 And **the people came to the house of God,** and abode there till even [*evening*] before God, **and lifted up their voices, and wept sore** [*bitterly*];

3 And said, **O LORD God of Israel, why is this come to pass in Israel, that there should be to day one tribe lacking** [*one less tribe*] **in Israel?**

As you can see, in verse 4, next, the people increase their attention to religious duties when trouble presses upon them.

4 And it came to pass on the morrow, that **the people rose early, and built there an altar, and offered burnt offerings and peace offerings.**

In verses 5, next, as the eleven tribes start trying to come up with solutions to the dilemma, they look around to see if there are any pockets of Israelites who did not join and support the eleven tribes in their civil war against Benjamin.

5 And the children of Israel said, **Who is there among all the tribes of Israel that came not up with the congregation unto the LORD?** For they had made a great oath concerning him that came not up to the LORD to Mizpeh, saying, He shall surely be put to death [*they had vowed to put any such traitors to death*].

An idea is beginning to hatch. It will be put into action, beginning with verse 8. Meanwhile, verses 6 and 7 review the problem they are facing.

6 And **the children of Israel repented them for Benjamin** [*grieved for the loss of the tribe of Benjamin*] their brother, and said, There is one tribe cut off from Israel this day.

7 How shall we do for [*where will we get*] **wives for them that remain,** seeing we have sworn by the LORD that we will not give them of our daughters to wives?

In verses 8–12, they come up with a plan that demonstrates the low level upon which their apostate minds operate. If they can discover an Israelite city whose people did not support

the war against Benjamin, they can simply kill all the men, married women, and children, then give any virgins to the remaining Benjamite men to marry. They determine that the city of Jabesh-gilead qualifies. It is about 50 miles north of Jerusalem and 2 miles east of the Jordan River.

8 ¶ And they said, **What one** [*what city*] is there of the tribes of Israel that **came not up to Mizpeh** to the LORD? And, behold, there came none to the camp from **Jabesh-gilead** to the assembly.

9 For the people were numbered [*were accounted for*], and, behold, there were none of the inhabitants of Jabesh-gilead there [*none of the residents of Jabesh-gilead supported us in the war against Benjamin*].

10 And the congregation [*the eleven tribes*] sent thither [*to Jabesh-gilead*] twelve thousand men of the valiantest, and commanded them, saying, Go and **smite the inhabitants of Jabesh-gilead with the edge of the sword, with the women and the children.**

11 And this is the thing that ye shall do, Ye shall **utterly destroy every male, and every woman that hath lain by man** [*who is not a virgin*].

12 And **they found** among the inhabitants of Jabesh-gilead **four hundred young virgins,** that had known no man by lying with any male: and they brought them unto the camp to Shiloh, which is in the land of Canaan.

> While four hundred wives is not enough for the six hundred men left in the tribe of Benjamin, it is nevertheless a good start.

13 And **the whole congregation** [*the eleven tribes*] **sent some** [*a delegation*] **to speak to the children of Benjamin** [*the 600 Benjamite men*] that were in the rock Rimmon [*who had fled to the rock of Rimmon*], and **to call peaceably unto them** [*to offer peace*].

14 And Benjamin came again at that time; and **they gave them wives which they had saved alive of the women of Jabesh-gilead:** and yet so they sufficed them not [*there weren't enough wives to go around*].

> As a side issue, have you noticed that the writers of some Old Testament books sometimes give credit to the Lord for things He probably does not want credit for? An example of this might be verse 15, next.

15 And the people repented them [*felt remorse*] for Benjamin [*the tribe of Benjamin*], **because that the LORD had made a breach** [*a gap*] **in the tribes of Israel.** [*In other words, the people felt sorry for the few remaining members of the tribe of Benjamin because of what the Lord had done to them. In reality, it was the*

vengeful attitude and over-reaction of the other tribes that caused the slaughter and the ensuing problem.]

Going back to the problem of finding wives for the other two hundred Benjamites, the leaders of the other tribes come up with a plan designed to solve the problem without causing them to break their oath not to let Benjamites marry any of their daughters. Verses 16–23, next, explain what they decided to do. It shows their twisted way of thinking and reminds us that the farther people move away from God, the less rationally they are capable of thinking. Basically, their plan was as follows:

There was an annual feast and celebration held in Shiloh (about twenty-five miles northeast of Jerusalem). There would be many young ladies there, participating and putting on a dance performance during the festival. So the leaders of the other tribes told the men of Benjamin to hide themselves among the grape vines near where the dance would take place. When the young ladies were dancing, they could kidnap them and haul them off to become their wives. Since it was a kidnapping, it would not violate the oath that the fathers had made, since they would technically not be "giving" them in marriage. The plan worked.

16 ¶ Then the elders of the congregation [*the leaders of the eleven tribes*] said, How [*what*] shall we do for wives for them that remain, seeing the women are destroyed out of Benjamin? [*since we have killed off the* *women of the tribe of Benjamin—see verse 10.*]

17 And they said, There must be an inheritance for them that be escaped of Benjamin [*the survivors of Benjamin must have posterity*], that a tribe be not destroyed out of Israel.

18 Howbeit [*however*] **we may not give them wives of our daughters:** for the children of Israel have sworn, saying, Cursed be he that giveth a wife to Benjamin.

19 Then they said, Behold, there is a feast of the LORD in Shiloh yearly in a place which is on the north side of Beth-el, on the east side of the highway that goeth up from Beth-el to Shechem, and on the south of Lebonah.

20 Therefore they commanded [*instructed*] the children of Benjamin [*the remaining Benjamite men*], saying, **Go and lie in wait in the vineyards;**

21 And see, and, behold, if the daughters of Shiloh come out to dance in dances, then come ye out of the vineyards, and **catch you every man his wife of the daughters of Shiloh, and go to the land of Benjamin.**

22 And it shall be, when their fathers or their brethren come unto us to complain, that we will say unto them, Be favourable unto them for our sakes [*do us a favor*]: because we reserved not to each man his wife in the war: for **ye did not give unto them at this time, that ye should be guilty** [*you didn't actually "give" your daughters to them, so you are not guilty of breaking your oath not to allow your daughters to marry Benjamites*].

23 And the children [*descendants*] of Benjamin did so, and **took them wives,** according to their number, of them that danced, **whom they caught: and they went and returned** unto their inheritance, and repaired the cities, and dwelt in them.

The civil war is over and the problem of survival for the tribe of Benjamin is solved. The men of the other tribes of Israel go home to their families and relative peace returns to the land.

24 And **the children of Israel departed thence at that time, every man to his tribe and to his family,** and they went out from thence every man to his inheritance.

Next, a final reminder from the writer of Judges, whoever that was, that there was no strong central government at this time and people were still making their own rules, rather than adhering strictly and faithfully to the Law of Moses.

25 In those days **there was no king**

in Israel: **every man did that which was right in his own eyes.**

The tribe of Benjamin, already the smallest tribe, remained comparatively small thereafter. By the way, the Apostle Paul was from the tribe of Benjamin (Romans 11:1) and Saul, the first king of Israel was likewise from this tribe (1 Samuel 9:1).

RUTH

RUTH IS A favorite of many who read the Old Testament. She is an example of fidelity and loyalty, love, generosity, humility, and gentleness. She was a hard worker and shared her meager possessions with her mother-in-law, Naomi.

Naomi also has exemplary qualities. Among them is her unselfishness as she seeks to support the emotional needs of her two daughters-in-law after the deaths of their husbands. Naomi tells them that she will support their decision if they determine to go back to their own people and culture. She demonstrates strength during adversity.

One of the important doctrinal truths of the book of Ruth is that non-Israelites can join the Church and become part of covenant Israel, receiving all the blessings of Abraham, Isaac, and Jacob (the blessings of exaltation) if they remain worthy.

The story of Ruth takes place approximately 1250 BC to 1200 BC, sometime during the later period of the book of Judges.

RUTH 1

Selection: all verses

BECAUSE OF SEVERE famine, Naomi (Hebrew: "sweet, pleasant") and her husband, Elimelech (Hebrew: "my God is king"), are forced to leave their home in Bethlehem with their two sons, Mahlon and Chilion, and find a place in which they can survive. They go to the land of Moab (east, across the Jordan River, along the eastern shore of the Dead Sea), and settle perhaps thirty to fifty miles from Bethlehem in the non-Israelite culture of the Moabites.

While living in the land of Moab, Naomi's husband dies. Her two sons marry Moabite women, Orpah and Ruth, and they continue to live in the land for about ten years. Eventually, both husbands die. Naomi has heard that the famine is over in the land of Judah, which includes Bethlehem, so she determines to return to her own people. She tells her two daughters-in-law of her decision and tenderly explains that she will understand if they want to remain in their country and get on with their lives. Orpah decides to stay in Moab, and Ruth desires to go with Naomi.

1 Now it came to pass in the days when the judges ruled [*during the period covered by the book of Judges*], that **there was a famine in the land**. And **a certain man of Bethlehem-judah** [*Bethlehem of Judea*] **went to sojourn** [*live*] **in the country of Moab, he, and his wife, and his two sons.**

2 And the name of the man *was* **Elimelech**, and the name of his wife **Naomi**, and the name of his two sons **Mahlon** and **Chilion**, Ephrathites [*residents of Bethlehem—see Genesis 35:19*] of Beth-lehem-judah. And

they came into the country of Moab, and continued [*lived*] there.

3 And Elimelech **Naomi's husband died**; and she was left, and **her two sons.**

4 And they **took them wives of the women of Moab** [*their wives were not Israelites*]; the name of the one *was* **Orpah**, and the name of the other **Ruth**: and **they dwelled there about ten years.**

5 And **Mahlon and Chilion died also** both of them; and the woman was left of [*was thus left by*] her two sons and her husband.

6 ¶ **Then she arose with her daughters in law, that she might return** [*to Bethlehem*] from the country of Moab: **for she had heard** in the country of Moab how **that the LORD had visited his people** [*had blessed His people in Judea*] **in giving them bread** [*food*].

7 Wherefore [*this is the reason*] she went forth out of the place where she was [*where she was living in Moab*], and her two daughters in law with her; and **they went** on the way **to return unto the land of Judah** [*which was located in southern Israel*].

Naomi's gentle personality and unselfishness are seen in verses 8–9, next.

8 And Naomi said unto her two

daughters in law, Go, return each to her mother's house: the LORD deal kindly with you, as ye have dealt with the dead [*your dead husbands and my deceased husband*], and with me.

9 The LORD grant you that ye may find rest, each *of you* in the house of her husband [*with your husbands' families*]. Then she kissed them; and they lifted up their voice, and wept.

> At this point, both Orpah and Ruth determine to go with their mother-in-law back to her home in Bethlehem.

10 And they said unto her, Surely we will return with thee unto thy people.

11 And Naomi said, Turn again [*go back to Moab*], my daughters: why will ye go with me? *are* there yet *any* more sons in my womb, that they may be your husbands [*in other words, do you think I will have more sons for you to marry*]?

12 Turn again, my daughters, go *your way*; for I am too old to have an husband [*I'm too old to remarry*]. If I should say, I have hope, *if I should have an husband also to night, and should also bear sons* [*and even if I did remarry and conceived this very night, and had sons*];

13 Would ye tarry [*wait*] for them till they were grown? Would ye

stay for them from having husbands [*would you remain unmarried and wait to marry them after they grow up*]? Nay, my daughters; for **it grieveth me much for your sakes** that the hand of the LORD is gone out against me [*in effect, I am so sorry that the trials that the Lord has given me have caused much sorrow for you*].

14 And they lifted up their voice, and wept again: and Orpah kissed her mother in law [*good-bye*]; but Ruth clave unto [*stayed with*] her.

15 And she [*Naomi*] said, Behold, thy sister in law is gone back unto her people, and unto her gods: return thou after thy sister in law.

> Next, Ruth exemplifies the virtues of loyalty and commitment. Verses 16 and 17 are among the most beautiful and best-known in the Bible.

16 And Ruth said, Intreat me not [*do not ask me*] to leave thee, or to return from following after thee: for whither thou goest, I will go; and where thou lodgest, I will lodge: thy people *shall be* my people, and thy God my God:

17 Where thou diest, will I die, and there will I be buried: the LORD do so to me, and more also, *if* ought [*anything*] but death part thee and me.

18 When she saw that she was

stedfastly minded to go with her, then she left speaking unto her [*stopped trying to convince her to go back to her own people*].

19 ¶ So they two went until they came to Beth-lehem. And it came to pass, when they were come to Beth-lehem, that all the city was moved about them [*word spread rapidly that Naomi and her daughter-in-law were back; everyone was excited*], and they said, Is this Naomi?

> In the Holy Land culture and language, emotions and setting are often communicated with the skillful use of just one or two words. We see this next. It is helpful to know that Naomi means "pleasant" or "sweet," and Mara means "bitter" (footnotes 20a and 20b in your Bible).

20 And she said unto them [*the residents of Bethlehem*], Call me not Naomi, call me Mara: for the Almighty hath dealt very bitterly with me [*the Lord has seen fit to put bitter trials in my life*].

21 I went out [*to Moab*] full [*with a husband and two sons*], and the LORD hath brought me home again empty: why *then* call ye me Naomi, seeing the LORD hath testified against me [*humbled me—see footnote 21a in your Bible*], and the Almighty hath afflicted me?

22 So Naomi returned, and Ruth the Moabitess, her daughter in law, with her, which returned out of the country of Moab: and they came to Beth-lehem in the beginning of barley harvest.

RUTH 2

Selection: all verses

THE PRACTICE OF gleaning was an important part of the Law of Moses for taking care of the poor and the needy.

In harvesting grain, the person doing the harvesting went into the field, gathered several stalks of grain into one hand, and cut the stalks off close to the ground with a knife or sickle (a curved knife specially designed for this work) with the other hand. The cut stalks of grain were then bundled together in sheaves for convenient carrying and handling.

As the harvesters worked rapidly, a number of stalks of grain fell to the ground. Under the Law of Moses, it was required that these stalks of grain be left for the poor and the needy to glean—in other words, to gather. We will quote this part of the Law of Moses:

> Leviticus 19:9–10
> 9 ¶ And when ye reap the harvest of your land, thou shalt not wholly reap [*completely harvest*] the corners of thy field, neither shalt thou gather the gleanings of thy harvest.
> 10 And thou shalt not glean thy vineyard, neither shalt

thou gather *every* grape of thy vineyard; **thou shalt leave them for the poor and stranger:** I *am* the LORD your God.

In this chapter, Ruth gleans barley, and also wheat (verse 23), in order to sustain Naomi and herself. She attracts the attention of a wealthy man, Boaz, who is a close relative of Naomi's deceased husband, Elimelech.

1 And **Naomi had a kinsman** [*a relative*] **of her husband's,** a **mighty man of wealth,** of the family of Elimelech [*Naomi's husband*]; and **his name** *was* **Boaz.**

2 And **Ruth** the Moabitess **said unto Naomi, Let me now go to the field, and glean ears of corn** [*grain*] after *him* in whose sight I shall find grace. And she said unto her, Go, my daughter.

3 **And she** went, and came, and **gleaned in the field after the reapers** [*following the people who were doing the harvesting*]: **and her hap was to light on** [*she happened to land on*] **a part of the field** *belonging* **unto Boaz,** who *was* of the kindred of Elimelech.

We see the hand of the Lord in what happens next. Boaz just "happens" to return from town at the right moment and goes out into the field to greet his harvesters.

4 ¶ And, behold, Boaz came from Bethlehem, and said unto the reapers, The LORD *be* with you. And they answered him, The LORD bless thee.

Something about Ruth attracts the attention of Boaz, and he asks about her.

5 **Then said Boaz unto his servant** that was set over the reapers [*who was in charge of his harvesters*], **Whose damsel** *is* **this?**

6 And **the servant** that was set over the reapers **answered** and said, **It** *is* **the Moabitish damsel that came back with Naomi out of the country of Moab:**

7 And she said, I pray you, let me glean and gather after the reapers among the sheaves [*she asked me to please let her glean here*]: so **she came, and hath continued even from the morning until now,** that she tarried a little in the house [*she rested for a little while in the shade shelter*].

Next, Boaz asks Ruth not to go anywhere else to glean but to continue gleaning in his fields.

8 **Then said Boaz unto Ruth,** Hearest thou not, my daughter [*in other words, are you listening*]? **Go not to glean in another field,** neither go from hence [*don't go anywhere else*], **but abide** [*stay*] **here fast by** [*close by*] **my maidens** [*my servant girls*]:

9 *Let* thine eyes *be* on the field that they do reap, and **go thou after them** [*follow them*]: **have I not charged the young men that they shall not touch thee?** [*In other words, you don't have to worry about being safe because I have told the young men to leave you strictly alone.*] **And when thou art athirst, go unto the vessels, and drink of** *that* **which the young men have drawn** [*and anytime you get thirsty, feel free to get a drink from the pitchers of water the young men have filled from the well*].

10 **Then she fell on her face** [*a sign of humility, respect, and reverence in their culture*], **and bowed herself to the ground, and said** unto him, **Why have I found grace in thine eyes, that thou shouldest take knowledge of me, seeing I** *am* **a stranger** [*why are you being so kind to me, knowing that I am a non-Israelite*]?

Boaz has already heard much good about Ruth.

11 **And Boaz answered** and said unto her, **It hath fully been shewed me** [*I have been told all about you*], all that thou hast done unto thy mother in law since the death of thine husband: and *how* thou hast left thy father and thy mother, and the land of thy nativity [*birth*], and art come unto a people which thou knewest not heretofore.

12 **The LORD recompense** [*reward*] **thy work, and a full reward be given thee of the** LORD God of Israel, under whose wings thou art come to trust.

Ruth humbly asks that his favor continue upon her and expresses appreciation for the kindness Boaz is showing her.

13 Then she said, **Let me find favour in thy sight, my lord; for that thou hast comforted** me, **and for that thou hast spoken friendly unto thine handmaid,** though I be not like unto one of thine handmaidens [*even though I do not have the same standing as your servant girls*].

Next, Boaz invites Ruth to eat lunch with him and his servants.

14 **And Boaz said** unto her, **At mealtime come thou hither, and eat of the bread, and dip thy morsel in the vinegar** [*the sauce*]. And she sat beside the reapers: and **he reached her parched** *corn* [*he handed her some roasted grain*], **and she did eat,** and was sufficed [*until she was full*], and left [*and had plenty left over*].

After lunch, Boaz instructs his young men servants, who are harvesting, to make it easy for Ruth to be successful in her gleaning.

15 And when she was risen up to glean, **Boaz commanded his young men,** saying, **Let her glean even among the sheaves,** and reproach [*rebuke*] her not:

16 And let fall also *some* of the handfuls of purpose for her [*drop extra stalks of grain on the ground on purpose just for her*], **and leave *them*,** that she may glean *them*, and rebuke her not.

17 So she gleaned in the field until even [*evening*], and beat out that she had gleaned [*and beat the kernels of grain out of the stalks she had gleaned*]: and it was about an ephah of barley [*about twenty-two liters or eight gallons*].

18 ¶ And she took *it* up, and went into the city: and her mother in law saw what she had gleaned: and she brought forth, and gave to her that she had reserved after she was sufficed.

19 And her mother in law said unto her, Where hast thou gleaned to day? and where wroughtest thou [*where did you work*]? blessed be he that did take knowledge of thee. And she shewed her mother in law with whom she had wrought, and said, The man's name with whom I wrought [*whose field I worked in*] to day *is* Boaz.

> Imagine Naomi's pleasant surprise when she finds out that Ruth had gleaned in Boaz's field that day!

20 And Naomi said unto her daughter in law, Blessed *be* he of the LORD, who hath not left off his kindness to the living and to the dead [*in other words, the Lord is blessing us even though our husbands are dead*]. And Naomi said unto her, The man *is* near of kin unto us, one of our next kinsmen [*a close relative*].

21 And Ruth the Moabitess said, He said unto me also, Thou shalt keep fast by my young men, until they have ended all my harvest [*Boaz told me to stick close to the harvesters for the entire rest of the harvest*].

22 And Naomi said unto Ruth her daughter in law, *It is* good, my daughter, that thou go out with his maidens, that they meet thee not in any other field.

23 So she kept fast by the maidens of Boaz to glean unto the end of barley harvest and of wheat harvest; and dwelt with her mother in law.

RUTH 3

Selection: all verses

IN ORDER TO understand this chapter, it will be helpful for you to have a bit of background about marriage customs and laws in this culture. You can read the basic law governing a case in which a husband has died without having any children, in Deuteronomy 25:5-10. We will use a quote to summarize this law:

"These verses define the levirate law of marriage, which provided that a dead man's brother should marry the widow and raise a family to the dead man. 'The custom insured the security of a widow who might otherwise be left destitute and friendless. . . . If no brother existed, some more distant male relative was required to perform this duty. Whichever relative married the widow became her "go'el" (redeemer or protector). The first son born to the widow by the new marriage was counted as a child of the dead husband and inherited his property.' (*Great People of the Bible and How They Lived,* p. 132.)" (quoted in the *Old Testament Student Manual,* page 230).

Watch now as Ruth's mother-in-law instructs her in how to propose to Boaz. Remember that what you are seeing is being done according to the custom of the day. It was discreet and honorable, even though, to the uninformed, it may appear to push the limits of proper behavior.

1 Then Naomi her mother in law **said** unto her, **My daughter, shall I not seek rest for thee, that it may be well with thee** [*don't you think it would be a good idea if I helped you gain security by marrying again*]?

2 And now is **not Boaz of our kindred** [*wouldn't Boaz make a good husband since he is a close relative and could fulfill the law of marriage for you*], with whose maidens thou wast? Behold, he winnoweth barley to night in the threshingfloor [*he will be threshing the barley tonight and*

will stay there all night to guard it].

3 Wash thyself therefore, and anoint thee [*clean yourself up so you look real nice*], **and put thy raiment upon thee** [*dress nicely*], **and get thee down to the floor** [*the threshing floor*]: **but** make not thyself known unto the man, until he shall have done eating and drinking [*but not until the time is right*].

> What Naomi tells Ruth to do next was a formal proposal for marriage, according to custom, from a woman in Ruth's situation to a man who could fulfill the requirements of the law for her.

4 And it shall be, when he lieth down, that thou shalt mark [*pay attention to*] **the place where he shall lie, and thou shalt go in, and uncover his feet, and lay thee down; and he will tell thee what thou shalt do.**

5 And she said unto her, All that thou sayest unto me I will do.

6 ¶ And she went down unto the floor [*the grain threshing floor*], **and did according to all that her mother in law bade her.**

7 **And when Boaz had eaten and drunk, and his heart was merry** [*and he was pretty comfortable and content*], **he went to lie down at the end of the heap of corn** [*at the far end of the pile of grain*]: **and she**

came softly, and uncovered his feet [*pulled the blanket back from his feet*], **and laid her down** [*by his feet*].

Boaz was a man of high moral principles and integrity, and so he was startled when he discovered a woman lying at his feet.

8 ¶ And it came to pass **at midnight**, that **the man was afraid, and turned himself: and, behold, a woman lay at his feet.**

Next, Ruth makes the formal marriage proposal.

9 And **he said, Who** *art* **thou?** And she answered, I *am* Ruth thine handmaid: **spread therefore thy skirt** [*Hebrew: "wing"*] **over thine handmaid; for thou** *art* **a near kinsman** [*in other words, spread your wing over me, take me under your wing, be my protector, my husband, because you are a near relative*].

Next, Boaz puts Ruth at ease (no doubt she was nervous) and promises to marry her, provided that a man he knows, who is a closer relative, renounces his right to marry her. It appears from verse 10 that Boaz is somewhat older than she is.

10 And **he said, Blessed** *be* **thou** of the LORD, my daughter: *for* thou hast shewed more kindness in the latter end than at the beginning, **inasmuch as thou followedst not young men** [*since you have not pursued younger men to marry*], whether poor or rich.

11 And now, my daughter, fear not; **I will do to thee all that thou requirest:** for all the city of my people doth know that thou *art* a virtuous woman.

12 And now **it is true that I** *am* *thy* **near kinsman: howbeit** [*however*] **there is a kinsman nearer than I** [*you have a closer relative than I am*].

Next, Boaz tells Ruth to get some rest, and in the morning they will see if the other man, the closer relative, wants to marry her. If he does, Boaz will respect his right to do so. If not, Boaz will marry her.

13 Tarry this night, and it shall be **in the morning,** *that* **if he will perform unto thee the part of a kinsman, well** [*if he desires to fulfill the requirement of the Law of Moses and marry you, fine*]; let him do the kinsman's part: **but if he will not do the part of a kinsman to thee, then will I do the part of a kinsman to thee,** *as* the LORD liveth [*I give you my solemn word*]: lie down until the morning.

14 ¶ And she lay at his feet until the morning: and **she rose up before one could know another** [*before it was light enough to recognize a person walking*]. And **he said, Let it not be known that a woman came into the floor** [*in other words, don't give the gossips anything to talk about*].

15 Also he said, Bring the vail that

thou *hast* upon thee, and hold it. And when she held it, he measured six *measures* of barley, and laid *it* on her [*gave it to her to carry home*]: and she went into the city.

16 And when she came to her mother in law, she said, Who *art* **thou, my daughter** [*in other words, are you Boaz's fiancée*]? And she told her all that the man had done to her.

17 And she said, These six *measures* of barley gave he me; for he said to me, Go not empty unto thy mother in law.

18 Then said she, **Sit still, my daughter, until thou know how the matter will fall** [*stay put until we see what happens with the closer relative*]: for **the man** [*Boaz*] **will not be in rest, until he have finished the thing this day** [*Boaz will not rest until he gets this settled*].

RUTH 4

Selection: all verses

CAN YOU IMAGINE the feelings that Ruth and Naomi, as well as Boaz, had as they waited to see what the nearer kin would say? We will review the part of the Law of Moses that describes the rules to follow in such a situation. We will use **bold** as usual to point things out.

Deuteronomy 25:5–10

5 ¶ If brethren dwell together,

and **one of them die, and have no child**, the wife of the dead shall not marry without [*outside the family*] unto a stranger: **her husband's brother shall** go in unto her, and **take her to him to wife**, and perform the duty of an husband's brother unto her.

6 And it shall be, *that* **the firstborn which she beareth shall succeed in the name of his brother which is dead** [*will inherit the dead brother's property and will handle his estate*], that his name be not put out of Israel [*so that the dead brother's name is perpetuated*].

Next, in verses 7–9, is the clause of the law that we are currently interested in and that dictates what happens next for Ruth and Boaz.

7 And **if the man** [*in this case, the next of kin, a closer relative than Boaz*] **like not to take his brother's wife, then let his brother's wife go up to the gate** [*the gate of the city, where such business as this is conducted before witnesses*] **unto the elders, and say, My husband's brother** [*in Ruth's case, the nearest relative*] **refuseth to raise up unto his brother a name in Israel**, he will not perform the duty of my husband's brother.

8 **Then the elders of his city** [*the city officials who handle such things*] **shall call him, and speak unto him:** and **if he stand to it** [*if he stands*

firmly by his decision not to marry her], **and say, I like not to take her;**

9 Then shall his brother's wife come unto him in the presence of the elders, and loose his shoe from off his foot, and spit in his face, and shall answer **and say, So shall it be done unto that man that will not build up his brother's house** [*who will not build up a posterity for his dead brother*].

10 And his name shall be called in Israel, The house of him that hath his shoe loosed.

> Verses 7–9, above, will particularly apply to what we read next. Remember that the city gate was the place where much official business was transacted. There were scribes and witnesses, specialists, and city officials there on a routine, daily basis.
>
> It appears that Boaz, Ruth, and Naomi have come up with a plan that will increase Boaz's chances of marrying Ruth. The plan is to offer the next of kin the opportunity to buy the piece of land that belonged to Elimelech, Naomi's dead husband, which now belongs to Naomi. Since Ruth's husband was the heir to Elimelech, the property also belongs to Ruth. If a next of kin buys it, he must also marry the dead man's widow, Ruth, in order to maintain the name of the dead with his property.
>
> Let's see what happens.

1 Then went Boaz up to the gate [*the city gate, where such business was transacted*], **and sat** him **down** there: and, behold, **the kinsman of whom Boaz spake came by;** unto whom **he** [*Boaz*] **said, Ho,** such a one [*"so and so"—in other words, whatever the man's name was*]! **turn aside, sit down here** [*come over here and sit down*]. And he turned aside, and sat down.

2 And **he** [*Boaz*] **took ten men** of the elders of the city, **and said, Sit ye down here**. And they sat down [*to serve as witnesses*].

3 And he said unto the kinsman, Naomi, that is [*who has*] come again out of the country of Moab, selleth a parcel of land, which *was* our brother Elimelech's [*which belonged to her departed husband*]:

4 And I thought to advertise [*alert*] thee, saying, Buy *it* before the inhabitants, and before the elders of my people [*in other words, in front of these witnesses*]. If thou wilt redeem *it*, redeem *it*: but if thou wilt not redeem *it*, *then* tell me, that I may know: for *there is* none to redeem *it* beside thee; and I *am* after thee [*I am next in line after you*]. And **he said, I will redeem it.**

5 Then said Boaz, What day thou buyest the field of the hand of Naomi, thou must buy *it* also of Ruth the Moabitess, the wife of the dead, **to raise up the name of**

the dead upon his inheritance [*in other words, if you buy this piece of property from Naomi, you must also buy it from Ruth, which would include marrying her and having posterity with her for her dead husband, which means her firstborn son will inherit the property*].

6 ¶ And **the kinsman said, I cannot redeem** it **for myself**, lest I mar mine own inheritance [*lest I endanger my own estate*]: **redeem thou my right to thyself** [*you go ahead and take it*]; for I cannot redeem it.

7 **Now this** *was* **the manner** in **former time in Israel** concerning redeeming and concerning changing [*this was the customary way of handling such a transaction*], for **to confirm all things** [*to make everything legal*]; **a man plucked off his shoe, and gave** it **to his neighbour:** and this *was* a testimony in Israel.

8 **Therefore the kinsman said unto Boaz, Buy** it **for thee** [*buy it for yourself*]. **So he** [*the kinsman*] **drew off his shoe** [*and gave it to Boaz as a witness that he had agreed to the deal*].

9 ¶ **And Boaz said** unto the elders, and *unto* all the people, **Ye** *are* **witnesses** this day, that I have bought all that *was* Elimelech's, and all that *was* Chilion's and Mahlon's, of the hand of Naomi.

10 **Moreover Ruth** the Moabitess, the wife of Mahlon, **have I purchased to be my wife,** to raise up the name of the dead [*Mahlon*] upon his inheritance, that the name of the dead be not cut off from among his brethren [*to perpetuate Mahlon's name*], and from the gate of his place: ye *are* witnesses this day.

Next, the witnesses and people who have gathered pronounce a customary blessing of posterity and fame upon Ruth.

11 And all the people that *were* in the gate, and the elders, said, We *are* witnesses. **The LORD make the woman** [*Ruth*] **that is come into thine house like Rachel and like Leah** [*Jacob's wives*]**, which two did build the house of Israel** [*who were the mothers, along with Jacob's servant wives, Zilpah and Bilhah, of the twelve sons of Israel (Jacob)*]: and do thou worthily in Ephratah [*may you do well in Bethlehem—see Genesis 35:19*], **and be famous in Beth-lehem:**

12 And let thy house be like the house of Pharez, whom Tamar bare unto Judah, of the seed which the LORD shall give thee of this young woman.

13 ¶ **So Boaz took Ruth, and she was his wife:** and when he went in unto her, the LORD gave her conception, **and she bare a son.**

Next, in verses 14–15, the women

of town give Grandmother Naomi a beautiful tribute.

14 And the women said unto Naomi, **Blessed** *be* **the LORD, which hath not left thee this day without a kinsman, that his name may be famous in Israel.**

15 And **he shall be unto thee a restorer of** *thy* **life, and a nourisher of thine old age: for thy daughter in law, which loveth thee, which is better to thee than seven sons, hath born him.**

16 And Naomi took the child, and laid it in her bosom, and became nurse unto it.

17 And **the women her neighbours gave it a name,** saying, There is a son born to Naomi; and they called his name **Obed:** he *is* the father of Jesse, the father of David.

Thus, Ruth became the great-grandmother of David and a direct ancestor of Jesus Christ.

Next, in verses 18–22, we are given a brief genealogy for Boaz and Ruth's son, Obed. It will end with David, the shepherd boy who became king. Christ's genealogy will come through David and thus back through Ruth.

18 ¶ Now these are the generations of Pharez: Pharez begat Hezron,

19 And Hezron begat Ram, and Ram begat Amminadab,

20 And Amminadab begat Nahshon, and Nahshon begat Salmon,

21 And Salmon begat **Boaz,** and Boaz begat **Obed,**

22 And Obed begat Jesse, and Jesse begat David [*the shepherd boy who became king*].

1 SAMUEL

THE BOOKS OF 1 and 2 Samuel go together and cover a period of approximately one hundred and thirty years, beginning with the birth of Samuel, who became a very influential prophet and ending with the final days of the reign of David the king. We do not know who the author was, nor do we know when he wrote the record. Most Bible scholars agree that Samuel was born somewhere between 1150 BC and 1100 BC.

During the reign of the judges, Israel did not have a strong central government, nor did it have a prophet. As the Bible picks up the story here in First Samuel, Eli is the Aaronic Priesthood high priest but is weak-willed. He has two sons, Hophni and Phinehas, who are serving as priests. Eli is lax in disciplining them and they corrupt the office of priest. After Eli's death, Samuel, who had been called by the Lord, becomes the prophet and judge of Israel. He unites the nation, restores law and order, and brings back regular religious devotion and worship. He is a powerful force for good in a nation that has been fragmented by apostasy and personal wickedness.

During this era, the Philistines are fierce enemies of Israel. Among other things, Israel demands a king in spite of advice to the contrary and Samuel anoints Saul to be their first king. David the shepherd boy kills Goliath, and King Saul becomes jealous of David. Saul changes from an honorable and righteous man to a self-centered paranoid king. David remains loyal to Saul against all odds. After a tumultuous life without inner peace, Saul finally violates the laws of God again by seeking to contact the dead prophet Samuel through the witch of En-dor. His life ends when he takes his own life by falling on a sword.

We will now proceed with chapter one.

1 SAMUEL 1

Selection: all verses

IN THIS CHAPTER, we meet Hannah, a woman of great faith and one of the heroines of the Bible. She was one of two wives of a man named Elkanah. She had not been able to have children, which caused her great sadness, especially since being barren carried with it a serious stigma in her culture. Elkanah's other wife, Peninnah, had both sons and daughters (verse 4) and took advantage of her position as a mother to mock Hannah because she was barren (verse 6).

In this chapter, we will also meet Eli and his two sons, Hophni and Phinehas, who are serving in the Tabernacle which is located at Shiloh (about 20 miles north and a bit east of Jerusalem). Eli was the Aaronic Priesthood high priest at this time and his two corrupt sons served under him as priests.

Each year, Elkanah and his wives made a pilgrimage to Shiloh (verse 3). There, Hannah prayed for a son and wept because she was barren.

1 NOW there was a certain man of Ramathaim-zophim, of mount Ephraim, and his name was **Elkanah**, the son of Jeroham, the son of Elihu, the son of Tohu, the son of Zuph, an Ephrathite:

2 And he **had two wives**; the name of the one was **Hannah**, and the name of the other **Peninnah**: and **Peninnah had children, but Hannah had no children.**

3 And **this man went up out of his city yearly to worship and to sacrifice unto the LORD of hosts in Shiloh.** And the two sons of Eli, Hophni and Phinehas, the priests of the LORD, were there.

4 ¶ And when the time was that **Elkanah** offered, he **gave to Peninnah his wife, and to all her sons and her daughters, portions:**

> The "portions," referred to at the end of verse 4, above, and in verse 5, next, likely refer to the portion of the sacrifice given back to the offerer (Elkanah) after the priest had received his portion, which was usually the breast and right shoulder of the sacrificial animal, and after the fat, kidneys, and other parts were burned, as specified in the Law of Moses.

5 **But unto Hannah he gave a worthy portion** [NIV: "double portion"]; **for he loved Hannah**: but the LORD had shut up her womb [she was barren, unable to have children].

> Next, we are told that Peninnah mocked Hannah mercilessly because of her inability to have children.

6 And **her adversary** [Peninnah, Elkanah's other wive] also **provoked her sore,** for to make her fret, because the LORD had shut up her womb.

7 And as he did so year by year [this happened year after year], when she went up to the house of the LORD, so **she provoked her; therefore she wept, and did not eat.**

> Next, in verse 8, Hannah's husband tries to comfort her.

8 Then said Elkanah her husband to her, Hannah, why weepest thou? and why eatest thou not? and why is thy heart grieved? am not I better to thee than ten sons [don't I mean more to you than ten sons would]?

> In verse 9, next, we meet Eli, the Aaronic Priesthood high priest, a direct descendant of Aaron through Aaron's youngest son, Ithamar. It appears that he was seated nearby on a backless seat or stool, as was customary, hearing cases and making judgments. It was common for such officials to place their stool against a wall, post, column or whatever to provide a backrest.

9 ¶ So Hannah rose up after they had eaten in Shiloh, and after they had drunk. Now **Eli the priest sat upon a seat by a post of the temple** [NIV: "tabernacle"] **of the LORD.**

10 And she was in bitterness of soul, and prayed unto the LORD, and wept sore.

At this point, Hannah determined to make a vow with the Lord. If he would take away her barrenness, she would dedicate her firstborn son to Him.

11 And **she vowed a vow**, and said, O LORD of hosts, **if thou wilt** indeed look on the affliction of thine handmaid, and remember me, and not forget thine handmaid, but wilt **give unto thine handmaid a man child, then I will give him unto the LORD all the days of his life,** and there shall no razor come upon his head [*in other words, he would become a Nazarite, one dedicated to the service of the Lord—in this case, full-time service for life—see Bible Dictionary, under "Nazarite"*].

Eli happened to see Hannah praying silently and got the impression that she was drunk.

12 And it came to pass, **as she continued praying** before the LORD, that **Eli marked** [*noticed*] **her mouth.**

13 Now Hannah, she spake in her heart; only her lips moved, but her voice was not heard: therefore **Eli thought she had been drunken.**

14 And **Eli said unto her, How long wilt thou be drunken?** put away thy wine from thee.

15 And **Hannah answered** and said, No, my lord, I am a woman of a sorrowful spirit: **I have drunk neither wine nor strong drink, but have poured out my soul before the LORD.**

We infer from verse 16, next, that he had approached her and accused her of being a "daughter of Belial," a term that means "good-for-nothing, base, wicked, evil, worthless." She responded with a sincere explanation of her situation.

16 Count not thine handmaid for a daughter of Belial: for out of the abundance of my complaint and grief have I spoken hitherto.

When he understood what the situation actually was, Eli pronounced a blessing upon Hannah, and she went on her way happy and filled with faith.

17 Then Eli answered and said, Go in peace: and **the God of Israel grant thee thy petition** that thou hast asked of him.

18 And she said, Let thine handmaid find grace in thy sight. So **the woman went her way,** and did eat [*remember, she had refused to eat, in verses 7–8*], and her countenance **was no more sad.**

Major Message

Faith has the power to make us happy while we are waiting for the promised blessings of the Lord.

At the end of verse 19, next,

we are informed that Hannah successfully conceived, as promised by the Lord.

19 ¶ And they rose up in the morning early, and worshipped before the LORD, and returned, and came to their house to Ramah [*about 7 miles north of Jerusalem*] and **Elkanah knew Hannah his wife; and the LORD remembered her.**

In due time a baby boy was born.

20 Wherefore it came to pass, when the time was come about after **Hannah** had conceived, that she **bare a son, and called his name Samuel,** saying, Because I have asked him of the LORD.

When it was time for the annual pilgrimage to Shiloh, verse 21, Hannah chose to stay home with her baby Samuel, telling her husband that she desired to wait to go until the time arrived to fulfill her promise to give their son to the Lord for life-long service, verses 22–23.

21 And the man Elkanah, and all his house, went up to offer unto the LORD the yearly sacrifice, and his vow.

22 But **Hannah** went not up; for she **said unto her husband, I will not go up until the child be weaned, and then I will bring him, that he may appear before the LORD, and there abide for ever.**

Next, Elkanah shows respect

for Hannah by honoring her decision.

23 And Elkanah her husband said unto her, **Do what seemeth thee good;** tarry until thou have weaned him; only the LORD establish his word. So the woman abode, and gave her son suck [*nursed him*] until she weaned him.

After he was weaned (normally about three years among Israelite women), Hannah fulfilled her promise to the Lord and brought the young child to the Tabernacle and gave him to Eli to begin his training for his lifelong ministry.

24 ¶ And **when she had weaned him, she took him up with her,** with three bullocks, and one ephah [*a little over 8 US gallons*] of flour, and a bottle of wine, **and brought him unto the house of the LORD in Shiloh: and the child** *was* **young.**

25 And they slew a bullock [*offered a bull as a sacrifice*], **and brought the child to Eli.**

26 And she said, O my lord, *as* thy soul liveth, my lord, **I** *am* **the woman that stood by thee here, praying unto the LORD.**

27 For this child I prayed; **and the LORD hath given me my petition which I asked of him:**

28 Therefore also I have lent him to the LORD; **as long as he liveth**

he shall be lent to the LORD. And he worshipped the LORD there.

1 SAMUEL 2

Selection: all verses

OFTEN, A BLESSING is more appreciated if it has taken a long time to come. Such was the case with Hannah who was barren for many years despite her pleas to be blessed to bear children. Now, her prayers have been answered and she has the satisfaction of having kept her promise to give Samuel to the Lord. The words of her prayer of gratitude and praise to the Lord, in verses 1–11, next, show her to be a well-educated, faithful woman of great strength who has the gift of prophecy (Doctrine & Covenants 46:22).

1 AND Hannah prayed, and said, **My heart rejoiceth in the LORD,** mine horn [*symbolic of power and strength*] is exalted in the LORD [*made great because of the Lord*]: my mouth is enlarged over mine enemies [*I am now able to reply in triumph over my enemies (probably including Peninnah) who taunted me when I was barren*]; because I rejoice in thy salvation.

2 There is none holy as the LORD: for there is none beside thee: neither is there any rock [*foundation, protection*] like our God.

3 Talk no more so exceeding proudly; let not arrogancy come out of your mouth: for the LORD is a God of knowledge, and by him actions are weighed [*God is fair, after all is said and done*].

4 The bows of the mighty men are broken [*God is more powerful than the mighty*], and they that stumbled are girded with strength [*those who are burdened down with trials are eventually strengthened by them, like Hannah was*].

> Next, in verses 5–10, Hannah exults that the Lord is indeed all-powerful and can and does humble and bless as needed.

5 They that were full have hired out themselves for bread [*the once prosperous are now in poverty*]; and they that were hungry ceased [*those who once did not know where their next meal would come from, now have no such worries*]: so that the barren hath born seven [*children*]; and she that hath many children is waxed feeble.

6 The LORD killeth, and maketh alive: he bringeth down to the grave, and bringeth up.

7 The LORD maketh poor, and maketh rich: he bringeth low, and lifteth up.

8 He raiseth up the poor out of the dust, and lifteth up the beggar from the dunghill [*the garbage heap*], to set them among princes, and to make them inherit the throne of glory:

for the pillars of the earth are the LORD's, and he hath set the world upon them.

9 He will keep the feet of his saints [*bless the faithful saints*], and the wicked shall be silent in darkness; for by strength [*his own strength*] shall no man prevail.

Verse 10, next, is an allusion to the Messiah, the "Anointed One," the Savior. Hannah is prophesying of the coming Messiah.

10 The adversaries of the LORD shall be broken to pieces; out of heaven shall he thunder upon them: the LORD shall judge the ends of the earth; and **he shall give strength unto his king, and exalt the horn** [power] **of his anointed.**

Young Samuel's family returns home and he stays in Shiloh and continues his education with Eli.

11 And **Elkanah went to Ramah to his house.** And **the child did minister unto the LORD before Eli the priest.**

One of the sad lessons in this chapter is Eli's failure to discipline his sons. He allowed them to serve as priests and make a mockery of sacred things.

Perhaps you recall that the priests and Levites among the children of Israel were the only men assigned to function in the Aaronic Priesthood. According to the Law of Moses, they received a portion of burnt offerings and other offerings brought by the Israelites, with which to feed their families because they were called to full-time service of the Lord. There were definite rules and regulations as to which portion of the offerings the priests could take, which were to be consumed by fire upon the altar, and which portions were to be returned to the offerer and his family. Eli's sons took unauthorized portions of meat, often by force, thus offending the worshipers and causing disrespect for the work of the Lord. We see this in verses 12–16, next.

12 ¶ Now the **sons of Eli** *were* **sons of Belial** [*wicked and causing much trouble*]; **they knew not** [*had no respect for*] **the LORD.**

13 And the priests' custom with the people was, that, when any man offered sacrifice, the priest's servant came, while the flesh was in seething [*in the pot, boiling*], with a fleshhook of three teeth [*a three-pronged fork*] in his hand;

14 And he struck it into the pan, or kettle, or caldron, or pot; all that the fleshhook brought up the priest took for himself. So they did in Shiloh unto all the Israelites that came thither [*this was the usual approach to getting a portion of the meat for the priest and his family*].

But the sons of Eli were corrupting their office and position by demanding raw meat, contrary to the laws governing proper sacrifice.

15 Also before they burnt the fat, the priest's servant [*who worked under the direction of Eli's corrupt sons*] came, and said to the man that sacrificed [*the man who was offering the sacrifice*], Give flesh to roast for the priest; for he will not have sodden [*boiled*] flesh of thee, but raw.

16 And if any man [*who was offering a sacrifice*] said unto him, Let them not fail to burn the fat presently [*the fat must be burned first (according to proper procedure)*], and *then* take *as much as* thy soul desireth; then he would answer him, *Nay*; but thou shalt give *it me* now: and if not, **I will take *it* by force.**

17 Wherefore the sin of the young men was very great before the LORD: for men abhorred the offering of the LORD [*the people began to hate offering sacrifices*].

> We will include a quote from a Bible commentary to help with understanding the seriousness of what Eli's sons were doing in verses 13–16, above.

> "Of these offerings, the portion which legally fell to the priest as his share was the heave-leg and wave-breast. And this he was to receive after the fat portions of the sacrifice had been burned upon the altar [see Leviticus 7:30–34]. To take the flesh of the sacrificial animal and roast it before this offering had been made, was a crime which was equivalent to a robbery of God. . . . Moreover, the priests

could not claim any of the flesh which the offerer of the sacrifice boiled for the sacrificial meal, after burning the fat portions upon the altar and giving up the portions which belonged to them, to say nothing of their taking it forcibly out of the pots while it was being boiled [see 1 Samuel 2:12–17]. Such conduct as this on the part of the young men (the priests' servants), was a great sin in the sight of the Lord, as they thereby brought the sacrifice of the Lord into contempt." (Keil and Delitzsch, Commentary, 2:2:35–36.)

Meanwhile, Samuel was learning his duties and continuing his education. He even had his own little linen ephod (vest or apron) patterned after the ephod worn by the high priest.

18 ¶ But Samuel ministered before the LORD, being a child, girded with a linen ephod.

Each year, when Hannah came with her husband to offer their annual sacrifice in Shiloh, she brought a new little coat or robe for Samuel. No doubt he was growing rapidly and needed a new one that fit him better each time.

19 Moreover **his mother made him a little coat, and brought it to him from year to year**, when she came up with her husband to offer the yearly sacrifice.

> Because of her faithfulness to her vow to give Samuel to full-time service of the Lord, the Lord blessed Hannah with more children.

20 ¶ And Eli blessed Elkanah and

his wife, and said, The LORD give thee seed of this woman for the loan [*Samuel, see chapter 1, verse 28*] which is lent to the LORD. And they went unto their own home.

21 And the LORD visited [*blessed*] Hannah, so that she conceived, and bare **three sons and two daughters.** And the child Samuel grew before the LORD.

> Beginning with verse 22, next, we see that Eli fails to discipline his sons, allowing them to corrupt the priest's office and serve as a terrible example for the people. It appears that he made no real effort to curb their vile behaviors or to even remove them from serving.

> **Major Message**
>
> Parents have an obligation to do their best to discipline their children and to teach them respect for sacred things.
>
> One of the worst things his sons did was to engage in illicit sexual activity with women who came to the tabernacle to worship.

22 ¶ Now **Eli** was very old, and **heard all that his sons did** unto all Israel; **and how they lay** [*engaged in sex*] **with the women that assembled** *at* **the door of the tabernacle** of the congregation.

> Eli's attempts to discipline his sons, in verses 23–25, next, seem rather weak-willed and feeble.

23 And he said unto them, **Why do ye such things?** for I hear of your evil dealings by all this people [*everybody's talking about your wicked behavior*].

24 Nay, my sons; for it is no good report that I hear: **ye make the LORD's people to transgress** [*you are causing the Lord's covenant people to commit sin*].

25 If one man sin against another, the judge shall judge him: but if a man sin against the LORD, who shall intreat [*intercede, plead his case*] for him? Notwithstanding **they hearkened not unto the voice of their father**, because the LORD would slay them [*perhaps Eli had warned them that the Lord would destroy them if necessary to remove them from office; compare with verse 34*].

> Samuel continues to grow and learn. He is well thought of by God and the people.

26 And the child **Samuel grew on, and was in favour both with the LORD, and also with men.**

> We don't know who the "man of God" was in verse 27, next. But the message he delivered to Eli in the following verses was a scathing rebuke, reminding him first of his very serious responsibility as the high priest.

27 ¶ And **there came a man of God unto Eli**, and said unto him, Thus saith the LORD, **Did I plainly appear unto the house of thy**

father, when they were in Egypt in Pharaoh's house? [*did I leave any doubt that this is My work back when I first established the office of high priest?*]

> Next, Eli is reminded of the responsibility upon his shoulders to carry on the tradition of his ancestors in honorably discharging the duties of the Aaronic Priesthood high priest.

28 And did I choose him out of all the tribes of Israel to be my priest, to offer upon mine altar, to burn incense, to wear an ephod before me? and did I give unto the house of thy father all the offerings made by fire of the children of Israel? [*perhaps asking why the prescribed portions of the meat offerings were not sufficient for Eli and his sons. Why were they cheating?*]

> The questions asked in verse 29 must have hit Eli very hard. He is being forced to face reality.

29 Wherefore kick ye at [*why are you rejecting the rules and laws for*] **my sacrifice and at mine offering,** which I have commanded in my habitation; and **honourest thy sons above me** [*why do you honor your sons above Me*], **to make yourselves fat** with the chiefest of all the offerings of Israel my people [*by taking the best cuts of meat of the offerings for yourselves*]?

> Did you notice the principle being violated, in verse 29, above? Eli

and his sons were appropriating the best cuts of meat from the sacrificial animals for their own use rather than for the Lord.

One of the principles faithful saints follow is that of giving their best to the Lord. For example, we do it in building temples. It would be like a builder in our day under contract to build one of our temples, who, on the sly, takes the best materials from the temple construction and builds a house for himself, substituting lesser quality materials for use on the temple.

Major Message

The promises of the Lord can be revoked because of wickedness (compare with Doctrine & Covenants 58:32–33; 82:10).

Next, Eli is told that the promised blessings given his ancestors to be fulfilled continuing with him and his posterity will be revoked.

30 Wherefore the LORD God of Israel saith, I said indeed that thy house, and the house of thy father, should walk before me for ever [*I previously promised your father rich blessings of ministering in the priesthood, that would continue through you and your posterity*]: **but now the LORD saith, Be it far from me; for them that honour me I will honour, and they that despise me shall be lightly esteemed.**

31 Behold, the days come, that I will cut off thine arm [*symbolic of power and influence*], and the arm of thy father's house, **that there shall not be an old man in thine house** [*your family line will now see much trouble, such that none will live to a ripe old age*].

32 And thou shalt see an enemy in my habitation, in all the wealth which God shall give Israel: and [*God will still bless Israel, but*] **there shall not be an old man in thine house for ever.**

33 And the man of thine, whom I shall not cut off from mine altar [*any of your descendants who are allowed to serve in the Tabernacle*], shall be to consume thine eyes, and to grieve thine heart [*will cause you to wish that you and your sons had lived worthy to continue serving*]: and **all the increase of thine house shall die in the flower of their age** [*your descendants will die in their prime*].

In verse 34, next, we see a sad prophecy concerning the untimely deaths of Eli's two wicked sons, Hophni and Phinehas.

34 And **this shall be a sign unto thee,** that shall come upon thy two sons, on **Hophni and Phinehas; in one day they shall die both of them** [*will be fulfilled in 1 Samuel 4:11*].

The prophecy goes on to say that Eli and his sons will be replaced with a righteous man who will fulfill the priest's office faithfully. In context, this could easily be referring to Samuel.

35 And **I will raise me up a faithful priest,** that shall do according to that which is in mine heart and in my mind: and I will build him a sure house; and he shall walk before mine anointed for ever.

Verse 36 indicates that Eli's posterity will be reduced to poverty such that some will request being allowed to function as priests as a matter of desperation in order to secure even a meager meal.

36 And it shall come to pass, that every one that is left in thine house shall come and crouch to him for a piece of silver and a morsel of bread, and shall say, **Put me, I pray thee, into one of the priests' offices, that I may eat a piece of bread.**

1 SAMUEL 3

Selection: all verses

WHILE ELI'S SONS were mocking the Lord and terrorizing worshipers at the tabernacle, the young boy Samuel was faithfully learning his duties as a servant of the Lord. It was a time when there was no "open vision" (verse 1) in Israel because of gross wickedness among the people. In this chapter, you will see that Samuel hears the voice of the Lord but thinks that it is Eli calling. Finally, he finds out that it is the Lord and is given a sobering message that Eli will be cut off from the Lord because he has allowed his evil sons to continue in their priesthood service.

Samuel grows to adulthood and is known throughout all of Israel. Because of Samuel's righteousness, there is once again "open vision" (1 Samuel 3:21).

1 AND **the child Samuel ministered unto the LORD before Eli** [*under Eli's supervision*]. And the word of the LORD was precious [*scarce*] in those days; **there was no open vision.**

> This dark era of having no "open vision" will change with the calling of Samuel, in verses 2–10, and subsequent appearance of the Lord to him, in verse 21.

2 And it came to pass at that time, when Eli was laid down in his place [*NIV: "his usual place"*], and his eyes began to wax dim, that he could not see [*he was getting to the point that he could hardly see*];

3 And ere the lamp of God [*menorah, see Exodus 27:20–21*], went out in the temple [*Tabernacle*] of the LORD, where the ark of God was, and **Samuel was laid down to sleep;**

4 That **the LORD called Samuel:** and he answered, Here am I.

> Young Samuel thought that it was Eli who had called to him. It wasn't.

5 And **he ran unto Eli, and said, Here am I**; for thou calledst me.

And **he said, I called not**; lie down again. And he went and lay down.

6 And **the LORD called yet again,** Samuel. And Samuel arose and went to Eli, and said, Here am I; for thou didst call me. And he answered, I called not, my son; lie down again.

> As indicated in verse 7, next, this was a new, unfamiliar experience for young Samuel. In a way, it might be compared to the First Vision, where Joseph Smith, too, was initially unfamiliar with direct communication with God.

7 Now **Samuel did not yet know the LORD, neither was the word of the LORD yet revealed unto him.**

> Finally, to his credit, Eli recognized that it was the Lord who was calling Samuel.

8 And **the LORD called Samuel again the third time.** And he arose and went to Eli, and said, Here am I; for thou didst call me. And **Eli perceived that the LORD had called the child.**

9 Therefore Eli said unto Samuel, Go, lie down: and it shall be, if he call thee, that thou shalt say, Speak, LORD; for thy servant heareth. So Samuel went and lay down in his place.

10 And the LORD came, and stood, and called as at other times, Samuel, Samuel. Then **Samuel**

answered, Speak; for thy servant heareth.

Samuel is given a sobering message that Eli will be cut off from the Lord because he has allowed his evil sons to continue in their priesthood offices. It would seem that this was a very important message for Samuel, whose young, impressionable mind had seen much hypocrisy and dishonor with Eli's sons. He no doubt wondered how they could be priests of God and still do such evil deeds, which brought dishonor to the office and the commandments of the Lord. He likely wondered why Eli didn't do more to stop his sons. Now he will have clear in his mind that such behavior is not ignored by the Lord.

11 ¶ And the LORD said to Samuel, Behold, I will do a thing in Israel, at which both the ears of every one that heareth it shall tingle [*it will scream in their ears, jar them*].

12 In that day I will perform against Eli all things which I have spoken concerning his house: when I begin, I will also make an end [*everything I have said, from beginning to end*].

13 For I have told him that **I will judge** [*punish*] **his house for ever** for the iniquity which he knoweth; **because his sons made themselves vile, and he restrained them not.**

14 And therefore I have sworn unto the house of Eli, that the iniquity of Eli's house shall not be purged with sacrifice nor offering for ever [*outward ordinances and offerings cannot cleanse inward corruption, unrepented of*].

It is likely that Samuel did not get back to sleep, with so much now on his mind. It might be similar to Joseph Smith's situation when "sleep had fled from my eyes" (Joseph Smith—History 1:46) during the night of Moroni's visits.

In the morning, Samuel goes about his duties, which include opening the doors of the Tabernacle. He is nervous about telling Eli about the message in the vision.

15 ¶ And **Samuel lay until the morning,** and opened the doors of the house of the LORD. And **Samuel feared to shew Eli the vision.**

16 Then **Eli called Samuel,** and said, Samuel, my son. And he answered, Here am I.

Next, in verse 17, Eli, who is aware that the Lord spoke to young Samuel during the night, gives him strict instructions to tell him everything.

17 And he said, **What is the thing that the LORD hath said unto thee? I pray thee hide it not from me:** God do so to thee, and more also [*God deal with you very severely*], if thou hide any thing from me of all the things that he said unto thee.

18 And **Samuel told him every whit**, and **hid nothing from him**. And he [*Eli*] said, It is the LORD: let him do what seemeth him good [*His will be done*].

In verses 19–21, Samuel continues to grow and mature to adulthood and becomes known throughout the land.

19 ¶ And **Samuel grew, and the LORD was with him, and did let none of his words fall to the ground** [*everything the Lord prophesied about Samuel and Eli and his sons was fulfilled. Compare with Doctrine & Covenants 1:38*].

20 And **all Israel from Dan even to Beer-sheba** [*from the far north to the far south*] **knew that Samuel was established to be a prophet of the LORD.**

The wonderful message in verse 21, next, is that "open vision" (see verse 1) had resumed once more in Israel, because there was once more a prophet, namely, Samuel.

21 And **the LORD appeared again in Shiloh** [*where the Tabernacle was*]: for **the LORD revealed himself to Samuel in Shiloh** by the word of the LORD.

1 SAMUEL 4

Selection: all verses

THIS IS A tragic chapter which gives the account of the fulfillment of the prophecy in chapter 3 against Eli and his sons. First, in verses 1–10, we see the Philistines from the west successfully attacking Israel and capturing the ark of the covenant.

1 AND the word of Samuel came to all Israel. Now Israel went out against the Philistines to battle, and pitched beside Eben-ezer: and the Philistines pitched in Aphek.

2 And the Philistines put themselves in array against Israel: and when they joined battle, Israel was smitten before the Philistines: and they slew of the army in the field about four thousand men.

With open apostasy and wickedness crippling their ability to think rationally, the Israelite leaders make a very foolish decision. They decide to bring the sacred ark of the covenant from the Tabernacle in Shiloh and bring it to their encampment to protect them from the Philistines.

3 ¶ And when the people were come into the camp, the elders of Israel said, Wherefore [*why*] hath the LORD smitten us to day before the Philistines? Let us fetch the ark of the covenant of the LORD out of Shiloh unto us, that, when it cometh among us, it may save us out of the hand of our enemies.

4 So the people sent to Shiloh, that they might bring from thence the ark of the covenant of the LORD of hosts, which dwelleth between the cherubims: and the two sons of Eli, Hophni and Phinehas, were there with the ark of the covenant of God.

> The great shouting and rejoicing among the Israelite forces when the ark was brought into camp caused much anxiety among the Philistine soldiers, who were camped nearby. But they talked themselves out of fear, rallied their troops, and attacked anyway.

5 And when the ark of the covenant of the LORD came into the camp, all Israel shouted with a great shout, so that the earth rang again.

6 And when the Philistines heard the noise of the shout, they said, What meaneth the noise of this great shout in the camp of the Hebrews? And they understood that the ark of the LORD was come into the camp.

7 And the Philistines were afraid, for they said, God is come into the camp. And they said, Woe unto us! for there hath not been such a thing heretofore.

> Adding to the fear and trepidation among the Philistine soldiers was the fact that they

had heard of the great miracles performed by Jehovah in bringing the children of Israel to the Holy Land from Egypt.

8 Woe unto us! who shall deliver us out of the hand of these mighty Gods? these are the Gods that smote the Egyptians with all the plagues in the wilderness.

> The Philistines had men who stirred their troops up and rallied them to the fight, despite their initial misgivings.

9 **Be strong, and quit yourselves like men** [*be men!*], O ye Philistines, that ye be not servants unto the Hebrews, as they have been to you: **quit yourselves like men, and fight.**

10 ¶ And the Philistines fought, and Israel was smitten, and they fled every man into his tent: and there was a very great slaughter; for there fell of Israel thirty thousand footmen.

> Next, in verse 11, the Philistine troops go to the Tabernacle in Shiloh, kill Hophni and Phinehas, and take the ark of the covenant. This fulfills the prophecy that both of Eli's sons would be slain the same day (1 Samuel 2:34).

11 And the ark of God was taken; and the two sons of Eli, Hophni and Phinehas, were slain.

> Next, an Israelite soldier, of the tribe of Benjamin, comes in great mourning and breathlessly reports the bad news to ninety-eight-year-old Eli.

12 ¶ And there ran a man of Benjamin out of the army, and came to Shiloh the same day with his clothes rent, and with earth upon his head [*signs of great distress and mourning in that culture*].

13 And when he came, lo, Eli sat upon a seat [*generally a backless chair or stool used by the high priest as he judged cases brought before him*] by the wayside watching: for his heart trembled for the ark of God [*he was very upset by the loss of the ark*]. And when the man came into the city, and told it, all the city cried out.

14 And when Eli heard the noise of the crying, he said, What meaneth the noise of this tumult? And the man came in hastily, and told Eli.

15 Now Eli was ninety and eight years old; and his eyes were dim, that he could not see.

16 And the man said unto Eli, I am he that came out of the army, and I fled to day out of the army. And he said, What is there done, my son?

17 And the messenger answered and said, Israel is fled before the Philistines, and there hath been also a great slaughter among the people, and thy two sons also, Hophni and Phinehas, are dead, and the ark of God is taken.

When Eli heard the bad news, it was too much for him.

18 And it came to pass, when he made mention of the ark of God, that he [*Eli*] fell from off the seat backward by the side of the gate, and his neck brake, and he died: for he was an old man, and heavy. And he had judged Israel forty years.

In verses 19–20 yet another tragedy strikes Eli's family. His daughter-in-law dies in child-birth. She was near full-term and all the bad news caused her to go into labor.

19 ¶ And his daughter in law, Phinehas' wife, was with child, near to be delivered: and when she heard the tidings that the ark of God was taken, and that her father in law and her husband were dead, she bowed herself and travailed; for her pains came upon her.

20 And about the time of her death the women that stood by her said unto her, Fear not; for thou hast born a son. But she answered not, neither did she regard it.

21 And she named the child I-chabod [*meaning, in this context, "Where has Israel's glory gone?"*], saying, The glory is departed from Israel: because the ark of God was taken, and because of her father in law and her husband.

22 And she said, The glory is departed from Israel: for the ark of God is taken.

1 SAMUEL 5

Selection: verses 2–4, 6, 9, 11–12

THE PHILISTINES HAVE triumphantly taken the ark of the covenant from the Israelites and placed it in the shrine of their pagan god, Dagon, right next to their statue of Dagon, in their city of Ashdod.

We will briefly view verses in this chapter which detail the calamities that befell the Philistines as a result. Such verses are no doubt part of the truths from the Bible that have formed the basis for much of the popular folklore that surrounds the ark of the covenant in our day. We will begin our selection with verse 2.

2 When **the Philistines took the ark of God**, they brought it into the house of Dagon [*their shrine*], **and set it by Dagon** [*one of their idols, a fish god*].

> Imagine the horror on the faces of the Philistines as their triumph over the Israelites turns to fear and great concern.

3 ¶ And when they of Ashdod arose early on the morrow, behold, **Dagon was fallen upon his face to the earth before the ark of the LORD** [*as if he were worshipping the ark of the covenant*]. And **they took Dagon, and set him in his place again.**

4 And when they arose early **on the morrow morning, behold,**

Dagon was fallen upon his face to the ground before the ark of the LORD; and **the head of Dagon and both the palms of his hands were cut off upon the threshold; only the stump of Dagon was left to him.**

> Not only was there great concern over what had happened to their idol, Dagon, but it became very personal as plagues of hemorrhoids or tumors came upon them. Some Bible scholars suspect that it might have been bubonic plague, based on the description and symptoms (see *Old Testament Student Manual, Genesis--2 Samuel,* page 270).

6 But the hand of **the LORD** was heavy upon them of Ashdod, and he destroyed them, and **smote them with emerods** [*hemorrhoids or tumors, see Deuteronomy 28:27, footnote c, in your LDS Bible*], even Ashdod and the coasts thereof.

9 And it was so, that, after they had carried it about, the hand of the LORD was against the city with a very great destruction: and he smote the men of the city, both small and great [*NIV: "both young and old"*], and **they had emerods in their secret parts** [*private parts of their bodies*].

> Because of the destruction and personal plagues that beset them, the Philistines sent the ark from place to place, and finally determined to take it back to the Israelites.

11 So they sent and gathered together all the lords of the Philistines, and said, **Send away the ark of the God of Israel, and let it go again to his own place**, that it slay us not, and our people: for there was a deadly destruction throughout all the city; the hand of God was very heavy there.

12 And **the men that died not were smitten with the emerods: and the cry of the city went up to heaven.**

1 SAMUEL 6

Selection: verses 1–15; 19–21

IN THIS CHAPTER, the Philistines finally agree among themselves upon a way to return the ark of the covenant to the Israelites. This was after seven months of plagues and disasters associated with their possession of the ark.

1 AND the ark of the LORD was in the country of the Philistines **seven months.**

2 And **the Philistines called for the priests and the diviners** [*their magicians, fortune tellers, and so forth*], saying, What shall we do to the ark of the LORD? tell us wherewith we shall send it to his place [*tell us what we should send with the ark when we return it*].

3 And they said, If ye send away the ark of the God of Israel, **send it not empty**; but in any wise return him a trespass offering: then ye shall be healed, and it shall be known to you why his hand is not removed from you.

The mice mentioned in verse 4, next, imply that a plague of mice accompanied the plagues mentioned in chapter 5. In the thinking of the Philistines, making gold replicas of emerods and mice would help appease the Israelite god.

4 Then said they, What shall be the trespass offering which we shall return to him? They answered, **Five golden emerods, and five golden mice,** according to the number of the lords of the Philistines: for one plague was on you all, and on your lords.

5 Wherefore ye shall make images of your emerods, and images of your **mice that mar the land** [*implies a plague of mice*]; and ye shall give glory unto the God of Israel: peradventure he will lighten his hand from off you, and from off your gods, and from off your land.

6 Wherefore then do ye harden your hearts, as the Egyptians and Pharaoh hardened their hearts? when he had wrought wonderfully among them, did they not let the people go, and they departed?

The Philistine soothsayers and wise men recommend a

means of getting the ark of the covenant back to the Israelites, in verses 7–9, next.

7 Now therefore **make a new cart**, and **take two milch kine** [*milk cows*], on which there hath come no yoke [*that have never been broken to the yoke*], and **tie the kine to the cart**, and bring their calves home from them:

Cows who have been separated from their calves tend to get frantic and will do almost anything not to leave their calves. Therefore, it sounds like the priests and diviners (verse 2, above), are devising a test to see if the god of the Israelites will cause the milk cows to take the ark home to Israel.

8 And **take the ark of the LORD, and lay it upon the cart**; and put the jewels of gold, which ye return him for a trespass offering, in a coffer by the side thereof; and send it away, that it may go.

In verse 9, next, the Philistine priests and wise men explain the test they have devised to see if it is really the Israelite god who has plagued them. If the cows leave their calves and pull the cart with the ark directly to the Israelite city of Beth-shemesh, a city of the tribe of Judah set aside for Levite priests to live in, about twelve miles southeast of Ekron, then it is the God of Israel who is punishing them for having the ark. Otherwise, the plagues and troubles were just coincidental.

By the way, Ekron was the Philistine city where the ark finally ended up, see 1 Samuel 5:10.

9 And **see, if it goeth up** by the way of his own coast **to Beth-shemesh**, then he [*the Israelite god*] hath done us this great evil: but **if not, then we shall know that it is not his hand that smote us; it was a chance that happened to us.**

10 ¶ And **the men did so**; and took two milch kine, and tied them to the cart, and shut up their calves at home:

11 And they laid the ark of the LORD upon the cart, and the coffer with the mice of gold and the images of their emerods.

12 And **the kine took the straight way to the way of Beth-shemesh**, and went along the highway, lowing as they went, and turned not aside to the right hand or to the left; and the lords of the Philistines went after them unto the border of Beth-shemesh.

13 And **they of Beth-shemesh** [*inhabitants of this Israelite city*] were reaping their wheat harvest in the valley: and they **lifted up their eyes, and saw the ark, and rejoiced to see it.**

14 And the cart came into the field of Joshua, a Beth-shemite, and stood there, where there was a great stone:

and they clave the wood of the cart, and offered the kine a burnt offering unto the LORD.

> In verse 15, next, authorized Levite priests lifted the ark off of the cart, and the wood of the cart was used to fuel the fire for burnt offerings to the Lord, verse 14, above.

15 And **the Levites took down the ark of the LORD,** and the coffer that was with it, wherein the jewels of gold were, and put them on the great stone: and **the men of Beth-shemesh offered burnt offerings and sacrificed sacrifices the same day unto the LORD.**

> The Philistine leaders who had followed the cart from a safe distance were satisfied and returned to Ekron.

> The Bible does not tell us what the men of Beth-shemesh did to incur the wrath of God, in verse 19, next. No doubt it was some grossly inappropriate behavior. However, the Old Testament Student Manual, Genesis–2 Samuel, page 270, does indicate that seventy men were slain, rather than fifty thousand. The NIV also says seventy were killed, as opposed to fifty thousand.

19 ¶ And he smote the men of Beth-shemesh, because they had looked into the ark of **the LORD,** even he **smote** of the people fifty thousand and **threescore and ten men:** and the people lamented, because the LORD had smitten many of the people with a great slaughter.

One technique for scripture marking is to just highlight key words in a verse, such that they form a clause or sentence by themselves explaining a key concept or meaning of the verse. You can see an example of this approach in verse 19, above.

20 And the men of Beth-shemesh said, Who is able to stand before this holy LORD God? and to whom shall he go up from us [*where should the ark go from here*]?

21 ¶ And they sent messengers to the inhabitants of Kirjath-jearim [*about 7 to 8 miles northwest of Jerusalem*], saying, **The Philistines have brought again the ark of the LORD; come ye down, and fetch it up to you.**

1 SAMUEL 7

Selection: verses 1–4; 6–13

AS REPORTED IN the last verses of chapter 6, the Israelites in Beth-shemesh were anxious to have the ark of the covenant transported from their town to Kirjath-jearim, a few miles north of Jerusalem. The men of that city were quick to grant their request. It remained there for twenty years.

1 AND **the men of Kirjath-jearim came, and fetched up the ark** of the LORD, and brought it into the house of Abinadab in the hill, and sanctified Eleazar his son to keep the ark of the LORD.

2 And it came to pass, while **the ark abode in Kirjath-jearim**, that the time was long; for it was **twenty years**: and all the house of Israel lamented after the LORD.

The Philistines are still a strong threat to the Israelites who have again strayed from the Lord. In verse 3, next, Samuel calls the people to repentance and promises deliverance from the Philistines if they will return to the Lord.

3 ¶ And Samuel spake unto all the house of Israel, saying, **If ye do return unto the LORD with all your hearts**, *then* put away the strange gods and Ashtaroth [*worshipped in association with Baal*] from among you, **and prepare your hearts unto the LORD, and serve him only: and he will deliver you out of the hand of the Philistines.**

The people accept Samuel's call to repentance and return to the Lord.

4 Then the children of Israel did put away Baalim and Ashtaroth, and served the LORD only.

As you know, one of the key steps of repentance is confession. The Israelites complied willingly with this step as reported in verse 6, next.

6 And they gathered together to Mizpeh [*about 10 miles northwest of Jerusalem*], and drew water, and

poured it out before the LORD, and fasted on that day, **and said there, We have sinned against the LORD.** And Samuel judged the children of Israel in Mizpeh.

Remember the promise of the Prophet Samuel, near the end of verse 3, above, that the Lord would free them from the oppression of the Philistines, if they would repent. Remember also, that promised blessings often come after the trial of our faith (Doctrine & Covenants 58:4). This "trial of faith" is about to begin for these Israelites. Without such trials, faith seldom leads to increased spiritual strength.

Many Israelites have gathered at Mizpeh, a town about ten miles north and a bit west of Jerusalem, to listen to Samuel and recommit to live in obedience to the Lord. In verse 7, next, the Philistines learn of this and see it as a perfect opportunity to attack.

7 And **when the Philistines heard that the children of Israel were gathered together to Mizpeh, the lords of the Philistines went up against Israel.** And when **the children of Israel** heard it, they **were afraid** of the Philistines.

Instead of losing faith, the Israelites increase their efforts to get the promised help from the Lord against the Philistines.

8 And **the children of Israel said to Samuel, Cease not to cry unto the LORD** our God for us, **that he**

will save us out of the hand of the Philistines.

9 ¶ And Samuel took a sucking lamb, and offered it for a burnt offering wholly unto the LORD: and **Samuel cried unto the LORD for Israel; and the LORD heard him.**

10 And as Samuel was offering up the burnt offering, the Philistines drew near to battle against Israel: but **the LORD thundered with a great thunder on that day upon the Philistines, and discomfited** [*frightened and confused*] **them**; and they were smitten before Israel.

> As is often the case, the Lord expects us to do all we can to answer our own prayers and then He does the rest. Verse 11, next, has an example of this.

11 And **the men of Israel** went out of Mizpeh, and **pursued the Philistines, and smote them**, until they came under Beth-car.

> Have you noticed the word "Ebenezer" in one of our LDS Hymns? It was in the old 1948 Hymn Book, #70, *Come Thou Fount of Every Blessing*, and is in the second verse. It is often sung by the Tabernacle Choir. It means "stone of help." Samuel set up such a stone to show gratitude for the help of the Lord in defeating the Philistines, as recorded in verse 12, next.

12 Then Samuel took a stone, and set it between Mizpeh and Shen,

and called the name of it **Eben-ezer,** saying, Hitherto hath **the LORD helped us.**

Major Message

By following their prophet, the Israelites triumphed over one of their most feared enemies. So also can we, with patience and following our modern prophets, overcome our enemies of temptation and sin.

13 ¶ So the Philistines were subdued, and they came no more into the coast of Israel: and **the hand of the LORD was against the Philistines** all the days of Samuel.

1 SAMUEL 8

Selection: all verses

SEVERAL YEARS HAVE passed since Samuel became the prophet and he has now become old. During his time as the prophet, Israel's government was a "theocracy," meaning government under the direction of God. During his administration, the Philistines returned several cities they had taken from Israel and there was peace between Israel and their enemies (see 1 Samuel 7:14). Samuel governed in righteousness, traveling around the country (1 Samuel 7:15-17), much as did Alma and other chief judges in the Book of Mormon.

As Samuel's age took its toll, he turned many of the functions of governing over to his sons (see verses 1-2, next).

1 AND it came to pass, when Samuel was old, that he made his sons judges over Israel.

2 Now the name of his firstborn was Joel; and the name of his second, Abiah: they were judges in Beer-sheba.

Unfortunately, his sons were materialistic, took bribes, and corrupted the government.

3 And his sons walked not in his ways, but turned aside after lucre, and took bribes, and perverted judgment.

Sadly, the people used the misbehavior of Samuel's sons as an excuse to demand a king so that they could be like other nations around them (see verses 19–20), even though those nations were corrupt and wicked. The fact that they requested a king rather than a prophet shows that they had once again fallen into the cycle of apostasy themselves.

4 Then all the elders [leaders of the various tribes] of Israel gathered themselves together, and came to Samuel unto Ramah,

5 And said unto him, Behold, thou art old, and thy sons walk not in thy ways: now make us a king to judge us like all the nations.

This would have been very disheartening to Samuel and he went to the Lord for direction.

6 ¶ But the thing displeased Samuel, when they said, Give us a king to judge us. And Samuel prayed unto the LORD.

Jehovah, the premortal Christ, instructed Samuel to grant the people's request, reminding him that ultimately, the people were rejecting Him with their short-sighted request.

7 And the LORD said unto Samuel, Hearken unto the voice of the people in all that they say unto thee: for they have not rejected thee, but they have rejected me, that I should not reign over them.

8 According to all the works which they have done since the day that I brought them up out of Egypt even unto this day, wherewith they have forsaken me, and served other gods, so do they also unto thee.

One of the principles of agency and accountability is that we must have sufficient knowledge and understanding in order to be held accountable. Therefore, the Lord instructs Samuel to teach the people in considerable detail what the consequences of such a choice will be. This way, they can make an informed choice and will own the consequences.

9 Now therefore hearken unto their voice [do what they ask]: howbeit yet protest solemnly unto them [warn them in all seriousness], and shew them the manner of the king that shall reign over them.

Samuel obeys. Verses 10–18 are a record of his warnings to them.

10 ¶ And Samuel told all the words of the LORD unto the people that asked of him a king.

11 And he said, This will be the manner of the king that shall reign over you: He will take your sons, and appoint them for himself, for his chariots, and to be his horsemen; and some shall run before his chariots.

12 And he will appoint him captains over thousands, and captains over fifties; and will set them to ear [*plow, cultivate*] his ground, and to reap his harvest, and to make his instruments of war, and instruments of his chariots.

13 And he will take your daughters to be confectionaries [*to make perfume, ointments, and the like*], and to be cooks, and to be bakers.

14 And he will take your fields, and your vineyards, and your oliveyards, even the best of them, and give them to his servants.

> In verse 15, next, Samuel warns them that a king will levy taxes to support his government.

15 And he will take the tenth of your seed, and of your vineyards, and give to his officers, and to his servants.

16 And he will take your menservants, and your maidservants, and your goodliest young men, and your asses, and put them to his work.

17 He will take the tenth of your sheep: and ye shall be his servants.

18 And ye shall cry out in that day because of your king which ye shall have chosen you; and the LORD will not hear you in that day.

> Against all wisdom and revealed warnings from the Lord, the people insist on a king.

19 ¶ Nevertheless the people refused to obey the voice of Samuel; and they said, Nay; but we will have a king over us;

20 That we also may be like all the nations; and that our king may judge us, and go out before us, and fight our battles.

> Verses 21–22, next, are a good reminder that, although God already knows our thoughts and needs, we are invited to verbalize them in prayer in order to get answers and help from Him.

21 And Samuel heard all the words of the people, and he rehearsed them in the ears of the LORD.

22 And the LORD said to Samuel, Hearken unto their voice, and make them a king. And Samuel said unto the men of Israel, Go ye every man unto his city.

1 SAMUEL 9

Selection: all verses

EVEN THOUGH IT was an unwise request by the people to have a king (chapter 8), the Lord instructs Samuel to find a good man and anoint him to be Israel's king. Saul, a young man from the tribe of Benjamin will fill this role.

Perhaps there is a lesson for us here. We are not always wise and we, too, make mistakes. Nevertheless, the Lord in His patience and wisdom still blesses us with the best He can under the circumstances. In this chapter and several that follow, we see this principle in action.

Perhaps you've noticed that sometimes we start out at the beginning of a rather routine day and things take a turn that changes the whole course of our lives. Starting with verse 1, next, Saul has this kind of a day.

1 NOW there was a man of Benjamin [*of the tribe of Benjamin*], whose name was Kish, the son of Abiel, the son of Zeror, the son of Bechorath, the son of Aphiah, a Benjamite, a mighty man of power.

2 And he had a son, whose name was Saul, a choice young man, and a goodly: and there was not among the children of Israel a goodlier person than he: from his shoulders and upward he was higher than any of the people [*he was a head taller than any others*].

It was a serious economic matter to lose donkeys and in verse 3, next, Saul's father sends him with a servant to find and recover the beasts of burden that have apparently strayed.

3 And the asses of Kish Saul's father were lost. And Kish said to Saul his son, Take now one of the servants with thee, and arise, go seek the asses.

The hand of the Lord is in their lack of success in finding the donkeys, because it will ultimately lead them to Samuel.

4 And he passed through mount Ephraim [*he searched the hill country of Ephraim, north of Jerusalem*], and passed through the land of Shalisha, but they found them not: then they passed through the land of Shalim, and there they were not: and he passed through the land of the Benjamites, but they found them not.

5 And when they were come to the land of Zuph [*the area in which Samuel lived*], Saul said to his servant that was with him, Come, and let us return; lest my father leave caring for the asses, and take thought for us [*we must return home or father will forget about the donkeys and worry about us instead*].

Young Saul's servant knew that the prophet, Samuel, lived close by and was familiar with his reputation. He suggested to Saul that Samuel might be able to point them in the right direction to find the missing animals.

6 And he said unto him, Behold now, there is in this city a man of God, and he is an honourable man; all that he saith cometh surely to pass: now let us go thither; peradventure [*perhaps*] he can shew us our way that we should go.

> In verses 7–10, next, we see that Saul is desirous of bringing a gift of some sort to show their respect for Samuel.

7 Then said Saul to his servant, But, behold, if we go, what shall we bring the man? for the bread is spent in our vessels, and there is not a present to bring to the man of God: what have we?

8 And the servant answered Saul again, and said, Behold, I have here at hand the fourth part of a shekel of silver [*NIV: about a tenth of an ounce*]: that will I give to the man of God, to tell us our way.

9 (Beforetime in Israel, when a man went to enquire of God, thus he spake, Come, and let us go to the seer: for he that is now called a Prophet was beforetime called a Seer.)

> The term "seer," in verse 9, above, is very significant. A "seer" is one who "sees" the future, and also the past (Mosiah 8:17). We sustain the First Presidency and the Twelve as "prophets, seers, and revelators." They "see" the future and alert us to coming dangers and events to look forward to. Joseph Smith defined the term "seer" and described what "seers" in past dispensations have seen, as they saw prophetically into the future:
>
> "Wherefore, we again say, search the revelations of God; study the prophecies, and rejoice that God grants unto the world Seers and Prophets. They are they who saw the mysteries of godliness; they saw the flood before it came; they saw angels ascending and descending upon a ladder that reached from earth to heaven; they saw the stone cut out of the mountain, which filled the whole earth; they saw the Son of God come from the regions of bliss and dwell with men on earth; they saw the deliverer come out of Zion, and turn away ungodliness from Jacob; they saw the glory of the Lord when he showed the transfiguration of the earth on the mount; they saw every mountain laid low and every valley exalted when the Lord was taking vengeance upon the wicked; they saw truth spring out of the earth, and righteousness look down from heaven in the last days, before the Lord came the second time to gather his elect; they saw the end of wickedness on earth, and the Sabbath of creation crowned with peace; they saw the end of the glorious thousand years, when Satan was loosed for a little season; they saw the day of judgment when all men received according to their works, and they saw the heaven and the earth flee away to make room for the city of God, when the

righteous receive an inheritance in eternity." (Joseph Smith, *Teachings of the Prophet Joseph Smith*, selected and arranged by Joseph Fielding Smith [Salt Lake City: Deseret Book Co., 1977], pages 12–13.)

Saul agrees with his servant's recommendation and they go to find Samuel, asking directions as they proceed.

10 Then said Saul to his servant, Well said; come, let us go. So they went unto the city where the man of God was.

11 ¶ And as they went up the hill to the city, they found young maidens going out to draw water, and said unto them, Is the seer here?

12 And they answered them, and said, He is; behold, he is before you [*he is ahead of you*]: make haste now, for he came to day to the city; for there is a sacrifice of the people to day in the high place:

13 As soon as ye be come into the city, ye shall straightway find him, before he go up to the high place to eat: for the people will not eat until he come, because he doth bless the sacrifice; and afterwards they eat that be bidden. Now therefore get you up; for about this time ye shall find him.

Little does Saul know that the man of God, Samuel, received a revelation yesterday that he was coming and would be in town for Samuel to meet with today.

14 And they went up into the city: and when they were come into the city, behold, Samuel came out against [*toward*] them, for to go up to the high place.

15 ¶ Now the LORD had told Samuel in his ear a day before Saul came, saying,

16 To morrow about this time I will send thee a man out of the land of Benjamin, and thou shalt anoint him to be captain over my people Israel, that he may save my people out of the hand of the Philistines: for I have looked upon my people, because their cry is come unto me.

"Anointing," as seen in verse 16, above, was to consecrate for service to God and the people.

17 And when Samuel saw Saul, the LORD said unto him, Behold the man whom I spake to thee of! this same shall reign over my people.

In verse 18, next, little does Saul know that the man of whom he asks directions to the Seer is the Seer!

18 Then Saul drew near to Samuel in the gate, and said, Tell me, I pray thee, where the seer's house is.

19 And Samuel answered Saul, and said, I am the seer: go up before me unto the high place; for ye shall eat with me to day, and to morrow I will let thee go, and will tell thee all that is in thine heart.

Did you notice that the Lord, in His kindness, is giving Saul a strong witness that Samuel is indeed His prophet?

20 And as for thine asses that were lost three days ago, set not thy mind on them [*don't worry about them*]; for they are found. And on whom is all the desire of Israel [*do you realize that you are the one for whom all Israel has been looking to become their king*]? Is it not on thee, and on all thy father's house?

Saul immediately hesitates and begins presenting reasons why he should not become the king. This is much the same response that Moses gave and that Enoch gave when they were called (Exodus 3:11; Moses 6:31).

21 And Saul answered and said, Am not I a Benjamite, of the smallest of the tribes of Israel? and my family the least of all the families of the tribe of Benjamin? wherefore then speakest thou so to me [*why are you speaking of my becoming king*]?

Samuel ignores Saul's protests and proceeds with the business at hand.

22 And Samuel took Saul and his servant, and brought them into the parlour, and made them sit in the chiefest place among them that were bidden, which were about thirty persons.

23 And Samuel said unto the cook, Bring the portion which I gave thee, of which I said unto thee, Set it by thee [*bring the piece of meat I told you to set aside*].

24 And the cook took up the shoulder, and that which was upon it, and set it before Saul. And Samuel said, Behold that which is left! set it before thee, and eat: for unto this time hath it been kept for thee since I said, I have invited the people. So Saul did eat with Samuel that day.

25 ¶ And when they were come down from the high place into the city, Samuel communed with Saul upon the top of the house [*Samuel took Saul up onto the flat roof of the house where they could talk in private*].

26 And they arose early: and it came to pass about the spring of the day, that Samuel called Saul to the top of the house, saying, Up, that I may send thee away. And Saul arose, and they went out both of them, he and Samuel, abroad.

As Samuel accompanied Saul and his servant to the outskirts of town, Samuel asks Saul to send the servant on ahead so he can instruct Saul in private.

27 And as they were going down to the end of the city, Samuel said to Saul, Bid the servant pass on before us, (and he passed on,) but stand thou still a while, that I may shew thee the word of God [*that I may do what God told me to do with you*].

Chapter 10, verse 1, tells us what Samuel did next.

1 SAMUEL 10

Selection: all verses

SAMUEL HAS CALLED Saul to be the king of Israel, as instructed by the Lord. Now, in verse 1, Samuel will anoint Saul to be "captain" over Israel, in other words, to be Israel's first king.

1 THEN Samuel took a vial of oil, and poured it upon his head, and kissed him, and said, Is it not because the LORD hath anointed thee to be captain over his inheritance?

2 When thou art departed from me to day, then thou shalt find two men by Rachel's sepulchre in the border of Benjamin at Zelzah; and they will say unto thee, The asses which thou wentest to seek are found: and, lo, thy father hath left the care of the asses, and sorroweth for you, saying, What shall I do for my son?

> In verses 3–8, Samuel's role as a seer is clearly demonstrated, no doubt as a witness to Saul that God was indeed involved in his call to be king.

3 Then shalt thou go on forward from thence, and thou shalt come to the plain of Tabor, and there shall meet thee three men going up to God to Beth-el, one carrying three kids [*young goats*], and another carrying three loaves of bread, and another carrying a bottle of wine:

4 And they will salute [*greet*] thee, and give thee two loaves of bread; which thou shalt receive of their hands.

5 After that thou shalt come to the hill of God, where is the garrison [*military outpost*] of the Philistines: and it shall come to pass, when thou art come thither to the city, that thou shalt meet a company of prophets coming down from the high place with a psaltery [*lyre, a stringed music instrument*], and a tabret [*tambourine*], and a pipe [*flute*], and a harp, before them; and they shall prophesy:

> Next, in verse 6, Samuel prophesies that Saul will be given the gift of prophecy (see Doctrine & Covenants 46:22, Moroni 10:13, 1 Corinthians 12:10).

6 And the Spirit of the LORD will come upon thee, and thou shalt prophesy with them, and shalt be turned into another man [*you will become a different person*].

> In verse 7, Samuel tells Saul to view the signs he will be given as witnesses and assurances that God is with him.

7 And let it be, when these signs are come unto thee, that thou do as occasion serve thee; for God is with thee.

8 And thou shalt go down before

me to Gilgal; and, behold, I will come down unto thee, to offer burnt offerings, and to sacrifice sacrifices of peace offerings: seven days shalt thou tarry, till I come to thee, and shew thee what thou shalt do.

9 ¶ And it was so, that when he had turned his back to go from Samuel, God gave him another heart [*he is spiritually reborn*]: and all those signs came to pass that day.

10 And when they came thither to the hill, behold, a company of prophets met him; and the Spirit of God came upon him, and he prophesied among them.

In verses 11–12 we see that people who knew Saul before notice a change in him.

11 And it came to pass, when all that knew him beforetime saw that, behold, he prophesied among the prophets, then the people said one to another, What is this that is come unto the son of Kish? Is Saul also among the prophets?

12 And one of the same place answered and said, But who is their father? Therefore it became a proverb, Is Saul also among the prophets?

13 And when he had made an end of prophesying, he came to the high place.

While all this has been going on with Saul and his servant, his father and family back home have been worried that something might have happened to them as they searched high and low for the missing donkeys.

14 ¶ And Saul's uncle said unto him and to his servant, Whither went ye? And he said, To seek the asses: and when we saw that they were no where, we came to Samuel.

As Saul relates the things that happened during their absence, the uncle is curious about what Samuel had to say. Saul tells him some things but holds back on the things pertaining to his becoming king.

15 And Saul's uncle said, Tell me, I pray thee, what Samuel said unto you.

16 And Saul said unto his uncle, He told us plainly that the asses were found. But of the matter of the kingdom, whereof Samuel spake, he told him not.

The time has now come for Samuel to present Saul to the people as their king. As he does so, he chastises the people for choosing a king and thus rejecting God.

17 ¶ And Samuel called the people together unto the LORD to Mizpeh;

18 And said unto the children of Israel, Thus saith the LORD God of Israel, I brought up Israel out of Egypt, and delivered you out of the hand of the Egyptians, and out of the hand of all kingdoms, and of them that oppressed you:

19 And ye have this day rejected your God, who himself saved you out of all your adversities and your tribulations; and ye have said unto him, Nay, but set a king over us. Now therefore present yourselves before the LORD by your tribes [*gather yourselves together by tribes*], and by your thousands.

20 And when Samuel had caused all the tribes of Israel to come near, the tribe of Benjamin was taken.

> Imagine the anticipation and drama among the people as Samuel first selected the tribe of Benjamin and then began selecting groups from Benjamin, family by family or clan by clan. He was narrowing it down bit by bit to the man who would be their king.
>
> In verse 21, next, when it came time for Saul to step forward, he was nowhere to be found.

21 When he had caused the tribe of Benjamin to come near by their families, the family of Matri was taken, and Saul the son of Kish was taken: and when they sought him, he could not be found.

22 Therefore they enquired of the LORD further, if the man should yet come thither [*they were wondering if maybe Saul hadn't arrived yet*]. And the LORD answered, Behold,

he hath hid himself among the stuff [*NIV: "baggage"*].

23 And they ran and fetched him thence: and when he stood among the people, he was higher than any of the people from his shoulders and upward.

24 And Samuel said to all the people, See ye him whom the LORD hath chosen, that there is none like him among all the people? And all the people shouted, and said, God save the king.

25 Then Samuel told the people the manner of the kingdom [*described the rules and regulations governing being ruled by a king*], and wrote it in a book, and laid it up before the LORD. And Samuel sent all the people away, every man to his house.

26 ¶ And Saul also went home to Gibeah; and there went with him a band of men, whose hearts God had touched [*who were loyal to Saul*].

> Not all the people were thrilled to have Saul as their new king and they let it be known.

27 But the children of Belial [*dissidents, troublemakers*] said, How shall this man save us? And they despised him, and brought him no presents. But he held his peace [*didn't pay any attention to them*].

> As you continue reading 1 Samuel in your Bible, you will see that Saul united Israel in

battle against their enemies and was successful in conquering them.

1 SAMUEL 11

Selection: all verses

AT THIS POINT, Saul is humble, willing to listen to counsel from Samuel and others, quick to give the Lord credit, has the Spirit of the Lord upon him, and is willing to forgive his detractors and critics. Having been anointed to be Israel's first king, Saul now shows his leadership and ability to unite the Israelites in battle against their enemies.

The Ammonites, descendents of Lot who live in the territory east of the Jordan River, east of Mount Gilead, and south of the Jabbok River, have come to attack and subdue the settlement of Jabesh. It is an Israelite settlement about twenty miles south of the Sea of Galilee and just a bit east across the Jordan River. Initially, in verse 1, the frightened men of Jabesh cower and offer to make a treaty with Nahash, the Ammonite leader, in which they would serve the Ammonites in return for their lives.

1 THEN Nahash [*king of the Ammonites, see 1 Samuel 12:12*] the Ammonite came up, and encamped against Jabesh-gilead: and **all the men of Jabesh said unto Nahash, Make a covenant** [*treaty*] **with us, and we will serve thee.**

With malicious enjoyment, Nahash informs the frightened Israelites that he will agree to their offer on one condition, that they all submit to having their right eyes gouged out.

2 And **Nahash** the Ammonite **answered** them, **On this condition will I make a covenant with you, that I may thrust out all your right eyes,** and lay it for a reproach [*to bring disgrace and contempt*] upon all Israel.

The leaders of Jabesh ask for a grace period of seven days to explore possibilities of rescue from their fragmented fellow tribes of Israel.

3 And the elders of Jabesh said unto him, **Give us seven days' respite, that we may send messengers unto all the coasts of Israel: and then, if there be no man to save us, we will come out to thee.**

In verses 4–7, next, Saul hears about the threat from the Ammonites and exercises strong "persuasion" to unite and rally the men of Israel to fight the Ammonites.

4 ¶ **Then came the messengers** to Gibeah of Saul, **and told the tidings** in the ears of the people: **and all the people lifted up their voices, and wept.**

5 And, behold, Saul came after the herd out of the field [*Saul happened to be coming along behind his animals*]; and **Saul said, What aileth the people that they weep?** And they told him the tidings of the men of Jabesh.

6 And the Spirit of God came upon Saul when he heard those tidings, and **his anger was kindled greatly.**

Saul used very persuasive means to get his message across to the trembling Israelites.

7 And **he took a yoke of oxen, and hewed them in pieces, and sent them throughout all the coasts of Israel** by the hands of messengers, saying, **Whosoever cometh not forth after Saul and after Samuel, so shall it be done unto his oxen.** And the fear of the LORD fell on the people, and they came out with one consent [*they all agreed to come together and fight*].

As a result of Saul's tactics, he gathered an army of three hundred and thirty thousand.

8 And when he numbered them in Bezek, **the children of Israel were three hundred thousand,** and the **men of Judah thirty thousand.**

9 And they said unto the messengers that came [*from the threatened area of Jabesh-gilead*], Thus shall ye say unto the men of Jabesh-gilead, **To morrow, by that time the sun be hot, ye shall have help.** And the messengers came and shewed it to the men of Jabesh; and they were glad.

Encouraged, the men of Jabesh set a trap for the Ammonites.

10 Therefore the men of Jabesh said, **To morrow we will come out unto you, and ye shall do with us all that seemeth good unto you.**

11 And it was so on the morrow [*the next day*], that Saul put the people in three companies; and they came into the midst of the host [*the Ammonite armies*] in the morning watch [*went from 2 a.m. to sunrise*], and slew the Ammonites until the heat of the day: and it came to pass, that they which remained were scattered, so that two of them were not left together.

With this resounding victory behind him, Saul is invited by enthusiastic followers to execute the dissidents and critics who publicly criticized him after being anointed king (see chapter 10, verse 27).

12 ¶ And the people said unto Samuel, **Who is he that said, Shall Saul reign over us? bring the men, that we may put them to death.**

Saul shows his personal righteousness and willingness to forgive in his response, verse 13, next.

13 And Saul said, **There shall not a man be put to death this day:** for to day the LORD hath wrought salvation in Israel [*he gives the Lord credit for the victory*].

Next, in verses 14–15, Samuel calls the people to gather in

Gilgal and join in reaffirming Saul's kingship.

14 Then said Samuel to the people, Come, and let us go to Gilgal [*about a mile northeast of Jericho*], **and renew the kingdom there.**

15 And all the people went to Gilgal; and **there they made Saul king before the LORD** in Gilgal; and there they sacrificed sacrifices of peace offerings before the LORD; and there Saul and all the men of Israel rejoiced greatly.

1 SAMUEL 12

Selection: verses 1–5; 14–25

SAMUEL HAS NOW grown old. He calls the children of Israel to gather and reviews his dealings as their prophet with them. His speech to them is quite similar to that of King Benjamin to his people, in Mosiah 2:14.

1 AND Samuel said unto all Israel, Behold, I have hearkened unto your voice in all that ye said unto me, and have made a king over you.

2 And now, behold, the king walketh before you: and I am old and gray-headed; and, behold, my sons are with you: and I have walked before you from my childhood unto this day.

In verses 3–5, Samuel asks the people to be the judge as to whether or not he has been honest and fair with them all his life. They respond, affirming that he has not taken advantage of them in any way.

3 Behold, here I am: witness against me before the LORD, and before his anointed: whose ox have I taken? or whose ass have I taken? or whom have I defrauded? whom have I oppressed? or of whose hand have I received any bribe to blind mine eyes therewith? and I will restore it you.

4 And they said, Thou hast not defrauded us, nor oppressed us, neither hast thou taken ought of any man's hand [*you have never taken any bribe at all*].

5 And he said unto them, The LORD is witness against you, and his anointed is witness this day, that ye have not found ought in my hand. And they answered, He is witness.

In the next several verses, Samuel rehearses the Lord's dealings with Israel, from the time He freed them from Egyptian bondage to the present day.

We will pick it up again with verses 14–15, where Samuel uses "if-then" clauses to warn the people.

14 If ye will fear [*respect and honor*] the LORD, and serve him, and obey his voice, and not rebel against the commandment of the LORD, then shall both ye and also the king that

reigneth over you continue following the LORD your God:

15 But if ye will not obey the voice of the LORD, but rebel against the commandment of the LORD, then shall the hand of the LORD be against you, as it was against your fathers [*ancestors*].

> Next, Samuel invites the Israelites to witness a spectacular demonstration of the power of the Lord to remind them of their dependency on Him and to chastise them for demanding a king. It is harvest season and severe thunder showers would be disastrous to them.

16 ¶ Now therefore stand and see this great thing, which the LORD will do before your eyes.

17 Is it not wheat harvest to day? I will call unto the LORD, and he shall send thunder and rain; that ye may perceive and see that your wickedness is great, which ye have done in the sight of the LORD, in asking you a king.

18 So Samuel called unto the LORD; and the LORD sent thunder and rain that day: and all the people greatly feared the LORD and Samuel.

> Next, the people admit their sin and foolishness in asking for a king.

19 And all the people said unto Samuel, Pray for thy servants unto the LORD thy God, that we die not: for we have added unto all our sins this evil, to ask us a king.

> Despite their wickedness and foolishness, the Lord gives them yet another chance and invites them to repent and be loyal to Him. This can remind us of a verse in the Book of Mormon.
>
> **Mosiah 26:30**
> Yea, and as often as my people repent will I forgive them their trespasses against me.

20 ¶ And Samuel said unto the people, Fear not: ye have done all this wickedness: yet turn not aside from following the LORD, but serve the LORD with all your heart;

21 And turn ye not aside: for then should ye go after vain things, which cannot profit nor deliver; for they are vain [*worthless, of no value to you*].

22 For the LORD will not forsake his people for his great name's sake [*He has a reputation of being a loving and forgiving God*]: because it hath pleased the LORD to make you his people.

23 Moreover as for me, God forbid that I should sin against the LORD in ceasing to pray for you: but I will teach you the good and the right way:

24 Only fear the LORD, and serve him in truth with all your heart: for consider how great things he hath done for you.

Samuel concludes the meeting with a severe warning.

25 But if ye shall still do wickedly, ye shall be consumed, both ye and your king.

1 SAMUEL 13

Selection: all verses

AFTER ABOUT TWO years as king, a subtle change begins to occur in Saul. Pride begins to take over his thinking. He rejects the counsel of the Lord's prophet and begins to apostatize. He takes upon himself authority he does not have and offers a burnt offering. As a result, he is rejected by the Lord.

As the Philistine armies penetrate deep into Israelite territory (clear to Michmash, verses 2 and 5, about ten miles northeast of Jerusalem), Saul calls for Samuel to come and offer sacrifice to get the Lord's help against the Philistines. Samuel doesn't come as soon as Saul thinks he should, so Saul takes things into his own hands and offers the sacrifice himself. He has no priesthood authority to do so, and it is a grievous sin.

1 SAUL reigned one year; and when he **had reigned two years over Israel,**

2 Saul chose him **three thousand men of Israel;** whereof two thousand were with Saul in Michmash [*about 10 miles northeast of Jerusalem*] and in mount Beth-el, and a thousand were with Jonathan [*Saul's son*] in Gibeah [*about 2 miles north of Jerusalem*] of Benjamin: and the rest of the people he sent every man to his tent [*he sent the rest of his troops home*].

In verse 3, next, Jonathan attacks a Philistine outpost in Geba, located right between Saul's forces in Michmash and his forces in Gibeah, which stirs up the Philistines to launch a major attack against Israel.

3 And **Jonathan smote** [*attacked*] **the garrison of the Philistines that was in Geba,** and the Philistines heard of it [*and were mad*]. And Saul blew the trumpet throughout all the land, saying, Let the Hebrews hear.

Verse 4, next, shows that word of the attack against the Philistine outpost spread rapidly and worried the Israelites greatly. They feared that Saul's men had unwisely angered the Philistines and made Israel "stink" in the eyes of the Philistines.

4 And **all Israel heard say that Saul had smitten a garrison of the Philistines,** and that Israel also was had in abomination [*NIV: "had become a stench"*] with the Philistines. And the people were called together after Saul to Gilgal [*Saul called the people to join him in Gilgal, a few miles north of Jericho*].

Bible scholars suggest that the "thirty thousand chariots," in verse 5, next, was more likely 3,000 chariots. It is a translation error (see *Old Testament Student Manual, Genesis–2 Samuel*, p 273). Even at 3,000 chariots, it would still be a frightening and formidable enemy presence.

5 ¶ And the Philistines gathered themselves together to fight with Israel, thirty thousand chariots, and six thousand horsemen, and people as the sand which is on the sea shore in multitude: and they came up, and pitched in Michmash, eastward from Beth-aven.

Many of the terrified Israelites hid wherever they could.

6 When the men of Israel saw that they were in a strait [*a tight situation*], (for the people were distressed,) then **the people did hide themselves in caves, and in thickets, and in rocks, and in high places, and in pits.**

Some of the Israelite men deserted Saul and fled east across the Jordan River.

7 And **some of the Hebrews went over Jordan to the land of Gad and Gilead.** As for Saul, he was yet in Gilgal, and all the people followed him trembling [*terrified*].

According to verse 8, next, Samuel had agreed to join Saul in Gilgal in seven days, but was delayed.

8 ¶ And **he tarried seven days,** **according to the set time that Samuel had appointed:** but Samuel came not to Gilgal; and the people were scattered from him [*more of Saul's soldiers started deserting*].

Saul's worry and impatience overcame him and he justified himself in offering the sacrifices that Samuel was to offer when he arrived. This was a gross misstep and a grievous sin. Patience and obedience are part of our mortal test and Saul failed them both in this instance.

9 And Saul said, Bring hither a burnt offering to me, and peace offerings. **And he offered the burnt offering.**

In verses 10-14, next, Samuel arrives on the scene just as Saul finishes the sacrifices. He tries to explain and justify his disobedience but it doesn't work.

10 And it came to pass, that **as soon as he had made an end of offering the burnt offering, behold, Samuel came;** and Saul went out to meet him, that he might salute [*greet*] him.

11 ¶ And **Samuel said, What hast thou done?** And Saul said, Because I saw that the people were scattered from me, and that thou camest not within the days appointed, and that the Philistines gathered themselves together at Michmash;

12 Therefore said I, The Philistines will come down now upon me to

Gilgal, and I have not made supplication unto the LORD: **I forced myself therefore, and offered a burnt offering.**

13 And **Samuel said to Saul, Thou hast done foolishly: thou hast not kept the commandment of the LORD thy God,** which he commanded thee: for now would the LORD have established thy kingdom upon Israel for ever.

14 But **now thy kingdom shall not continue:** the LORD hath sought him a man after his own heart [*David, see 1 Chronicles 10:14*], and the LORD hath commanded him to be captain over his people, because thou hast not kept that which the LORD commanded thee.

> In verses 15–18, next, Samuel leaves and goes to Gibeah. Saul is left with only about six hundred men. They also return to Gibeah, about three miles north of Jerusalem. The Philistines send out raiding parties from their encampment in Michmash.

15 And **Samuel arose, and gat him up from Gilgal unto Gibeah** of Benjamin. And Saul numbered the people that were present with him, **about six hundred men.**

16 And Saul, and Jonathan his son, and the people that were present with them, abode in Gibeah of Benjamin: but **the Philistines encamped in Michmash.**

17 ¶ And the spoilers [*raiding parties*] came out of the camp of the Philistines in three companies: one company turned unto the way that leadeth to Ophrah, unto the land of Shual:

18 And another company turned the way to Beth-horon: and another company turned to the way of the border that looketh to the valley of Zeboim toward the wilderness.

> In verses 19–22, we see that the Israelites did not have blacksmiths among them. Rather, in times past, they had relied on Philistine blacksmiths. This now became a very serious detriment to their war efforts. Some scholars believe that the Israelites did not know much about how to work with iron and so relied on softer metals such as brass (see *Old Testament Student Manual Genesis—2 Samuel*, page 274).

19 ¶ Now **there was no smith** [*no blacksmith*] **found throughout all the land of Israel:** for the Philistines said, Lest the Hebrews make them swords or spears:

20 But **all the Israelites went down to the Philistines, to sharpen** every man his **share** [*plow, cutting edge of a plow*], and his **coulter** [*garden hoe*], and his **axe**, and his **mattock** [*a grubbing axe*].

21 Yet they had a file [*the Philistines have files for sharpening*] for the mattocks, and for the coulters, and for the forks, and for the axes, and to sharpen the goads [*a sharp rod about 8 feet long, used to prod animals*].

22 So it came to pass in the day of battle, that there was neither sword nor spear found in the hand of any of the people that were with Saul and Jonathan: but with Saul and with Jonathan his son was there found [*only Saul and Jonathan had them*].

23 And the garrison of the Philistines went out to the passage of Michmash.

1 SAMUEL 14

Selection: all verses

THE PHILISTINES CONTINUE to be a major military threat to the Israelites in the promised land. Saul continues his downward spiral as he focuses on himself and makes uninspired decisions which seriously handicap his men in the battles against the Philistines.

In this chapter, we will get better acquainted with Saul's son, Jonathan, who will become known for his deep friendship and loyalty to David. He is a young man of courage and great faith in the Lord. In verses 1–15, he and his armor bearer courageously enter the Philistine outpost and, with the help of the Lord, cause a major disturbance among the enemy. They did not tell anyone else, including Saul, that they were going.

1 NOW it came to pass upon a day, that Jonathan the son of Saul said unto the young man that bare his armour, **Come, and let us go over to the Philistines' garrison** [*military outpost*], that is on the other side. But **he told not his father.**

Verses 2–3, next, indicate that Saul, with about six hundred men including troops plus the men in verse 3, were gathered together but not actively engaged in battle at the time Jonathan and his armor bearer quietly left.

2 And **Saul tarried** in the uttermost part of Gibeah under a pomegranate tree which is in Migron: and the people that were with him were about six hundred men;

3 And Ahiah, the son of Ahitub, I-chabod's brother, the son of Phinehas, the son of Eli, the LORD'S priest in Shiloh, wearing an ephod. And the people knew not that Jonathan was gone.

4 ¶ And between the passages, by which Jonathan sought to go over unto the Philistines' garrison, there was a sharp rock on the one side, and a sharp rock on the other side: and the name of the one was Bozez, and the name of the other Seneh.

5 The forefront of the one was situate northward over against Michmash, and the other southward over against Gibeah.

Jonathan goes with faith that
God will help them.

6 And Jonathan said to the young
man that bare his armour, Come,
and let us go over unto the garrison
of these uncircumcised [*non-Israelites*]: **it may be that the LORD will
work for us**: for there is no restraint
to the LORD to save by many or
by few [*there is no limit on God; He
can use many or just a few to save His
people*].

Next, in verse 7, we gain insight
into the strength of character
and faith of Jonathan's armor
bearer.

7 And **his armourbearer said** unto
him, **Do all that is in thine heart**:
turn thee [*NIV: "go ahead"*]; behold,
**I am with thee according to thy
heart.**

In verses 8–14, next, the two
execute a plan to boldly walk in
among some Philistine troops.
With the help of the Lord, they
slay about twenty of the enemy
in an area about one half acre
in size.

8 Then said Jonathan, Behold, we
will pass over unto these men, and
we will discover [*reveal, show*] ourselves unto them.

9 If they say thus unto us, Tarry
until we come to you; then **we will
stand still** in our place, and will not
go up unto them.

10 But if they say thus, **Come up
unto us**; then **we will go up**: for the
**LORD hath delivered them into
our hand**: and this shall be a sign
unto us.

11 And both of them discovered
themselves unto the garrison of the
Philistines: and the Philistines said,
Behold, the Hebrews come forth
out of the holes where they had hid
themselves.

12 And **the men of the garrison
answered** Jonathan and his armourbearer, and said, **Come up to us**,
and we will shew you a thing [*we will
teach you a lesson*]. And Jonathan
said unto his armourbearer, Come
up after me: **for the LORD hath
delivered them into the hand of
Israel.**

Again we see Jonathan's faith in
the Lord, at the end of verse 12,
above. His armor bearer follows
right behind him as they attack
and slay about twenty enemies,
in verses 13–14.

13 And Jonathan climbed up upon
his hands and upon his feet, and
his armourbearer after him: and
they fell before Jonathan [*Jonathan
killed several enemy soldiers*]; and **his
armourbearer slew after him.**

14 And **that first slaughter, which
Jonathan and his armourbearer
made, was about twenty men**,
within as it were an half acre of land,
which a yoke of oxen might plow.

This unexpected turn of events
resulted in great panic and

confusion among the Philistines. It was greatly magnified by an earthquake.

15 And there was trembling in the host [*panic among the whole Philistine army*], in the field, and among all the people: the garrison, and the spoilers [*raiding parties who burned homes and fields as part of the Philistine strategy against Israel*], they also trembled, and the earth quaked [*the Lord sent an earthquake*]: so it was a very great trembling [*there was great panic and disarray among the enemies*].

Next, in verse 16, Saul's lookouts see the Philistine army scattering in panic in every direction.

16 And **the watchmen of Saul** in Gibeah of Benjamin **looked**; and, behold, **the multitude** [*Philistine army*] **melted away**, and they went on beating down one another.

Saul is curious as to who of his group might have snuck away and caused the panic among the Philistine soldiers in the garrison. He calls for a roll call.

17 Then said Saul unto the people that were with him, Number now, and see who is gone from us. **And when they had numbered, behold, Jonathan and his armourbearer were not there.**

In verses 18–46, we watch again as Saul's downward spiral of disobedience and personal power seeking lead to unrighteous and unwise decisions. In

verse 18, next he calls for the ark of the covenant to be brought to his location, hoping that it will protect his army. He is failing to learn from past experience.

Perhaps you recall that previously the Israelite leaders likewise requested that the ark be brought to their encampment to protect them from the Philistines (1 Samuel 4:3-4). Their real protection consisted in repenting and returning to the Lord. The ark was captured by the Philistines and caused much trouble among them (chapters 4–7) and was eventually returned to Israel. Now, Saul is willing to repeat past mistakes of his people.

18 And Saul said unto Ahiah [*the high priest in Shiloh, see verse 3*], **Bring hither the ark of God.** For the ark of God was at that time with the children of Israel [*had been returned back to Israel previously by the Philistines*].

As a result of Jonathan and his armor bearer's faith and courage and the Lord's help, the Philistine soldiers have been routed. Saul and his men take advantage of it and, in verses 19–23, next, they all join in the battle, even the ones who had previously deserted return and join the fight (verse 22).

19 ¶ And it came to pass, while Saul talked unto the priest, that the noise that was in the host of the Philistines went on and increased: and Saul said unto the priest, Withdraw thine hand.

20 And **Saul and all the people that were with him assembled themselves, and they came to the battle:** and, behold, every man's sword was against his fellow, and there was a very great discomfiture [*the Philistines were in total confusion, even to the point of attacking each other with their own swords*].

21 Moreover the Hebrews [*Israelites*] that were with the Philistines before that time [*who had previously joined with the Philistines for safety*], which went up with them into the camp from the country round about, **even they also turned to be with the Israelites that were with Saul and Jonathan.**

22 Likewise **all the men of Israel which had hid themselves in mount Ephraim**, when they heard that the Philistines fled, even they also **followed hard after** [*close behind*] them in the battle.

23 So the LORD saved Israel that day: and the battle passed over unto Beth-aven.

> Next, beginning with verse 24, Saul made an uninspired decision and commanded that his men fast all day, even though they were in the heat of battle and needed strength. We would wish that his motive for demanding that they fast would be to request the help of the Lord. But, not so. It is so that he can get revenge on his enemies. Sadly, his apostasy is leading to extreme self-centeredness.

24 ¶ And the men of Israel were distressed that day: for **Saul had adjured the people, saying, Cursed be the man that eateth any food until evening, that I may be avenged on mine enemies.** So none of the people tasted any food.

25 And all they of the land came to a wood; and **there was honey** upon the ground.

26 And when the people were come into the wood, behold, the honey dropped; but **no man put his hand to his mouth: for the people feared the oath** [*they all feared Saul's oath and command not to eat anything*].

> Jonathan and his armor bearer were away from camp, wreaking havoc among the Philistines in their garrison at the time Saul gave orders to his men to fast. So, they were unaware of the order.

27 **But Jonathan heard not when his father charged the people with the oath:** wherefore he put forth the end of the rod that was in his hand, and dipped it in an honeycomb, and put his hand to his mouth; and his eyes were enlightened [*he received strength and nourishment*].

28 Then answered [*responded*] one of the people, and said, Thy father straitly [*strictly*] charged the people with an oath, saying, Cursed be the man that eateth any food this day. And the people were faint [*very hungry and weak from lack of nourishment*].

29 Then said Jonathan, **My father hath troubled the land** [*my father gave a foolish command*]: see, I pray you, how mine eyes have been enlightened, because I tasted a little of this honey.

30 How much more, if haply [*it would have been much better if*] the people had eaten freely to day of the spoil of their enemies which they found? for had there not been now a much greater slaughter among the Philistines?

31 And they smote the Philistines that day from Michmash to Aijalon: and **the people were very faint** [*extremely hungry*].

> Next, in verse 32, Saul's soldiers in their famished condition grab up some animals left behind by the fleeing Philistines, slaughter them and eat them blood and all. They did not drain the blood first, which is a serious violation of the law of Jehovah (Genesis 9:4).

32 And the people flew upon the spoil, and took sheep, and oxen, and calves, and slew them on the ground: and **the people did eat them with the blood.**

> In verses 33–35, next, the tragedy of Saul's spiritual decline continues as he immediately seeks to undo the sin of his people by offering sacrifices, which he has no authority to do. He obviously did not learn his previous lesson from Samuel (1 Samuel 13:9–14).

33 ¶ Then they told Saul, saying, Behold, the people sin against the LORD, in that they eat with the blood. And he said, Ye have transgressed: roll a great stone unto me this day.

34 And Saul said, Disperse yourselves among the people, and say unto them, Bring me hither every man his ox, and every man his sheep, and slay them here, and eat; and sin not against the LORD in eating with the blood. And **all the people brought every man his ox with him that night, and slew them there.**

35 And Saul built an altar unto the LORD: the same was the first altar that he built unto the LORD.

> Next, Saul determines to pursue the Philistines and attack them by night. His men agree to follow him. But he wants to check with the Lord as to whether or not such an attack would be wise.

36 ¶ And **Saul said, Let us go down after the Philistines by night,** and spoil them until the morning light, and let us not leave a man of them. And they said, Do whatsoever seemeth good unto thee. Then said the priest, Let us draw near hither unto God.

Saul tries to get revelation from God, but no answer comes.

37 And **Saul asked counsel of God, Shall I go down after the Philistines?** wilt thou deliver them into the hand of Israel? **But he answered him not that day.**

Rather than looking inwardly to find the cause of his lack of an answer from the Lord, he blindly seeks to find out which of his men have offended the Lord, thus causing lack of revelation.

38 And Saul said, **Draw ye near hither, all the chief of the people: and know and see wherein this sin hath been this day.**

He swears an oath that whoever is guilty of sin, even if it is his own son, Jonathan, will be put to death. Jonathan did indeed eat some honey, but was not guilty of breaking his father's command because he did not know about it. Still, Saul, when he finds out that his son ate some honey, he pridefully and unfairly determines to have him executed. The people protest and rescue Jonathan. Saul's power and hold on his people is beginning to erode.

39 For, **as the LORD liveth** [*the strongest, most serious oath possible in their culture*], which saveth Israel, though it be in Jonathan my son, he shall surely die. **But there was not a man among all the people that answered him** [*they are silently taking Jonathan's side*].

Through the casting of lots, Saul determines that Jonathan is the guilty party (verses 40–43).

40 Then said he unto all Israel, Be ye on one side, and I and Jonathan my son will be on the other side. And the people said unto Saul, Do what seemeth good unto thee.

41 Therefore Saul said unto the LORD God of Israel, Give a perfect lot. And Saul and Jonathan were taken: but the people escaped.

42 And Saul said, Cast lots between me and Jonathan my son. And Jonathan was taken.

43 **Then Saul said to Jonathan, Tell me what thou hast done.** And Jonathan told him, and said, I did but taste a little honey with the end of the rod that was in mine hand, and, lo, I must die.

44 And **Saul answered**, God do so and more also: for **thou shalt surely die, Jonathan.**

45 And the people said unto Saul, Shall Jonathan die, who hath wrought this great salvation in Israel? God forbid: as the LORD liveth, there shall not one hair of his head fall to the ground; for he hath wrought with God this day. So **the people rescued Jonathan, that he died not.**

Verses 46–48 summarize Saul's success militarily as he leads Israel into battle against other enemies of the Israelites.

46 Then Saul went up from following the Philistines: and the Philistines went to their own place.

47 ¶ So **Saul took the kingdom over Israel, and fought against all his enemies on every side**, against Moab, and against the children of Ammon, and against Edom, and against the kings of Zobah, and against the Philistines: and whithersoever he turned himself, he vexed them.

48 And he gathered an host, and smote the Amalekites, and delivered Israel out of the hands of them that spoiled them.

> Verses 49–51 are a basic family history chart of Saul and his family.

49 Now the sons of Saul were Jonathan, and Ishui, and Melchishua: and the names of his two daughters were these; the name of the firstborn Merab, and the name of the younger Michal:

50 And the name of Saul's wife was Ahinoam, the daughter of Ahimaaz: and the name of the captain of his host was Abner, the son of Ner, Saul's uncle.

51 And Kish was the father of Saul; and Ner the father of Abner was the son of Abiel.

> Verse 52, next, is a partial fulfillment of Samuel's warning and prophecy when the people requested a king, back in chapter 8. He warned them, among other things, that a king would take their best and strongest sons into his service (1 Samuel 8:11).

52 And there was sore war against the Philistines all the days of Saul: and **when Saul saw any strong man, or any valiant man, he took him unto him.**

1 SAMUEL 15

Selection: all verses

EARLY IN THE history of the exodus of the children of Israel from Egypt, the Amalekites (whose territory was west of the southern end of the Dead Sea) attacked them (Exodus 17:8–16). Now, once again, the Amalekites come to battle against Israel in the Holy Land.

As we see in verses 1–3, the Lord gives Saul yet another chance to demonstrate strict obedience as he leads the Israelites against the Amalekites. This can remind us of how patient He is with us.

Sadly, despite being warned so emphatically, Saul continues to openly disobey the Lord and the instructions he is given by Samuel the prophet.

1 Samuel also said unto Saul, **The LORD sent me to anoint thee to be king over his people,** over Israel: **now therefore hearken thou unto the voice of the words of the LORD.**

2 Thus saith the LORD of hosts, I remember that which Amalek did to Israel, how he laid wait for him in the way, when he came up from Egypt [*when Moses was leading the children of Israel from Egypt toward the promised land*].

> Strict instructions are now given to Saul. While they seem merciless to us, it was common in the culture of the day to completely destroy the enemy and all associated therewith. In fact, archeological digs show that often the destruction included undermining city walls, propping them up with timbers, then setting fire to the timbers so that the walls crumbled completely.

3 Now go and smite Amalek, and **utterly destroy all that they have, and spare them not**; but slay both man and woman, infant and suckling, ox and sheep, camel and ass.

> In verses 4–9, next, we see that Saul made his own rules and did not completely obey the word of the Lord given through Samuel. He had not yet learned.

4 And Saul gathered the people together, and numbered them in Telaim, two hundred thousand footmen, and ten thousand men of Judah.

5 And **Saul came to a city of Amalek, and laid wait in the valley.**

6 ¶ And Saul said unto the Kenites, Go, depart, get you down from among the Amalekites, lest I destroy you with them: for ye shewed kindness to all the children of Israel, when they came up out of Egypt. So the Kenites departed from among the Amalekites.

7 And **Saul smote the Amalekites** from Havilah until thou comest to Shur, that is over against Egypt.

8 And **he took Agag the king of the Amalekites alive**, and utterly destroyed all the people with the edge of the sword.

9 But Saul and the people spared Agag, and the best of the sheep, and of the oxen, and of the fatlings, and the lambs, and all that was good, and would not utterly destroy them: but every thing that was vile and refuse, that they destroyed utterly.

> As a result, Saul was rejected. This was a sad time for Samuel, who had Christlike love for Saul in his heart.

10 ¶ Then came the word of the LORD unto Samuel, saying,

11 It repenteth me that I have set up Saul to be king: for he is turned back from following me, and hath not performed my commandments. And **it grieved Samuel; and he cried unto the LORD all night.**

> The Lord does not repent. He is perfect. We need the JST to correct verse 11, above.

JST 1 Samuel 15:11

11 I have set up Saul to be a king, and he repenteth not that he hath sinned, for he is turned back from following me, and hath not performed my commandments. And it grieved Samuel; and he cried unto the Lord all night.

It appears, in verse 12, next, that Saul intentionally avoids Samuel.

12 And **when Samuel rose early to meet Saul in the morning, it was told Samuel, saying, Saul came to Carmel** [*an Israelite town in Judea*], and, behold, he set him up a place [*NIV: "has set up a monument in his own honor"*], and is gone about, and passed on, and gone down to Gilgal [*just north of Jericho*].

Samuel finally catches up with Saul and Saul acts like all is well and he has obeyed the instructions given him by the Lord through Samuel. When Samuel challenges him, asking why he can hear the Amalekite's animals, Saul immediately begins making flimsy excuses, justifying his own behavior or blaming others for it.

13 And **Samuel came to Saul: and Saul said unto him, Blessed be thou of the LORD: I have performed the commandment of the LORD.**

14 And **Samuel said, What meaneth then this bleating of the sheep** in mine ears, **and the lowing of the oxen which I hear?**

15 And Saul said, They have brought them from the Amalekites: for **the people spared the best of the sheep and of the oxen, to sacrifice unto the LORD** thy God; and the rest we have utterly destroyed.

16 Then Samuel said unto Saul, Stay, and I will tell thee what the LORD hath said to me this night. And he said unto him, Say on.

There is a major message for all of us in verse 17, next. When we are humble, we are far more likely to be obedient to the Lord's commandments.

17 And Samuel said, **When thou wast little in thine own sight,** wast thou not made the head of the tribes of Israel, and the LORD anointed thee king over Israel?

18 And the LORD sent thee on a journey [*a mission*], and said, Go and utterly destroy the sinners the Amalekites, and fight against them until they be consumed.

19 Wherefore [*why*] then didst thou not obey the voice of the LORD, but didst fly upon the spoil [*NIV: "pounce on the plunder"*], and didst evil in the sight of the LORD?

In verse 20, next, Saul seems to have lost the ability to discern when he is disobedient. Satan has succeeded in deceiving him and getting him to believe his own lies.

20 And Saul said unto Samuel, Yea, I have obeyed the voice of the LORD, and have gone the way which the LORD sent me, and have brought Agag the king of Amalek, and have utterly destroyed the Amalekites.

He is still blaming others.

21 But **the people took of the spoil**, sheep and oxen, the chief of the things which should have been utterly destroyed, **to sacrifice unto the LORD thy God in Gilgal.**

The bolded statement in verse 22, next, is one of the most important and best-known verses in scripture.

22 And Samuel said, Hath the LORD as great delight in burnt offerings and sacrifices, as in obeying the voice of the LORD? Behold, **to obey is better than sacrifice, and to hearken than the fat of rams.**

23 For rebellion is as the sin of witchcraft, and stubbornness is as iniquity and idolatry. **Because thou hast rejected the word of the LORD, he hath also rejected thee from being king.**

Saul tries again to get out of the mess he has created for himself, but to no avail.

24 ¶ And **Saul said unto Samuel, I have sinned**: for I have transgressed the commandment of the LORD, and thy words: because I feared the people, and obeyed their voice.

25 Now therefore, I pray thee, pardon my sin, and turn again with me, that I may worship the LORD.

26 And **Samuel said unto Saul, I will not return with thee: for thou hast rejected the word of the LORD, and the LORD hath reject-ed thee from being king over Israel.**

27 And as Samuel turned about to go away, he laid hold upon the skirt of his mantle, and it rent [*tore it*].

28 And Samuel said unto him, **The LORD hath rent the kingdom of Israel from thee this day, and hath given it to a neighbour of thine** [*David, 2 Samuel 3:9–10*], that is better than thou.

29 And also **the Strength of Israel** [*Jehovah*] **will not lie nor repent: for he is not a man, that he should** repent.

Did you notice, in verse 29, above, that "Strength of Israel" is capital-ized? When capitalized like this, it means, Deity, in this case, Jehovah.

Next, Samuel shows compassion for Saul.

30 Then he said, I have sinned: yet honour me now, I pray thee, before the elders of my people, and before Israel, and turn again [*come back*] with me, that I may worship the LORD thy God.

31 So Samuel turned again after Saul; and **Saul worshipped the LORD.**

> Next, Samuel is forced to carry out the demands of justice because Saul has failed to.

32 ¶ **Then said Samuel, Bring ye hither to me Agag the king of the Amalekites.** And Agag came unto him delicately. And Agag said, Surely the bitterness of death is past.

33 And Samuel said, As thy sword hath made women childless, so shall thy mother be childless among women. **And Samuel hewed Agag in pieces** before the LORD in Gilgal.

34 ¶ Then Samuel went to Ramah; and Saul went up to his house to Gibeah of Saul.

35 And Samuel came no more to see Saul until the day of his death: nevertheless **Samuel mourned for Saul:** and **the LORD repented** that he had made Saul king over Israel.

JST 1 Samuel 15:35

35 And Samuel came no more to see Saul until the day of his death; nevertheless, Samuel mourned for Saul; and **the Lord rent** [*tore*] **the kingdom from Saul whom he had made king over Israel.**

1 SAMUEL 16

Selection: all verses

IN THIS CHAPTER, you will see that David was anointed to be king (verse 13), long before he actually became king of Israel.

Anointing is often used in the work of the Lord to prepare His people for future blessings. For example, as Melchizedek Priesthood holders administer to the sick, consecrated oil is used to prepare the person for the blessings that will be pronounced a few moments later in the sealing of the anointing. In summary, anointing is often a preliminary ordinance to later blessings.

Because of Saul's repeated disobedience, the Lord rejected him and told him that another would be made king in his place (1 Samuel 15:28). Samuel, a man of deep love and compassion, is still mourning for Saul. In verse 1, the premortal Christ instructs Samuel to curtail his mourning sufficiently to move ahead with anointing a new king.

1 AND the LORD said unto Samuel, **How long wilt thou mourn for Saul, seeing I have rejected him from reigning over Israel?** fill thine horn with oil [*olive oil, used for anointing*], and go, I will send thee to Jesse [*David the shepherd boy's father*] the Beth-lehemite: for **I have provided me a king among his sons.**

> We get an idea of Saul's deteriorating emotional state from Samuel's concern in verse 2, next.

2 And Samuel said, **How can I go? if Saul hear it, he will kill me.** And the LORD said, Take an heifer with thee, and say, I am come to sacrifice to the LORD.

3 And call Jesse to the sacrifice, and I will shew thee what thou shalt do: and thou shalt anoint unto me him whom I name unto thee.

It appears that the community leaders in Bethlehem were worried that they might be in trouble, when they saw the prophet Samuel coming.

4 And Samuel did that which the LORD spake, and came to Bethlehem. And **the elders of the town trembled at his coming, and said, Comest thou peaceably?**

5 And **he said, Peaceably:** I am come to sacrifice unto the LORD: sanctify yourselves, and come with me to the sacrifice. And he sanctified [*to be made clean by the Atonement*] Jesse and his sons, and called them to the sacrifice.

Verses 6–13 contain the fascinating account of the Lord's inspiration to Samuel as he sought out a new king of Israel from Jesse's sons. This process of seeking the Lord's choice and obtaining revelation during the process is repeated weekly throughout the world as General Authorities travel on assignments to search out, interview, select, and call new stake presidents.

6 ¶ And it came to pass, when they were come, that he looked on Eliab [*David's oldest brother, see 1 Samuel 17:13*], and said, Surely the LORD's anointed is before him [*Samuel thought that this was for sure the Lord's choice to be king*].

Verse 7, next, is quite well known. It contains great wisdom and insight as to how God sees us.

7 But the LORD said unto Samuel, Look not on his countenance, or on the height of his stature; because I have refused him: for **the LORD seeth not as man seeth; for man looketh on the outward appearance, but the LORD looketh on the heart.**

8 Then Jesse called Abinadab [*the next oldest son*], and made him pass before Samuel. And he said, Neither hath the LORD chosen this.

9 Then Jesse made Shammah [*Jesse's third son*] to pass by. And he said, Neither hath the LORD chosen this.

10 Again, **Jesse made seven of his sons to pass before Samuel. And Samuel said unto Jesse, The LORD hath not chosen these.**

11 And **Samuel said unto Jesse, Are here all thy children?** And he said, There remaineth yet the youngest [*David*], and, behold, he keepeth the sheep. And Samuel said unto Jesse, Send and fetch him: for we will not sit down till he come hither.

> Finally, with the bringing of young David to be considered by Samuel, Samuel's assignment is completed. David is a healthy looking and handsome young man. The Lord confirmed to Samuel that this was the next king.

12 And he sent, and brought him in. Now he was ruddy, and withal of a beautiful countenance, and goodly to look to. **And the LORD said, Arise, anoint him: for this is he.**

13 Then **Samuel took the horn of oil, and anointed him** in the midst of his brethren: **and the Spirit of the LORD came upon David from that day forward.** So Samuel rose up, and went to Ramah [*his home*].

> Beginning with verse 14, next, we are shown that Saul has become a very troubled, guilt-ridden man, unable to find peace.
>
> We need the help of the JST to get correct doctrine from verses 14–16. These are examples of what the eighth Article of Faith means when it says, "We believe the Bible to be the word of God as far as it is translated correctly. . . ." God does not communicate through evil spirits nor send them to trouble people.

14 ¶ But the Spirit of the LORD departed from Saul, and an evil spirit **from the LORD** troubled him.

JST 1 Samuel 16:14
14 But the Spirit of the Lord departed from Saul, and an evil spirit which was not of the Lord troubled him.

15 And Saul's servants said unto him, Behold now, an evil spirit **from God** troubleth thee.

JST 1 Samuel 16:15
15 And Saul's servants said unto him, Behold now, an evil spirit which is not of God troubleth thee.

16 Let our lord now command thy servants, which are before thee, to seek out a man, who is a cunning player on an harp: and it shall come to pass, when the evil spirit **from God** is upon thee, that he shall play with his hand, and thou shalt be well.

JST 1 Samuel 16:16
16 Let our lord now command thy servants, which are before thee, to seek out a man, who is a cunning player on a harp; and it shall come to pass, when the evil spirit, **which is not of God**, is upon thee, that he shall play with his hand, and thou shalt be well.

> In verse 16, above, Saul is trying to find relief from his troubled soul. But he ignores the only solution. It is repentance and keeping God's commandments thereafter. He seeks other means to sooth and calm his soul, which only provide occasional temporary relief via distraction.

17 And **Saul said unto his servants, Provide me now a man that can play well, and bring him to me.**

18 Then answered one of the servants, and said, Behold, I have seen a son [*David*] of Jesse the Bethlehemite, that is cunning [*skilled*] in playing, and a mighty valiant man, and a man of war, and prudent in matters, and a comely person, and the LORD is with him.

19 ¶ Wherefore **Saul sent messengers unto Jesse, and said, Send me David** thy son, which is with the sheep.

20 And Jesse took an ass laden with bread, and a bottle of wine, and a kid, and sent them by David his son unto Saul.

> David quickly found favor with Saul. Saul will love him, but soon will hate him and attempt to kill him. A troubled soul is unstable.

21 And David came to Saul, and stood before him: and he loved him greatly [*NIV: "Saul liked him very much"*]; and he became his armourbearer.

22 And Saul sent to Jesse, saying, Let David, I pray thee, stand before me; for he hath found favour in my sight.

23 And it came to pass, when the evil spirit **from God** was upon Saul, that David took an harp, and

played with his hand: so Saul was refreshed, and was well, and the evil spirit departed from him.

JST 1 Samuel 16:23
23 And it came to pass, when the evil spirit, which was not of God, was upon Saul, that David took a harp, and played with his hand; so Saul was refreshed, and was well, and the evil spirit departed from him.

1 SAMUEL 17

Selection: all verses

IN THIS CHAPTER, Saul's armies are engaged in pitched battle with the Philistines, who have come up east toward Jerusalem from their homes in the coastal regions of the Mediterranean Sea.

One of the most popular and stirring stories in the Old Testament is the account of David and Goliath. Goliath was a giant in the Philistine army. If we calculate his height, based on 1 Samuel 17:4, we come up with a height of about nine feet, six inches. He came from a family of exceptionally tall sons. We see very tall men in our day among professional basketball teams, but Goliath was even taller than they are.

In this chapter, you will see the purity of David's soul and his simple faith in the Lord. In response to Goliath's mocking challenge, David simply replies that the Lord will help him.

1 NOW **the Philistines gathered together their armies to battle,** and were gathered together at Shochoh, which belongeth to Judah, and pitched between Shochoh and Azekah, in Ephes-dammim.

2 And **Saul and the men of Israel** were gathered together, and pitched by the valley of Elah [*almost directly west and a bit south of Jerusalem*], and **set the battle in array against the Philistines.**

3 And the Philistines stood on a mountain on the one side, and Israel stood on a mountain on the other side: and there was a valley between them.

> A common practice in ancient warfare was for each side to select a "champion" from their forces to represent them in a fight with the champion selected by the opposing army. These two fought and the outcome determined the victory In verses 4–11, next, this approach appears to be the strategy for this battle between the Philistines and Saul's forces.

4 ¶ And **there went out a champion out of the camp of the Philistines, named Goliath,** of Gath, whose height was six cubits [*a cubit is about 18 inches*] and a span.

5 And he had an helmet of brass upon his head, and he was armed with a coat of mail [*iron mesh*]; and the weight of the coat was five thousand shekels of brass [*NIV: "about 125 pounds"*].

6 And he had greaves [*shin armor*] of brass upon his legs, and a target [*armor protection for the neck*] of brass between his shoulders.

7 And the staff of his spear was like a weaver's beam; and his spear's head weighed six hundred shekels of iron [*NIV: "about 15 pounds"*]: and one bearing a shield [*an armor bearer*] went before him.

> Goliath taunted and mocked Saul's armies on a daily basis. It was very discouraging and disheartening to Israel's soldiers.

8 And **he stood and cried unto the armies of Israel,** and said unto them, Why are ye come out to set your battle in array? am not I a Philistine, and ye servants to Saul? **choose you a man for you, and let him come down to me.**

9 **If he be able to fight with me, and to kill me, then will we be your servants: but if I prevail against him, and kill him, then shall ye be our servants, and serve us.**

10 And the Philistine said, **I defy the armies of Israel** this day; **give me a man, that we may fight together.**

11 When Saul and all Israel heard those words of the Philistine, they **were dismayed, and greatly afraid.**

Verses 12–20, next, appear to be a brief flashback employed by the writer of 1 Samuel to bring the reader up to date with how David came on the scene.

12 ¶ **Now David was the son of** that Ephrathite of Beth-lehem-judah, whose name was **Jesse**; and he had eight sons: and the man went among men for an old man in the days of Saul.

13 And **the three eldest sons of Jesse went and followed Saul to the battle**: and the names of his three sons that went to the battle were Eliab the firstborn, and next unto him Abinadab, and the third Shammah.

14 And **David was the youngest**: and the three eldest followed Saul.

Even though David was Saul's armor bearer (1 Samuel 16:21), it appears that he was allowed to return home on occasions and help with the sheep and chores.

15 But **David went and returned from Saul to feed his father's sheep at Beth-lehem.**

Goliath taunted the Israelite army for days on end.

16 And **the Philistine drew near morning and evening, and presented himself forty days.**

In verses 17–20, next, Jesse sends David with provisions for his brothers and their commander and to see how his brothers are doing.

17 And Jesse said unto David his son, Take now for thy brethren an ephah [*a little over a half bushel*] of this parched corn [*roasted grain*], and these ten loaves, and run to the camp to thy brethren;

18 And carry these ten cheeses unto the captain of their thousand, and look how thy brethren fare, and **take their pledge** [*bring back word and some token from them that shows they're okay*].

19 Now Saul, and they, and all the men of Israel, were in the valley of Elah, fighting with the Philistines.

20 ¶ And David rose up early in the morning, and left the sheep with a keeper, and took, and went, as Jesse had commanded him; and he came to the trench, as the host was going forth to the fight, and shouted for the battle.

21 For Israel and the Philistines had put the battle in array, army against army [*had lined up again, facing each other*].

22 And **David left his carriage** in the hand of the keeper of the carriage, **and ran into the army**, and came and saluted his brethren [*greeted his brothers*].

23 And **as he talked with them, behold, there came up** the champion, the Philistine of Gath, **Goliath** by name, out of the armies of the

Philistines, and spake according to the same words [*repeated the same taunts*]: **and David heard them.**

24 And **all the men of Israel,** when they saw the man, **fled from him,** and were sore afraid.

> In verses 25–31, next, David is aghast and outraged at the words of Goliath as he, a Gentile, defies the armies of the living God! He has faith, while the Israelite soldiers around him, including his brothers, have only fear and trembling.

25 And the men of Israel said, Have ye seen this man that is come up? surely to defy Israel is he come up: and it shall be, that the man who killeth him, the king will enrich him with great riches, and will give him his daughter, and make his father's house free [*free from taxes*] in Israel.

26 And **David spake to the men that stood by him, saying,** What shall be done to the man that killeth this Philistine, and taketh away the reproach from Israel? for **who is this uncircumcised** [*Gentile, non-Israelite, non-covenant man*] **Philistine, that he should defy the armies of the living God?**

27 And the people answered him after this manner, saying, So shall it be done to the man that killeth him.

> David's oldest brother, Eliab, is embarrassed and furious at David's seemingly naive comments and chastises him for leaving his flocks.

28 ¶ And Eliab his eldest brother heard when he spake unto the men; and Eliab's anger was kindled against David, and he said, Why camest thou down hither? and with whom hast thou left those few sheep in the wilderness? **I know thy pride, and the naughtiness of thine heart; for thou art come down that thou mightest see the battle.**

> David does not cower before his brother's rebuke, but rather responds with a bold question. His question is a valid question for all of us who claim to be on the Lord's side.

29 And **David said,** What have I now done? **Is there not a cause?**

> David speaks with other soldiers and is told the same thing about the rewards that await the man who kills Goliath.

30 And he turned from him toward another, and spake after the same manner: and the people answered him again after the former manner.

> Word of David's boldness and confidence gets to Saul who sends for him.

31 And when the words were heard which David spake, they rehearsed them before **Saul:** and he **sent for him.**

> In verse 32, next, David, filled with faith and confidence that comes from faithfulness to God, volunteers to fight Goliath.

32 ¶ And David said to Saul, Let no man's heart fail because of him; **thy servant will go and fight with this Philistine.**

> In verses 33–37, Saul rejects David's well-meaning but to him naive offer, but David persists, expressing his faith in the Lord's help.

33 And **Saul said to David, Thou art not able to go against this Philistine to fight with him:** for thou art but a youth, and he a man of war from his youth.

34 And David said unto Saul, Thy servant kept his father's sheep, and there came a lion, and a bear, and took a lamb out of the flock:

35 And I went out after him, and smote him, and delivered it out of his mouth: and when he arose against me, I caught him by his beard, and smote him, and slew him.

36 Thy servant slew both the lion and the bear: and this uncircumcised Philistine shall be as one of them, seeing he hath defied the armies of the living God.

37 David said moreover, **The LORD that delivered me out of the paw of the lion, and out of the paw of the bear, he will deliver me out of the hand of this Philistine.** And Saul said unto David, Go, and the LORD be with thee.

> David's faith and confidence inspire confidence in Saul and he agrees.

38 ¶ And **Saul armed David with his armour, and he put an helmet of brass upon his head; also he armed him with a coat of mail** [*heavy, woven metal mesh*].

39 And David girded [*put on*] his sword upon his armour, and he assayed to go [*tried walking around*]; for he had not proved it. And David said unto Saul, I cannot go with these; for I have not proved them [*I can't use these; I'm not used to them*]. And David put them off him.

> David was an expert with the sling, no doubt having had many hours of practice during idle time tending his flocks. In fact, slingers were used fairly commonly in the ancient Near East in battles and showed amazing accuracy.
>
> Imagine the attention it drew in both armies as this young shepherd boy representing Israel's army stepped forward to meet Goliath!

40 And **he took his staff in his hand, and chose him five smooth stones out of the brook, and put them in a shepherd's bag** which he had, even in a scrip [*another name for a bag in which food and supplies were carried*]; and **his sling was in his hand: and he drew near to the Philistine.**

41 And **the Philistine came on**

and drew near unto David; and the man that bare the shield went before him.

42 And **when the Philistine looked about, and saw David, he disdained him** [*looked upon him with scorn and ridicule*]: for he was but a youth, and ruddy, and of a fair countenance.

> Goliath's roar of ridicule toward David is very well-known among Bible readers.

43 And the Philistine said unto David, **Am I a dog, that thou comest to me with staves** [*sticks; a shepherd's staff*]? And the Philistine cursed David by his gods.

> Goliath taunts and attempts to intimidate David.

44 And the Philistine said to David, **Come to me, and I will give thy flesh unto the fowls of the air, and to the beasts of the field.**

> Verses 45–47, next, are a thrilling affirmation that one faithful individual plus the Lord make a winning team.

45 Then said David to the Philistine, **Thou comest to me with a sword, and with a spear, and with a shield: but I come to thee in the name of the LORD of hosts**, the God of the armies of Israel, whom thou hast defied.

46 **This day will the LORD deliver thee into mine hand;** and I will smite thee, and take thine head from thee; and I will give the carcases of the host of the Philistines this day unto the fowls of the air, and to the wild beasts of the earth; **that all the earth may know that there is a God in Israel.**

47 And **all this assembly shall know that the LORD saveth not with sword and spear: for the battle is the LORD's, and he will give you into our hands.**

48 And it came to pass, when the Philistine arose, and came and drew nigh to meet David, that **David hasted, and ran toward the army to meet the Philistine.**

> David did all he could and the Lord did the rest.

49 And **David put his hand in his bag, and took thence a stone, and slang it, and smote the Philistine in his forehead, that the stone sunk into his forehead; and he fell upon his face to the earth.**

50 **So David prevailed over the Philistine** with a sling and with a stone, and smote the Philistine, and slew him; but there was no sword in the hand of David.

51 Therefore David ran, and stood upon the Philistine, and took his sword, and drew it out of the sheath thereof, and slew him, and cut off his head therewith. And **when the**

Philistines saw their champion was dead, they fled.

52 And the men of Israel and of Judah arose, and shouted, and pursued the Philistines, until thou come to the valley, and to the gates of Ekron [*a major Philistine city about 30 miles down the mountains west of Jerusalem*]. And the wounded of the Philistines fell down by the way to Shaaraim, even unto Gath [*Goliath's home town*], and unto Ekron.

53 And the children of Israel returned from chasing after the Philistines, and they spoiled [*pillaged, plundered*] their tents.

54 And David took the head of the Philistine, and brought it to Jerusalem; but he put his [*Goliath's*] armour in his tent.

> Saul is now very curious as to who his young harp playing musician and armor bearer (1 Samuel 16:21–23) really is.

55 ¶ And when Saul saw David go forth against the Philistine, he said unto Abner, the captain of the host [*the commander of his army*], Abner, whose son is this youth? And Abner said, As thy soul liveth, O king, I cannot tell [*NIV: "I don't know"*].

56 And the king said, Enquire thou whose son the stripling is.

57 And as David returned from the slaughter of the Philistine, Abner took him, and brought him before Saul with the head of the Philistine in his hand.

58 And Saul said to him, Whose son art thou, thou young man? And David answered, I am the son of thy servant Jesse the Beth-lehemite.

1 SAMUEL 18

Selection: all verses

AFTER HIS TRIUMPH over Goliath, Saul insisted that David not return to his home but that he come to the palace and stay there (verse 2). In verse 1, one of the greatest friendships in the scriptures continues to grow, that between Saul's son, Jonathan, and David.

1 AND it came to pass, when he had made an end of speaking unto Saul, that the soul of Jonathan was knit with the soul of David, and Jonathan loved him as his own soul.

2 And Saul took him that day, and would let him go no more home to his father's house.

3 Then Jonathan and David made a covenant, because he loved him as his own soul.

> As a token of their friendship, Jonathan gave David a gift.

4 And Jonathan stripped himself

of the robe that was upon him, and gave it to David, and his garments, even to his sword, and to his bow, and to his girdle.

5 ¶ And **David went out whithersoever Saul sent him, and behaved himself wisely:** and Saul set him over the men of war, and he was accepted in the sight of all the people, and also in the sight of Saul's servants.

> Verses 6–9, next, show Saul's instability and pride as he becomes insanely jealous of David's popularity. Over time, he will make repeated attempts to kill David.

6 And it came to pass as they came, **when David was returned from the slaughter of the Philistine, that the women came out of all cities of Israel, singing and dancing, to meet king Saul,** with tabrets, with joy, and with instruments of musick.

7 And the women answered [*joyfully shouted to*] one another as they played, and said, **Saul hath slain his thousands, and David his ten thousands.**

8 And **Saul was very wroth, and the saying displeased him;** and he said, **They have ascribed unto David ten thousands, and to me they have ascribed but thousands:** and what can he have more but the kingdom [*what is to keep him from*

taking over the kingdom right now]?

> There is no indication that, at this time, Saul was aware that Samuel had anointed David to become king of Israel, in his place (1 Samuel 16:13).

9 And **Saul eyed** [*was wary and jealous of*] **David from that day and forward.**

> Saul's jealousy overcomes reason and he makes two attempts to kill David with a javelin, in verses 10–11, next.

10 ¶ And it came to pass on the morrow, that the evil spirit **from God** came upon Saul, and he prophesied in the midst of the house: and **David played** [*his harp*] with his hand, as at other times: and **there was a javelin in Saul's hand.**

<u>JST 1 Samuel 18:10</u>
10 And it came to pass on the morrow, that the evil spirit which was not of God came upon Saul, and he prophesied in the midst of the house; and David played with his hand, as at other times; and there was a javelin in Saul's hand.

11 And **Saul cast the javelin; for he said, I will smite David even to the wall with it.** And David avoided out of his presence twice.

> Next, Saul tries to get David killed in battle by making him a captain over a thousand soldiers.

12 ¶ And **Saul was afraid of David,** because the LORD was with him, and was departed from Saul.

13 Therefore **Saul removed him from him, and made him his captain over a thousand**; and he went out and came in before the people.

14 And David behaved himself wisely in all his ways; and **the LORD was with him.**

> Jealousy can be a damaging combination of pride and fear. We see this next, in verse 15.

15 Wherefore when Saul saw that he behaved himself very wisely [*was a skilled and successful military tactician*], **he was afraid of him.**

16 But all Israel and Judah loved David, because he went out and came in before them [*NIV: "because he led them in their campaigns"*].

> In verses 17–22, Saul pretends publicly to favor David by giving him a wife from his own daughters, but secretly, he still hopes that David will be killed in battle against the Philistines.

17 ¶ And Saul said to David, Behold my elder daughter Merab, her will I give thee to wife: only be thou valiant for me, and fight the LORD's battles. For Saul said, Let not mine hand be upon him, but **let the hand of the Philistines be upon him.**

18 And David said unto Saul, Who am I? and what is my life, or my father's family in Israel, that I should be son in law to the king?

19 But it came to pass at the time when Merab Saul's daughter should have been given to David, that she was given unto Adriel the Meholathite to wife.

20 And Michal Saul's daughter loved David: and they told Saul, and the thing pleased him.

21 And Saul said, I will give him her, that she may be a snare to him, and **that the hand of the Philistines may be against him.** Wherefore Saul said to David, Thou shalt this day be my son in law in the one of the twain [*you have a second chance now to become my son-in-law, by marrying Michal*].

22 ¶ And **Saul commanded his servants, saying, Commune with David secretly, and say, Behold, the king hath delight in thee, and all his servants love thee**: now therefore be the king's son in law.

23 And Saul's servants spake those words in the ears of David. And David said, Seemeth it to you a light thing to be a king's son in law, seeing that I am a poor man, and lightly esteemed?

24 And the servants of Saul told him, saying, On this manner spake David.

> Next, Saul intensifies his efforts to get David killed in battle by demanding a dangerous dowry from him for the privilege of

marrying Michal. This gift would require that he and his men kill one hundred Philistine men.

25 And Saul said, Thus shall ye say to David, The king desireth not any dowry, but an hundred foreskins of the Philistines, to be avenged of the king's enemies. **But Saul thought to make David fall by the hand of the Philistines.**

26 And when his servants told David these words, it pleased David well to be the king's son in law: and the days were not expired [*the allotted time to acquire the dowry had not yet expired*].

> David shows his loyalty to Saul by doubling the required gift and Saul has no choice but to keep his word.

27 Wherefore **David arose and went, he and his men, and slew of the Philistines two hundred men;** and David brought their foreskins, and they gave them in full tale to the king, that he might be the king's son in law. **And Saul gave him Michal his daughter to wife.**

28 ¶ And **Saul saw and knew that the LORD was with David, and that Michal Saul's daughter loved him.**

29 And Saul was yet the more afraid of David; and **Saul became David's enemy continually.**

> In verse 30, next, we are told

that the leaders of the Philistine armies continued to attack Israel and every time David was more successful in leading his troops to victory against them than any other of Saul's officers.

30 Then the princes [*leaders*] of the Philistines went forth: and it came to pass, after they went forth, that David behaved himself more wisely [*was more successful*] than all the servants of Saul; so that his name was much set by [*David became more and more famous and popular*].

1 SAMUEL 19

Selection: all verses

ONE OF THE sad accounts in the Old Testament is the ongoing story of Saul's attempts to kill David. He fails to control his jealousy, and it eats away at his common sense. We see this throughout this chapter.

1 AND Saul spake to Jonathan his son, and to all his servants, that they should kill David.

> In verses 2–17, both Jonathan, Saul's oldest son and heir apparent to the throne, and Michal, David's wife and Saul's daughter, help David escape their father's paranoid efforts to murder him.

2 But Jonathan Saul's son delighted much in David: and Jonathan told David, saying, Saul my father seeketh to kill thee: now therefore, I pray thee, take heed to thyself until the morning, and abide in a secret place, and hide thyself:

3 And I will go out and stand beside my father in the field where thou art, and I will commune with my father of thee; and what I see, that I will tell thee.

4 ¶ And Jonathan spake good of David unto Saul his father, and said unto him, Let not the king sin against his servant, against David; because he hath not sinned against thee, and because his works have been to thee-ward very good:

5 For he did put his life in his hand, and slew the Philistine, and the LORD wrought a great salvation for all Israel: thou sawest it, and didst rejoice: wherefore then wilt thou sin against innocent blood, to slay David without a cause?

> Next, in verse 6, Saul makes an oath not to kill David. He will break it repeatedly.

6 And Saul hearkened unto the voice of Jonathan: and Saul sware, As the LORD liveth, he shall not be slain.

7 And Jonathan called David, and Jonathan shewed him all those things. And Jonathan brought David to Saul, and he was in his presence, as in times past.

8 ¶ And there was war again: and David went out, and fought with the Philistines, and slew them with a great slaughter; and they fled from him.

> You have no doubt noticed in your studies of the Old Testament so far that some Old Testament writers incorrectly attribute some things to the Lord for which He does not want credit. Here again, in verse 9, we see the false doctrine that the Lord puts evil thoughts in people's minds. The JST will correct it.

9 And the evil spirit from the LORD was upon Saul, as he sat in his house with his javelin in his hand: and David played with his hand [*played his harp*].

JST 1 Samuel 19:9

9 And the evil spirit which was not of the Lord was upon Saul, as he sat in his house with his javelin in his hand; and David played with his hand.

10 And Saul sought to smite David even to the wall with the javelin; but he slipped away out of Saul's presence, and he smote the javelin into the wall: and David fled, and escaped that night.

11 Saul also sent messengers unto David's house, to watch him, and to slay him in the morning: and Michal David's wife told him, saying, If thou save not thy life to night, to morrow thou shalt be slain.

12 ¶ So Michal let David down through a window: and he went, and fled, and escaped.

Next, Michal makes it look like David is still sleeping in his bed.

13 And Michal took an image, and laid it in the bed, and put a pillow of goats' hair for his bolster [*a long pillow or cushion used for sleeping*], and covered it with a cloth.

14 And when Saul sent messengers to take David, she said, He is sick.

Saul, unwilling to give up, orders his servants to bring David, bed and all, to him so he can kill him.

15 And Saul sent the messengers again to see David, saying, Bring him up to me in the bed, that I may slay him.

16 And when the messengers were come in, behold, there was an image in the bed, with a pillow of goats' hair for his bolster.

Michal makes up an excuse that protects her from her father's anger.

17 And Saul said unto Michal, Why hast thou deceived me so, and sent away mine enemy, that he is escaped? And Michal answered Saul, He said unto me, Let me go; why should I kill thee? [*Don't make me kill you.*]

In order to better understand verses 18–24, next, we will include a quote from the

Old Testament Student Manual Genesis–2 Samuel, pages 279–280:

"After David escaped from Saul through the help of his wife, Michal, Saul sent messengers to kill him. But David had sought refuge with Samuel in what scholars called the 'Schools of the Prophets' (Keil and Delitzsch, Commentary, 2:2:199)."

These scholars showed that such prophets as Samuel, Elijah, and Elisha conducted special schools that were called here "the company of the prophets" (verse 20). Elsewhere, the men who attended these schools were called "sons of the prophets" (1 Kings 20:35). This fact is of interest to Latter-day Saints because Joseph Smith set up a similar school in Kirtland, Ohio, to help teach priesthood holders their special duties.

When the messengers from Saul and finally Saul himself came, they came under the influence of the Spirit, and thus David's life was spared. The fact that the people said, "Is Saul also among the prophets?" (verse 24) is explained this way:

Saul "threw off his royal robes or military dress, retaining only his tunic; and continued so all that day and all that night, uniting with the sons of the prophets in prayers, singing praises, and other religious exercises, which were unusual to kings and warriors; and this gave rise to the saying, Is Saul also among the prophets? By bringing both him and his men thus under a Divine influence, God prevented them from injuring the person of David." (Clarke,

Bible Commentary, 2:274.)

This remarkable event has a parallel in latter-day Church history. During his mission to Great Britain, Elder Wilford Woodruff was delivered from the hands of government authorities through the influence of the Spirit.

"When I arose to speak at Brother Benbow's house, a man entered the door and informed me that he was a constable, and had been sent by the rector of the parish with a warrant to arrest me. I asked him, 'For what crime?' He said, 'For preaching to the people.' I told him that I, as well as the rector, had a license for preaching the gospel to the people, and that if he would take a chair I would wait upon him after meeting. He took my chair and sat beside me. For an hour and a quarter I preached the first principles of the everlasting gospel. The power of God rested upon me, the spirit filled the house, and the people were convinced. At the close of the meeting I opened the door for baptism, and seven offered themselves. Among the number were four preachers and the constable. The latter arose and said, 'Mr. Woodruff, I would like to be baptized.' I told him I would like to baptize him. I went down into the pool and baptized the seven. We then came together. I confirmed thirteen, administered the Sacrament, and we all rejoiced together.

"The constable went to the rector and told him that if he wanted Mr. Woodruff taken for preaching the gospel, he must go himself and serve the writ; for he had heard him preach the only true gospel sermon he had ever listened to in his life. The rector did not know what to make of it, so he sent two clerks of the Church of England as spies, to attend our meeting, and find out what we did preach. They both were pricked in their hearts, received the word of the Lord gladly, and were baptized and confirmed members of the Church of Jesus Christ of Latter-day Saints. The rector became alarmed, and did not venture to send anybody else." (In Cowley, Wilford Woodruff, page 118.)

18 ¶ So David fled, and escaped, and came to Samuel to Ramah, and told him all that Saul had done to him. And he and Samuel went and dwelt in Naioth.

19 And it was told Saul, saying, Behold, David is at Naioth in Ramah.

20 And Saul sent messengers to take David: and when they saw the company of the prophets prophesying, and Samuel standing as appointed over them, the Spirit of God was upon the messengers of Saul, and they also prophesied [*joined in the discussion and activities being conducted by Samuel*].

21 And when it was told Saul, he sent other messengers, and they prophesied likewise. And Saul sent messengers again the third time, and they prophesied also.

22 Then went he also to Ramah, and came to a great well that is in Sechu: and he asked and said, Where are Samuel and David? And one said, Behold, they be at Naioth in Ramah.

23 And he went thither to Naioth in Ramah: and the Spirit of God was upon him also, and he went on, and prophesied, until he came to Naioth in Ramah.

24 And he stripped off his clothes [*his kingly robes and trappings*] also, and prophesied before Samuel in like manner, and lay down naked [*dressed only in his tunic*] all that day and all that night. Wherefore they say, Is Saul also among the prophets?

1 SAMUEL 20

Selection: verses 1–4, 24–33, 35–42

IN THIS CHAPTER, David and Jonathan continue their loyalty and friendship one to another. David asks Jonathan to find out if it would be safe for him to return to Saul's presence. In verse 1, we see that David is still perplexed as to why Saul continues his attempts to kill him.

1 AND **David** fled from Naioth in Ramah, and **came and said before Jonathan, What have I done? what is mine iniquity? and what is my sin before thy father, that he seeketh my life?**

In verse 2, next, Jonathan reassures David that he will know of any attempts by his father on David's life.

2 And he said unto him, God forbid; thou shalt not die: behold, **my father will do nothing either great or small, but that he will shew it me**: and why should my father hide this thing from me? it is not so.

But David expresses deep concern to Jonathan that he is indeed just one step from death when he is around Saul.

3 And David sware moreover, and said, Thy father certainly knoweth that I have found grace in thine eyes; and he saith, Let not Jonathan know this, lest he be grieved: but truly as the LORD liveth, and as thy soul liveth, **there is but a step between me and death.**

4 Then said Jonathan unto David, **Whatsoever thy soul desireth, I will even do it for thee.**

In the next verses, David and Jonathan devise a plan to let David know if it is safe to resume his duties serving Saul in his court. We will pick it up again with verses 24–33 for our verse-by-verse commentary.

24 ¶ **So David hid himself in the field**: and when the new moon [*one of the feasts and sacrifices established by the Law of Moses that accompanied* the new moon, see Numbers 10:10; 28:11] was come, the king sat him down to eat meat.

25 And the king sat upon his seat, as at other times, even upon a seat by the wall: and Jonathan arose, and Abner sat by Saul's side, and **David's place was empty.**

26 Nevertheless Saul spake not any thing that day: for he thought, Something hath befallen him, **he is not clean; surely he is not clean** [*Saul thought David perhaps had not ritually cleansed himself and thus could not attend the feast*].

The next day, Saul brought up the subject of David's absence.

27 And it came to pass on the morrow, which was the second day of the month, that **David's place was empty: and Saul said unto Jonathan his son, Wherefore cometh not the son of Jesse to meat, neither yesterday, nor to day?**

28 And **Jonathan answered** Saul, **David earnestly asked leave** [*permission*] **of me to go to Beth-lehem:**

29 And he said, Let me go, I pray thee; for our family hath a sacrifice in the city; and my brother, he hath commanded me to be there: and now, if I have found favour in thine eyes, let me get away, I pray thee, and see my brethren. **Therefore he**

cometh not unto the king's table.

Saul launches into a tirade against Jonathan, who is his firstborn son and thus would be heir apparent to the throne.

30 Then **Saul's anger was kindled against Jonathan,** and he said unto him, Thou son of the perverse rebellious woman [*accusing Jonathan's mother of fostering his loyalty to David instead of Saul*], do not I know that thou hast chosen the son of Jesse to thine own confusion, and unto the confusion of thy mother's nakedness [*NIV: "to the shame of the mother who bore you"*]?

31 For **as long as the son of Jesse** [*David*] **liveth** upon the ground, **thou shalt not be established, nor thy kingdom** [*you won't become king*]. Wherefore now send and **fetch him unto me, for he shall surely die.**

Next, in verses 32–33, Jonathan stands up for David and in a fit of rage Saul attempts to kill him with a javelin.

32 And **Jonathan answered** Saul his father, and said unto him, **Wherefore shall he be slain** [*why should David be killed*]? **what hath he done?**

33 **And Saul cast a javelin at him to smite him:** whereby Jonathan knew that it was determined of his father to slay David.

Did you catch the understatement

at the end of verse 33, above? It can remind us of the understatement spoken by Abraham, in Abraham 1:1. After his father had cooperated with the local priest in an attempt to have Abraham sacrificed, Abraham said, "I, Abraham, saw that it was needful for me to obtain another place of residence. . . ."

Next, in verses 35–40, Jonathan carries out a prearranged plan to signal to David to come out of hiding and meet him.

35 ¶ And it came to pass in the morning, that **Jonathan went out into the field at the time appointed with David**, and a little lad with him.

36 And he said unto his lad, Run, find out now the arrows which I shoot. And as the lad ran, he shot an arrow beyond him.

37 And when the lad was come to the place of the arrow which Jonathan had shot, Jonathan cried after the lad, and said, Is not the arrow beyond thee?

38 And Jonathan cried after the lad, Make speed, haste, stay not [*a message to David, who is in hiding but is within earshot*]. And Jonathan's lad gathered up the arrows, and came to his master.

39 But the lad knew not any thing: only Jonathan and David knew the matter [*understood the prearranged message*].

40 And Jonathan gave his artillery unto his lad, and said unto him, Go, carry them to the city.

41 ¶ And **as soon as the lad was gone, David arose out of a place toward the south**, and fell on his face to the ground, and bowed himself three times: and **they kissed one another, and wept one with another, until David exceeded** [*David's sadness and distress at their parting exceeded even Jonathan's*].

42 **And Jonathan said to David, Go in peace**, forasmuch as we have sworn both of us in the name of the LORD, saying, The LORD be between me and thee, and between my seed and thy seed for ever. And he arose and departed: and Jonathan went into the city.

In the next several chapters of 1 Samuel, Saul continues his attempts to catch and kill David. Despite Saul's crazed attempts to destroy him, David continues to have success in battle and to gather men loyal to him. He has opportunities to kill Saul, but refuses to do so because of his reverence for the Lord's anointed, respecting the office of king above the need to protect himself.

Major Message

"The Lord's anointed" is a phrase often used in our day to refer to the leaders of the Church. It is vital that we respect the office and not engage in criticizing our Church leaders.

We will pick up the account in more detail now, with chapter 24.

1 SAMUEL 24

Selection: verses 3–6; 8–17

AS MENTIONED IN the transition note, between chapter 20 and 24, above, respect for the Lord's anointed is a vital aspect of maintaining order and effectiveness in the Lord's Church. It was also an important aspect of the culture in which David lived. Showing respect for those in authority, duly placed by proper process, is a vital part of successful societies. David exemplified this principle many times despite personal danger to himself from King Saul.

One such example comes when Saul and his armies were relentlessly pursuing David and the men who had joined him. David and his companions were hiding in a cave when Saul and his soldiers stopped just outside. Saul came into the cave alone to go to the bathroom, and David could easily have killed him. Instead, he very quietly cut off a piece of Saul's robe to later show Saul that he could have killed him. Even though David had exercised such restraint, he still felt deep sorrow that he had shown disrespect for the Lord's anointed.

3 And he [Saul] came to the sheep-cotes [shepherd's caves] by the way, where was a cave; and Saul went in to cover his feet [NIV: "to relieve himself; Hebrew idiom: to use the bathroom"]: and David and his men remained in the sides [the deepest part] of the cave.

Next, David's men tell him, in effect, "Now is your chance."

4 And the men of David said unto him, Behold the day of which the LORD said unto thee, Behold, I will deliver thine enemy into thine hand, that thou mayest do to him as it shall seem good unto thee. Then David arose, and cut off the skirt of Saul's robe [the hem or border, which symbolized Saul's authority as king—see footnote 4a in your Bible] privily [secretly].

5 And it came to pass afterward, that David's heart smote him [he felt sorry], because he had cut off Saul's skirt.

6 And he said unto his men, The LORD forbid that I should do this thing unto my master, the LORD's anointed, to stretch forth mine hand against him, seeing he is the anointed of the LORD.

In fact, David felt so bad about what he had done that he ran out of the cave, called after Saul and apologized!

8 David also arose afterward, and went out of the cave, and cried after Saul, saying, My lord the king. And when Saul looked behind him, David stooped with his face to the earth, and bowed himself.

9 ¶ And David said to Saul, Wherefore hearest thou men's words, saying, Behold, David seeketh thy hurt [*why do you keep believing rumors that I am out to harm you*]?

10 Behold, this day thine eyes have seen how that the LORD had delivered thee to day into mine hand in the cave [*I could easily have killed you today in the cave*]: and *some* bade me [*told me to*] kill thee: but *mine eye* spared thee; **and I said, I will not put forth mine hand against my lord; for he *is* the LORD's anointed.**

11 Moreover, my father [*a term of respect*], see, yea, **see the skirt of thy robe in my hand: for in that I cut off the skirt of thy robe, and killed thee not**, know thou and see that *there is* neither evil nor transgression in mine hand, and **I have not sinned against thee; yet thou huntest my soul to take it.**

12 The LORD judge between me and thee, and the LORD avenge me of thee: but **mine hand shall not be upon thee.**

13 As saith the proverb of the ancients, Wickedness proceedeth from the wicked: but mine hand shall not be upon thee.

14 After whom is the king of Israel come out? **after whom dost thou pursue?** after a dead dog, after a flea.

15 **The LORD therefore be judge, and judge between me and thee** [*compare with Doctrine & Covenants 64:11*], and see, and plead my cause, and deliver me out of thine hand.

16 ¶ And it came to pass, **when David had made an end of speaking** these words unto Saul, that **Saul said, *Is this thy voice, my son David?* And Saul** lifted up his voice, and **wept.**

17 And **he said to David, Thou *art* more righteous than I: for thou hast rewarded me good, whereas I have rewarded thee evil.**

1 SAMUEL 25

Selection: verse 1

WE WILL REFER to just one verse in this chapter, in order to say goodbye to a truly courageous prophet who united Israel again after almost two hundred years of weakness and apostasy during the time of the judges.

1 And **Samuel died**; and all the Israelites were gathered together, and lamented him, and buried him in his house at Ramah. And David arose, and went down to the wilderness of Paran.

1 SAMUEL 26

Selection: verses 7–11

IN THIS CHAPTER, David has yet another chance to kill Saul. Saul has pursued David and his forces with three thousand men, has pitched camp, and, as we pick up the account, is asleep, surrounded by sleeping guards. David has asked two trusted men to accompany him into the enemy camp at night.

7 So **David and Abishai came** to the people **by night**: and, behold, **Saul lay sleeping within the trench**, and his spear stuck in the ground at his bolster: but Abner and the people lay round about him.

8 **Then said Abishai to David,** God hath delivered thine enemy into thine hand this day: now therefore **let me smite him,** I pray thee, with the spear even to the earth at once, and I will not *smite* him the second time.

In verse 9, next, David yet again shows committed respect for "the Lord's anointed," in this case, King Saul, as he refuses to take advantage of another opportunity to kill him.

9 And **David said** to Abishai, Destroy him not: for **who can stretch forth his hand against the LORD's anointed**, and be guiltless?

10 David said furthermore, *As* the LORD liveth, **the LORD shall smite him; or his day shall come to die; or he shall descend into battle, and perish.**

11 **The LORD forbid that I should stretch forth mine hand against the LORD's anointed**: but, I pray thee, take thou now the spear that *is* at his bolster, and the cruse of water, and let us go.

As you continue to read this chapter in your Bible, you will see that, the next day, David uses Saul's spear and water container as proof to Saul and his men that he had quietly entered into their camp and could have killed Saul.

1 SAMUEL 28

Selection: verses 6–19

ONE OF THE most serious and rebellious sins among the Israelites was to go to a witch, often referred to as one who has a "familiar spirit" (Leviticus 19:31)— in other words, a fortune teller who claims to contact the dead. Saul's constant disobedience to the Lord has stopped his ability to get answers from the Lord to his prayers.

6 And when Saul enquired of the LORD, **the LORD answered him not**, neither by dreams nor by Urim, nor by prophets.

Consequently, Saul violates another law of God and

determines to go to the witch of En-dor, in verse 7, next.

7 ¶ Then said Saul unto his servants, Seek me a woman that hath a familiar spirit, that I may go to her, and enquire of her. And his servants said to him, Behold, there is a woman that hath a familiar spirit at En-dor.

In verses 8–19, next, Saul, in disguise, arrives at the fortune teller's house in the middle of the night, and asks her to contact the dead prophet Samuel. She claims to do so, and Saul is given the message that he and his sons will die in battle the next day (verse 19). We will use JST corrections for several of the next verses.

8 And Saul disguised himself, and put on other raiment, and he went, and two men with him, and they came to the woman by night: and he said, I pray thee, divine unto me by the familiar spirit, and bring me him up, whom I shall name unto thee.

The occultist woman fears a trap and reminds the stranger that King Saul has expelled mediums from the land. Wary, the woman at first claims not to be able to contact the dead, as you can see in the JST translation of verse 9, next.

9 And the woman said unto him, Behold, thou knowest what Saul hath done, how he hath cut off those that have familiar spirits, and the wizards, out of the land: wherefore

then layest thou a snare for my life, to cause me to die?

JST 1 Samuel 28:9
9 And the woman said unto him, Behold, thou knowest what Saul hath done, how he hath cut off those that have familiar spirits, and the wizards, out of the land; wherefore then layest thou a snare for my life, to cause me to die also, who hath not a familiar spirit?

10 And Saul sware to her by the LORD, saying, As the LORD liveth, there shall no punishment happen to thee for this thing.

11 Then said the woman, Whom shall I bring up unto thee? And he said, Bring me up Samuel.

JST 1 Samuel 28:11
11 Then said the woman, The word of whom shall I bring up unto thee? And he said, Bring me up the word of Samuel.

12 And when the woman saw Samuel, she cried with a loud voice: and the woman spake to Saul, saying, Why hast thou deceived me? for thou art Saul.

JST 1 Samuel 28:12
12 And when the woman saw the words of Samuel, she cried with a loud voice; and the woman spake to Saul, saying, Why hast thou deceived me? for thou art Saul.

13 And the king said unto her, Be not afraid: for what sawest thou? And the woman said unto Saul, I saw gods ascending out of the earth.

JST 1 Samuel 28:13
13 And the king said unto her, Be not afraid; for what sawest thou? And the woman said unto Saul, I saw the words of Samuel ascending out of the earth. And she said, I saw Samuel also.

14 And he said unto her, What form is he of? And she said, An old man cometh up; and he is covered with a mantle. And Saul perceived that it was Samuel, and he stooped with his face to the ground, and bowed himself.

JST 1 Samuel 28:14
14 And he said unto her, What form is he of? And she said, I saw an old man coming up, covered with a mantle. And Saul perceived that it was Samuel, and he stooped, his face to the ground, and bowed himself.

15 ¶ And Samuel said to Saul, Why hast thou disquieted me, to bring me up? And Saul answered, I am sore distressed; for the Philistines make war against me, and God is departed from me, and answereth me no more, neither by prophets, nor by dreams: therefore I have called thee, that thou mayest make known unto me what I shall do.

JST 1 Samuel 28:15
15 And these are the words of Samuel unto Saul, Why hast thou disquieted me, to bring me up? And Saul answered, I am sore distressed; for the Philistines make war against me, and God is departed from me, and answereth me no more, neither by prophets, nor by dreams; therefore I have called thee, that thou mayest make known unto me what I shall do.

Did the witch of En-dor actually get in touch with Samuel the prophet? The answer is absolutely not! That is not how the Lord works. Obviously, Satan provided a counterfeit Samuel, and Saul could not discern between a messenger from God and a messenger from the devil.

In the book of Revelation, we are reminded that the devil and his evil spirits can indeed perform miracles.

Revelation 16:14
14 For they are the spirits of devils, working **miracles**, which go forth unto the kings of the earth and of the whole world, to gather them to the battle of that great day of God Almighty.

The devil is highly skilled in the art of deceiving, mixing truth with falsehood. We see some of the truths he added to the mix in verses 16–18, next.

16 Then said Samuel, Wherefore then dost thou ask of me, seeing the

LORD is departed from thee, and is become thine enemy?

17 And the LORD hath done to him, as he spake by me: for the LORD hath rent the kingdom out of thine hand, and given it to thy neighbour, even to David:

18 Because thou obeyedst not the voice of the LORD, nor executedst his fierce wrath upon Amalek, therefore hath the LORD done this thing unto thee this day.

> Next, in verse 19, Saul is given the message that he and his sons will die in battle the next day. We suspect that it is a falsehood that he, himself, would be safe and comfortable with the Lord after his death.

19 Moreover the LORD will also deliver Israel with thee into the hand of the Philistines: and to morrow shalt thou and thy sons be with me [*in other words, you will all be killed and return home to be with the Lord*]: the LORD also shall deliver the host of Israel into the hand of the Philistines.

1 SAMUEL 31

Selection: verses 2–4

SAUL'S THREE SONS are killed in battle, and Saul, wounded, takes his own life.

2 And the Philistines followed hard [*close*] upon Saul and upon his sons; and **the Philistines slew** Jonathan, and Abinadab, and Malchi-shua, **Saul's sons.**

3 And the battle went sore against Saul, and **the archers hit him**; and he was sore [*severely*] wounded of the archers.

4 Then said Saul unto his armourbearer, Draw thy sword, and thrust me through therewith; lest these uncircumcised [*Gentiles*] come and thrust me through, and abuse me. But his armourbearer would not; for he was sore afraid. Therefore **Saul took a sword, and fell upon it.**

2 SAMUEL

THE FIRST SEVERAL chapters of Second Samuel deal with the great success of King David as he continues the wars against their enemies and unites the twelve tribes of Israel together as one nation. During his administration, Israel reached its high point, its "golden age." Under David's leadership, the armies of Israel were finally able to conquer and occupy all territories of the promised land originally given and promised by the Lord. Also, David established Jerusalem as the political and spiritual headquarters of Israel.

Initially, though, upon Saul's death, the tribes of Israel did not immediately accept David as their king. 2 Samuel 2:1-7, shows that the tribe of Judah anointed David to be their king. However, Abner, Saul's commander-in-chief of his army, set up Ish-bosheth, one of Saul's sons as the king over Israel (2 Samuel 2:8-9). This situation with two opposing kings resulted in a long civil war between the two kings and their followers (2 Samuel 3:1).

In chapter 4, verses 5-8, Ish-bosheth is assassinated, and, as a result, the leaders of the other tribes of Israel came to David and negotiated a treaty with him to take them and the rest of Israel under his wing and become their king also.

The book of Second Samuel also contains the tragic account of the fall of King David, beginning in chapter 11 with his adultery with Bathsheba and the subsequent murder of Uriah in an unsuccessful attempt to cover up his adultery with Uriah's wife.

We will include a few selections that detail the background given above, up to the account of David and Bathsheba.

2 SAMUEL 1

Selection: verses 1–16

WHEN DAVID HEARD the news that Saul and his son, Jonathan, had both been killed in battle against the Philistines (1 Samuel 31:1-6), he had just returned from leading his forces in a successful battle against the Amalekites, an Arab tribe living southwest of the Dead Sea. These long time enemies of Israel sometimes ranged as far north as Mount Ephraim, north of Jerusalem. At the time a messenger brought the news, David had been resting up in Ziklag, about thirty-five miles southwest of Jerusalem, for a few days.

1 NOW it came to pass after the death of Saul, when David was returned from the slaughter of the Amalekites, and David had abode [*had stayed*] two days in Ziklag;

> The account of Saul's death in verses 2-10, next, differs from the account in 1 Samuel 31:1-6, which states that Saul had been wounded by arrows and then committed suicide by falling on his own sword to avoid letting the Philistines capture him.

2 It came even to pass on the third day, that, behold, a man came out of the camp from Saul with his clothes rent [*torn*], and earth upon his head [*a sign of deep mourning*]: and so it was, when he came to David, that he fell to the earth, and did obeisance [*he bowed before David*].

3 And David said unto him, From whence comest thou? And he said unto him, Out of the camp of Israel am I escaped.

4 And David said unto him, How went the matter [*how did the battle go*]? I pray thee, tell me. And he answered, That the people are fled from the battle, and many of the people also are fallen and dead; and Saul and Jonathan his son are dead also.

5 And David said unto the young man that told him, How knowest thou that Saul and Jonathan his son be dead?

6 And the young man that told him said, As I happened by chance upon mount Gilboa, behold, Saul leaned upon his spear [*preparing to take his own life*]; and, lo, the chariots and horsemen followed hard after him [*the Philistines were closing in on him*].

7 And when he looked behind him, he saw me, and called unto me. And I answered, Here am I.

8 And he said unto me, Who art thou? And I answered him, I am an Amalekite.

9 And he said unto me again, Stand, I pray thee, upon me, and slay me: for anguish is come upon me, because my life is yet whole in me [*NIV: "I am in the throes of death, but I'm still alive"*].

10 So I stood upon him, and slew him, because I was sure that he could not live after that he was fallen: and I took the crown that was upon his head, and the bracelet that was on his arm, and have brought them hither unto my lord.

11 Then David took hold on his clothes, and rent them [*tore them, an act of mourning*]; and likewise all the men that were with him:

12 And they mourned, and wept, and fasted until even [*evening*], for Saul, and for Jonathan his son, and for the people of the LORD, and for the house of Israel; because they were fallen by the sword.

> Next, in verses 13–14, David appears to challenge the truthfulness of the young man's story.

13 ¶ And David said unto the young man that told him, Whence art thou? And he answered, I am the son of a stranger [*a Gentile, a non-Israelite*], an Amalekite.

14 And David said unto him, How wast thou not afraid to stretch forth thine hand to destroy the LORD's anointed [*King Saul*]?

Next, in verses 15–16, David has the young Amalekite executed.

15 And David called one of the young men, and said, Go near, and fall upon him. And he smote him that he died.

16 And David said unto him, Thy blood be upon thy head; for thy mouth hath testified against thee, saying, I have slain the LORD's anointed.

David's action in verses 14–16, above, seems harsh, but, on closer look, the young Amalekite's story about killing Saul seems to be made up and he appears to be a opportunistic plunderer who tries to obtain favor with David. We will quote from a Bible commentary concerning this:

"The whole account which this young man gives is a fabrication: in many of the particulars it is grossly self-contradictory. There is no fact in the case but the bringing of the crown, or diadem, and bracelets of Saul; which, as he appears to have been a plunderer of the slain, he found on the field of battle; and he brought them to David, and told the lie of having despatched Saul, merely to ingratiate himself with David." (Clarke, Bible Commentary, 2:308.)

David's own words in chapter 4, verse 10, indicate that he saw through the Amalekite's story and knew he was lying.

2 SAMUEL 2

Selection: verses 1–17, 28–32

IN THIS CHAPTER, David becomes king over the tribe of Judah, but Saul's son, Ish-bosheth, is pronounced king over all of Israel by Abner, Saul's commanding general. This sets the stage for a long war between the followers of David and those of Ish-bosheth.

In verses 1–4, David asks the Lord where he should set up his headquarters and is told, Hebron. Consequently he moves his family to Hebron, which is about twenty miles southwest of Jerusalem. Likewise, his men and their families move to the same area.

1 AND it came to pass after this, that David enquired of the LORD, saying, Shall I go up into any of the cities of Judah? And the LORD said unto him, Go up. And David said, Whither shall I go up? And he said, Unto Hebron.

Remember that having plural wives was a common thing during Old Testament times. Two of David's wives come to Hebron with him but his first wife, Michal (Saul's daughter) left him some time ago and has remarried. David will force things to get her back, in chapter 3, verses 13–16.

2 So David went up thither, and his two wives also, Ahinoam the Jezreelitess, and Abigail Nabal's wife [*widow, see 1 Samuel 25:38–44*] the Carmelite.

3 And his men that were with him did David bring up, every man with his household: and they dwelt in the cities of Hebron.

4 And the men of Judah [*the tribe of Judah*] came, and there they anointed David king over the house of Judah. And they told David, saying, That the men of Jabesh-gilead were they that buried Saul.

5 ¶ And David sent messengers unto the men of Jabesh-gilead, and said unto them, Blessed be ye of the LORD, that ye have shewed this kindness unto your lord, even unto Saul, and have buried him.

6 And now the LORD shew kindness and truth unto you: and I also will requite [*reward you for*] you this kindness, because ye have done this thing.

7 Therefore now let your hands be strengthened, and be ye valiant: for your master Saul is dead, and also the house of Judah have anointed me king over them.

In verses 8–11, next, we see that Abner, who was commander-in-chief of the army before Saul's death, still exercises leadership and has determined that Saul's son, Ish-bosheth, should be the next king.

8 ¶ But Abner the son of Ner, captain of Saul's host, took Ish-bosheth the son of Saul, and brought him over to Mahanaim [*a city about 15–20 miles east of the Jordan River and about half way between the Sea of Galilee and the Dead Sea*];

9 And made him king over Gilead, and over the Ashurites, and over Jezreel, and over Ephraim, and over Benjamin, and over all Israel.

10 Ish-bosheth Saul's son was forty years old when he began to reign over Israel, and reigned two years. But the house of Judah followed David [*was loyal to David as their king*].

11 And the time that David was king in Hebron over the house of Judah was seven years and six months.

Abner was the commander of the forces loyal to Ish-bosheth, and Joab was the commander of David's armies. The two armies gathered to Gibeon (about eight miles northwest of Jerusalem) to face each other. In verses 12–16, the two opposing sides determine to settle the issue by choosing twelve "champions" (similar to the situation involving David and Goliath) from each side to fight against each other. The outcome would decide who would surrender to whom.

12 ¶ And Abner the son of Ner, and the servants of Ish-bosheth the son of Saul, went out from Mahanaim to Gibeon.

13 And Joab the son of Zeruiah,

and the servants of David, went out, and met together by the pool of Gibeon: and they sat down, the one on the one side of the pool, and the other on the other side of the pool.

14 And Abner said to Joab, Let the young men now arise, and play before us [*engage in a fight to the death while we observe*]. And Joab said, Let them arise.

15 Then there arose and went over by number twelve of Benjamin, which pertained to [*represented*] Ish-bosheth the son of Saul, and twelve of the servants of David.

Next, in verses 16–17, all twenty-four of the fighters die, leaving the issue unresolved. Consequently, both armies engage in a fierce battle and David's forces triumph.

16 And they caught every one his fellow by the head, and thrust his sword in his fellow's side; so they fell down together [*all of them died*]: wherefore that place was called Helkath-hazzurim [*NIV: "field of daggers or field of hostilities"*], which is in Gibeon.

17 And there was a very sore battle that day; and Abner was beaten, and the men of Israel, before the servants of David.

Finally, after relentless pursuit of Abner by Joab and his brothers, the two sides call a truce.

We will pick the account up with verse 28.

28 So Joab blew a trumpet, and all the people stood still, and pursued after Israel no more, neither fought they any more.

Abner and the remnants of Saul's army plodded all night and finally returned to Ish-bosheth's headquarters east of the Jordan River. Joab and his men likewise traveled all night, finally arriving at David's headquarters in Hebron.

29 And Abner and his men walked all that night through the plain, and passed over Jordan, and went through all Bithron, and they came to Mahanaim.

David's forces had lost twenty men and Abner's army had lost three hundred and sixty.

30 And Joab returned from following Abner: and when he had gathered all the people together, there lacked of David's servants nineteen men and Asahel.

31 But the servants of David had smitten of Benjamin, and of Abner's men, so that three hundred and threescore men died.

32 ¶ And they took up Asahel, and buried him in the sepulchre of his father, which was in Beth-lehem. And Joab and his men went all night, and they came to Hebron at break of day.

2 SAMUEL 3

Selection: verses 1–30

ALONG WAR BETWEEN David's followers and those loyal to Ish-bosheth (King Saul's son) follows now. Verse 1 informs us that David's forces gradually gained the upper hand.

1 NOW there was long war between the house of Saul and the house of David: but David waxed [*grew*] stronger and stronger, and the house of Saul waxed weaker and weaker.

> Verses 2–5, next, show that David's own family is growing during the years he spends in Hebron. We see six wives and six sons born. It is highly likely that there were also daughters born during these years.

2 ¶ And unto David were sons born in Hebron: and his firstborn was Amnon, of Ahinoam the Jezreelitess;

3 And his second, Chileab [*also knows as Daniel*], of Abigail the wife of [*widow of*] Nabal the Carmelite; and the third, Absalom the son of Maacah the daughter of Talmai king of Geshur;

4 And the fourth, Adonijah the son of Haggith; and the fifth, Shephatiah the son of Abital;

5 And the sixth, Ithream, by Eglah David's wife. These were born to David in Hebron.

6 ¶ And it came to pass, while there was war between the house of Saul and the house of David, that Abner made himself strong for the house of Saul [*Abner grew in power and influence*].

> In verse 7, next, Ish-bosheth accuses Abner of having an affair with one of Saul's concubine.

7 And Saul had a concubine, whose name was Rizpah, the daughter of Aiah: and Ish-bosheth said to Abner, Wherefore hast thou gone in unto my father's concubine?

8 Then was Abner very wroth for the words of Ish-bosheth, and said, Am I a dog's head [*am I a traitor*], which against Judah do shew kindness this day unto the house of Saul thy father, to his brethren, and to his friends, and have not delivered thee into the hand of David, that thou chargest me to day with a fault concerning this woman?

> Next, in verses 9–10, Abner swears a vow to use his influence to get Ish-bosheth's followers to transfer their loyalty to David.

9 So do God to Abner, and more also, except, as the LORD hath sworn to David, even so I do to him [*persuade the people to transfer their allegiance to David*];

10 To translate the kingdom from the house of Saul, and to set up the throne of David over Israel and over Judah, from Dan even to Beer-sheba [*over the whole country, from the far north to the far south*].

11 And he [*Ish-bosheth*] could not answer Abner a word again, because he feared him.

> In verse 12, Abner negotiates with David to use his influence to sway all of the people to support David as king.

12 ¶ And Abner sent messengers to David on his behalf, saying, Whose is the land? saying also, Make thy league [*treaty*] with me, and, behold, my hand shall be with thee, to bring about all Israel unto thee.

> David agrees, but makes it conditional on getting his first wife, Michal (one of Saul's daughters, 1 Samuel 18:20–27), forcibly brought back to him. She had deserted David earlier and had married another man.

13 ¶ And he said, Well; I will make a league with thee: but one thing I require of thee, that is, Thou shalt not see my face, except thou first bring Michal Saul's daughter, when thou comest to see my face.

14 And David sent messengers to Ish-bosheth Saul's son, saying, Deliver me my wife Michal, which I espoused to me for an hundred foreskins of the Philistines.

15 And Ish-bosheth sent, and took her from her husband, even from Phaltiel the son of Laish.

16 And her husband went with her along weeping behind her to Bahurim. Then said Abner unto him, Go, return [*go back home*]. And he returned.

> Next, in verses 17–21, Abner proceeds with his agreement to persuade the rest of the people to switch their loyalty over to king David.

17 ¶ And Abner had communication with the elders [*leaders*] of Israel, saying, Ye sought for David in times past to be king over you:

18 Now then do it: for the LORD hath spoken of David, saying, By the hand of my servant David I will save my people Israel out of the hand of the Philistines, and out of the hand of all their enemies.

19 And Abner also spake in the ears of Benjamin: and Abner went also to speak in the ears of David in Hebron all that seemed good to Israel, and that seemed good to the whole house of Benjamin.

20 So Abner came to David to Hebron, and twenty men with him. And David made Abner and the men that were with him a feast.

21 And Abner said unto David, I will arise and go, and will gather all

Israel unto my lord the king, that they may make a league with thee, and that thou mayest reign over all that thine heart desireth. And David sent Abner away; and he went in peace.

> Joab, David's commander-in-chief of his military forces, has a grudge against Abner, because Abner killed his brother, Asahel, after giving him repeated fair warnings not to attempt to fight him (2 Samuel 2:20-23). Now Joab sees an opportunity to avenge his brother's death. David knows nothing of the plot.

22 ¶ And, behold, the servants of David and Joab came from pursuing a troop, and brought in a great spoil with them: but Abner was not with David in Hebron; for he had sent him away, and he was gone in peace.

> People excitedly told Joab what had happened during his absence concerning the peace negotiations between Abner and David.

23 When Joab and all the host that was with him were come, they told Joab, saying, Abner the son of Ner came to the king, and he hath sent him away, and he is gone in peace [*King David has made peace with Abner*].

> Next, in verses 24-25, Joab tries to convince King David that it is all a plot on Abner's part to deceive King David and to gain entrance to David's headquarters so that he can spy things out.

24 Then Joab came to the king, and said, What hast thou done? behold, Abner came unto thee; why is it that thou hast sent him away, and he is quite gone?

25 Thou knowest Abner the son of Ner, that he came to deceive thee, and to know thy going out and thy coming in, and to know all that thou doest.

> Joab secretly sends messengers to ask Abner to return.

26 And when Joab was come out from David, he sent messengers after Abner, which brought him again from the well of Sirah: but David knew it not.

> In verse 27, Joab pulls Abner aside as if to speak to him privately and kills him. According to verse 30, Joab's brother, Abishai, helped him carry out the deed.

27 And when Abner was returned to Hebron, Joab took him aside in the gate to speak with him quietly, and smote him there under the fifth rib, that he died, for the blood of Asahel his brother [*to get revenge for Abner's killing of Joab's brother, Asahel*].

> David is aghast at what has taken place. He pronounces a curse on Joab's posterity.

28 ¶ And afterward when David heard it, he said, I and my kingdom are guiltless before the LORD for ever from the blood of Abner the son of Ner:

29 Let it rest on the head of Joab, and on all his father's house; and let there not fail from the house of Joab [*let Joab's posterity never cease to be cursed with*] one that hath an issue, or that is a leper, or that leaneth on a staff [*is a cripple*], or that falleth on the sword, or that lacketh bread.

30 So Joab and Abishai his brother slew Abner, because he had slain their brother Asahel at Gibeon in the battle.

We will now fast forward to chapter 11 for the tragic story of David and Bathsheba. Note that David conquered Jerusalem and made it the capital city of his kingdom, as recorded in 2 Samuel 5:6–10.

2 SAMUEL 11

Selection: all verses

AFTER DAVID BECAME king over all of Israel, he continued the wars against the enemies of Israel. Then comes one of the saddest accounts in the whole Bible. Noble and valiant David makes terrible choices which cause suffering for himself and others, including Bathsheba, and falls from his potential exaltation (Doctrine & Covenants 132:39). There is a major message in this.

Major Message

Position and power do not make one immune to Satan's wiles.

It is important to be aware that plural marriage was still a common practice at this time in the history of Israel. David already had several wives and concubines, all authorized and approved by the Lord. The Doctrine & Covenants explains this:

Doctrine & Covenants 132:39

39 David's wives and concubines were given unto him of me, by the hand of Nathan, my servant, and others of the prophets who had the keys of this power; and in none of these things did he sin against me save [*except*] in the case of Uriah [*Bathsheba's husband*] and his wife; and, therefore he hath fallen from his exaltation, and received his portion; and he shall not inherit them out of the world, for I gave them unto another, saith the Lord.

In verse 1, David has sent his armies off to battle under the leadership of Joab, his commander-in-Chief, but has remained home in Jerusalem himself.

1 AND it came to pass, after the year was expired, at the time when kings go forth to battle [*NIV: "In the spring, at the time when kings go off to war"*], that David sent Joab, and his servants with him, and all Israel; and they destroyed the children of Ammon, and besieged Rabbah. But David tarried still at Jerusalem.

David was restless one night and was walking back and forth on the flat roof of his palace when he spotted Bathsheba. As we read the account, ask yourself this question: "At what point did David begin to compromise the commandments of God?"

2 ¶ And it came to pass in an eveningtide, that David arose from off his bed, and walked upon the roof of the king's house: and from the roof he saw a woman washing herself; and the woman *was* **very beautiful to look upon.**

3 And David sent and enquired after the woman. And *one* said, *Is* **not this Bath-sheba,** the daughter of Eliam, the **wife of Uriah** the Hittite?

At the very least, David should have stopped any further interest in Bathsheba upon finding out that she was a married woman. He did not.

4 And David sent messengers, and took her; and she came in unto him, and he lay with her [*committed adultery with her*]; **for she was** purified from her uncleanness: and she returned unto her house.

5 And the woman conceived, and sent and told David, and said, I am with child.

Many students ask about Bathsheba's responsibility and accountability in this tragic affair. Since we do not have any specific information in the Bible at all regarding this question, we may be wise to simply give

her the benefit of the doubt. (The implication in Doctrine & Covenants 132:39, quoted above, is that she will attain exaltation, since she will be given "unto another" in eternal marriage.) If we do, we might think of her as being intimidated by the king, who was the Lord's anointed, and afraid to disobey his orders or even his suggestions. Whatever the case, discussions about her culpability are fruitless.

Part of the continuing tragedy of David is that he could have been forgiven of adultery had he chosen to go through the deepest remorse and repentance at this stage of things. An example of this is Alma's son Corianton, who repented and later was described by Mormon as a righteous man (Alma 48:17; 49:30).

Rather than repenting, David first tried to get Bathsheba's husband, Uriah (who was a valiant soldier in David's army), to come home from battle and spend time with Bathsheba so that it would look like it was Uriah's baby.

This plot did not work. Uriah would not go home because he felt that in doing so, it would be disloyal to his fellow soldiers for him to enjoy the comforts of home while they were dying in battle.

6 ¶ And David sent to Joab, saying, Send me Uriah the Hittite. And Joab sent Uriah to David.

7 And when Uriah was come

unto him, David demanded of him how Joab did, and how the people did, and how the war prospered.

8 And **David said to Uriah, Go down to thy house, and wash thy feet** [*relax and spend time at home*]. And Uriah departed out of the king's house, and there followed him a mess of meat [*a gift of food*] from the king.

Much to David's disappointment and frustration, noble Uriah did not go home, but rather slept in the servant's quarters of the palace.

9 But **Uriah** slept at the door of the king's house with all the servants of his lord, and **went not down to his house.**

10 And when they had told David, saying, Uriah went not down unto his house, **David said unto Uriah, Camest thou not from thy journey? why then didst thou not go down unto thine house?**

11 And **Uriah said unto David, The ark** [*of the covenant*], **and Israel, and Judah, abide in tents** [*have to live in battlefield conditions*]**; and my lord Joab, and the servants of my lord, are encamped in the open fields; shall I then go into mine house, to eat and to drink, and**

to lie with my wife? as thou livest, and as thy soul liveth, I will not do this thing.

Next, David tries to get him drunk so that he will go home and spend time with Bathsheba.

12 And David said to Uriah, Tarry here to day also, and to morrow I will let thee depart. So Uriah abode in Jerusalem that day, and the morrow.

13 And when David had called him, he did eat and drink before him; and **he made him drunk: and at even he went out to lie on his bed with the servants of his lord, but went not down to his house.**

In deepest frustration and desperation, David commanded that Uriah be placed in a position in battle where he would certainly be killed.

14 ¶ And it came to pass in the morning, that **David wrote a letter to Joab,** and sent it by the hand of Uriah.

15 And he wrote in the letter, saying, **Set ye Uriah in the forefront of the hottest battle, and retire ye from him** [*pull the other soldiers back so that Uriah is left alone*]**, that he may be smitten, and die.**

16 And it came to pass, when **Joab** observed the city, that he **assigned Uriah unto a place where he knew**

that valiant men [*powerful enemy soldiers*] were.

17 And the men of the city went out, and fought with Joab: and there fell some of the people of the servants of David; and **Uriah the Hittite died** also.

> Thus, David committed murder in an attempt to cover up his adultery. He then quickly married Bathsheba, hoping to quell any evidence of his adultery.

18 ¶ **Then Joab sent and told David all the things concerning the war;**

> Next, Joab is worried that David might be angry with him for putting his men in extra danger in the battle. But he knows that David will not pursue the issue if he knows that Uriah died in the heat of that battle (verse 21).

19 And charged the messenger, saying, When thou hast made an end of telling the matters of the war unto the king,

20 And if so be that the king's wrath arise, and he say unto thee, Wherefore approached ye so nigh unto the city when ye did fight? knew ye not that they would shoot from the wall?

21 Who smote Abimelech the son of Jerubbesheth? did not a woman cast a piece of a millstone upon him from the wall, that he died in Thebez? why went ye nigh the wall? then say thou, Thy servant **Uriah the Hittite is dead also.**

22 ¶ **So the messenger went, and came and shewed David all that Joab had sent him for.**

23 And the messenger said unto David, Surely the men prevailed against us, and came out unto us into the field, and we were upon them even unto the entering of the gate.

24 And the shooters shot from off the wall upon thy servants; and some of the king's servants be dead, and **thy servant Uriah the Hittite is dead also.**

> Joab's strategy with David works, and, in verse 25, next, David, in effect, says don't worry about it.

25 Then **David said unto the messenger, Thus shalt thou say unto Joab, Let not this thing displease thee**, for the sword devoureth one as well as another [*one man can die as easily as another in battle*]: make thy battle more strong against the city, and overthrow it: and encourage thou him.

> As you can imagine, this whole thing has been very hard on Bathsheba. As is often the case, one man's sin has taken many victims.

26 ¶ And **when the wife of Uriah [*Bathsheba*] heard that Uriah her**

husband was dead, she mourned for her husband.

27 And **when the mourning was past, David sent and fetched her to his house, and she became his wife**, and bare him a son. **But the thing that David had done displeased the LORD.**

2 SAMUEL 12

Selection: verses 1–13

HAVING COMMIT-TED MURDER to try to cover up for adultery, David now tries to settle in and live his lie in peace. It doesn't work. The Lord knows and sends Nathan, the prophet to confront David. He presents a parable to David and invites him to pass judgment at the end of it.

1 And **the LORD sent Nathan unto David.** And **he came unto him, and said unto him**, There were two men in one city; the one rich [*symbolic of David*], and the other poor [*symbolic of Uriah*].

2 The rich *man* had exceeding many flocks and herds:

3 But the poor *man* had nothing, save one little ewe lamb [*symbolic of Bathsheba*], which he had bought and nourished up: and it grew up together with him, and with his children; it did eat of his own meat, and drank of his own cup, and lay in his bosom, and was unto him as a daughter.

4 And there came a traveler unto the rich man, and he spared to take of his own flock and of his own herd, to dress for the wayfaring man that was come unto him; **but took the poor man's lamb**, and dressed it for the man that was come to him.

5 And **David's anger was greatly kindled** against the man; and he said to Nathan, *As* the LORD liveth, **the man that hath done this** *thing* **shall surely die:**

6 And he shall restore the lamb fourfold, because he did this thing, and because he had no pity.

7 ¶ **And Nathan said** to David, **Thou** *art* **the man.** Thus saith the LORD God of Israel, I anointed thee king over Israel, and I delivered thee out of the hand of Saul;

8 And I gave thee thy master's house, and thy master's wives into thy bosom, and gave thee the house of Israel and of Judah; and if *that had been* too little, I would moreover have given unto thee such and such things.

9 Wherefore hast thou despised the commandment of the LORD, to do evil in his sight? **thou hast killed Uriah** the Hittite with the sword, **and hast taken his wife** *to be* thy

wife, and hast slain him with the sword of the children of Ammon.

> Next, Nathan severely chastises David and pronounces a prophecy of doom upon him and his household. This is a sad reminder that "wickedness never was happiness" (Alma 41:10).

10 Now therefore **the sword** [*symbolic of calamity and bloodshed*] **shall never depart from thine house**; because thou hast despised me, and hast taken the wife of Uriah the Hittite to be thy wife.

11 Thus saith the LORD, Behold, **I will raise up evil against thee out of thine own house**, and I will take thy wives before thine eyes, and give them unto thy neighbour, and he shall lie with thy wives in the sight of this sun.

12 For **thou didst it secretly: but I will do this thing before all Israel,** and before the sun [*in the full light of day*].

> Having been caught, rather than voluntarily confessing, David now pleads for forgiveness. The JST makes a vital change to verse 13, next.

13 And David said unto Nathan, I have sinned against the LORD. And Nathan said unto David, **The LORD also hath put away thy sin;** thou shalt not die.

JST 2 Samuel 12:13

13 And David said unto Nathan, I have sinned against the Lord. And Nathan said unto David, The Lord also hath not put away thy sin that thou shalt not die.

The Doctrine & Covenants confirms that David was not forgiven of murder. In other words, he "died" with respect to gaining exaltation.

Doctrine & Covenants 132:39

39 David's wives and concubines were given unto him of me, by the hand of Nathan, my servant, and others of the prophets who had the keys of this power; and in none of these things did he sin against me save [*except*] in the case of Uriah and his wife; and, therefore he hath fallen from his exaltation, and received his portion; and he shall not inherit them out of the world, for I gave them unto another, saith the Lord.

As suggested earlier, we note from the above quote that David's wives were not held back because of the transgression of their husband. They have been given another husband or other husbands (they would surely make the final choice) "out of the world".

Sadly, David's last recorded words are filled with desire for revenge. See 1 Kings 2:5–6.

SOURCES

Book of Mormon Student Manual. Salt Lake City: The Church of Jesus Christ of Latter-day Saints, 1982.

Bryant, T. Alton. *The New Compact Bible Dictionary.* Grand Rapids, Mich.: Zondervan, 1981.

Clark, James R., comp. *Messages of the First Presidency of The Church of Jesus Christ of Latter-day Saints.* 6 vols. Salt Lake City: Bookcraft, 1965–75.

Conference Reports of The Church of Jesus Christ of Latter-day Saints. Salt Lake City: The Church of Jesus Christ of Latter-day Saints, 1898 to present.

Doctrines of the Gospel Student Manual. Salt Lake City: The Church of Jesus Christ of Latter-day Saints (Institutes of Religion), 2000.

Encyclopedia of Mormonism. Edited by Daniel H. Ludlow. 5 vols. New York: Macmillan, 1992.

Hymns of The Church of Jesus Christ of Latter-day Saints. Salt Lake City: The Church of Jesus Christ of Latter-day Saints, 1985.

International Bible Society. *The Holy Bible: New International Version (NIV).* Grand Rapids, Mich.: Zondervan, 1984.

Josephus. *Antiquities of the Jews.* Philadelphia: John C. Winston Co., n.d.

Journal of Discourses. 26 vols. London: Latter-day Saints' Book Depot, 1854–86.

Kiel, C. F., and F. Delitzsch. *Commentary on the Old Testament.* 10 vols. Grand Rapids, Mich.: William B. Eerdmans Publishing, 1991.

Kimball, Spencer W. *Faith Precedes the Miracle.* Salt Lake City: Deseret Book, 1972.

Ludlow, Victor L. *Isaiah: Prophet, Seer, and Poet.* Salt Lake City: Deseret Book, 1982.

Maxwell, Neal A. *Deposition of a Disciple.* Salt Lake City: Deseret Book, 1976.

McConkie, Bruce R. *A New Witness for the Articles of Faith.* Salt Lake City: Deseret Book, 1985.

———. *Doctrinal New Testament Commentary.* 3 vols. Salt Lake City: Deseret Book, 1972.

———. *Mormon Doctrine.* 2d ed. Salt Lake City: Bookcraft, 1966.

———. *The Millennial Messiah.* Salt Lake City: Deseret Book, 1982.

———. *The Promised Messiah—The First Coming of Christ.* Salt Lake City: Deseret Book, 1978.

Nyman, Monte S. *Great Are the Words of Isaiah.* Salt Lake City: Bookcraft, 1980.

Old Testament Gospel Doctrine Teacher's Manual. Salt Lake City: The Church of Jesus Christ of Latter-day Saints (Institutes of Religion), 2001.

Old Testament Student Manual: Genesis–2 Samuel. Salt Lake City: The Church

of Jesus Christ of Latter-day Saints
(Institutes of Religion), 1981.

*Old Testament Student Manual, I Kings–
Malachi* (Religion 302). Salt Lake City:
The Church of Jesus Christ of Latter-
day Saints, 1981.

Petersen, Mark E. *Moses, Man of Miracles.*
Salt Lake City: Deseret Book, 1977.

Rasmussen, Ellis. *An Introduction to the
Old Testament and its Teachings.* 2d
ed. 2 vols. Provo, Utah: BYU Press,
1972–74.

Richards, LeGrand. *Israel! Do You Know?*
Salt Lake City: Deseret Book, 1954.

Smith, Joseph. *History of The Church of Jesus
Christ of Latter-day Saints.* Edited by
B. H. Roberts. 2d ed. rev., 7 vols. Salt
Lake City: The Church of Jesus Christ
of Latter-day Saints, 1932–1951.

————. *Teachings of the Prophet Joseph
Smith.* Selected by Joseph Fielding
Smith. Salt Lake City: Deseret Book,
1977.

ABOUT THE AUTHOR

DAVID J. RIDGES taught for the Church Educational System for thirty-five years and taught for several years at BYU Campus Education Week. He taught adult religion classes and Know Your Religion classes for BYU Continuing Education for many years. He has also served as a curriculum writer for Sunday School, seminary, and institute of religion manuals.

He has served in many callings in the Church, including Gospel Doctrine teacher, bishop, stake president, and patriarch. He and Sister Ridges have served two full-time CES missions together. They are the parents of six children and grandparents of eleven grandchildren so far. They make their home in Springville, Utah.